Julian Maclaren-Ross
Selected Letters

for Alex Maclaren-Ross

Julian Maclaren-Ross self-portrait: detail from a mock-up
film poster for his radio serial *The Girl in the Spotlight*.

JULIAN MACLAREN-ROSS
Selected Letters

edited by Paul Willetts

**BLACK
SPRING
PRESS**

Published in 2008 by Black Spring Press Ltd
Curtain House
134–146 Curtain Road
London EC2A 3AR

www.blackspringpress.co.uk

ISBN 978-0-948238-38-3

A full CIP record for this book is available from the British Library

Cover design Ken Leeder, based on an original design by Hanna Sundén;
front cover: Julian Maclaren-Ross, sitting in the garden of Greenleaves,
Bognor Regis, 1940, © C.K. Jaeger.

Typeset in Minion by Dexter Haven Associates Ltd, London
Printed and bound in Great Britain by CPI Cox and Wyman Ltd, Reading

CONTENTS

Acknowledgements
Paul Willetts

This book wouldn't have been possible without the generous assistance of the following people and institutions. Copies of privately owned Maclaren-Ross letters were obtained with the help of Max Eden, Matt Thomas, John Powell, Marc Glendening, Crispin Jackson and Nicholas Worskett of Christie's, South Kensington, plus C.K. Jaeger and his children, Nick Jaeger and Karel Bartholemew, who patiently responded to my questions. The bulk of the letters were, however, provided by the Department of Special Collections at the University of Bristol Library (Ref: DM1 352/1/1), England; the Archives of Jonathan Cape Ltd at the University of Reading, England; the McFarlin Library, Department of Special Collections at the University of Tulsa, Oklahoma, USA; the Harry Ransom Humanities Research Center, the University of Texas at Austin, USA; the BBC Written Archives Centre at Caversham, England; the Archives of the Royal Literary Fund, England; the Lehmann Family Archive at the Manuscripts Division, Department of Rare Books and Special Collections, Princeton University Library, USA; the General and Literary Manuscripts Collection, Wilson Library, the University of North Carolina at Chapel Hill, USA; and the Manuscripts and Archives Section (MS-Papers-5079-186) of the Andrew Turnbull Library, Wellington, New Zealand.

Extensive and invaluable background research, which yielded a significant proportion of the raw material for the footnotes, was quarried by four of the interns at Black Spring Press: Chris Underwood, Sofia Zanabria, Alyssa Levy and especially Amber Manko. Thanks are also due to Gretchen Ladish and Robert Hastings at Black Spring Press. As well as lending his support and enthusiasm to the project, Robert provided some useful comments which have been dovetailed into the book's introduction.

I'm similarly grateful to Alex and Kirsty Maclaren-Ross; D.J. Taylor; Brigid Sandford-Smith; Alan Brownjohn; Craig Dickson; Gerry Harrison, author of the forthcoming biography of R.D. 'Reggie' Smith; the ever-helpful Rachel Bowles at the BBC Written Archives Centre;

the Maclaren-Ross literary estate's indefatigable agent, Andrew Lownie; and Robert Nedelkoff, who solved the mystery surrounding the wartime disappearance of Maclaren-Ross's friend G.S. Marlowe.

Introduction
Paul Willetts

Even before the advent of e-mail, letter-writing was often portrayed as a lost art. Julian Maclaren-Ross, that quintessential literary bohemian, belonged to what was probably the last generation to practise it with widespread vigour. For someone who claimed to detest writing letters, Maclaren-Ross produced an unexpectedly large and engaging body of them. The extent of his output as a correspondent is also surprising in view of the circumstances of his troubled life, circumstances scarcely conducive to staying in touch with people by post. A brisk trawl through his letters reveals frequent changes of address, many of these enforced by landladies or hoteliers to whom he owed money. Sudden departures, leaving behind no forwarding address, only a sense of smouldering grievance, were commonplace. As if that didn't make correspondence hard enough, his pub and club-going – which came to dominate his daily routine from the summer of 1943 onwards – allowed him little time for anything but paid writing, necessary to fund his drinking and prolong his precarious tenure at his current address. Those addresses ranged from cramped lodgings to suites in luxurious hotels, the grandeur of his accommodation bearing scant relation to his income.

A significant proportion of his letters were written on luxurious, complimentary stationery dispensed by imposing London hotels. Down the lefthand margins, there are usually small sepia photos of that establishment's facilities: ornate turkish baths, winter gardens, ball-rooms and cavernous, chequerboard-floored entrance halls, evocative of a world that's remote from our own. Yet Maclaren-Ross's letters, in common with his other writing, are never remote, their crisp, unadorned manner lending his travails considerable immediacy.

With rare exceptions, marking moments of extreme stress, his letters are masterpieces of penmanship, each tiny, carefully delineated character as reluctant to come into contact with its neighbour as a neurotic on a crowded tube train. In his entertaining *Memoirs of the Forties*, he describes an occasion when someone asked him how he did it. His curtly dismissive response was, 'With a pen.' I wonder what a graphologist would make of his handwriting. It's certainly the handwriting of an obsessive, its creepy restraint offering a paradoxical contrast to his flamboyance and exhibitionism, to the lack of restraint that permeated so many other aspects of his existence. That said, there's a remarkable continuity between his handwriting and prose style. Both share the hallmarks of clarity and precision, traits conspicuous in all but the rambling letters which he wrote during the height of his obsession with George Orwell's widow Sonia. These letters pore over every nuance of her behaviour, their overloaded sentences and tortured syntax mirroring his state of mind.

Unfortunately there are long stretches of his life from which little if any of his correspondence appears to have survived. There is, for instance, nothing from his childhood or adolescence. A high proportion of the surviving letters, spanning most of his adult years, focus on his work. Far from endorsing the clichéd view of him as a feckless barfly, content to squander his time and energy, his letters draw attention to his diligence and productivity, not to mention the humility that lurked beneath the veneer of self-confidence. Here was a man who, as his friend Anthony Powell so eloquently described, somehow succeeded in combining a multitude of contradictory roles, each of them enacted with similar conviction. The serious-minded, professional writer coexisted with the boozy bohemian, the impervious dandy with the vulnerable middle-aged man, the victim with the aggressor, the gentle and considerate friend with the nightmarish egotist.

Besides illuminating his relationships with fellow writers, as well as publishers, radio producers and the like, his letters offer a fascinating insight into the literary milieu of that halcyon period when John Lehmann, Cyril Connolly and other perceptive editors wielded such influence. In selecting material for this volume, I've included a smattering of purely functional business letters on the grounds that these represent small steps in an evolving story, more often than not the story of how Maclaren-Ross alienated yet another valuable contact.

Like his previously published writings, his letters are wide-ranging in tone and subject matter. They can be formal, gossipy, observant, irreverent and amusing. Unlike the work for which he is celebrated, though, they can also be paranoid, irascible and disturbing in their monomaniacal intensity. The majority of them are nonetheless vivid, lively and stylish.

Chronological outline

1912	7 July: born at 18 Whitworth Road, South Norwood, London.
1916–17	Family moves to 80 Paisley Road, Southbourne, Bournemouth.
1921	Family moves to Marseilles and then Nice.
1925	Attends a boarding school near Antibes.
c.1926–28	Attends the Collège Roustan, a boarding school in Antibes.
1928–29	Attends boarding school in Paris. Expelled from school.
1929–33	Lives with his parents on the French Riviera.
1933	Returns to England, funded by an allowance from his paternal grandfather's estate.
1936	September: Father dies. Marries Elizabeth Gott, a young actress, and moves from London to Bognor Regis.
1937	Separates from his wife.
1938	His allowance stops. Finds a job as as a door-to-door vacuum-cleaner salesman. Sells a radio play, *The Stars Foretell*, to the BBC.
1940	June: publishes first fiction, a short story in *Horizon*. July: conscripted into the army. Stationed in Dorset. October: transferred to an infantry unit in Bury St Edmunds.
1941	June: assigned as a clerk to a Territorial Army unit in Ipswich. October: transferred to clerical duties with the garrison at Felixstowe.
1942	January: writes and immediately sells the first in what will become a sequence of popular short stories about army life. April: mother dies.
1943	January: deserts from the army. Gaoled and then sent to Northfield Military Hospital.

May: sent to the Military Detention Barrack in
Colchester.

June: transferred to the Infantry Depot in Southend.

August: declared 'unfit for military service' and
discharged from the army. Settles in London and finds
job working as a screenwriter on government-funded
documentaries.

1944   January: loses screenwriting job.

July: publishes *The Stuff to Give the Troops: 25 Stories of
Army Life*.

1945   November: publishes second short-story collection,
Better than a Kick in the Pants.

1946   February: publishes novella, *Bitten by the Tarantula: A
Story of the South of France*.

October: publishes third collection of short stories, *The
Nine Men of Soho*.

1947   October: publishes first full-length novel, *Of Love and
Hunger*.

December: starts writing for *Times Literary
Supplement*.

1948   August: lands job as one of a team of screenwriters
working on *The Naked Heart*.

1950   October: publishes *Pierrot*, a translation of Raymond
Queneau's *Pierrot mon ami*.

1951–53   Works as a journalist and screenwriter for both film and
television.

1953   March: publishes *The Weeping and the Laughter*, a
childhood memoir.

May: starts writing for *Punch*.

1954   August: moves to Oxford.

1955   November: publishes translation of Georges Simenon's
Maigret et la grande perche, released in England as
Maigret and the Burglar's Wife.

1956   January: moves back to London, mainly motivated by
the need to be close to Sonia Orwell, whom he has
begun to stalk.

March: briefly homeless.

April: begins romance with Leonard Woolf's niece,
Diane Bromley.

	July: publishes *The Funny Bone*, a collection of short stories, parodies and memoirs.
1957	April: briefly imprisoned.
	June: writes first of numerous radio serials for the BBC.
1958	7 July: Diane Bromley gives birth to his only child, Alex.
	August: marries Diane Bromley.
1960	January: publishes *Until the Day She Dies*, a novel based on one of his radio serials.
1961	June: publishes *The Doomsday Book*, a novel based on one of his radio serials.
	December: moves with Diane and Alex to a flat in Hove.
1962	April: separates from Diane and moves back to London.
	November: becomes a regular contributor to the *London Magazine*.
1964	January: publishes *My Names Is Love*, a novel based on one of his radio serials.
	August: completes the first instalment of his *Memoirs of the Forties*, which is serialised in the *London Magazine*. The uncompleted book is published to considerable acclaim the following year.
	3 November: suffers a fatal heart attack. Buried in an unmarked grave in Paddington Cemetery, Mill Hill, north London.

In 2006 a fundraising campaign led by the writer Virginia Ironside culminated in the installation of a headstone, featuring an inscription carved by Evelyn Waugh's grandson Tom.

PART I
(1938–45)

Board Residence and Apartments

Proprietress:
Mrs. C. Francis

St. Helens
Stocker Road, Bognor Regis

Telephone: Bognor Regis 1461

April 7th 1938
=

Dear Sir,

Two months ago, I read in the Daily Telegraph that you were complaining of the shortage of new radio plays and new radio playwrights. For the past two years I have been writing plays for broadcasting purposes, but have not submitted any for your consideration as I did not think they were sufficiently good for production, and I believe in applying to my own work the same searching criticism which I should apply to the work of others. On February 18th, however, I sent to you a play entitled "Gallows Alley" adapted by me from a novel by Anthony Skene, which might be worthy of your notice if you have not already considered and rejected it. In this play, I endeavoured to produce a realistic thriller equivalent to such films as "Winterset" and "Dead End"; it is not for me to say whether or not I have succeeded: indeed, I do not know.

I have listened to many plays on the air, and it seems to me that, while some of them achieve a very high standard, the full possibilities of this medium have not yet been exploited. For example, it should not be necessary for the announcer to outline the scene where the play is being enacted, or for stage-directions to be read aloud; everything should be conveyed to the listener by means of sound and dialogue. This latter, by the way, is often stilted and unnatural: especially in the case of historical plays. As it is one of my aims to provide completely naturalistic dialogue, I am particularly interested in this matter.

I shall be in London on Saturday afternoon and during the following week, and if you would favour me with an interview, I should be extremely grateful. I think, without undue conceit, that you would find some of my ideas profitable in application, and I should grateful for your advice on some technical points. Could you let me know, by return if possible, whether you would grant me an interview at any time on Saturday afternoon?

Yours faithfully, J. Maclaren-Ross

The seeds of Julian Maclaren-Ross's unsettled life were sown by his similarly itinerant parents. Born in 1912, he was baptised James McLaren Ross, the youngest of three children, two of whom were already living away from home. At that time his part-Cuban, part-Scottish, part-Indian parents had lodgings in suburban South London. From there, his father – supported by a modest private income – took the family to live in a succession of seaside towns, among them Bournemouth and Ramsgate. In the autumn of 1921, the family moved to the French Riviera, where they had relatives and where they were exempt from British income tax. Maclaren-Ross would later portray his early experiences in *The Weeping and the Laughter*, a poignant childhood memoir that prompted *The Times* to declare him 'one of the most gifted writers of his generation'.

Prior to his family's cross-channel move, Maclaren-Ross had had no formal education. At the age of twelve he was sent to a small French boarding school. Over the next few years he would attend other such schools in Antibes and then Paris. In 'Monsieur l'Abbé', a fragment from the uncompleted sequel to *The Weeping and the Laughter*, he mentions letters that he received from his father, letters that were, at the behest of the headmaster, written in French. He probably replied to these, yet none of the correspondence between him and his cantankerous father has survived. Nor have any other letters that Maclaren-Ross wrote during his teens.

Ultimately expelled from school on account of his bad behaviour, the sixteen-year-old Maclaren-Ross went back to live with his parents, who had rented a villa near Nice. He soon began to explore the city's vibrant and cosmopolitan café society. An obsession with Oscar Wilde prompted him to reinvent himself in the guise of an 1890s dandy, a process that would lead to him adopting the grand-sounding moniker of Julian Maclaren-Ross. He also conceived an ambition to become either a painter or a writer. Financed by an allowance from the huge estate of his paternal grandfather, he returned to England in 1933, initially basing himself in Bognor Regis before gravitating to London. It was there that he began an ill-advised relationship with Elizabeth Gott, a young actress who became his first wife. Right after their marriage, they settled in Bognor, where his freshly widowed mother was living. But he and his wife separated only about six months later.

Lonely and distraught, he found sanctuary with C.K. and Lydia Jaeger, a young local couple whom he had befriended. Through the Jaegers, he met Eileen Cooke, the proprietress of a local café. Much to the disapproval of Cooke's father, she and Maclaren-Ross began what would be a lengthy romance.

Encouraged by C.K. Jaeger, who also harboured literary ambitions, Maclaren-Ross turned his hand to writing short stories and radio plays. His earliest surviving letter dates from 1938, when he tried to get his work published in *New Writing*, edited by John Lehmann, who would go on to launch the more popular *Penguin New Writing*.

Though he would become well known as a writer of prose fiction, Maclaren-Ross first made headway as a radio dramatist. Most of his early letters chronicle his stuttering progress in this genre, a genre in which he wouldn't achieve success until the late 1950s. With war looming and his relationship with the BBC descending into acrimony, he concentrated on producing short stories. Meanwhile, his allowance had abruptly ended and he'd taken on a sequence of jobs, the longest-running of these being as a door-to-door vacuum-cleaner salesman.

Just before he was conscripted into the army, he made his debut as a writer of published fiction, courtesy of Cyril Connolly's seminal, recently launched magazine *Horizon*. By the summer of 1940, he was undergoing infantry training in Dorset, but a chronic knee problem resulted in him being confined to clerical duties in various garrisons and depots. Drawing on his experiences, he penned numerous short stories about military life that were published in literary magazines such as *Horizon*, *English Story* and *Penguin New Writing*. These earned him a reputation as one of England's most promising writers. Nonetheless, he felt increasingly frustrated by the knowledge that the army wasn't making best use of his talents, which included fluency in French.

While on leave in London during August 1942 he met Scylla Yates, a member of the Women's Auxilliary Air Force. She quickly usurped Eileen Cooke's role as his supportive girlfriend. In January 1943 he spent his leave with her in the capital, where he tried to find a job more suited to his talents. Determined to secure a fresh posting before he left London, he failed to return to the Infantry Depot in Southend where he was based. Fourteen days later, the Military Police arrested him for desertion. During his incarceration in the Regimental Gaol, pending a court martial, he suffered a breakdown. He responded by seeking help from Rupert Hart-Davis, now an army officer but formerly a director of Jonathan Cape, a publishing firm which had expressed interest in releasing a collection of his short stories. Maclaren-Ross explained his predicament to Hart-Davis in a lengthy statement, followed by a flurry of desperate letters written in the wake of his transfer to Northfield Military Hospital, a bleak psychiatric establishment where his suitability to face a court martial was being assessed.

In the course of his unhappy sojourn at Northfield, he also wrote regular letters to Jaeger, who was by that stage serving as an artilleryman in North Africa. According to Jaeger, these lost letters catalogued the daily humiliations of hospital life, their grim flavour unleavened by the humour that his friend used to find in most circumstances.

Maclaren-Ross's darkest fear, expressed in his letters to Hart-Davis, was that he'd be certified insane, but this never happened. His spell at Northfield provided the prelude to his brief incarceration in the Detention Barrack at Colchester, after which he was declared 'unfit for military service'. On his release from the army in August 1943, Maclaren-Ross settled in London, the city with which he would become synonymous. He celebrated his release from the discipline and restrictions of military life by immersing himself in the world of bohemian London, a world he would memorialise in numerous short stories and in the 'Fitzrovian Nights' chapter of *Memoirs of the Forties*.

During the latter stages of the war, the epicentre of literary London was the Wheatsheaf pub on Rathbone Place. Maclaren-Ross became a ubiquitous presence at the bar, where he crossed paths with an extraordinary range of people, encompassing Dylan Thomas, George Orwell, Anthony Burgess and Aleister Crowley. Even among his more flamboyant contemporaries, he stood out, thanks to his gangsterish dress sense as well as his habit of wearing dark glasses and clutching a cane.

The cramped, smokey confines of the Wheatsheaf offered the backdrop to his first encounter with Scylla Yates's successor, Monica Foster, who worked at the Ministry of Information, based in nearby Bloomsbury. Before long, they were living together in a series of West End hotels, the cost of which stretched their slender resources. Following his discharge from the army, Maclaren-Ross earned a meagre and erratic income as a screenwriter, working alongside Dylan Thomas for a company specialising in government-funded propaganda documentaries. He supplemented these earnings by selling short stories and film journalism to *Penguin New Writing* and other popular magazines, which had flourished in wartime conditions. By the end of 1945, he had published two volumes of stories – *The Stuff to Give the Troops* and *Better than a Kick in the Pants* – which helped to consolidate his reputation as a leading new English writer.

to THE BBC's FEATURES AND DRAMA (SOUND) DEPARTMENT

St Helen's[1]/Stocker Road/Bognor Regis/Sussex

7-4-38

Dear Sir,

Two months ago, I read in *The Daily Telegraph* that you were complaining of the shortage of new radio plays and new radio playwrights. For the past two years I have been writing plays for broadcasting purposes, but have not submitted any for your consideration as I did not think they were sufficiently good for production, and I believe in applying to my own work the same searching criticism which I should apply to the work of others. On February 18th, however, I sent to you a play entitled *Gallows Alley*,[2] adapted by me from a novel by Anthony Skene, which might be worthy of your notice if you have not already considered and rejected it. In this play, I endeavoured to produce a realistic thriller equivalent to such films as *Winterset*[3] and *Dead End*;[4] it is not for me to say whether or not I have succeeded; indeed, I do not know.

I have listened to many plays on the air, and it seems to me that, while some of them achieve a very high standard, the full possibilities of this medium have not yet been exploited. For example, it should not be necessary for the announcer to outline the scene where the play is being enacted, or for stage-directions to be read aloud; everything should be conveyed to the listener by means of sound and dialogue. This latter, by the way, is often stilted and unnatural, especially in the case of historical plays. As it is one of my aims to provide completely naturalistic dialogue, I am particularly interested in this matter.

I shall be in London on Saturday afternoon and during the following week, and if you would favour me with an interview, I should be extremely grateful. I think, without undue conceit, that you would find some of my ideas profitable in application, and I should be grateful for your advice on some technical points. Could you let me know, by return if possible, whether you would grant me an interview at any time on Saturday afternoon?

Yours faithfully,

J. Maclaren-Ross

1 Most likely because he could no longer afford to continue living at the Chelsea Hotel, also on Stocker Road, Maclaren-Ross moved to this boarding house at the beginning of 1938. The Chelsea Hotel was described in his unpublished novel *House of Cards*, a surviving fragment of which appeared in *Bitten by the Tarantula and Other Writing* (Black Spring Press, 2005).

2   A 1934 novel which, in its feeling of tragic inevitability and in the way it subjects its characters to such cold-blooded scrutiny, anticipates the novels of Patrick Hamilton (1904–62). *Gallows Alley* follows the fortunes of the beautiful but manipulative and unscrupulous daughter of a south London greengrocer. Capitalising on her looks, she changes her name and embarks on a career as an actress, her innate talent for deception ensuring her success. By her late thirties, though, she has become a cocaine addict. This addiction leads her into an ill-fated relationship with the crooked 'Dr Gath'.

3   A 1936 film, set on the New York waterfront. It starred Burgess Meredith and the Italian actor Eduardo Ciannelli (1887–1969). The latter – mainly typecast as a villain – was one of Maclaren-Ross's favourite movie actors. Maclaren-Ross liked to impersonate him.

4   A 1937 New York lowlife drama, scripted by Lillian Hellman and directed by William Wyler. It starred Joel McCrea, Sylvia Sidney and Humphrey Bogart. It also featured 'the Dead End Kids', a group of juvenile actors who played young New York hooligans in numerous other Hollywood films.

to   THE BBC's DIRECTOR OF FEATURES AND DRAMA (SOUND) DEPARTMENT
St Helen's / Stocker Road / Bognor Regis / Sussex
18-2-38

Dear Sir,

I have much pleasure in submitting herewith the MS of *Gallows Alley*, a radio-play adapted from the novel by Anthony Skene. I have Mr Skene's full permission to make this adaptation; his only condition being that, in the event of the play proving acceptable to you, it should be produced before the end of 1938. If there are any alterations you wish made in the play, I am perfectly ready to make them if you will communicate with me to the above address. A stamp for return postage is enclosed should the play prove unsuitable to you.

Yours faithfully,

J. Maclaren-Ross

to   MORAY McLAREN[1]
St Helen's / Stocker Road / Bognor Regis / Sussex
25-4-38

Dear Mr McLaren,

Many thanks for your letter received yesterday. It is very kind of you to take an interest in my play,[2] and I shall certainly be very pleased to revise the ending. With regard to the girl Julia, perhaps I did not give sufficient indication that she had fallen in love with Gath, and if I included a scene early in the play which would make this plain, I think it would be to advantage. I shall also stress the sympathetic side of Dr Gath; in my original version, the play began with a scene in which the doctor performed a free operation on a poor man's dog; this was intended to show his humanitarian instincts, but the beginning was later altered by Mr Skene. I did not intend to glorify Gath, but only to show him as an average decent individual who, through a fatal weakness for experiment, drifted into criminal practices. However, I think you will find my revised version a great improvement; I am working on it now, in the intervals between hawking Hoovers,[3] and directly it is completed, I intend to arrange a reading to hear how it sounds. Would you consider coming down here one weekend to be present at this, say in the course of the next two weeks? I know it is rather much to ask, but at the same time, as you are interested, it would give you a really good idea of how the play goes. I am sorry I cannot arrange this in London, but as you know, I am tied to my work down here. However, if you have a free weekend in the near future, I should esteem it a great favour if you would be present at the reading (I myself shall play the part of Blindy Ludder, the gunman).[4]

I am enclosing herewith the first part of one of my early efforts: I thought, if revised, it might make a good serial for radio. In any case, I am sending it for your opinion; it was written two years ago.[5]

Yours sincerely,

J. Maclaren-Ross

1 Moray McLaren (1901–?) was BBC Radio's Assistant Director of Features and Drama (Sound), the BBC's radio section.

2 *Gallows Alley*, adapted from the novel of the same title by Patrick Skene, pseudonym of J. Evans (1924–2000).

3 From around the beginning of that month, Maclaren-Ross had been working as a door-to-door salesman, selling Hoover vacuum cleaners.

4 The reading of the play was held in May 1938. Maclaren-Ross persuaded Mrs Francis, the owner of the boarding house, to let him stage it in her dining room. He recruited a cast that included Anthony Skene, C.K. 'Mac' Jaeger and Jaeger's wife Lydia, who had been a professional actress. According to C.K. Jaeger, their performances were – aside from Maclaren-Ross's own hammy contribution – uniformly leaden. In view of that, it was just as well that Moray McLaren was unable to attend.

5 The play in question was called *The Witch Doctor*. The script has not survived.

to MORAY McLAREN

St Helen's/Stocker Road/Bognor Regis/Sussex

22-5-38

Dear Mr McLaren,

Herewith please find the revised version of *Gallows Alley*; I have not carried out completely the scheme outlined in my synopsis,[1] but I think you will find that the two scenes which I have added, will show clearly that Julia is in love with Gath and also prevent any confusion arising in the mind of the listener with regard to the two girls. If they were brought on together, as I had originally planned, it might be too confusing, and I have therefore left the actual ending as before. If there are any further alterations which to facilitate production you find it necessary to make, you have my full permission to do so. Also, if you could give me a decision fairly soon, I should be very grateful. You will understand, I am sure, that I am not trying to hurry you; but my financial position is very insecure at present and I may not be able to hold onto my job much longer.[2] So, if when you have decided, even if you do not accept the play, you would give me another interview, I should be greatly obliged; but I trust that the alterations made will prove satisfactory.

Yours faithfully,

J. Maclaren-Ross

1 On 14 May 1938 Maclaren-Ross had written to Moray McLaren outlining the ways in which he intended to revise his script. McLaren encouraged him to go ahead with these changes.
2 His pessimism was justified. In mid-July that year, he lost his job working for Hoover as a door-to-door vacuum-cleaner salesman.

to VAL GIELGUD[1]

St Helen's/Stocker Road/Bognor Regis/Sussex

11-6-38

Dear Sir,

From Mr Moray McLaren's letter of June 8th, I understand that you would like to talk to me regarding my radio play *Gallows Alley*.[2] I shall be coming up to London one day next week, and should be delighted to call at Broadcasting House if you would name a date and time convenient to you. Would Wednesday afternoon be suitable?[3]

As Mr McLaren may have told you, I am very anxious to write broadcast plays and would like to devote my whole time to this work, but my present employment does not allow me to do so. I have, however, various plans for new plays and if you would care to discuss these or any alterations for *Gallows Alley*, I shall be very glad to do so. The plays which I am preparing include dramatisations of the Mayfair Men Case[4] and also the Stavisky Scandal[5] – naturally, in fictionised form.

Sincerely,

J. Maclaren-Ross

1   Val Gielgud (1900–81), brother of the actor John Gielgud, was the Director of Features and Drama (Sound), the BBC's radio section.

2   Though Gielgud had rejected the play on the grounds that it was too bleak, he was 'very interested in [Maclaren-Ross's] way of writing'. (Letter from Moray McLaren to Julian Maclaren-Ross, 17 June 1938.) Both McLaren and Gielgud regarded Maclaren-Ross as a talented writer worth nurturing.

3   On 14 June 1938, Maclaren-Ross paid his second visit to Broadcasting House, where he met McLaren and Gielgud. McLaren offered Maclaren-Ross 'some preliminary help over plot outline', the facet of his work which, they felt, let him down. (Letter from Moray McLaren to Julian Maclaren-Ross, 17 June 1938.)

4   'The Mayfair Men', sometimes known as 'the Mayfair Playboys', were the stars of one of the most widely publicised British criminal cases of that era. They consisted of four suave London jewel thieves whose arrest at the Hyde Park Hotel in December 1937 led to an Old Bailey trial. They subsequently received stiff sentences, ranging from eighteen months' hard labour to seven years' imprisonment and 20 strokes of the cat-o'-nine-tails.

5   Named after the embezzler Alexandre Stavisky (1888–1934), the 'Stavisky Affair' was a French financial scandal that reached its grim climax in 1934. The well-connected fraudster at the centre of the story had been selling large numbers of bonds which turned out to be worthless. When the scheme was exposed, he appears to have committed suicide, though there was widespread speculation that he had, at the behest of his erstwhile allies, been murdered by the police.

to MORAY McLAREN

St Helen's / Stocker Road / Bognor Regis / Sussex

12-6-38

Dear Mr McLaren,

Many thanks for your letter of June 8th. I have written to Mr Gielgud, and hope to be seeing him this week. With regard to *The Witch Doctor*, I have the complete MS and will type the rest out for you; I fear, however, that it will not be long enough for a serial: it should run about an hour. It is one of my very early efforts and I do not like it much because of the melodramatic plot, but I will submit it to you if you think anything could be done with it. There is in my work an unfortunate tendency towards melodrama, which I am endeavouring to subdue by means of realistic treatment; in my future plays, I hope to succeed in doing this.

Yours sincerely,

J. Maclaren-Ross

to VAL GIELGUD

St Helen's / Stocker Road / Bognor Regis / Sussex

20-6-38

Dear Mr Gielgud,

Many thanks for your letter received this morning. *The Witch Doctor* was the first play I ever wrote, and so I did not expect you to like it very much. I shall certainly send you something for the autumn, and over the weekend will prepare some synopsis of projective plays. Paramount have given me permission to adapt *Gun for Sale* provided that only one performance is given over the air.[1]

If, after seeing the synopses, you would let me know which you think is most suitable, I will begin the script without further delay; I am anxious to secure an acceptance as soon as possible, as this would provide me with the means to carry on writing for radio uninterrupted by the necessity for taking irksome and unprofitable jobs which, as at present, leave me little leisure for concentrating on plays.[2]

Yours sincerely,

J. Maclaren-Ross

1 Paramount, the Hollywood studio, owned the dramatic rights to *A Gun for Sale*, Graham Greene's 1936 novel. In 1942 the studio released its film adaptation under the title *The Gun For Hire*. The film starred Alan Ladd and Veronica Lake.

2 He hadn't yet lost his job working for Hoover as a door-to-door vacuum-cleaner salesman.

to VAL GIELGUD

St Helen's / Stocker Road / Bognor Regis / Sussex

25-6-38

Dear Mr Gielgud,

Many thanks for yours received this morning. Enclosed herewith is a synopsis of the play which I plan to write from one of Anthony Skene's shorter stories.[1] Others follow as soon as possible.

Yours sincerely,

J. Maclaren-Ross

This play will be presented in a very much lighter vein than *Gallows Alley*; despite its occasional grim passages, there is a strong atmosphere of comedy about it – in the scenes between the pompous professor, who believes quite sincerely in his own powers, while being not averse to making money out of them, and his foolish adoring secretary; and also in conversations between Heapey and his henchman, who begs to be allowed to play 'jokes' on people whom he dislikes. I shall attempt here a mixture of farce and tragedy, not incompatible ingredients if the mixture is properly stirred.

1 Maclaren-Ross's play *The Stars Foretell Murder* was adapted from the short story 'Predicted Murder'.

to VAL GIELGUD

c/o C. Collins[1] / Heathfield / Eastergate / near Chichester / Sussex

8-8-38

Dear Mr Gielgud,

I have been in touch with Paramount over the radio rights of *Gun for Sale*, and the agreement is not satisfactorily settled. I've also discussed the script with Graham Greene himself,[2] and the adaptation is progressing pretty well.

Unfortunately, owing to a remittance which I expected not coming through, I find myself very awkwardly situated, and I was wondering whether you could employ me in any capacity, if it were only a temporary job. Mr McLaren spoke to me about a position in April, and said there might be a vacancy later on, otherwise I would not trouble you in the matter. Any sort of job would do, if it gave me the means to carry on and allowed me time to finish the plays which I am writing for your autumn schedule. Otherwise I shall not be able to complete them, as there are unfortunately no jobs vacant down here which would enable me to keep going.[3] I must apologise for intruding my personal and financial troubles upon you, but if you happened to have any sort of vacancy, it would assist me tremendously, and I feel sure you will understand and excuse me for bothering you.

Yours sincerely,

J. Maclaren-Ross

1 After losing his job with Hoover, Maclaren-Ross must have been unable to afford to remain at St Helen's boarding house. Collins must have been a friend who had offered him temporary accommodation.

2 Maclaren-Ross had visited Greene at his London home during the second week of July 1938. He later wrote about the visit in *Memoirs of the Forties* (*Collected Memoirs*, Black Spring Press, 2004, pp. 194–206).

3 In desperation, Maclaren-Ross had teamed up with C.K. Jaeger, who had set up a garden maintenance business, though neither of them knew much about gardening. Unsurprisingly, the venture soon failed. Their friend Martin Jordan offers a comical account of their antics in 'Maclaren-Ross at the Mower' (*London Magazine*, December 1971/January 1972).

to VAL GIELGUD

c/o C. Collins / Heathfield / Eastergate / near Chichester / Sussex

17-9-38

Dear Mr Gielgud,

Here is the adaption of *Gun for Sale*; I have dispatched, at the same time, a copy for Graham Greene's approval. It is possible that after he has read it he may wish to make some alterations, but that should not affect the general plot and atmosphere of the play, which follows the book closely.

I have not been able to hold a reading this time, so cannot give you any accurate time for the play to run, but if you find it too long, there are scenes which can easily be deleted.

In view of the present political situation, would it not be to advantage to change the names of the countries concerned?

Hoping you will be satisfied.

Yours sincerely,

J. Maclaren-Ross

to VAL GIELGUD

3 Argyle Road[1]/Bognor Regis/Sussex
30-10-38

Dear Mr Gielgud,

As it is now over 6 weeks since I submitted to you the MS of *A Gun For Sale*, and 4 weeks in the case of *Stars Foretell Murder*, I wonder if you could manage to give me a decision within the next seven days? You'll appreciate that, while I have no wish to hurry you in the matter and while I fully realise that you're a busy man, I am at the same time anxious to know the result of these two plays; and as my financial position is now worse than ever,[2] I should naturally like to know whether there's any chance of an acceptance and a consequent cheque. I've no desire to intrude my personal and monetary troubles upon you; I merely mention these facts as an excuse for asking you, if possible, to hasten your decision. As you will see by above, I have changed my address again; but this will only find me for the following week: after that I've no idea where I shall be.

Yours sincerely,

J. Maclaren-Ross

1 By late September 1938, Maclaren-Ross had left Heathfield and moved into a ground-floor bedsit at 15 Kimbell Terrace on Belmont Street in Bognor Regis. During the penultimate week of October, though, he had been turfed out of these lodgings due to non-payment of rent. He'd then moved to 3 Argyll Road, a tiny Victorian terraced house near the centre of Bognor.
2 When the garden maintenance business, on which he and C.K. Jaeger had been working failed, he'd found a job at the Butlin's funfair on the Eastern Esplanade at Bognor Regis. Sacked from that, he had recently been forced to register for Unemployment Assistance.

to MORAY McLAREN

3 Argyle Road/Bognor Regis/Sussex
1-11-38

Dear Mr McLaren,

Many thanks for your letter received this evening, with regard to the acceptance of *Gun for Sale*. You will, I'm sure, understand that I would not have asked you to hasten your decision if it were not for the fact that things have been really bad with me of late.

I will certainly make any minor alterations necessary and will get in touch with Mr Greene in this connection. I am also preparing two more plays which should be ready for your consideration in the near future.

Yours sincerely,

J. Maclaren-Ross

to VAL GIELGUD

3 Argyle Road / Bognor Regis / Sussex

26-11-38

Dear Mr Gielgud,

Early in the week, I submitted a script *The Last Passenger*, a radio-play adapted by me from a play by Eugene Ertz.[1] Mr Ertz dispatched this, addressed to Mr McLaren, whom we have just heard is away on the Continent; so perhaps you would get the script from his secretary and look it over, if you're interested? I think you will like it.

During the next four weeks, I plan to send you five new plays, as follows:

Adaptations

Reply to an Echo   (from a play by Eugene Ertz)
I Am Your Brother   (from novels by G.S. Marlowe)[2]
Caracas[3]

Original MSS

Newgate Calendar   (the life and death of Jack Sheppard)
Nightshade   (a play about the French underworld)[4]

I hope to be in London the week after next, and would like to have a talk with you about these one day when you are not too busy.

With regard to *Gun for Sale*, I have now prepared a revised version in accordance with Graham Greene's suggestions, which I will let you have directly it is typed out.

Yours sincerely,

J. Maclaren-Ross

1   Eugene Horsfall-Ertz was a Bognor Regis eccentric and aspiring writer who had become friendly with Maclaren-Ross and his circle.
2   *I Am Your Brother* (1935), a Gothic fantasy novel which had acquired a cult following. 'G.S. (Gabriel) Marlowe' was the pseudonym of Gabriel Beer-Hoffman (1901–71), a Jewish Viennese writer living in London.

3 Based on a G.S. Marlowe short story of the same name, from his collection *Their Little Lives* (1938).
4 No synopsis or script of the play has survived.

to VAL GIELGUD

Greenleaves[1]/Robins Drive/Aldwick/Bognor Regis/Sussex

2-1-39

Dear Mr Gielgud,

Thank you for your letter. I quite understand the position[2] and am sorry to hear of the illness of your staff. I hope you have not been ill yourself.

With regard to *The Stars Foretell*, I shall be pleased to get another copy typed out for you, but first I think I shall have to revise the script, as on re-reading it, I am very dissatisfied. I also thought of rewriting my first play *Gallows Alley* at some later date.

The script of my adaptation of G.S. Marlowe's *I Am Your Brother* is now ready and the bulk of it has been approved by Marlowe himself, but there are still some minor alterations to be made. When Marlowe has been through the MS, I will forward a copy on to you, with a list of the corrections appended. I hope to get this done next week.

Yours sincerely,

J. Maclaren-Ross

1 The ramshackle bungalow where Maclaren-Ross was living as the sub-tenant of the married couple C.K. Jaeger (1912–) and Lydia Jaeger (1906–79), who had a young daughter, Karel. The four of them had moved into Greenleaves in December 1938.
2 Gielgud had written to him, apologising for the fact that the BBC had mislaid the script of *The Stars Foretell*.

to VAL GIELGUD

Greenleaves/Robins Drive/Aldwick/Bognor Regis/Sussex

14-1-39

Dear Mr Gielgud,

I am enclosing under separate cover the typescript of *Jack Sheppard*, which I have written in collaboration with Martin Jordan.[1] As you will see, the dialogue is completely modernised in so far as is compatible with the eighteenth-century characters; the thieves' slang of the period is used in moderation, and with regard to oaths, phrases such as 'Go to hell' are employed instead of 'Devil rot your bones' etc. No 'Zounds' or

'Gadzooks', although 'God's blood' is used now and then, to remind listeners that after all they are listening to a gangster-drama over 200 years old.

A friend of mine listened-in to *The Small*, the play on Jonathan Wild[2] which was produced last month, and reported to me that the character of Wild therein, differed considerably from my conception of him, so I hope that the production of this play will not debar your acceptance of ours, should you think it deserving of performance.

The play is a very free adaptation of Ainsworth's book, written 100 years ago;[3] in fact only a very few scenes of the novel remain, as we did not think that the romantic story which Ainsworth imposed upon the historical facts was suitable for modern listeners.

I shall be in London one day next week, and if you could at any rate glance through the play quickly, I should be most grateful, although I appreciate that you are a busy man and hope you will not think that I am attempting to hurry your decision in any way.

I am not quite certain which day I am coming to town yet, but will let you know beforehand, as I should very much like to see you. I have to meet Mr G.S. Marlowe to discuss my adaptation of *I Am Your Brother*; this is now finished and will probably be submitted to you the week after next.

Yours sincerely,

J. Maclaren-Ross

1   Martin Jordan was a friend of both Maclaren-Ross and C.K. Jaeger. Maclaren-Ross had first met Jordan in 1936 when Jordan, also an aspiring writer, had been working in an estate agent's office near Bognor Regis.
2   Jonathan Wild (1683–1725), notorious criminal.
3   *Jack Sheppard: A Romance* (1839), by William Harrison Ainsworth.

to VAL GIELGUD

Greenleaves / Robins Drive / Aldwick / Bognor Regis / Sussex

14-2-39

Dear Mr Gielgud,

I am sending you herewith my radio adaptation of G.S. Marlowe's novel *I Am Your Brother*. The script is well over the usual length, but considering the success which the book had when it was first published, I thought you might make an exception in its favour should the play meet with your approval. The script is still subject to Mr Marlowe's final approval, but he has seen most of it and requires only a few minor alterations to be made.[1] If you would have a look at the MS and let me know what you think, Mr Marlowe and I can then discuss and correct, once you have reached a decision. I dispatched a copy of the script to him last week, but have not yet had a reply.

Yours sincerely,

J. Maclaren-Ross

1 Accompanied by C.K. Jaeger, another fan of Marlowe's work, Maclaren-Ross had first met him in December 1938. Marlowe turned out to be an intriguing, slightly mysterious figure. A section of Maclaren-Ross's *Memoirs of the Forties* (*Collected Memoirs*, Black Spring Press, 2004, pp. 215–21) is devoted to Marlowe. It describes Marlowe's disappearance, following his ill-fated decision to travel to Norway in early 1940, just before the country was invaded by the Nazis. Maclaren-Ross mentions encountering a man who claimed to have met Marlowe in the early 1960s. Recent research by the American writer Robert Nedelkoff has revealed that Marlowe somehow survived his Norwegian trip and resurfaced in Scotland. In *Love Stronger Than Death* (Fordham University Press, 2000), Father Ronald J. Walls describes meeting Marlowe there between 1947 and 1948. Walls refers to Marlowe as a 'Jewish Catholic convert' who had 'written screenplays in Hollywood'.

to THE BBC

Greenleaves / Robins Drive / Aldwick / Bognor Regis / Sussex

15-2-39

Dear Sir,

Thank you for your letter of February 13th, which has just been forwarded to me at above address.

I shall be pleased to accept the fee of twenty guineas for a single broadcast of my adaptation *The Stars Foretell* as offered. I am writing to Mr Anthony Skene today, asking him to get in touch with you directly, unless you have already written to him. I had made no definite arrangement financially with him, but will leave him to make what arrangement commends itself to him with regard to division of the fee.

Yours faithfully,

J. Maclaren-Ross

to THE BBC

Greenleaves / Robins Drive / Aldwick / Bognor Regis / Sussex

18-2-39

Sir,

With reference to my play *The Stars Foretell*. I have just received a letter from Mr Anthony Skene saying that all he requires from the production is the mention of his name as author at every performance. I should like also the title of his story to be announced, as follows:

The Stars Foretell
A play for broadcasting by J. Maclaren-Ross
adapted from a story *The Predicted Murder* by Anthony Skene

If an advance of the fee of 20 guineas could be made to me as soon as possible, I should be very grateful.

Yours faithfully,

J. Maclaren-Ross

to VAL GIELGUD

Greenleaves / Robins Drive / Aldwick / Bognor Regis / Sussex

14-3-39

Dear Mr Gielgud,

With regard to the play *Jack Sheppard*, written by me in collaboration with Martin Jordan, and submitted to you two months ago, I should be grateful to hear your decision as soon as possible.[1]

Yours sincerely,

J. Maclaren-Ross

1 On 31 March 1939, Moray McLaren wrote Maclaren-Ross a rejection letter.

to MORAY McLAREN

Greenleaves / Robins Drive / Aldwick / Bognor Regis / Sussex

16-3-39

Dear Mr McLaren,

Thank you for your letter and the revised script of *Gun for Sale;*[1] I have read this through and think it is all right. I should like to know, however, an approximate date for production of this play, and also my

19

other play *The Stars Foretell*, which was accepted last month. I agreed to a fee of 20 guineas for one performance of this, and wrote asking for an advance to Mr Hamilton Marr,[2] who informed me that none could be made but that the sum was payable on production only. In the circumstances I should be grateful to know when this is likely to take place, particularly as the script of *Stars Foretell* was held up for five months before acceptance and was believed by Mr Gielgud to have been lost. I had furthermore understood, from an article published by Jonah Barrington in *The Daily Express*, that payment was made on acceptance. However, I hope that the production of the play will take place as soon as possible, and hope you will be able to confirm this.

Yours sincerely,

J. Maclaren-Ross

1 With Graham Greene's approval, Moray McLaren had instructed a junior member of his staff to produce an abbreviated version of Maclaren-Ross's adaptation of *A Gun For Sale*.
2 An employee in the BBC's Copyright Department.

to VAL GIELGUD

Greenleaves / Robins Drive / Aldwick / Bognor Regis / Sussex

10-4-39

Dear Mr Gielgud,

Thank you for your letter regarding *Jack Sheppard*. Perhaps you would care to consider an entirely different and less elaborate version, which follows more truthfully the facts of Sheppard's life? If so, perhaps you would let me know, when I will immediately start work on the script. In this new version I will endeavour to lighten the technical complications and expense entailed in production. As you must be aware, a play on *Jack Sheppard* by Mr Mervyn Mills was produced on television a week or two ago, but apparently this does not affect the chances of a radio play on the same subject. I have not seen Mr Mills's play, purposely, as I did not wish to be influenced in any way on my treatment of Sheppard's life, a theme which I have studied for some considerable time.

Yours sincerely,

J. Maclaren-Ross

to VAL GIELGUD

Greenleaves/Robins Drive/Aldwick/Bognor Regis/Sussex

22-4-39

Dear Mr Gielgud,

Enclosed herewith a synopsis for a new version of Jack Sheppard. My proposed treatment is in the form of a play based on these events. If you would mark the main incidents which, in your view, form the most suitable for inclusion and which would reduce over-elaboration and expense in production, I should be greatly obliged.[1]

Yours sincerely,

J. Maclaren-Ross

1 The new script of *Jack Sheppard* was rejected. Retitled *The Bowl of St Giles*, the script by Maclaren-Ross and Martin Jordan was eventually broadcast on the BBC Home Service on 1 August 1947. Maclaren-Ross's interest in Sheppard also spawned a completed but unproduced filmscript, entitled *Jack Sheppard*.

to MORAY McLAREN

Greenleaves/Robins Drive/Aldwick/Bognor Regis/Sussex

25-7-39

Dear Mr McLaren,

Thank you for your letter of yesterday's date. With regard to *The Stars Foretell*, I am enclosing herewith a revised script which I should be obliged if you would forward to the producer concerned. It contains a new opening which I consider an improvement and some minor changes in the dialogue.

I enclose also a new play, *Caracas*, adapted from a story by G.S. Marlowe. I must apologise for this being in manuscript, but my present employment does not allow me very much time for getting MSS typed.[1]

Mr Marlowe has not yet seen this adaptation, but if you would kindly read the script and let me know whether the play is acceptable, any minor changes which Mr Marlowe desires could be made in the event of a favourable decision. He is a very busy man and as I am anxious for quick results I thought it best to let you see the script first, and approach Mr Marlowe in the event of acceptance. He gave me his permission to adapt the story last November.

Yours sincerely,

J. Maclaren-Ross

1 The nature of his 'present employment' remains unclear.

to MORAY McLAREN

Greenleaves/Robins Drive/Aldwick/Bognor Regis/Sussex

8-8-39

Dear Mr McLaren,

Many thanks for your letter of August 3rd. I am sorry that the date of *Gun for Sale* is postponed, although I can quite see your point in view of the international situation.[1]

I shall probably be in London one day next week, when if possible I should like to see you. In the meantime I hope that *Caracas* will prove suitable for inclusion in your programme.

Yours sincerely,

J. Maclaren-Ross

1 *A Gun for Sale*, previously included in the BBC's July to September schedule, had been postponed by the Programme Committee. On 3 August 1939 the Committee had declared that 'any play, however fantastic, dealing with the possibility of a general war or with such controversial subjects as an armaments racket is certain of a hostile reception.'

to MORAY McLAREN

Greenleaves/Robins Drive/Aldwick/Bognor Regis/Sussex

13-8-39

Dear Mr McLaren,

I am enclosing herewith the script of a new play *Hold-up in Harley Street* adapted from a story by G.S. Marlowe.[1] I have permission to adapt this, although Mr Marlowe has not yet seen the script. However, as it follows the story almost exactly as to dialogue, with only a few minor changes necessary for broadcasting, I think he will approve. In any case, to save time, I am sending it to you first to see what you think of the idea. If you could give me a quick decision I should be greatly obliged. I shall probably be in London next week and can then see both you and Mr Marlowe about the play and also the other play *Caracas*, if you will give me an interview.[2]

Yours sincerely,

J. Maclaren-Ross

1 The story features in the 1938 collection *Their Little Lives* (1938).

2 His meeting with McLaren is described in *Memoirs of the Forties* (see *Collected Memoirs*, Black Spring Press, 2004, pp. 207–10).

to MORAY McLAREN

Greenleaves/Robins Drive/Aldwick/Bognor Regis/Sussex

16-9-39

Dear Mr McLaren,

At the outbreak of war I was engaged in writing two new radio plays; I abandoned work on these as I had no means of knowing whether plays would be produced as usual. Now that programmes are returning to normal, I am still not sure whether you are accepting any new material and whether it is a waste of time to continue work on the plays. Perhaps you could let me know about this? And also in the event of your willingness to consider new plays, must these be necessarily of a light or fantastical nature? Is there for instance a chance of *Hold-up in Harley Street* being accepted?

I am sorry to worry you with questions at a time like this, when you must be so busy and worried, but I am sure you will understand and appreciate my reasons for asking them.

Yours sincerely,

J. Maclaren-Ross

to MORAY McLAREN

Greenleaves/Robins Drive/Aldwick/Bognor Regis/Sussex

13-3-40

Dear Mr McLaren,

As it is now over a year since my play *Stars Foretell* was accepted for broadcasting, I wonder if you could now arrange for the second half of the fee, 10 guineas, to be paid to Mr J. Evans,[1] of No 2 Park Avenue, Maidstone, Kent; that is, unless an early date for broadcasting the play has been fixed. I should be very much obliged if you could arrange this.

Listening to recent programmes I note that thrillers have been reinstated; I wonder therefore if you would care to consider further plays by me? I have several themes in mind, not necessarily of the thriller variety, and some historical themes, such as the Jack Sheppard play which I once mentioned to you. If you would care for any further material, perhaps you would let me know at above address?

Yours faithfully,

J. Maclaren-Ross

1 The real name behind the pseudonym Anthony Skene.

to THE BBC

Greenleaves/Robins Drive/Aldwick/Bognor Regis/Sussex

4-4-40

Dear Sir,

With regard to my play *The Stars Foretell*, adapted from a story by Anthony Skene, and accepted for broadcasting on February 13th last year, I wonder if it would be possible to arrange for the remainder of the fee, 10 guineas, to be paid to Mr J. Evans of 2, Park Avenue, Maidstone, Kent.

While I do not wish to appear unreasonable or impatient, the play has been held up for over a year, and Mr Moray McLaren informs me that there is no possibility of production in the near future. I therefore suggest that since production is usual within a year from the date of acceptance, the fee should now be forthcoming.

In the case of my other adaptation, Graham Greene's *Gun For Sale*, a cheque was paid to me in December, just over a year from the date of acceptance, although owing to the war, the play was not produced in September as scheduled. I hope therefore that you will be able to make a similar arrangement with regard to *Stars Foretell* as soon as possible.

Yours Faithfully,

J. Maclaren-Ross

to THE BBC

Greenleaves/Robins Drive/Aldwick/Bognor Regis/Sussex

3-5-40

Dear Sir,

In reply to your letter of April 23rd, I have considered the matter of *Stars Foretell* carefully, and have come to the conclusion that I am not prepared to wait indefinitely for payment of the fee to be made.

It is already a year and three months since the play was accepted and so far only half the fee has been paid over. I consider that I have waited quite long enough. If it is your practice to pay on production, then production should be made within a reasonable time.

In no other branch of literary activity are authors expected to wait for over a year before payment is made for work accepted, and unless a cheque for 10 guineas is forthcoming by return of post, I shall be obliged to employ legal aid to recover the sum due to me.[1]

Yours faithfully,

J. Maclaren-Ross

1   Legal action was rendered unnecessary when, on 8 May, the BBC paid the outstanding money. This was accompanied by a note informing him that *The Stars Foretell* had been 'cancelled due to the war'.

to RUPERT HART-DAVIS[1]
           4 Platoon / 'Z' Coy / ITC Suffolk Regiment / Bury St Edmunds / Suffolk[2]
                                                                                  9-3-41

Dear Hart-Davis,

I have been meaning to write you for some time, but as I daresay you realise, one gets very little time for anything in the army; and I use almost every spare moment I have for writing. How are you doing? When I last heard from you in July last, you expected to be called up either for the army or some other form of national service. I have often wondered how you were getting on, and would appreciate a brief note if you have the time to write one. I get few letters, but that's my fault for being myself such a rotten correspondent.

I managed to finish a long short story of the Riviera, *The Simple Life*[3] (35,000 words) and if you are still at Cape's and at all interested, this can be obtained from William Makins[4] of *Horizon*. In any case I should value your opinion as a critic. Makins doesn't like this new story as well as some of the former ones and I should like to see if you agree with him.

I am now writing two novels, the Russian exiles[5] and the vacuum-cleaner salesman:[6] both are doing tolerably well. I've also collected some material for a book on life in the army training camps. I have read Anthony Cotterell's book[7] and do not like it at all. Mine would be a more personal record. I am unable, as Cotterell did, to sink my personality entirely in the army life or to forego what ambitions I have as a writer because I happen to have been enlisted. I mean to carry on and do what writing I can in whatever conditions.

Did you read *Angels on Horseback* by Karel Jaeger?[8] He is a great friend of mine[9] and as a matter of fact I typed the MS for him. I am very anxious to read Hemingway's *For Whom the Bell Tolls*, but cannot get it at all down here. In fact it is very difficult to get any good books at all in the army.

I have landed a job connected with Intelligence work in the tropics,[10] and may be going any time now. It will mean promotion, possibly

a commission, when I get there. I should value a letter from you before
I go.

With my very best wishes,
Yours sincerely,
J. Maclaren-Ross

Please excuse the paper: it's all I get down here.

1   In his capacity as a director of the publishing firm of Jonathan Cape, Rupert
Hart-Davis (1907–99) had first encountered Maclaren-Ross just over six months
earlier. The encounter was prompted by the June 1940 issue of the literary
magazine *Horizon*, which published 'A Bit of a Smash', the story that marked
Maclaren-Ross's debut as a published writer. Impressed by it, Hart-Davis wrote to
him expressing interest in releasing a collection of his short stories.
2   Maclaren-Ross had been conscripted into the army as a private the previous
summer. Due to a chronic knee problem, caused by a bicycle accident at the age of
12, he'd been taken off active duties and hospitalised. According to a letter from his
girlfriend, Eileen Cooke, to C.K. Jaeger, written on 17 October 1940, the doctors at
the hospital had diagnosed that 'the tendons of his [left] knee are cut'. From his
original unit, Maclaren-Ross ended up being transferred to the ITC (Infantry
Training Centre) at Bury St Edmunds.
3   *The Simple Life* was eventually published under the title *Bitten By The
Tarantula* (Allan Wingate, 1946).
4   Bill Makins, the magazine's Business Manager, was acting as Maclaren-
Ross's literary agent.
5   The novel, entitled *Threnody on a Gramophone*, was never completed. A
brief section of the opening chapter surfaced among a cache of manuscripts
discovered during the autumn of 2007. This is reproduced in Appendix 4.
6   Originally entitled *The Salesman Only Rings Once*, this would later be
published as *Of Love and Hunger* (Allan Wingate, 1947).
7   *Oh it's Nice to Be in the Army* (Victor Gollancz, 1941).
8   *Angels on Horseback* was written under the name of 'C.K. Jaeger'. During the
1950s, Jaeger would switch his attention to children's books, written under the
name 'Karel Jaeger'.
9   Immediately before being conscripted into the army, Maclaren-Ross had
been sharing a house with C.K. Jaeger, along with Jaeger's wife Lydia and their
daughter, Karel.
10   Like so many of Maclaren-Ross's hopes and plans, the promised job never
materialised.

to CYRIL CONNOLLY[1]

The Lantern Café[2]/Aldwick Rd/Bognor Regis/Sussex
Late January 1942

Dear Mr Connolly,
    Attached herewith please find the MS of an army story called 'The
Tape'. The title refers to the strip which a lance-corporal wears on his

arm and not to the red tape which strangles all ranks in the army and especially those working in the orderly room.

Perhaps you'd be kind enough to glance through this when you've a moment and let me know whether it is acceptable to *Horizon* or if not, return it to above address, on Thursday morning. I shall be proceeding on 9 days leave.³ I am anxious for a quick decision as I am hard-up and if you don't want the story I can offer it elsewhere, possibly obtaining thereby some cash to tide me over whilst on my leave. If possible, I will give you a ring about 2 o'clock on that day when I stop off in town.

With apologies for seeming to hurry you,

Yours very sincerely,

J. Maclaren-Ross

1   Cyril Connolly (1903–74), editor of *Horizon*, the influential literary magazine which had first featured Maclaren-Ross's writing.
2   The business address of Maclaren-Ross's girlfriend Eileen Cooke. Her father so disapproved of their relationship that Maclaren-Ross would have been reluctant to send letters to her family home.
3   Maclaren-Ross visited Connolly en route to Bognor Regis, where he spent his leave with Eileen Cooke, most likely staying at a mutual friend's house.

to JOHN LEHMANN¹

'Z' Coy/70th Bn Suffolk Regiment/Felixstowe/Suffolk

c/o Miss E. Cooke/Beach Café²/Bognor Regis/Sussex

11-7-42

Dear Mr Lehmann,

You may remember that I sent you, in 1940, some stories which you did not feel inclined to publish: they were in fact what I call my civilian stories and some of them have, or are now, coming out (*Fortune Anthology, English Story* Series II & III).³

Now, having kept quiet for two years, since I've been in the army, (except for a 35,000 word story about the Riviera which may be published separately soon, and a novel which I'm endeavouring to finish now)⁴ I have suddenly embarked on a series of army stories and there are twelve of them so far, four already sold (*Horizon, Selected Writing, Tribune, Modern Reading*) and the others have not yet been circulated. I've read everything that's been written about the army up to now and find that most of the stuff is either journalese, like Cotterell, or deadly dull: I liked a story you printed called *They Kept Him On The Square*. The best actually are those written by Alun Lewis⁵ and not yet published, which I read in typescript when he was billeted in the house next door to me; and Gwynn-Browne's book *FSP*.[6] I hesitated at first to write anything about the army, my opinion was that one could not see it in proper perspective until afterwards and that one should therefore try to avoid it as much as possible and use the wartime period for recapitulation and a summing-up of the past; as Pritchett[7] seems to be doing in 'The Chestnut Tree' and 'Aunt Gertrude', both very fine, and Rosamond Lehmann in 'The Red Haired Miss Daintreys' and 'The Gipsy's Baby': this last a truly magnificent story and one which gave me, I think greater pleasure than anything you've ever printed – except perhaps 'The Sailor'.[8]

So I thought I'd leave the army alone, and then one afternoon I started a story and finished it, Cyril Connolly bought it,[9] meanwhile I wrote others and all of a sudden the material which I must have been subconsciously accumulating fell into place and I'm swamped under with subjects: yesterday in the train I thought of three and today am writing the stories.

Well if you'd like to see any drop me a card and I'll send you some. They're mostly between 1,500 to 3,000 words and comic in viewpoint, although the one *Horizon*'s taken is 7000 words. Meanwhile the best of luck for *New Writing*[10] and I'm anxiously awaiting your next series, also *Penguin New Writing* No 13: I have all the numbers so far.

Yours sincerely,

J. Maclaren-Ross

1   John Lehmann (1907–87) was the editor of the popular literary magazine *Penguin New Writing*.

2   The new establishment opened by Maclaren-Ross's girlfriend Eileen Cooke.

3   The first of these submissions was on 12 March 1938, when he sent Lehmann the manuscripts of 'a jazz poem "Dance Marathon"' and nine short stories. The stories were listed by Maclaren-Ross as follows: '"Five Finger Exercises" (3,000 words), "A Drink at Harrison's" (1,500 words), "Forever in My Heart" (1,500 words), "Birthplace" (6,000 words) "Nichevo" (3,000 words), "We've a Lot to Be Thankful For" (1,000 words), "As Others See Us" (1,500 words), "Moon Above" (2,000 words), "Action" (2,000 words)'. On 27 April 1938, Maclaren-Ross sent another letter to Lehmann, including further examples of his work. Of the stories in the list, 'We've a Lot to Be Thankful For', 'Forever In My Heart', 'As Others See Us' and 'Moon Above' were never published, and the manuscripts appear to have been lost. 'Five Finger Exercises', 'A Drink at Harrison's' (retitled 'The Hell of a Time'), 'Nichevo', 'Birthplace' (retitled 'The Snows of Yesterday') and 'Action' (retitled 'Action 1938') did, however, make it into print.

4   The novel in question was *The Salesman Only Rings Once*, subsequently published as *Of Love and Hunger*.

5   Alun Lewis (1915–44), Welsh poet and short-story writer.
6   Arthur Gwynn-Browne, *FSP: An NCO's Description of His and Others' First Six Months of War, January 1st–June 1st 1940* (Chatto & Windus, 1942).
7   V.S. Pritchett (1900–97), novelist, critic, memoirist and short-story writer.
8   A short story written by V.S. Pritchett (see previous note). It appeared in *Penguin New Writing* 12.
9   The short story was 'I Had to Go Sick', published in *Horizon* in August 1942.
10   The literary miscellany edited by John Lehmann and published by Leonard and Virginia Woolf's Hogarth Press.

to JOHN LEHMANN

30-7-42

Dear Mr Lehmann,

Thank you so much for your letter of July 17th and the issue of *Penguin New Writing* enclosed therewith. You must please excuse the delay in answering, but I wanted to send you the enclosed story and I could not get it typed out until today.

I think the issue you sent me was tremendous, quite one of your best, and I must thank you again for sending it to me. When you are stationed in a town like this[1] where hardly any books of importance penetrate, it means such a lot to receive anything like this: you can't imagine.

I like 'Report on Today'[2] and also '20 Cigarettes'[3] and I was very glad to read 'Making of a New Zealander'[4] which I had hitherto missed. I think the idea of a quarterly is very good if it permits you to enlarge the magazine and include more stuff. I liked Keith Vaughan's[5] drawings which are typical, especially the one of the Reading Room, which very much resembles the place where I used to work on Sunday afternoons when I was at the Training Camp at Bury. I look forward also to seeing *New Writing and Daylight*[6] and your article on *FSP*. I had an extraordinary letter from Arthur Gwynn-Browne in answer to one I wrote him saying how much I liked his book; the letter was very affected and I thought it such a pity that I may have been rather rude to him in my reply. But it annoys me when a man keeps up his character as an eccentric when he is not actually writing anything: it's as though one met Charles Laughton and he insisted on addressing one in the character of Captain Bligh.

Reference the enclosed story,[7] I hope you will like it: I think it is not too bad. It is at any rate true to hospital life in the army. If you don't like it, I hope you will continue to consider stuff from me; for although I've had five of my army stories accepted to date and am still awaiting decisions on the others, they are really only in the nature of five finger exercises so far and better examples will only be along later. Oh, and I would like to do you a 'Report on Today' all about life in the Company Office, which I think you will find sufficiently diverting: there is excellent material for satire all around.

I'm glad you have taken one of Alun Lewis' long ones: I hope, 'Private Jones'. If you want me to do the above mentioned 'Report', will you let me know soon as it looks as if I may have less leisure for writing in the very near future and I would like to get that done now? The above address will find me until the 12th of August, after which please write to the one on the enclosed MS.

With very best wishes,

Yours sincerely,

J. Maclaren-Ross

1   Maclaren-Ross was still stationed in Felixstowe.
2   A regular section of *Penguin New Writing*, devoted to documentary writing. The 'Report on Today' featured in Issue 13 contained the ballet dancer and former 'Bright Young Thing' William Chappell's army memoir 'The Sky Makes Me Hate It'; 'The Pilot's Diary', Richard Nugent's essay about his experiences in the RAF; and the New Zealand writer Dan Davin's short story 'Under the Bridge', set in wartime Crete. Maclaren-Ross would later strike up a close friendship with Davin. At this stage, however, the two of them had not yet met. Their first conversation, recounted in Davin's memoir *Closing Times*, featured a reference to 'Under the Bridge'.
3   Joseph Gurnard's brief, playful essay about cigarette-smoking. 'Gurnard' was the pseudonym for what the magazine described as 'a well-known London journalist'.
4   A short story by the New Zealand writer Frank Sargeson.
5   Keith Vaughan (1912–77), English painter and graphic designer.
6   Another literary miscellany edited by John Lehmann.
7   The story was 'Y-List', Maclaren-Ross's account of life in a military hospital.

to JOHN LEHMANN

'Z' Coy/70th Bn Suffolk Regiment/Felixstowe/Suffolk

5-8-42

Dear Mr Lehmann,

Thank you so much for your letter of Aug. 4. I shall certainly be pleased and proud to have 'Y List' printed in *New Writing*.[1] Regarding its defects, I'm well aware of them, in fact I hesitated before sending it to you, but in the end I didn't think I could do anything more to it in the limited time at my command and I don't think it will look too bad in print.

You see I'm obliged to write these things down at top speed usually, like 'Y List', in one day; as one's mood is so quickly altered by circumstances when in the army that otherwise I should never get anything done. And then in this story I am describing, by memory, experience over a year old and it is difficult to get anything down in the right order; when I write my complete army book *They Can't Give You a Baby*[2] I shall do it again but differently: it actually needs expansion.

But as a five finger exercise I think it can stand and I am very much encouraged by having something accepted by you; I have had all my stories written within the last month or so accepted now, except for *Lilliput*[3] and *Life and Letters*:[4] I sent them some stories and have heard nothing for over three weeks. Connolly and yourself replied within three days but from *Lilliput* nothing, although a stamped addressed envelope was enclosed for the return of the MS. It's annoying because I could quite easily sell the stories elsewhere. I should have at least one story a month appearing for the rest of this year, beginning with a long one in *Horizon*; I think this month's:[5] I've already corrected the proofs. All very encouraging.

I'm doing the Coy Office for you; it'll be along in a few days only I want to make sure it's good. Meantime here's one written yesterday which might amuse you.

When will *New Writing and Daylight* be out? I want to make sure of my copy.

You can keep on writing here; it will find me.

All the very best,

Yours sincerely,

J. Maclaren-Ross

1 'Y-List' eventually appeared in *Penguin New Writing* instead.
2 The book was never completed. Its title originated in a conversation recounted in the identically titled chapter of *Memoirs of the Forties* (*Collected Memoirs*, Black Spring Press, p. 250). '"They can do anything to you in the army bar give you a baby," an old London-Irish porter who'd had varicocele and served in four campaigns told me as I got aboard the train [bound for an Infantry Training Centre] in July 1940.'
3 A high-circulation magazine, edited by Kaye Webb, which featured short stories.
4 One of the few English wartime literary magazines which didn't include Maclaren-Ross's writing.
5 As expected, 'I Had to Go Sick' appeared in that month's edition of *Horizon*.

to JOHN LEHMANN

c/o Miss E. Cooke/Beach Café/Bognor Regis/Sussex

12-8-42

Dear Mr Lehmann,

Thank you for your last letter. I delayed replying until I had completed the enclosed.[1] This was finished today and I am forwarding it for what it's worth. It makes no attempt whatever to be a story, but *is* an accurate account of life in a particular Company Office. All the staff concerned have read their own portraits and were very pleased especially the sergeant known in the text as Smiler. But all liked the thing as a whole and wanted to know when it was going to be printed so they could buy copies. I myself didn't share their enthusiasm: I don't know whether I've done it well or not. It seemed to me the two extremes to avoid were hysteria and nostalgia. The effect of a constant boring routine on my own character I have not dealt with, but have relied on the cumulative effect of the various facts and incidents.

However that's enough apology. You may think it's too long but I thought it was better that way than just dashing off a 2,000 worder. Anyway I hope you'll like it. Please write to above address and not to the one on the MS itself as there's an impending move on.

Yours sincerely,

J. Maclaren-Ross

1 His submission, intended for the 'Report on Today' section of *Penguin New Writing*, was titled 'Are You Happy in Your Work'.

to RUPERT HART-DAVIS

'HQ' Company/No 3 Infantry Depot/Southend-on-Sea/Essex[1]

27-8-42

Dear Hart-Davis,

Thank you so much for your letter, twice re-directed, which gives me great pleasure. I've often wondered what is happening to you. Congratulations on being a Capt. and Adjt.[2] – I am still a private, graded at last B-2,[3] and employed as an Orderly Room clerk at the above address. I went in for OCTU[4] but was almost forcibly rejected at the War Office Selection Board Test, so now I'm resigned to a pipless and stripeless uniform for the duration. I'm glad you liked the story:[5] it's completely autobiographical and absolutely true. Everybody seems to like it and Evelyn Waugh wrote me very nicely. Yes, I've written 15 others and have placed most of them: *Selected Writing,*[6] *Modern Reading,*[7] *Tribune*[8] (2 short ones), *Bugle Blast,*[9] *New Writing* (2 long ones.) I've also a lot of stuff to appear in collections: *English Story*[10] is printing one of those I sent you in 1940 and 'Five Finger Exercises' came out in *Fortune Anthology.*[11] I am writing a complete book of army experiences called *They Can't Give You a Baby.* I am lucky because I will have an office to work in nights and a certain amount of free time. Well, let's hear from you again when you have a second to spare.

Meantime, the best of luck from

Yours sincerely,

J. Maclaren-Ross

1   Maclaren-Ross had been transferred to Southend-on-Sea, where he worked as a clerk in the Orderly Room at HQ Company.

2   In late 1941, Hart-Davis had been promoted to the rank of captain and appointed adjutant to the Sixth Battalion of the Coldstream Guards, based at Harrow, close to the outskirts of London.

3   A medical examination had resulted in Maclaren-Ross being re-graded 'B-2': suitable only for 'garrison duties at home and abroad'.

4   Officer Candidate Training Unit.

5   The story was 'I Had to Go Sick', which had appeared in that month's edition of *Horizon.*

6   A literary magazine edited by Reginald Moore, who was due to publish 'The Tape' in the September edition.

7   His story 'They Put Me in Charge of a Squad' appeared in the sixth issue of *Modern Reading.*

8   The Labour Party's weekly newspaper *Tribune* carried 'Death of a Comrade' in its 28 August 1942 issue, and 'The Mine' in its 23 October 1942 edition.

9   The May 1943 edition of *Bugle Blast: An Anthology of Writing from the Services* included Maclaren-Ross's short story 'Subject: Surprise Visit'.

10 *English Story,* edited by the future politician Woodrow Wyatt, featured Maclaren-Ross's pre-war story 'Happy as the Day Is Long' in its November 1942 issue.

11 The sole issue of *Fortune Anthology,* released in June 1942, was edited by Nicholas Moore, John Bayliss and Douglas Newton. It was published by the shady L.S. Caton, who would later be lampooned in Kingsley Amis's novel *Lucky Jim.*

to JOHN LEHMANN

'HQ' Company/No 3 Infantry Depot/Southend-on-Sea/Essex

2-9-42

Dear Mr Lehmann,

Proofs of 'Y List' corrected and returned herewith.

I shall be on leave and in London October 12th–14th; if you are free at all, perhaps we could meet.

Is *Penguin [New] Writing* 14 out yet? I haven't seen it.

With best wishes,

Yours sincerely,

J. Maclaren-Ross

to RUPERT HART-DAVIS

'HQ' Company/No 3 Infantry Depot/Southend-on-Sea/Essex

3-9-42

Dear Hart-Davis,

Thank you for your letter.

Reference the army book, *They Can't Give You A Baby*, it's getting on very nicely, though I don't know when it will be finished. No I have not promised it to anyone; the only thing that's promised is a 40,000 word novel to Reginald Moore for his Modern Reading Library. Collins[1] made an offer through Woodrow Wyatt of a £100 advance for my full-length novel *The Salesman Only Rings Once* – of which they had seen half – if satisfactorily completed; but God knows when I shall get that done.

As for the stories, there's nothing I should like better than to get them out as a collection. There are fifteen so far (in all approximately 40,000 words) and I am constantly adding to them. A list is appended. I have not got copies here because those that have been accepted are with the various editors but I could type them from the MSS if you are interested. It would not be necessary to do copies of 'I Had to Go Sick' or 'Death of a Comrade' (published in this week's *Tribune* August 28th) would it? And by the time I get the typing done I expect 'The Tape' will also be out in the September *Selected Writing*. Of the others, they are all awaiting decisions with editors but all should be printed in magazine form by the end of the year. Should you decide to do such a collection I suggest adding my short novel of the Riviera *The Simple Life* (35,000 words) as an effective contrast between the playboy life of the 30s and now.

Of the army stories only two, 'I Had To Go Sick' and 'Y List' (6,000 words, accepted by John Lehmann) are stories made of incidents which recur in the army book. I don't think that matters, though, as when introducing them in the latter, I am doing a chapter as a story, which should be interesting. The incidents are also considerably expanded in the army book.

Yes, I do find it hard to get books to read. If you have a copy of the Summer *New Writing and Daylight* and could lend it to me, I should appreciate it very much, or *Ulysses*, or any American story magazines. All my books are at home and I feel out of touch. There is *Death and Tomorrow* by Peter de Polnay[2] which I should very much like to read, but I don't think I could get it down here. What are you publishing lately?

If you let me know about the stories, I can get on with the typing.

Meantime, all the best from

J. Maclaren-Ross

'The Tape'	*Selected Writing*
'I Had to Go Sick'	*Horizon*
'Death of a Comrade'	*Tribune*
'They Put Me in Charge of a Squad'	*Modern Reading*
'This Mortal Coil'	
'Subject: Surprise Visit'	*Bugle Blast*
'From After Duty Sunday'[3]	
'Gas'	
'Jankers'	
'A Bit of a Stink'	
'The Mine'	*Tribune*
'Y List'	*New Writing*
'Last Time I Got My Leave'[4]	
'Are You Happy in Your Work'	
'A Sentimental Story'	

1 The publishing firm William Collins. Woodrow Wyatt had a connection with the firm, which published *English Story*, the literary anthology edited by him.

2 Published by Secker & Warburg in 1942.

3 This story appears to have been either retitled or lost.

4 Later retitled and published as 'Seven Days of Heaven'.

to RUPERT HART-DAVIS

'HQ' Company / No 3 Infantry Depot / Southend-on-Sea / Essex

15-9-42

Dear Hart-Davis,

Thank you for your letter received this morning. I agree with you about publishers except for the 40,000 word thing which the *Modern Reading* people would be doing at 2/6 a copy. I have something just that length that I want to write and you would not publish it anyway as it would be too short for you.

I have, as you know, always wanted Jonathan Cape to do my stuff for me. But it was Woodrow Wyatt who arranged with Collins about the novel and of course £100 is an attractive advance. I have to think of money more than ever now since on my 48 hour leave I arranged to get a divorce and re-marry almost immediately the decree is granted.[1] So it's important, both of us being in the Forces, to have a sum of money apart from Service pay and allowances to start us off with.

It sounds sordid but how much d'you think the army book would fetch as an advance if satisfactory? I'm very keen to get on with it but I shall have to do the novel first if it means immediate payment and the other doesn't. I have somebody else to think of now and as you say, I must get a book out with a bang since being in love has given me its attendant ambitious leanings.

So that is the position. And if the army book were successful what about doing the stories afterward? I do want the whole lot to come out, the ones you saw before and all. The army ones are doing very well, 13 sold out of 15 in less than three months. I've just sold another to *Horizon*[2] and one to *Lilliput*[3] (8 guineas a thousand).

Hoping to hear from you again shortly,

Yours ever,

J. Maclaren-Ross

1   In late August 1942 Maclaren-Ross had, whilst on leave in London, met and fallen in love with a girl named Scylla Yates, who was serving with the WAAF (Women's Auxilliary Air Force).

2   'This Mortal Coil', which appeared in the December 1942 issue.

3   *Lilliput* had purchased 'An Appreciation of Two Pictures', a spoof piece of art criticism. It was published in the magazine's December 1942 issue.

to JOHN LEHMANN

'HQ' Company / No 3 Infantry Depot / Southend-on-Sea / Essex

15-9-42

Dear Mr Lehmann,

I am sending you my new unit's address as above. I was posted here from Felixstowe on the 22nd August and shall be here for the duration unless somehow my position changes. I've not heard from you for some time and wondered perhaps if you had written and the letter had gone to my old unit; *Tribune* sent me a cheque addressed there on August 28th and it did not reach me until September 9th, as the unit had moved again twice. I've been doing very well and have sold thirteen out of fifteen stories written since the end of June. When the story came out in *Horizon* everyone wrote and Hart-Davis wrote and also Evelyn Waugh and other people wanting short stories. *Lilliput* took one of those I sent them (1,000 words) and is paying me 8 guineas for it. The money question is quite important because to get paid for the work one really wants to do gives one confidence I think. Also I have to think about it because I am getting a divorce and directly afterwards am getting married again: this happened suddenly on my last 48 hour leave. So it certainly seems as if everything is going to go all right. I look forward to hearing from you about the stories when you are not busy, but please don't take this letter as a reminder: I just wanted to write because you might have written and your letter gone astray.

I've not yet had a copy of *New Writing and Daylight* as you can't get anything down here. Will there be another *Penguin New Writing* soon and are you doing 'Y List' in it? Did the story arrive too late? I'd like to get them out because Hart-Davis wants to see the stories with a view to collecting them in book form and until they all come out, I can't do anything about it and I have still ten to appear, I hope, this year. But please don't think I'm attempting to hurry you, just do what you think best.

Meanwhile,

Yours sincerely,

J. Maclaren-Ross

to JOHN LEHMANN

'HQ' Company / No 3 Infantry Depot / Southend-on-Sea / Essex

17-9-42

Dear Mr Lehmann,

I received safely your letters of July 17th and August 4th; since then I wrote to you sending you a story 'When I Last Got My Leave', acknowledged in yours of August 6th, then later a 'Report on Today' 'Are You Happy in Your Work' acknowledged in a postcard from Miss Cooper[1] on August 14th. You had not then read the 'Report on Today' nor the second story, but said you would be writing shortly. It was a fear that owing to my recent moves (two of them)[2] the letters might have got lost that caused me to write again and not any attempt to hurry your decision in any way.

Yours sincerely,

J. Maclaren-Ross

1 Lehmann's assistant, Barbara Cooper.
2 He was referring to part of July 1942 which he'd spent on leave with his girlfriend, Eileen Cooke, in Bognor Regis. Soon afterwards he'd been posted from Felixstowe to Southend-on-Sea.

to THE OFFICER COMMANDING, HQ COMPANY, No 3 INFANTRY DEPOT

'HQ' Company / No 3 Infantry Depot / Southend-on-Sea / Essex

3-10-42

Sir,

I submit this application for 7 days' Privilege Leave from Monday 12 October to Monday 19 October 1942: reveille to 2359 hours.[1] Destination: Norwich. If granted, my address will be: ___ [2] but if permission could be granted for me to stay in London to see people for business reasons on the way through, I should be very grateful. It might be necessary for me to stay one night if the persons concerned are not actually accessible on the 12th.

Trusting that this application will meet with your kind consideration and approval,[3]

I have the honour to be, sir,

Your obedient servant,

J. Maclaren-Ross

1 Funerals and weddings were regarded as suitable reasons for granting 'privilege leave'. In this case, an impending wedding was probably the reason for the requested leave. When Maclaren-Ross had been on leave in London only a few weeks earlier, he'd met Scylla Yates, a member of the Women's Auxilliary Air Force, who was stationed near Norwich. They appear to have quickly hatched plans to marry. Maclaren-Ross wrote about the subject of his second marriage and long-overdue application for a divorce in the short story 'It Won't Be Long Now', first published in the December 1943 issue of the *Strand Magazine*. Under the title of 'Through the Usual Channels', the story was later included in his first short-story collection, *The Stuff to Give the Troops*.

2 This was left blank.

3 The request was granted, enabling Maclaren-Ross to travel to Norwich on 12 October 1942. Stopping off in London en route back to Southend-on-Sea, he had his first meeting with John Lehmann, who rejected not only 'Are You Happy in Your Work' but also the two stories Maclaren-Ross had sent him.

to JOHN LEHMANN

'HQ' Company/No 3 Infantry Depot/Southend-on-Sea/Essex

25-10-42

Dear Mr Lehmann,

Thank you so much for your letter and for sending back the stories so promptly. Yes, I will shortly let you have some more stuff which I hope you will like better.[1]

Your secretary has written to me asking for a reassurance that the characters and names used in 'Y List' are fictitious; they are and furthermore cannot be identified with any particular person.

The brief biography which she also asked for is appended below. It was indeed nice to meet you and I hope we shall be able to meet again when I am next in London.

Yours sincerely,

J. Maclaren-Ross

J. Maclaren-Ross was educated in Paris and the South of France. In England, during depression, sold vacuum-cleaners and adapted plays for broadcasting. Now in the army: an orderly room clerk: works ten hours a day and writes stories in spare time.

1 Despite being turned down by Lehmann, 'Are You Happy in Your Work' was eventually published in the third issue of *The Saturday Book*, released in October 1943.

to JOHN LEHMANN

'HQ' Company / No 3 Infantry Depot / Southend-on-Sea / Essex

27-10-42

Dear Mr Lehmann,

On Sunday last I sent off some MSS and unfortunately there was a mess up and the stories got put in the wrong envelopes by the man who was doing them for me, so that Kaye Webb[1] of *Lilliput* received a MS intended for John Atkins[2] of *Tribune,* and vice versa.

Unfortunately, Miss Webb imagined from the letter enclosed that it was intended for you and she has therefore forwarded it on to you. Would you be so kind as to send it on to John Atkins, please? I am sorry you have been troubled.

I will be sending you on another 'Report on Today' shortly. I am very anxious for you to do one by me as I think I can throw some new light on what is happening to people in the army and such a section is a great opportunity as it gives one a chance to write something that is neither a story nor mere reportage and in the end you may well be responsible for evolving a new medium by instituting such a platform for it.

I have been reading *New Writing and Daylight* and I was particularly pleased to see 'Colour Up' by John Close; he and I were fellow-recruits and great friends at Bury St Edmunds ITC and I remember well when this story was written, although I did not read it then. I have lost touch with him: would you be good enough to let me have his present address, please?

I was also very pleased with your own article,[3] particularly your remarks on *Music in the Park*[4] and the spy story being a true reflection of our times. It pleases me all the more since I half share the same opinion, to the extent of myself being engaged on a novel of this sort. Incidentally, in your article, you yourself have provided me with the title I wanted: *The Fields of Night.* From where does this quotation come: I cannot place it offhand?[5]

If you are interested, I would like to send you portions of my book as I write it, in your capacity as a critic. I am very diffident about trying anything of this genre and would welcome a criticism, especially as you are interested in the spy story as a reflection of our times. So if you can spare the time, I should be awfully grateful if you would read it and let me know what you think.

Yours sincerely,

J. Maclaren-Ross

1 Kaye Webb (1914–72) was the Assistant Editor of *Lilliput*.
2 John Atkins (1916– ?) was the Literary Editor of *Tribune* between 1942 and 1943.
3 The first instalment of a series called 'The Armoured Writer'.
4 *Music in the Park* (Michael Joseph, 1942) was a thriller by F.L. Green (1902–53).
5 The phrase comes from Virginia Woolf's *Between the Acts* (1941).

to RUPERT HART-DAVIS

'HQ' Company/No 3 Infantry Depot/Southend-on-Sea/Essex

10-11-42

Dear Hart-Davis,

My apologies for not answering your letter before. It arrived whilst I was myself on leave and of course when I returned the work had been piling up high enough to touch the Orderly Room roof. I've been working every night till 12 for a fortnight. Still, I did manage to revise the first few pages of army book[1] (enclosed). The beginning is I think the most important part, because it must present a clear picture of what I was like in civilian life – not an easy thing to do. Do tell me what you think.

Did you see my story in *Tribune*[2] two weeks ago. I think it's the best so far. There's also one in this month's *Lilliput*.[3]

If you have finished with *Death and Tomorrow*,[4] would you send it to me as soon as you can? I can't get a copy anywhere. You'll be doing me a great favour if you do.

Meantime,

Yours ever,

J. Maclaren-Ross

1 'They Can't Give You a Baby'.
2 'The Mine'.
3 'An Appreciation of Two Pictures' was, in fact, a brief parody, *not* a short story.
4 Peter de Polnay (Chatto and Windus, 1945).

to RUPERT HART-DAVIS

'HQ' Company/No 3 Infantry Depot/Southend-on-Sea/Essex

15-11-42

Dear Hart-Davis,

Thank you so much for your letter and the book.[1] I've not begun it yet but it looks good. I think de Polnay is a first class writer: his best book is *Children My Children*. I like that even more than *Angry Man's*

Tale, although *Angry Man* you might say should be more up my street. No, I haven't read *Scum*:[2] have you got it?

I'm glad you like my book or rather the beginning of it. I don't know when it'll be finished but not really so long now. I'll do my best to get it done as soon as possible and will certainly send you the first completed section and synopsis soon.

About the full colonel, yes I expect he was. Dumb insolence I've never come across myself, thank God, since I'm sure the set of my face sometimes would let me in for an entry on my 122.[3] But if the Guards are like General Kersh[4] then I supposed you would have dumb insolence as a punishable offence.

How do you like being an Adjutant? D'you make your Orderly Room staff work all night? Ours does. But he's rather nice really, he's just made me a lance/c.[5] and dated my appointment back on Part IIs so that I get paid right away. Which is always something. I'm sorry you won't do my army stories yet. There are 20 of them now and 45,000 words. I'm sure if you did them in Guild Books[6] at sixpence they'd have a large sale among army personnel. All the fellows in our mob are always anxious to get hold of them. It's a funny thing that blokes in the army want to read about it, especially if the stories show everybody browned off. There are enough for a Guild Six[7] and I should only expect a very small advance as I've made quite a lot of money out of them already. But still if you think better to wait until the complete book comes out, you know best.

Further instalment of *They Can't Give You a Baby* soon.

Meantime all the B. from

J.M.R.

1 Peter de Polnay's *Death and Tomorrow*.
2 The reference was to *Scum of the Earth*, a memoir released the previous year by Rupert Hart-Davis's firm. Written by the Hungarian émigré Arthur Koestler (1905–83), the book depicted its author's experiences in France between August 1939 and June 1940.
3 Army discipline record.
4 A reference to *They Die With Their Boots Clean* (1941) by Gerald Kersh (1911–68).
5 Lance-corporal.
6 An affordable paperback series produced by Jonathan Cape and the other members of the British Publishers' Guild.
7 A cheap series of paperback books produced by Guild, the imprint of the British Publishers' Guild.

to JOHN LEHMANN (LANCE-CORPORAL!!!!!)

'HQ' Company/No 3 Infantry Depot/Southend-on-Sea/Essex

26-11-42

Dear Mr Lehmann,

As I am extremely hard-up owing to unforeseen circumstances, I wonder if you could let me have the fee for my story 'Y List', unless it is strictly against your principles to pay before the date of publication.

You would be doing me a very great favour if you would let me have a money order for the amount, whatever it is; I should not be able to cash a cheque.

I shall be on leave again in January and look forward to seeing you again then, if convenient to you.

Meanwhile, with best wishes,

Yours sincerely,

J. Maclaren-Ross

to JOHN LEHMANN

'HQ' Company/No 3 Infantry Depot/Southend-on-Sea/Essex

3-12-42

Dear Mr Lehmann,

Thank you so much for responding to my appeal so promptly. It was very kind of you.

I don't know if I mentioned it in my last letter, but a filmscript on which I had been working for over a year, has been destroyed through malice on the part of the person who was entrusted with its safe keeping and I have applied for leave on compassionate grounds in the hope (I fear, a slight one) of putting the script together from the original MS.[1] So if this is granted I may be seeing you much sooner than I had expected; I hope so.

Meanwhile, with best wishes,

Yours sincerely,

J. Maclaren-Ross

1 When Maclaren-Ross's long-standing girlfriend, Eileen Cooke, discovered that he'd been unfaithful, he was led to believe that she had destroyed one of the manuscripts that he had left in her possession. The manuscript in question was the screenplay of *Jack Sheppard*, a filmscript he'd been writing about the eighteenth-century highwayman. After the break-up of her relationship with Maclaren-Ross, Eileen Cooke appears, however, to have passed this and other manuscripts over to their mutual friend C.K. Jaeger, among whose papers *Jack Sheppard* was discovered in 2007.

to RUPERT HART-DAVIS

'HQ' Company / No 3 Infantry Depot / Southend-on-Sea / Essex

4-2-43

Dear H.D.,

The other day you signed a warrant for two guardsmen to fetch me from Golders Green Police Station where I was being detained as an absentee. Queer isn't it? I only found out the day before where you'd moved to and phoned, but you were out. Next morning they got me. I was in bed. Someone had rung up Scotland Yard. I know who, but it's a long story.

The point is, I'd determined on this leave to land a job either at the War Office or the Ministry of Information. I had a War Office interview on my last leave but subsequently the man I saw and everybody connected with him was shifted. This time I had plenty of encouragement and contacts but the list of these had not expired when the time came to go back. So I just stayed on. You see, I knew it was my last chance. All category clerks at this depot are being shifted to be replaced by ATS,[1] which means I would either be transferred to somewhere, as a private, where I'd once more sweep out a Naffy,[2] or else a Maritime AA Bty,[3] where I should again have to go sick a million times before they found I was useless to them on account of my leg. Or as a third alternative, the Orderly Room Sergeant Major, who hates me, has threatened me with being sent abroad, to a depot where I'd spend all my time demobilising men for 2 years after the war ends.

He has already doublecrossed his own Orderly Room Sergeant in this way because of a trivial quarrel; had him demoted and sent abroad on the next draft, just when he was going to get married.

Well, I've stood enough in the army without that. So I overstayed my leave 14 days in the hope of getting a final decision from somebody. I still had to see Aneurin Bevan[4] and a girl in Foreign Affairs who's secretary to General de Gaulle.[5] I didn't see them; I was nabbed.

Then I spend a day in the civvy[6] clink, then a day at Great Scotland Yard, and now I'm back from the regimental gaol, a prisoner. Apparently the old CO,[7] prompted by the ORQMS,[8] is going to have me court martialled, although it's only 14 days absence, my first crime in the army and I'm an NCO.[9] I've had all my hair cut off and I had to wear handcuffs in London.

What infuriates me is that I honestly did it because I really hoped to be more use to the war effort in one of the ministries than sitting at a desk correcting the spelling and grammatical errors of my superior officers. And now of course they're going to pile it on.

It's no good – you can't do anything right: work for them night and day, put your personal life aside, sink yourself in an unimportant stupid job; and when you go absent from the best of motives, being fed-up with doing so little and the threat of doing even less, then you get treatment usually meted out to deserters only.

They seem to think I shall get detention, even though it's a first offence and they should only deprive me of my stripe for it. It's most unfair, although it'll only make my book[10] worse. Only with all this I don't know if I shall ever finish it. I wish I could have seen you before I was caught as I had with me a complete statement of my case which Tom Hopkinson[11] promised to publish: it's still in London and I can't get it typed now.

What course of action do you advise? From my knowledge of orderly room procedure I'm sure I'm being treated unfairly. I wish I could see you to talk things over. Down here there isn't any officer who could possibly defend me. They're all hopeless. And what makes me feel worse is seeing all my stories coming out: one in *Modern Reading* 6, one in *Penguin New Writing* 15, one in *Lilliput* and so on. It makes you feel that is the way writers are treated in this country, and to want to become a permanent deserter.

Be careful about what you write: censorship or one *can* dodge it.

All the best, hoping to hear from you,

J.M.R.

Monday

My God, my girlfriend's father[12] has landed me in the court. I had a box full of army stationery which I'd sent down there for him to look after, and he's sent it back to the orderly room, out of spite.

Now there's a 2nd charge of stealing public property and I shall get detention for sure, I come up before the CO today.

Any advice? It'll mean a court martial.

J.M.R.

1   The Auxilliary Territorial Service was the women's branch of the British army.
2   Slang version of NAAFI (Navy, Army and Air Force Institute). These establishments included canteens that could be used by members of the military.
3   Anti-aircraft battery.

4 A maverick Labour politician who edited *Tribune*. He was an outspoken critic of the wartime government and later held cabinet posts in the post-war Labour government.

5 General Charles de Gaulle (1890–1970) was the leader of the Free French forces, based in London.

6 Slang for 'civilian'.

7 Commanding officer.

8 Orderly Room Quartermaster Sergeant.

9 Non-commissioned officer, such as a lance-corporal.

10 His army memoir *They Can't Give You a Baby*.

11 Editor of the popular new magazine *Picture Post*.

12 He was referring to the father of Eileen Cooke, his *former* girlfriend.

to RUPERT HART-DAVIS (statement, by hand)[1]

14-2-43

I Had to Go Absent

I was on leave at the time and a lance-corporal. I had not been a lance-corporal for long. I had to make a frightful fuss before being made one. Not that I cared much about having a stripe. It was just that I thought I should be earning more than 4/9 a day for the work I was doing in the orderly room as a clerk. Everybody, including the authorities, agreed that I should be earning more but they did not do anything about it. They had not even granted me trade-pay.

I'd been in the army two years and six months. The first three months I spent on light duties awaiting medical boards. I tried to make myself useful in the Coy Office but my Company Commander soon put a stop to that. So then I did nothing. It seemed to be a satisfactory situation to all concerned except myself. They couldn't understand why I wasn't contented. 'You're cushy, aint you?' they said.

On the contrary. I did not join the army to be cushy, otherwise I would have made some attempt to get out of it, instead of allowing myself to be absorbed in a stream of conscripts.

Of course, when I first enlisted, I imagined myself to be A-1.[2] The doctors who passed me as such helped me in that belief. But in the army things are different and I was *not* A-1, oh no.

At last I had a medical board. It took place at the hospital where I stayed for three weeks awaiting it. But something went wrong with the proceedings. In other words, a mess-up.

I was drafted to another training centre to await another medical board which would not be a mess-up or at any rate less of a mess-up than the other.

Meanwhile I at last started my training. They discovered at once that I couldn't do drill. My left knee, apparently, without a tendon through being knocked down by a bicycle at the age of 12, would not allow me to even perform a correct about-turn. My platoon-sergeant was an extraordinarily decent chap. So were all the other NCOs. They spent endless time and trouble on me, and the other members of the awkward squad. At the same time to be in the awkward squad at all was humiliating.

Even more humiliating were the periodical interviews with the MO,[3] a man who'd taken a dislike to me on sight and moreover believed me to be a malingerer. So much humiliation combined to lower my spirits. I asked for leave.

They said, You haven't done your training yet.

I said, I've been in six months. The others are all going on leave.

They said, They've finished their training.

I said, I'd have finished mine if I hadn't been messed about by these medical boards.

They said, Have you had a board yet?

No, I said.

Then you can't go on leave, they said.

When can I go? I said.

When you've finished your training, they said. And anyway leave's a privilege.

I said, It's a privilege that seems to be granted to everyone except me.

You're a perfect lawyer, they said.

I'm a writer not a lawyer, I said.

Well if you write about this we'll drop you in the drink, they said. Now scram.

It's a free country, I said.

You're a bolshie, they said. Insolent to boot.

I hadn't meant to be insolent, so I was abashed. I returned to my barrack room and wrote a letter to the Coy Commander asking whether I could apply for a commission. I felt I had to do something.

The Coy Commander was doubtful at first. He knew I wasn't good on drill. On the other hand, my grandfather had been an Indian army colonel.[4] He passed me to a board of officers. They passed me to the CO. This took some time and meanwhile I'd been transferred to another Company, where the platoon sergeant could not by any stretch of imagination be described as a decent chap. He was in fact a pervert and a sadist.

As I was an OCTU candidate and excused marching, he used to stand me at the side of the square to take the salute from the platoon when the recruits were on saluting drill. He also put me on wiring[5] with bare hands.

As for leave: Never 'eard of it, he said.

Meanwhile I saw the CO.

What's your medical category? he said.

Awaiting a board, sir, I said.

Oh well, come back when you've had it.

In about another fortnight I had the board. B-2. I returned for interview with the CO.

No vacancies for B-2 officers except in the Pay Corps and that's full up, he said. Pity.

Yes sir, I said.

But next day the adjutant sent for me. There was a job going abroad, hush-hush, but a good one, and they needed an intelligent man. Would I volunteer?

I did so at once. I waited another three months, during which I had my leave.

Things don't happen at once of course, they said.

They were right. But perhaps things would have happened eventually if I had not contracted pleurisy and pneumonia.

I was in hospital and a convalescent home and on returning to the Depot they said Sorry, the job abroad is filled. How would you like one in the orderly room?

I said yes.

Will you start now? they said.

Yes, I said, although my leave was again well overdue.

In the orderly room they said, Do this job for a fortnight and then we'll give you a trade test.

All right, I said.

There was a heat wave on; it was July 1941 and I'd been in the army a year. Three of us sat typing in a room so small that both the others had to stand up if the third one wished to go out. The heat was such that in my weak condition, still convalescent, I almost passed out at my typewriter. The sun came in through the tiny window and melted the wax sheets on which we typed Depot Orders.

The fortnight passed and I said what about this trade test.

Oh, they said, not yet, but the ATS next door is due for a fortnight's privilege; will you put yours off till she comes back?

All right, I said.

Then we'll give you the test, they said.

So I typed and typed and the wax sheets melted; something about sausages was *secret* and you had to destroy whole stencils if you made a typing error because the CO was very particular.

Two more weeks and the ATS came back.

What about the test? I said.

They said, Better have your leave first otherwise you'll *never* get it.

All right, I said.

So I had my leave *now two months overdue* and when I came back they said No test because you're being posted.

I thought this job was permanent, I said.

You can't count on nothing permanent in the army, they said.

Where am I being posted to? I said.

It's secret, they said.

So I got in a train with some other fellows, all NCOs except me, and we went to a town where there was a Young Soldiers Battalion and I was to work in the Orderly Room.

What about a trade test, I said.

Nothing doing, they said, no vacancies on establishment.

All the other clerks had been trade-tested already. We're cushy, they said. So who cares.

I had letters from friends, some of whom were editors.

Why aren't you writing anything? they said.

I am, I said, a novel.

About the army?

No *not* about the army.

They were disappointed.

I wasn't writing a novel. I had been writing one but I stopped. I was dissatisfied with not being able to do something more in the army. Nobody could understand this.

You have time to write, they said, a cushy billet. What more do you want?

Then I was shifted as PRI's[6] clerk to a seaside town nearby, where the recruits were being trained. The recruits were always going absent. Many of them, although only about 18, had been burglars in civilian life and even civvy gaol appeared to them more like home than army discipline.[7] They used to avoid the detention barracks by committing some civil offence when they felt they could not hold out any longer

49

without being apprehended. Some remained at large for over a year. Some were never caught. I could quote you cases.

Take Cassidy, for instance, the one they used to call Texas – don't ask me why. He broke the regimental gaol eight times. Was finally nabbed and given a stretch at Chatham. Came back, was granted leave. The CO, I believe, shook hands with him. I don't know: he said so. Cassidy anyhow became a good soldier forever afterward.

He'd been given to understand he was a human being. Our CO was a very intelligent man, although a regular army officer. You see?

I, on the contrary, never having been absent, was imposed upon right and left, expected to work all hours while NCOs and warrant officers drew pay for the work I was doing. I wouldn't have minded the long hours, the fact that they took it for granted I never wanted any time off, if the work had been important. It wasn't. It was footling work, typing, copying letters, even drawing posters for battalion sports.

Anybody could have done it.

Well *somebody* has to, they said when I protested.

But why me? I said.

Why not? they said. Think you're better than anybody else? You're a private same as they are.

Maybe. But at the same time I was doing a job usually held by an NCO: all the other clerks were at least lance-corporals. Also I had to control a staff of 7 runners, who were supposed to take orders from me.

Two of my runners suddenly became lance-corporals. One could play cricket; the other had gone in for boxing and had his nose broken. Hence the stripes. They were immediately sent off on a cadre.

I remained a private. I wasn't envious, but I was a little amused. The other runners then became for a short while out of hand and I had to apply for a stripe.

No good, they said. Why, you can't do drill?

I'm not employed here to do drill, I said.

Can't have a stripe unless you're good on drill, they said.

Then one of the subalterns said, why don't you apply for a commission?

No good sir, I said. I'm B-2. I've already been rejected.

Plenty of vacancies now for B-2 officers, he said. Things have changed.

At first I said no. I was fed up. It seemed as though there was no place in the army for me. If they don't want me why the hell should I try. Then I thought perhaps I haven't tried hard enough.

So I wrote out another application.

Within three days I had a board.

B-2, they said, H'm. Where were you educated?

France, I said.

Do you speak French?

Fluently, sir.

H'm. Of course French isn't required much nowadays. What d'you do in civil life?

I'm a writer, sir.

Stories? Books?

Stories and radio plays so far.

Better put in for the pioneer corps, they said. Not much use in the army for a man who writes stories, ha ha.[8]

Two boys of nineteen who had both been about three months in the army were interviewed at the same time as me. Both were subsequently made lance-corporals. I was not made a lance-corporal.

Later we had to write essays and I corrected the spelling of the two lance-corporals for them. But an officer, I was told, doesn't have to spell to be a good officer: one of our subalterns was always coming to me asking how to spell loofah, and he was a *very* good officer.

That is, he was good on drill.

Later still I went before a War Office Selection Board. There was only one other private there. Most of the candidates were sergeants. Among other tests they gave me a paper and said Write what effect the army has had on you and what you think of it. Tell the truth.

I told the truth; they sent me to the psychiatrist.

I don't know what he thought about me at all. Next I saw the President.

He said, What kind of commission would you like?

I said, I want to go to Madagascar, sir.

Madagascar? Whatever for.

As a liaison officer, sir. After all I was brought up in France.

Oh, he said. Well how would you like a commission in the Pioneers?

No sir, I said.

You wouldn't like it?

No.

51

The President was puzzled.

After a while he said, Could you do administrative work d'you think?

I thought of the administration of the battalion I was in and said Yes.

The President said, A writer doesn't necessarily make a good administrator you know.

I said, He doesn't necessarily make a bad one either, and the President bowed. The interview was over.

I didn't get any commission. I was returned unsuitable. There had been one or two physical tests that on account of my leg I had been unable to pass, but I'm sure that these made no difference to the Board's unfavourable decision. In fact I'm sure that the test itself was fair in every way. Perhaps after all I was not cut out to be an officer. At the same time, looking around me at some examples, dispassionately and without malice, I could not entirely believe this. Surely in some way I could be more useful to the army than I was being in the battalion office.

I did my work as usual; the Padre, a very nice man, came in to have a chat. He was worried. Knowing something of my case he thought I might be bitter about being rejected if I were not given some local promotion or other.

I believe he had a talk to the CO about giving me a stripe, but the CO apparently felt he had to draw the line somewhere.

The sword in this case is mightier than the pen, he said.

Meantime there was Tobruk and the battalion sports became increasingly important. Cricket especially was de rigeur.

I typed and typed: mainly sports programmes, and in the evenings I wrote. I had begun now to write about the army, and in a space of two months I had written 17 short stories, which immediately began to appear in various reviews and magazines. Some of them are still doing so. *Horizon*, *English Story*, *Selected Writing*, *Modern Reading*, *Lilliput*, *Bugle Blast*, *Tribune*, *New Writing*, etc. all accepted more than one apiece.

As a writer I was now doing better than I had ever done in peacetime, but I was dissatisfied and unhappy. I saw the war going on and all I did was type sports programmes and write short stories.

Everyone said, What the hell are you worrying about? *You're* cushy.

Then suddenly the battalion moved and I was posted to another depot. At last, I thought, a more important job.

On the contrary. It was a job in the orderly room, much the same, with slightly longer hours. I was told it was permanent.

I said, what about a trade test?

They said at first, NBG.[9]

Then later, after a lot of this, All right, you'll get a test.

I didn't get a test. What I did get was a paid lance-stripe. I'm afraid it didn't make any difference. My stories came out right and left and they didn't make any difference either.

I wanted a job where I could use some intelligence. Looking around, I seemed to be the only writer of my particular kind who was not either an officer entrusted with something he *could* do without despising himself, or else out of the army and doing work of national importance.

It wasn't a matter of personal ambition – if I had wanted to be an army officer surely I could have, as a boy, fallen in with my father's suggestion that I should be one. Nor do I share the snobbery of those who believe that a commission makes a difference to one's social position. It does, of course (the enclosure at the All Ranks Dance; 'Whiskey reserved for officers'; the fact that most girls of the so-called upper-class will only be seen out with a pip). But I am not a social person. And I have been happy in the ranks. I would not want to leave them but for the fact that I know the more important jobs, where I could use for the war effort what talents I possess and which are now being wasted, usually carry a commission with them.

Personally, I should be better off where I am, writing stories in my spare time and preparing a novel. But I did not join the army to continue my career as a writer. I am perfectly prepared to sacrifice this if a job of national importance could be given me which absorbed all my time.

I had 9 days leave and through friends obtained a War Office interview.

It was a major and he was sympathetic. At the same time he didn't know what to do with me. I had no technical or mathematical ability and I wasn't a photographer.

I could do filmscripts, I said.

Oh yes, he said. And what about pamphlets.

I said, I could do pamphlets.

A staff captain came up and was invited to participate in the interview.

What qualities d'you think he's got? the major asked.

The captain said, after a long pause, Intelligence and imagination.

No good to the army, the major said.

No, the captain said gloomily.

And hope of getting out of the army? I said. One of the Ministries?

Not the faintest hope, they both said.

In the end I was given a cup of tea and the promise that something would be done sometime, if humanly possible.

Nothing was done. I wrote a long statement of my case and received no reply. Not surprisingly, because apparently the major and all his staff were shifted for some reason shortly after my interview with him.

Anyhow another 3 months passed and the New Year and meantime I heard that all category clerks at the Depot were to be shifted and replaced by ATSs.

Which meant that I should be drafted as a private to some other unit and probably return to my old occupation of naffy-sweeping. Clerical work in the army being all that my disability allows me to do, if that were closed to me, I should go back doubtless to the awkward squad, learning new drill movements which have surely been invented since I finished my training.

I wasn't going to let that happen. I felt I should go crazy if it did.

My leave was again due and I determined to pass it trying to find a job or someone who would take an interest in my case. I found plenty of the latter, but interest was as far as it went. With the best will in the world they could do nothing. Either they have no influence or the influential persons they knew were themselves handicapped by red tape or other obstructions.

However, I went on trying. I had a long list of contacts and I had not nearly exhausted these by the time my 9 days were up.

So I made a decision to overstay my leave. I had always disapproved of absence having in the YS.[10] Battalion seen so much of it, but it was the only thing to do. I refused, and still refuse, to believe that there were no intelligent people influential enough to procure my release from the army to a job where I could be of real use. (Apparently all the jobs where my gifts as a writer could really be employed to the best advantage are outside the army.)

If I had wanted to desert before, or just get out of the army, surely I would have tried before?

I don't mean to desert now: when I have exhausted every possible avenue, then I will return to my unit to take my punishment as an absentee.

I merely want to satisfy myself that an intelligent man of 31, travelled, educated abroad, sophisticated and an anti-fascist, a writer who can write over 17 stories in spare time and get them published, cannot be utilised, owing to his medical category, in any better capacity than an office boy in an orderly room.

I don't want to think that. But it will be worth any punishment to know that it is so, and if it is so, that the fault does not lie with me.

I've done my best, at any rate.

I can't do anymore. Except CB.[11]

J.M.R.

1 Hart-Davis responded to Maclaren-Ross's letter by visiting him at the Regimental Gaol in Southend. In the course of the visit, Maclaren-Ross thrust the crumpled manuscript of 'I Had to Go Absent' into Hart-Davis's hands. The manuscript had been written while Maclaren-Ross had been absent without leave. Its title is, of course, a reference to his much-praised short story 'I Had to Go Sick'.

2 Fit for all duties.

3 Medical Officer.

4 His mother's father, Fitzwilliam Thomas Pollok (1832–1909), had reached the rank of colonel in the Madras Staff Corps.

5 He was referring to the practice of laying coils of barbed wire.

6 President of the Regimental Institute.

7 This Young Soldiers training unit was so notoriously indisciplined that the regimental magazine had speculated on whether the regimental gaol was large enough to accommodate the entire unit.

8 Maclaren-Ross retold this story in *Memoirs of the Forties* and in the BBC television documentary *In the Shadow of Cain*, first broadcast during October 1964. Part of the story also recurs in the short story 'Warning to OCTU Wallahs', published in the July 1944 issue of *Summer Pie*.

9 One of numerous acronyms popular in wartime Britain. It stood for 'no bloody good'.

10 Young Soldiers.

11 He was referring to the punishment of being 'confined to barracks'.

to RUPERT HART-DAVIS

The usual address

14-2-43

Dear H.D.,

I was called up to have a further summary of evidence taken on Friday; it looks as if they're going to proceed shortly. When, I don't know.

Shall I start to write out a defence? There are several things I should like to consult you about first. I hope we are going to have time.

Nothing further about the psychiatrist. It seems, as usual, to have come to nothing.

If you have any instructions, would you please write them soon, as letters get to me usually a day late; they are hung up at the Orderly Room to be censored.

Calder-Marshall[1] writes that the MOI can do nothing while I am in charge; he hopes perhaps the psychiatrist will recommend me for some work more suitable to my abilities, but I doubt it. I am depressed.

Thank you again for the trouble you are taking.

Yours ever,

J.M.R.

By the way, if you read that synopsis of mine,[2] you'll see about my case and that I have cause to be dissatisfied. There are surely points mentioned that would help in my defence on the 1st charge of absence.

1 The writer Arthur Calder-Marshall (1908–92), who was working for the MOI (Ministry of Information).
2 'I Had to Go Absent'.

to RUPERT HART-DAVIS

16-2-43

Dear H.D.,

I'm getting this letter out to you by one of the chaps.

They're definitely piling it on to me here – it's enough to give one persecution mania. My girlfriend[1] sent me a wire she's coming over to see me today and the RSM[2] has refused permission. I'm positive that until I'm sentenced and while I'm awaiting court martial I am allowed visitors. They're simply doing this as an extra punishment because she was absent with me. My letters are being held up for two days at the Orderly Room because the ORQMS has it in for me – I told you about him.

Nothing more about the psychiatrist: I'm afraid I shall be rail-roaded to detention if something isn't done. Nor am I allowed my writing case: I have a feeling that the regulations are being especially tightened for me. This sort of thing induces exactly the state of mind that the psychiatrist wants to prevent, and the fault lies with that damned old fool of a CO and that knock-kneed broken-down old war-horse the RSM.

I've thought out several things for defence on the second charge.

Write soon, please, but be careful: censorship. I can read between the lines.

In haste,

Yours ever,

J.M.R.

1 Scylla Yates.
2 Regimental sergeant major.

to RUPERT HART-DAVIS

17-2-43

Dear H.D.,

Off to hospital Birmingham tomorrow.

You could get address off the Adjutant if you ring him: I don't know it yet.

In any case will write you on arrival.

If you don't hear from me within next 4 days, will you have enquiries made, please?

Am a little nervous: you would be if you knew the whole story.

All the best,

Julian

to RUPERT HART-DAVIS

Military Hospital/Northfields/Birmingham

22-2-43

Dear Rupert,

Thanks for your most encouraging letter. I've been very depressed here: this is a special psychiatric place and the man in charge of my case is called, funnily enough, Major Ross. No relation, unfortunately. We haven't got beyond my civilian life so far. He's reading my stories.

But I think there's a good chance of something happening, if only Calder-Marshall plays up. I've written him; you know he's the man I approached about a job in the Ministry, and he seemed hopeful, but later wrote and said nothing could be done whilst I was on a charge.

But Major Ross said there was a good chance of at any rate ameliorating the court-martial business – and he hasn't even heard what my case is yet.

I feel sure this is the chance I've been waiting for. Thank you for writing them – I'm sure if you tell them something about me it'll be good.

Have you got any more books? Nothing much to read here.

Thanks again for the trouble you're taking and please write again soon.

Yours ever,

Julian

to RUPERT HART-DAVIS

1-3-43

My Dear Rupert,

Could you please put these cheques through your bank and let me have cash registered as soon as you can?

They're quite OK. I can assure you: payment for stories.

Thanking you,

Yours ever,

Julian

We're only allowed 10/- a week here and I'm flat broke.

to MISHKA[1]

Military Hospital / Northfields / Birmingham
10-3-43

My dear Mishka,

Thank you so much for your letter and kind assistance, I wish I were able to help you instead. Still, that opportunity may shortly come.

I must apologise for not writing before; it must seem ungrateful but have been weighed down with worries and very depressed, also terribly hard at work writing some new stories in order to earn money.

I was very sorry to hear of your troubles and do hope they will right themselves shortly. Everything seems to come at once and everyone seems badly off; it depresses me awfully.

I believe you have seen Scylla; everything is all right again there; that is one good thing.

Please excuse me for not writing more this time; will write a long letter later but today have been in bed and am feeling rather shaky.

I haven't had the books and am rather worried lest they have been lost in the post.

Do drop me a line when you're not too busy and I will write more next time.

With kindest regards to Ilona, Michael, and yourself,

Yours ever,

Julian

1 A friend in whose North London flat Maclaren-Ross had, together with Scylla Yates, stayed while he had been absent without leave.

to RUPERT HART-DAVIS

Military Hospital / Northfields / Birmingham
10-3-43

Dear Rupert,

Last Monday (1st March) I posted two cheques to you, one for 6 guineas and one for £4, hoping you would put them through your account and cash them for me, as I cannot cash them myself and am in need of money.

I don't want to bother you if you're busy, but am rather worried to know if you received them, as they were endorsed and could have been stolen.[1]

If this is the case I should immediately wire Woodrow Wyatt and Reginald Moore and tell them to stop payment.

Yours ever,

Julian

1 Endorsed cheques, also known as 'opened' or 'uncrossed' cheques, didn't feature two parallel lines drawn across them. By adding these to a cheque, the sender ensured that the cheque could only be paid into the recipient's bank account. Without them, a cheque could be stolen and cashed by an obliging barman or shopkeeper.

to RUPERT HART-DAVIS

Military Hospital/Northfields/Birmingham

11-3-43

Dear Rupert,

Thank you for your letter.

There is no rule against your sending the money; patients are allowed to receive registered letters without any inquiry as to the contents, nor are they forbidden to have money sent to them.

If you still feel you need permission, please return the cheques, to reach Saturday, and I will try to get them cashed elsewhere. But I am very hard up and have a few debts which I must pay as soon as possible.

I think myself that to not send the money is pushing the scruples rather far, but you must do what you think fit.

Yes, a contract would definitely help.[1]

Major Ross is on leave till next Wednesday.

I'm glad you're in a better job now.

More later,

In haste,

Yours ever,

Julian

1 Maclaren-Ross was referring to the proposed contract to provide a collection of short stories for the publishing firm Jonathan Cape, of which Hart-Davis was still a director.

to RUPERT HART-DAVIS

Military Hospital/Northfields/Birmingham
17-3-43

My dear Rupert,

Very many thanks for your letter and for sending the necessary, which arrived yesterday.

I was so glad to hear that you may be able to come up here after all, and that I might be seeing you. Major Ross returns from leave today. I think that if you were bringing a contract with you, or if unable to, were to tell him that you were offering me one, it would do a lot of good. At our last interview I suggested to him that I should be released to civil life for 6 months or so in order that I might finish my book and have some established financial support for when the war ends. This could be granted easily, on the same grounds that they grant release to men whose businesses are failing etc. I also said that I could make use of this time to find a vacancy for myself in either the War Office or one of the Ministries. This should not be difficult if I were there to see people in person, but is never so easy by letter. Major Ross's present plan is simply to keep me here until a definite vacancy is suggested and then recommend me for it. Calder-Marshall has now definitely promised to do all he can to help, but I should feel happier if I were on the spot to see to things. So I could suggest that you recommend my plan to Major Ross in your capacity as publisher as it is quite true that the financial side is worrying me considerably. You'll find him entirely sympathetic and amenable and he does believe I acted all along for the best.

But you must do what you think: this is merely a suggestion. I myself don't want to return to civil life particularly except as a means to an end – getting the job. And of course I'd like to write the book. It seems to me that, rather than stay here for 3 months, say, as a patient, waiting for something to turn up, I would be doing just as much good outside where I could at least be active.

As for the book, it would be practically impossible to write it here. There are too many interruptions, whereas for any sustained effort I must have freedom of movement and not be disturbed. Once I have started I like to write straight on, not be suddenly ordered to break off and parade for PT,[1] or to go to bed at 9. No, it will only be possible to write short stuff here – if that.

I suggested at an ABCA[2] meeting the other day that publicity should be given to the valuable work given to the patients in this hospital and that the nature of the work itself should be made known to the public. I offered to have an article done in *Picture Post*, get photographs taken and write the article myself, from a patient's point-of-view. This met, apparently, with resounding approval from the hospital authorities.

Yet this morning, because I felt so rotten and depressed and did not get up on the dot of reveille (0630 hrs) I was shouted at and threatened with a charge by one of the staff. It's this sort of thing that makes one unwilling to do anything to help the army in any way – since every scheme that's any good is invariably spoilt by some stooge in a position of petty authority.

Hoping to see you soon,

Yours ever,

Julian

1 Physical training.
2 Army Bureau of Current Affairs.

to RUPERT HART-DAVIS

Military Hospital / Northfields / Birmingham
24-3-43

My dear Rupert,

Thank you for your letter.

I shall be awfully glad to see you again on Friday and I do hope nothing crops up to stop you.

Major Ross told me this morning that he'd arranged an interview with the CO for me today. The CO's also a psychiatrist and has to go away for the weekend so he won't be here when you come. The object of the interview is, so Major Ross told me, to attempt to decide whether anything can be found in the army for me or whether I should be discharged altogether.

Certainly in the ordinary way there is nothing in the army except clerical work and I think Major Ross knows this. It is also certain, and I have been told so, that I could easily obtain a job in one of the Ministries if I were a civilian again, whereas if I'm still in the army there's all the complicated machinery to be put into motion. This, taken in conjunction with my extremely bad financial position, seems to argue in favour of discharge.

You will probably be asked, in your capacity of publisher and critic, what your opinion of my chances if I were to return to civil life would be, so I leave everything to you.

I'm certain, feeling as I do, that I will never be any good so long as I am subject to petty discipline, whereas if discharged I should be of some real use to the war effort. Even Calder-Marshall agrees: in fact he suggested it, and I have come to agree with him.

I say this now because you'll be seeing Major Ross before you see me.

All my other news will keep till we meet.

Meantime,

Yours ever,

Julian

to RUPERT HART-DAVIS

Military Hospital/Northfields/Birmingham
31-3-43

My dear Rupert,

Had an interview with Major Ross yesterday, rather depressing. Apparently the CO hasn't been able to find anything for me at the War Office and by his manner I inferred that the major is bent on posting me to some other capacity in the army, which would be quite hopeless, as I am sick and tired of it and would feel incapable of carrying on. It would only lead to a repetition of last time's performance, which would benefit nobody. I'd much rather come out into civilian life and risk the Ministry of Labour, as I am confident of obtaining a suitable job in one of the Ministries if I were a civvy again. Many of the people whom I saw when on leave told me that as a civilian I could quite easily be employed but that the Ministries etc. had definite instructions not to take anybody out of the army if it could be avoided. Major Ross also asked me a lot of curious questions about fascism, who gave me away? Did I think he was a fascist? What were my political views? Did I think there were fascists in the War Office etc.? It looks like somebody with some pull is trying to do me harm. Else why that peculiar business about some member of the War Office staff who said I showed signs of a nervous breakdown, when I had seen nobody from the staff? It's all very disturbing.

However Major Ross doesn't think publishing the stories would do any harm, and as they would undoubtedly do me some personal good and possibly relieve the financial pressure I am sending you some of the MSS herewith: all I have by me at the moment, also a plan of the book. The other MSS should be here perhaps tomorrow or the next day and I will then send them on. The others will be typed but those in magazines which I enclose, could they afterwards be returned to me as they are the only copies of the magazines which I have? I hope you will like them.

It was so nice to see you and so kind of you to come. Also the book – I am enjoying it very much.

Yours ever,
Julian

to RUPERT HART-DAVIS

Military Hospital / Northfields / Birmingham
3-4-43

My dear Rupert,

Here are some more stories, making 22 out of the 33. Five of the others I have sent away for; the rest should be in print this month or next. Re-reading the ones I enclose they seem to be good.

I'm very depressed. Despite what you told him and what the colonel said, Major Ross seems determined to keep me in the army. He admits that if I were in civilian life again it would be easier for me to get an MOI job since apparently they have orders not to take staff from the army. But now he wants me to take another army clerical job, which I feel would probably lead to my either having a nervous breakdown or to my deserting the army altogether. Anything that has been done to help me here would be automatically nullified by my being forced into any more work of this sort.

I wish you would write to the CO here, he's much more reasonable, and suggest my discharge. I'd sooner work in a factory or on munitions or anything rather than have anything more to do with the army. As you said I've had enough, and any more would force me into committing some serious crime. I cannot stand being pushed around anymore. Even Calder-Marshall admits I'd be better off and more use as a civilian.

Will you try and do something?

I feel worse than when I was awaiting trial, since it seems that this, like every help I have been promised in the army, is leading nowhere or rather to another bloody orderly room. If only I could get to the CO again I feel sure he would listen, and a letter from you advocating discharge would undoubtedly bring about another interview.

Yours ever,
Julian

to RUPERT HART-DAVIS

Military Hospital/Northfields/Birmingham
8-4-43

My dear Rupert,

Awful shock this morning. Saw the CO, who said there was not only no chance of my getting a War Office job but that I would also have to return and face the court martial. He could not give any guarantee that I would not get detention, and also said that I would probably have to return to more clerical work after it.

Then I let him have it properly. I said definitely that I could not stand any more of the army. I gave him the works: he then said he would talk to Major Ross about that, but that I couldn't get out of the court martial anyway.

Afterwards I saw Major Ross and also told him the same. I nearly broke down completely. I've come to the end of my tether. He said that he believed I was sincere but couldn't give me any satisfaction other than that he would talk it over with the CO, although I asked for his help to get me out of the army.

I'm seeing him again tomorrow but think they have definitely decided to do nothing in my case. This is terrible. It's the worst I've had yet, and I do feel I can't carry on any longer.

Yours ever,
Julian

to RUPERT HART-DAVIS

Military Hospital/Northfields/Birmingham
10-4-43

My Dear Rupert,

As I told you over the phone and as you will see from my other letters, things are going very badly here. First of all I have the feeling that I am being railroaded. It seems to me significant that it is only after the CO's visit to the War Office that they started talking about sending me back to more clerical work and also about facing the court martial: before, that didn't come into it. The CO was apparently told definitely that there could never be anything for me at the War Office or the MOI and perhaps he was also told to send me back for the CM.[1] It's quite possible that there is someone who has connections at the War Office who wants me out of the way, and detention would do the trick. Before, there was no question of my doing detention; now the CO just said he hoped I wouldn't get it. I told him then that detention would finally finish my nerves, if I had to go back to clerical work in the army after it. I told him that I wouldn't go back into the army.

Apparently, you see, my case here must be cleared up before the CM comes off: they're not having me back here afterwards. Therefore they will just recommend more clerical work and send me off: the idea being that my stay here has made me in a fit state to undergo detention and return to duty, or if not detention, duty anyway. Actually my nerves are getting terrible: the suspense and alternate hope and despair are worse than any detention could be.

I've told Major Ross twice that I will not stay on in the army, I should only desert. I've seen enough stupidity and have been messed about enough to last me a lifetime, added to the three extremely unhappy years I spent prior to enlistment and my present financial troubles. Also my health is being seriously impaired by all this worry. He could not hold out any hope of discharge: he just says it's very difficult. I'm seeing him again on Monday. I've told him that any more army routine would bring about a breakdown but I don't think he believes that.

There's one loophole: they're very afraid of publicity here and they may not send me back in case I made the whole thing public. Please realise that it's not the CM that I'm afraid of, it's the thought that all this has again led to nothing that gets me down. I never realised how much I hated the army until recently.

About writing: I just can't at the moment. Also I feel, in view of the review of *Penguin New Writing* No 15, in the *Spectator* for April 2nd, which accords with my own ideas, that I should stop writing about the army for a while[2] after you do the stories (if you do), and then the army book later. After the stories should come a novel. I'm sorry you don't think *The Salesman*[3] contemporary. I intended it as a moral tale for those who think life before the war was a paradise. It ends on

September 1st 1939 and there follows an epilogue called 'A Happy Ending for Those Who Like Them' (May 1942) which shows Fanshawe as a candidate for Indian OCTU[4] and Roper as a naval officer, the idea being that it takes a war for the throw-outs to get back into their former position in life.

But if you don't like it, we'll scrap that. Then what kind of novel would you advise? I don't want to do anything too topical – it has no lasting value. I should really like to do something which will present a complete background of life as I knew it during the changing years from money and the Riviera to vacuum cleaners and the first days in the army. Not necessarily autobiographical. I think this would have value. What do you think? Please tell me. The only alternatives to this would be a completely Riviera novel or *The Fields of Night*, which for various reasons I cannot write just now. The topicality, I mistrust: I think it is better written in retrospect. Too many tales of invasion and occupied France kicking about for me to join in that racket.

At the moment I can't think: I want your advice. I will try to do what you suggest. My discharge is the most important thing to me at the moment – though what I'm going to live on if I get it and while I'm writing the novel, I don't know. That's why I wanted a contract and, if possible, an advance. Please don't think I'm pressing you for this: it's just trying to get the position clear to myself. It's pretty black.

Do write directly you have time,

Yours ever,

Julian

1   Court martial.
2   *The Spectator*'s unsigned review of *Penguin New Writing* 15 featured the following assessment of Maclaren-Ross's recent work: 'Surely all readers of contemporary literature have now had enough chance to digest Mr Maclaren-Ross's reports on Army Life, which are entertaining but not infinitely repeatable.'
3   *The Salesman Only Rings Once.*
4   Officer Training Candidate Unit.

to RUPERT HART-DAVIS

Military Hospital/Northfields/Birmingham
14-4-43

My dear Rupert,

Thank you for your letter which I received this morning.

No I'm not thinking about desertion, except that I thought it would be a pretty bad advertisement for this place, as I have been here for 2 months and nothing at all has been done for me. It is obviously silly for them to send me back for a court martial, since the general atmosphere and suspense of this could hardly do my nerves good. I'm not letting things get me down, but I know, and have told Major Ross, that any more of the army and especially more clerical work would definitely lead to a nervous breakdown. As you say, my writing and my whole life would suffer and I don't see why they should push me to this. I've tried my best for nearly 3 years, and if I had received less ridiculous treatment, I might have gone on with it. As it is, I cannot; I should only be useless, not only to the army but to myself. And I'm quite sure there is more use for me in civilian life than in the army.

Thank you for saying you will write to the CO; I think with you it won't do much good: a letter to Major Ross might. He is in charge of my case and on him the final decision depends. He admitted to me that his primary concern was to keep as many men in the army as possible, but a letter from you saying you consider me useless to it might influence him. At present he still thinks that more clerical work would meet the case, although I have told him frankly that I am through. He just says it's difficult. That's all very fine; but to me it means, if I don't get out, the ruin of my health and work, which naturally depends on having a clear mind. The army has never allowed me to do anything useful or important, but in civilian life I could and would. I don't care how hard I work but I must get away from the army routine and the charges and the shouting, otherwise I may do someone an injury, if not myself.

I hope you like these stories: I'm collecting the MSS of the rest for you. I think they'd make a good book. And about the novel I'll try. Riviera – vacuum cleaners – dole – the army: it's a wide range and how to connect it all. What a pity I can't do an autobiography: but it would be libellous and none would ever believe it to be true. Thanks for saying the financial pressure could be relieved: I'm sure I would do all right if only I could get Cat. 'E'.[1] But to go on in the army would mean my finish as a person and a writer.

Yours ever,
Julian

1 To be declared 'Category E' meant to be regarded as unfit for military service.

to RUPERT HART-DAVIS

Military Hospital / Northfields / Birmingham
22-4-43

My dear Rupert,

The latest news, and not too good.

The treatment here is getting me down terribly. Everybody or nearly everybody is getting put on a charge and punished right and left, the reason being that none of the RAMC[1] NCOs has the faintest idea of army rule. The other day a corporal had rushed in and put me *under arrest* for being absent off PT. Then it turned out to be a 'misunderstanding' and was of course washed out. (I was never formally charged with anything, by the way, just told I was under arrest.) Can you beat it? I complained to Major Ross about this and the bad effect it's having on my nerves; he then told me that he was leaving on Monday and proposes to turn my case over to Major Backus, the 2 i/c,[2] whom I believe you met. The CO is also leaving and a new CO is replacing him, so God knows what'll happen, with the only two men who did have a sympathetic view of my case going.

Major Ross told me that he was making a recommendation in my case but he would not tell me what it was.

It's absolutely heartbreaking; I don't know what to do.

Also, having first promised it to me, they won't let me have any leave now 'because I'm awaiting court martial'. I can't stand much more of this place the way it's being run now: more like a detention barracks than a hospital. You can't sleep for fear of charges: I had my name taken again today – another 'misunderstanding'.

Here are another 2 stories towards the collection.

Yours ever,
Julian

1 Royal Army Medical Corps.
2 Second in command.

to RUPERT HART-DAVIS

Military Hospital / Northfields / Birmingham
25-4-43

My dear Rupert,

Many new developments.

Scylla Yates, my girlfriend, has been up to see Major Ross before he left, and he told her that he was definitely recommending me for discharge, but that first I would have to face a court martial or do detention if it were awarded: after which the recommendation would come up before a Reviewing Board.

She asked isn't it possible for him to know that he will be discharged before he does detention; Major Ross said No, that was impossible, and that the CM couldn't be squashed as they could not say that I was irresponsible or unfit to plead.

Major Ross has now gone.

Can you come up again? It's urgent as you can see. I'm sorry to trouble you again but I think we should have an opportunity to talk over the case in surroundings more congenial than the regimental gaol; and also Major Backus who will be my new psychiatrist is an American with no respect for rules and regs, and you might, in your capacity as Defending Officer, persuade him to annul the CM on the grounds that the attendant conditions – detention whilst awaiting trial etc., irrespective of possible sentence – would aggravate my present state and possibly bring on a breakdown.

It might then be possible to discharge me from here whence; otherwise once I am RTU[1] the chance may be lost. Can you come please. I'm positive that your appearance will make all the difference – only it must be soon because I feel that I shall very shortly be sent back to the unit.

Yours ever,
Julian

1 Returned to unit.

to RUPERT HART-DAVIS

Military Hospital / Northfields / Birmingham

27-4-43

My dear Rupert,

I've just thought of a loophole. According to what I remember of court martial procedure, a man cannot be given an FGCM[1] if 8 weeks have elapsed since he was remanded for same. As I have now been in this hospital 10 weeks, I think the FGCM is automatically annulled. Could you find out definitely about this, please?

I haven't seen a new psychiatrist yet and am anxious not to leave the hospital to go before FGCM if this can be avoided, irrespective of possible sentence, since once I am RTU Major Ross's recommendation for my discharge might easily be lost sight of.

If that ruling re a time-limit on courts martial is definitely right, I could probably be graded 'E' within a very short time from here.

Yours ever,

Julian

1 Field General Court Martial. These were courts martial conducted anywhere away from headquarters.

to RUPERT HART-DAVIS

Military Hospital / Northfields / Birmingham

30-4-43

My dear Rupert,

Thank you for your letter.

Yes, I quite understand. And as Major Backus will be the supreme authority now as regards the cases, the new CO being not a psychiatrist but a regular army officer, should be alright.

A new psychiatrist, Major Foulks, has taken over Major Ross's patients; I haven't had an interview with him yet; but I hear that he's anxious to keep everyone on in the army, even those recommended for discharge. I suppose he'll make the FGCM the excuse in my case. If only that were squashed there would be no difficulty. I hope I'm right about the time limit – I know there is one. I'm sure if we could get the FGCM washed out I could get discharged straightaway.

Do write quickly and tell me about the time limit or is there some other way it could be squashed? Once I leave here for my unit I know the recommendation will be lost sight of.

Let me know your address at Staff College so that I can inform you of developments straightaway.

I'm so worried – it's awful to be so near and yet so far.

Yours ever,

Julian

to RUPERT HART-DAVIS

Military Hospital/Northfields/Birmingham
5-5-43

My dear Rupert,

Thank you for your letter.

I've looked up the *MML*,[1] and find that my court martial was not properly initiated: i.e. – I was merely remanded for the Summary of Evidence to be taken. After this I should have been re-charged by the Adjutant and remanded by CO for FGCM after which the charge goes forward with the summary to Higher Authority. Instead I was sent here, so I am not really awaiting CM at all.

If this could be impressed by you in a letter to Major Backus, I am sure he would put it to my unit not to proceed further. I've seen him and he's quite sympathetic, but it's important that the CM should not be proceeded with as the recommendation for discharge might be lost sight of if I am returned to unit.

I'm not at all afraid the court would punish me, I'm sure they wouldn't, but if the whole matter was annulled my discharge could go through at once. Also the suspense and further detention in the gaol while they start proceedings all over again would make my nerves even more unfit to face civilian life than they are at present. It seems ridiculous when the whole thing could be so easily squashed at its present stage, but these people don't understand court martial procedure and need to have it impressed upon them that the trial has not yet been initiated.

Yours ever,

Julian

1 *Manual of Military Law.*

to JOHN LEHMANN

Military Hospital/Northfields/Birmingham
5-5-43

Dear Mr Lehmann,

I am now preparing three long stories.

I. Based on my experiences as a prisoner in the Regimental Gaol
II. A report on life in this hospital, which is a psychiatric hospital for neurosis cases.
III. A story of life in the South of France in 1930.

The latter I think will have more value than the two more topical ones.
If you'd care to see any of these would you let me know, please.
I'm looking forward to *Penguin New Writing* 16: is it out yet?
Yours sincerely,
J. Maclaren-Ross

to RUPERT HART-DAVIS

'HQ' Company/No 3 Infantry Depot/Southend-on-Sea/Essex
10-5-43

Dear Rupert,

I was RTU this morning at a moment's notice and without seeing Major Backus before leaving; I haven't seen him for a week. So it seems the 3 months I spent in the hospital is a washout and they are not going to discharge me on Major Ross's recommendation at all.

I suggest you ring Major Backus, Priory 2677, and ask for details. I must know what is to happen. And please come to Southend at once, I'll go mad if I don't talk to someone. I'm writing this in the train, under escort so excuse scrawl.

It looks like the CM, detention and all, despite Major Ross's promises to Scylla Yates.[1] Major Backus saw that there was only the CM in the way to be cleared up and they could proceed. Now as he didn't even see me before I left it looks as though nothing is going to be done.

I'm in a very bad state: please come soon as you can.
Yrs ever,
Julian

1   The news that Maclaren-Ross was being returned to unit prompted him to write to Scylla Yates, asking her to contact Rupert Hart-Davis on his behalf. Her letter is reproduced in Appendix 1.

to RUPERT HART-DAVIS

Telegram

10-5-43

Come Southend immediately Julian

to RUPERT HART-DAVIS

'HQ' Company / No 3 Infantry Depot / Southend-on-Sea / Essex

14-5-43

My Dear Rupert,

Please come *at once*. Saw the medical officer this morning and he wants to have me sent to a Mental Home. I want you to come and help. Please ring up Major Backus at Northfield Hospital and find out what he thinks. Try and get the address of my specialist, Major Ross, and contact him before he goes abroad. I'm sure that was not his intention and I'm not going to be railroaded like this, with a stigma of insanity. Please come *immediately*: if I don't talk to someone I really should go mad!

Awaiting you,

Yours ever,

Julian

to RUPERT HART-DAVIS

'HQ' Company / No 3 Infantry Depot / Southend-on-Sea / Essex

15-5-43

My dear Rupert,

Further interview with the MO: he just said, 'So you don't like the idea of treatment' and got me to sign a paper for a Medical Board.

They've got me down as suffering from psychopathic personality: does this mean they'll try to certify me directly after the discharge?

Should you come down or not. I wish you could; there's a lot to talk over what I want to write, and I do feel some help is needed at this critical stage.

Sorry to bother you again but hope you will come.

Yours ever,

Julian

to RUPERT HART-DAVIS[1]

Telegram

19-5-43

Detention Colchester 28 days Friday can you come Julian

    1   Scylla Yates had, in the meantime, written to him again on behalf of Maclaren-Ross. Her letter is reproduced in Appendix 2.

to RUPERT HART-DAVIS

20-5-43

My dear Rupert,

    Why not a word from you?

    Court martial washed out; CO gave me 28 days detention yesterday; I start at Colchester Detention Barracks from tomorrow.

    I'm supposed to have a Medical Board when I come out but I don't know: I think you'll find the discharge will be washed out.

    There's a lot I can't write. Now listen, do please come and see me: you *must* – it's really necessary. This is what I told you might happen – remember? This is only the beginning of it.

    Do please come quickly: you can help me if you do. I may not be able to write from there so I rely on you.

    Yours ever,

    Julian

to RUPERT HART-DAVIS

5-6-43

My dear Rupert,

    I hope you're not ill, as I haven't heard a word from you since I came in here, except for a letter dated the 18th, in which you said my CO was giving me a suspended sentence of 28 days detention subject to re-examination by a Psychiatrist.

    This was what he also told me, but as you see it is not what happened. Instead I was sent here next day. The commandant here has been extremely kind to me and has given me a light job in the office. He also says that on expiration of sentence I should have a Medical Board as a matter of form and be subsequently discharged the service. I only hope he's right but so much has gone wrong that I don't know.

Anyhow, I'm coming out on Friday 11th unless I lose my remission, in which case it'll be the 15th.

I'm applying straightaway for leave – it's now five months since I had the one I overstayed – as I don't feel I can possibly carry on any longer if I don't get completely away from army life after the trouble I've had recently.

I expect they'll try and stop me, although it's well overdue and I think I have been punished enough for this offence (22 days in close arrest, 28 days detention, 28 days pay stopped!) and with 3 months in hospital I've had no liberty since February.

It might help if you would ring the Adjutant and confirm my statement that unless I get leave to see to my business I shall suffer financially, and suggest that I should be granted leave when I apply for it.

That is, if you still mean to give me a contract. You could mention that. My finances are very rocky, to say nothing of my health, and I must get away somewhere for peace of mind even if only for 10 days. Perhaps you could drop me a line about this, before Friday? My address after will be the same except for 'C' Coy instead of HQ.

Yours ever,

Julian

to RUPERT HART-DAVIS
'C' Company/No 3 Infantry Depot/Southend-on-Sea/Essex
13-6-43

My dear Rupert,

I came out on Friday. Back to a new company and a very unpleasant CSM. 'Leave? Not likely, not for 28 days and then only if you soldier properly.' And it's 5 months since I had any. I was told at the DB[1] I would get leave at once.

CSM also put me down to all duties, which I obviously can't otherwise I wouldn't be recommended for my ticket.[2] To do parades is going to bring on a breakdown for certain – I'm just back where I started. They say the Medical Board may come off in due course, meantime I'm to carry on normally. The idea being that if I can do parades I'm fit to be kept on in the army. You see? I knew it would all come to nothing, in fact I'm worse off.

I feel at the end of my tether – the next move will be to draft me abroad and get rid of me. I must do something to prevent this, but what? Down here I'm quite helpless, and they won't give me leave because they plan to get me drafted off quickly before I've time to communicate with anybody in London. The Mental Home didn't come off – it *wasn't* nonsense – so this is what they'll try next.

Can you help about leave, anyway? Or do something? Only quick, because otherwise it'll be too late. Please believe that – I *know*.

Yours ever,

Julian

1 Detention barrack.
2 An abbreviation of 'ticket of leave', prison slang for being paroled.

to JOHN LEHMANN
'C' Company/No 3 Infantry Depot/Southend-on-Sea/Essex
13-6-43

Dear Mr Lehmann,

Thank you so much for your letter and the copy of *PNW* 16; I couldn't acknowledge these before as when I received them I was doing 18 days in a Military Detention Barrack.

I am now recommended for my discharge from the army, but instead of this there may be an attempt to certify me insane! Can they certify you if you've never done anything more abnormal than go absent from the army or write 17 short stories in 2 months? I am telling everyone about this just now, as I don't think I should let this sort of attempt pass without raising hell about it.

If I'm not railroaded to the nut-house, I mean to write the book I told you about once – an essay in Hitchcockian melodrama called either *The Hunted Man* or *The Fields of Night*.[1] I mention this because of some remarks in an article of yours which impressed me very much at the time. You wrote of that world of underground intrigue where 'the individual has as little chance of survival as a sparrow striking a high tension cable,' or words to that effect. It seemed to me that perhaps you had had a glimpse of such a world – which to most people has no existence outside books by Graham Greene. As you seem to be alone among critics in recognising the existence of this world and valuing such serious books as might come from an attempt to portray it, I think my novel might be of interest to you. However, perhaps I shall soon be peering from behind the bars of some military madhouse and not allowed to write!

I've only just started reading *PNW* 16, but it seems a terrific number. I think Antony Verney's[2] the most talented new writer you've introduced for a long time – I haven't come across anyone else who portrays so well and so economically the crazy petty atmosphere of army life.

Well, best wishes from

Yours sincerely,

J. Maclaren-Ross

1   The novel was never completed.
2   Anthony Verney was the author of a piece entitled 'The Cat and the Soldier'.

to RUPERT HART-DAVIS
'C' Company / No 3 Infantry Depot / Southend-on-Sea / Essex
14-6-43

My dear Rupert,

Latest development. I was told to report to the Area Psychiatrist today. When I got there it wasn't Major Lock, the one who knows all about me, but another one, very detached and unsympathetic who knew nothing about me at all. 'Can't think why you've come. Who sent for you? Major Lock's ill and I don't want you.' Then he asked me, after looking through my papers, whether anything was being done about my discharge. I said I didn't know, and I was very worried. He said, what about? A recommendation's been made in your case, and that's final. I said, I want some leave. You can't have leave if you're going to be discharged, he said. I said, but that'll take months. He said certainly not. I'll get things moving right away. Only a matter of form.

I said, any chance of my being certified? He said, Not by us. Or by anyone else? I said. Not unless your conduct proves dangerous to persons at large, he said. I said, I don't see why it should. He said, Nor do I, or why you got the idea at all.

So that's that. It looks as if the discharge is finally coming off, and soon. As for the mental home, I think there was an attempt to control the machine in that direction, but that with this recommendation the machine is out of their control, and is this time in my favour. What terrifies me is the chance of the machine getting out of control *against me*. I don't think it can do that now. This man, though dispassionate and seemingly without human feelings at all, struck me as very efficient and the type to get things done at once. I prefer that to the inefficient sympathetic type, who can often be sidetracked from concrete action however well disposed they are. Well, we shall see.

Now my mind is a little more settled and I can turn to consideration of literary work. I am going to outline the plan of my novel, thought out while polishing buckets in the detention barrack, and I want you to write but if I can do it, I think it should be very popular. Also, probably very long.

The Hunted Man: A Melodrama

Theme
In our late youth we enter into possession of our minds. In early manhood we are damaged by the exterior world, of which we know so little. It often drives us out of the possessions of our original mind, and many people never return to their right mind again. After we have been wandering in the world for a long time we learn its ways through suffering. If we can then re-enter our mind, we are fortunate, we are adult.

George Buchanan, *Words For Tonight*[1]

The individual against the machine (in this case, the army, which represents the vast force of stifling mediocrity which in time of war temporarily gets power and the upper hand). Also the fact that the majority of people *prefer* a form of fascism (what else is the army system?) because it allows the mediocre to rise to authority (gauleiter or CSM).[2]

That the war against Nazism is merely part of a struggle against this inherent penchant for fascism in the average person, but that often the most frenzied flag wavers and haters are subconscious fascists, themselves. With the defeat of Hitler we may well have fascism here, because the little people having tasted temporary authority will be loth to give it up.

Therefore, while believing themselves patriots, they are used in the story as tools by crypto-fascists.

Plot
The central character, the hunted man, is Severn, a writer serving in the army. (He's *not* me; he has no real self-confidence. He typifies so many modern intellectuals in being basically weak and allowing

79

circumstances and people to divide his mind and purpose.) Whilst on leave he becomes involved with dictator-minded adventurer and neurotic crypto-fascist and plunges into intrigue to prove that he can indulge in violent action and restore his confidence by coming through it (as some modern writers went exploring jungles in peacetime). But Severn's jungle is underground London (tube stations play a large part) and he is the hunted not the hunter. Then of course I use my recent experiences an absentee, and subsequently the court martial business: used by the fascists as a means of putting him away for 6 months: economising on murder. After that follows the middle section, 'The Nightmare': the Kafka-like atmosphere of red tape, psychiatric ward and detention barrack.

Then, after discharge from the army, Severn goes back after the fascists. They haven't broken him; they've hardened him: they hadn't reckoned on his vanity. Action follows: in a communist theatre, at a literary party, in a deserted fun-fair; a pregnant woman gets murdered; a particularly revolting fascist dies by falling down an escalator (he has haemophilia).

And Severn is left with his girl whom he had formerly depended on for strength, but she needs him now, not the other way about. And he is happy because at last he needs no one, he is a complete man, he has come of age (Theme 1).

What d'you think?

Please write and tell me.

Yours ever,

Julian

1 Constable, 1936.
2 Company sergeant major.

to RUPERT HART-DAVIS

16-6-43

My dear Rupert,

Very many thanks for your letter; I was so pleased to hear from you again. I'd written you another letter, which I hadn't posted and I enclose it because it gives the latest developments in my case.

About what you say. I didn't demand a court martial because (1) the CO told me the Area Commander wouldn't allow him to give me one (2) because he told me the sentence was to be suspended until they'd given me a Medical Board.

Now this morning I met Moore, the phone orderly, who is on my side, and he told me he'd listened-in to a phone talk between the CO and Major Lock, the Area Psychiatrist; the CO asked what he should do and Major L. said I was to finish the sentence and have a Board immediately after. The CO then said he was adding his own recommendation for my discharge; so apparently we've misjudged him and he *is* on my side, as he told Woodrow Wyatt.

Major L. then rang up the Detention Barrack Commandant who in consequence had me put in the office and was extremely kind to me. Major L. is now ill and on Monday I saw a Major Rose, deputising for him: details on the other letter overleaf.

Now what is happening, 'C' Company is not too good, the CSM dislikes me, but I've got excused most parades by the MO. I still haven't heard anything about leave; am seeing the Welfare Officer again today. I'm sure they have no right to hold it back for 28 days because I've done detention: the Commandant told me they couldn't and I should proceed straightaway.

I definitely must have a break very soon and the discharge may still take time. I suggest if you found out definitely the rule about leave – it's 5 months since I had any – and whether a man should be penalised because he's committed one crime in 3 years and has done his punishment; and when you have found out, rang the CO, it would get me leave.

I'll tell you this from what I know: he's not at all anxious for it to appear that he has it in for me, and he's very much scared of both you and Wyatt. I was told that the RPs[1] had definite instructions to hold up any letters from me asking influential friends outside for help whilst I was in the Guardroom, and they're all afraid of a public scandal and accusations of persecution. (Hence no CM.)[2]

So I do think you could help there: considering that the CO promised to let you know how things went and he has not done so, he will think it quite natural for you to enquire.

Also you could say you wanted to see me for business reasons and your duty prevents you from coming down here, and when is my leave due as it's urgent?

If he comes out with this stuff about 28 days (I don't think he will) and you've found out there's a different ruling, then you could point it out. Only please do it soon, if you will, as the office has to know a week in advance and I'm anxious to go as soon as possible: next Monday or Tuesday if I can.

Will you do this?

And thank you again most awfully for your help, which has been a great comfort to me. I hope you'll like the plan of proposed book enclosed.

Yours ever,
Julian

1 Regimental Police.
2 Court martial.

to RUPERT HART-DAVIS
'C' Company/No 3 Infantry Depot/Southend-on-Sea/Essex
27-6-43

My dear Rupert,

I must write and tell you what is happening. I have filled up papers for a Medical Board again and I am to have this, I expect, Monday next. If all goes well, I've been told I shall be out on 28 days discharge leave by the following Friday; I hear there are three specialist recommendations and the CO's, so it does look hopeful.

But it's as well to be prepared, you never can tell. There may be someone interested in having me sent abroad after the war; it seems almost impossible but these things do happen. If the Board *doesn't* grade me E, it could be done quickly before I've time to get word out to you or anybody else. So if you don't hear anything from me by the Friday, would you please make enquiries and get ready to make a fuss? I will send you a card or a wire before that Friday unless this has happened and for 'security reasons' I'm not allowed to communicate. By then I should know definitely one way or the other unless something sinister's afoot.

I feel awfully low in my mind tonight, I'm very worried about money for one thing. I've been writing all day an account of life in the DB[1] but don't find this is going at all well. What I need if I do get my ticket is a rest, but I can't afford it. Life definitely doesn't seem worth living as things stand: my difficulties will only begin after my discharge; I'd had enough of money worries in peacetime. And yet to continue on in the army is impossible. I don't know at all what to do: there doesn't seem to be any hope anywhere. I wish I didn't feel like this, but there's nothing to dispel it.

Yours ever,
Julian

1 Detention barrack.

to RUPERT HART-DAVIS
PTE!!¹/'C' Company/No 3 Infantry Depot/Southend-on-Sea/Essex
3-7-43

My dear Rupert,

Thank you for your letter. I'm still awaiting the Board: it will be Monday I expect. They seem to think it will definitely be discharge. If you let me have a phone number where I can ring you during the day, we should be able to meet as if all goes well I should be on 28 days discharge leave next Friday.

I am enclosing what I consider my best story, 'The Tape', for the collection. On a separate sheet I've made out a list of the stories: these will now come to about 78,000 words; I'd hoped to include a 5,000 story 'The Boy Who Might Have Been With Luck the Chess Champion of the World' but Reginald Moore doesn't think this will be out in *Selected Writing* in time. The missing stories I shall be able to let you have directly I get to London, and the collection will then be complete.

Leonard Russell,² of *The Sunday Times* and *Saturday Book*,³ came down to see me in Southend the other day and he would like to do a short novel of mine, *Hangover*,⁴ at six bob in his Saturday Book Library. As this will mean immediate cash, of which I am sorely in need, I agreed; also the psychological effect of writing this book (it will take about a month to do) will be beneficial to me. It contains a lot of stuff I want to get rid of before my mind can be free. I do hope you won't mind? You did say you didn't mind if Moore published it, if you remember.

Then, while the stories are being printed and coming out, I can get cracking on either *They Can't Give You a Baby* or *The Hunted Man* for you, or both concurrently. We can talk about this in London. Let me know what you think.

I'm looking forward to seeing you – if all goes well. But I've been long enough in the army to know that in it nothing is ever certain: although it will be a definite scandal if the Board disregards the recommendations of 4 specialists.

A bientot (we hope).

Yours ever,

Julian

How about getting Connolly to do a preface for the stories? I think he would. He gave a very good criticism of them when he saw all the civvie ones first, and I know he likes the later ones. What d'you say?

1 Maclaren-Ross had been demoted from lance-corporal to private.
2 Leonard Russell (1906–74).
3 An annual hard-cover miscellany, published by Hutchinson. Its contents encompassed short stories, poems, memoirs and photographs.
4 The book appears never to have left the drawing-board.

to RUPERT HART-DAVIS

'C' Company / No 3 Infantry Depot / Southend-on-Sea / Essex

5-7-43

My dear Rupert,

Board graded me 'E'[1] today – papers should be through in about a week they said.

Will write again when I am coming up and we can meet.

And thanks again for your help.

Yours ever,

Julian

1 Unfit for military service.

to RUPERT HART-DAVIS

'C' Company / No 3 Infantry Depot / Southend-on-Sea / Essex

6-7-43

My dear Rupert,

Thank you for your letter, which I received on my return from the Medical Board.

Congratulations on the happy event[1] – I do hope everything turns out all right, as I'm sure it will. Good luck and good for you.

Reference the stories, I at first was about to disagree, because you know I don't want to get a reputation as an army writer. Still, I *have* told the truth about the army, which no one else seems to have done: Alun Lewis got very near it sometimes.

But these stories will only make about 40,000 words, easily collected once I'm free. I enclose a note to the stories which I should like to have printed.[2]

Now what about a title? *The Hell of a Time* will clearly have to be abandoned, since the story of that name is not included in the section. I'd use *They Can't Give You a Baby* only I want that for the book of army experiences later. *Hullo Soldier* wouldn't be bad – I am writing a story called that.[3]

By the way, I hope you will accept a dedication in view of what you have done for me.[4] It would give me great pleasure if you would.

Wishing you all the very best,

Yours ever,

Julian

Let's use *TCGYAB*[5] – we can call the other 'They Gave Me My Ticket' or something. Okay?

1 On 4 July 1943 Hart-Davis's third child, Adam, had been born.
2 The note wasn't included in the published volume.
3 The story may not have been completed. It was, in any case, never published.
4 Hart-Davis accepted. The book, ultimately titled *The Stuff to Give the Troops*, was dedicated to him.
5 *They Can't Give You a Baby*.

to RUPERT HART-DAVIS

29-12-43

My dear Rupert,

How are you? Haven't heard from you since God knows when. I got from Wren Howard[1] that you were down with the Coldstreams again and am sending this through them as I don't know your exact address. Are you having leave? If so do ring me up at my home number (PAD. 2832) in the morning and we must have a drink and some lunch. I met Nancy Cunard[2] and gave her your address; she remembered you as a boy.

I've had the hell of a time collecting the MSS for Cape. I got them all together and then Donald Taylor[3] wanted to make a film of them and didn't; but during this period the MSS were at the Strand Office and got distributed among members of the staff who wanted to read them.[4] So then Howard said the stories couldn't come out till April and now says he doesn't know *when* they're likely to get done. This is bad for me because it's no good following up with a novel which may not come out until 1945 if publication of the stories is held up until Summer 1944. Also people are saying everywhere that they're sick of war literature. And as for my future as a writer, it doesn't really start until the collected stories are out and followed by a novel. So it doesn't look, at this rate, as though I shall be at all established for over another year! I'm depressed.

The stories are all army ones (25). Provisional title: *Are You Happy in Your Work*. They won't have *TCGYAB*:[5] say women asking for it in shops would get given Marie Stopes[6] instead. Can you possibly have the typescript of *The Salesman* sent to me?[7] I want to rewrite it. Drop me a line when you've a moment. I hope you're well.

With very best wishes from Scylla and myself for the New Year,

Yours ever,

Julian

1   In the continued absence of Rupert Hart-Davis, C. Wren Howard was one of Maclaren-Ross's main contacts at Jonathan Cape.

2   Nancy Cunard (1896–1965) was an heiress who led a bohemian life and pursued a literary career. Her friends included the painter Augustus John and the poet Ezra Pound.

3   Donald Taylor (1911–66) was the founder and Managing Director of the Strand Film Company.

4   Soon after leaving the army, Maclaren-Ross was briefly employed alongside the poet Dylan Thomas as a screenwriter at the Strand Film Company, a firm dedicated to making government propaganda documentaries. The staff at Strand included the novelist Philip Lindsay (1906–58).

5   *They Can't Give You a Baby.*

6   Slang for condoms, Marie Stopes (1880–1958) being a famous birth-control campaigner.

7   On the evidence of numerous surviving fragments, this earlier draft may, unlike the published version, have been narrated in the third person.

to RUPERT HART-DAVIS

19 Park Place Villas[1]/London W2

3-6-44

My dear Rupert,

Thank you for your note the other day.

I think I should write to inform you of the general position with regard to Cape since I signed a contract with them in June 1943. Mr Howard, at this interview, told me that he was undecided whether to publish the army and civilian stories together or separately. He could not decide until he had seen the MSS of the civilian stories, which he told me you had not delivered to him. As you were then in the USA, it was arranged to await your return before deciding what form the collection would finally take. I asked whether this interval would not delay publication of the volume in January '44, as had been promised me. I was told it would make no difference. The MSS of the army stories were then returned to me and I left the office. An advance of £100 was paid to me next day.

Shortly afterwards I obtained a job as a scriptwriter to a film company.[2] When some time had elapsed, I think about 3 months, I rang up Mr Howard and said perhaps it would be better to do the army stories separately, and not wait to see the civilian stories on your return. He then told me it would be impossible now to print the collection before April. This disheartened me, as I had been told the interval would make no difference, and of course I was eager for publication as soon as possible. However, I started to collect the MSS of the army stories together: in the meantime many, through an accident, had been lost; some of the publications were out of print, and altogether it took until December to assemble and dispatch them. I was now told publication could not take place until July '44.

This did not encourage me to proceed with the novel on which I was engaged. Simultaneously I lost my job and was out of work for 6 weeks. I wrote to Mr Howard and asked if the firm would be willing to help me with money in any way. He said nothing could be paid until the book of stories was on sale. I was therefore far too worried to continue to work on a novel; it required peace of mind and ability to concentrate, which was denied me whilst I was forced to write more short stories in order to keep alive.

When, in April, the page proofs of the stories came through, a further sum of £50 (advance due on 1st printing) was paid to me.

Why couldn't this have been done in January, when I needed it most?

I had several conversations with Miss Wedgwood,[3] about projected novels; as with the various setbacks I had received, it was obvious that the longer novel could not be completed for publication even early in 1945, and I was forced to embark on something shorter.

I offered Mr Howard to write a completely revised version of *The Salesman*, as I was (and still am) again out of work and needed an advance on something which could be completed quickly. He refused *The Salesman*, adding in a letter dated 25th May '44, that he would receive all the material forthwith!

I wrote reminding him that the material had been on his desk during our first interview (June '43) and that it was his wish that he should see the civilian stories (which he told me had *not* been delivered to him) before deciding.

I received no reply to this letter, but was instead summoned to the office by telephone. There Mr Howard told me that if I would write out a one-page synopsis of a projected novel, it might be possible to pay me an immediate advance if the subject were approved. I delivered the synopsis, but Mr Howard rejected it.

I then suggested that if he could accommodate me with an advance on another civilian volume of stories (I have 25 collected), this would enable me to complete work on the long novel *Company of Shadows*[4] and the book of stories need not appear until after this latter. He agreed with me on this point, but regretted (once again) that he could not help me with any advance.

Now I find the civilian stories were in fact delivered by you with the army stories; there need have been no necessity to await your return from USA to obtain possession of them; Mr Howard could have read them there and then, decided immediately on the ultimate form of the collection, and the book would have been out in January.

The delay of 6 months – obviously not my fault, as can now be seen – has made a terrible difference to my position; I should have been established with 6 months sales behind me; instead of which I am down to my last shilling. That the civilian stories should have been all the time in the office, when Mr Howard definitely told me they had never been delivered to him, seems to me monstrous. Frankly, I am contemplating taking legal action for damages: the attitude all along has been consistently unhelpful and I fail to see why I should be penalised in this manner.

I am sorry that this position should have occurred; I know that had you not been away from the firm on army duty, these things would never have happened.

But I feel you should know the whole story; I have made every reasonable suggestion recently to obtain an advance; I can't do more.

Now I feel it is time to take some action to better my own position, which if all these delays had not occurred and the stories remained in the office, as in the June '43 interview, would have been so different.

I'm terribly sorry, but you can't blame me.

Do let me have all your news when you've a moment.

Yours ever,

Julian

1 He appears to have moved into a flat here immediately after being discharged from the army. The house was in Maida Vale, close to the Regent's Park Canal.
2 The Strand Film Company.
3 C. Wren Howard's colleague at Jonathan Cape, C.V. Wedgwood.
4 The new title of *The Hunted Man*, a never-to-be-completed novel.

to RUPERT HART-DAVIS

19 Park Place Villas / London W2

12-2-44

My dear Rupert,

How are you? Well, I hope? When are you coming on leave? Do let me know, so that we can meet.

I've seen Miss Wedgwood at Cape's and apparently the book is going to be done fairly soon; the only thing is, what to call it. There doesn't seem to be any real objection to the original title *They Can't Give You a Baby*; I myself don't think we shall find a better one. At present it's going to be advertised as *Are You Happy in Your Work* which I think is dull. The only other I can think of is: *Playing Soldiers*. What do you think? Any ideas? Or do you prefer the 1st one? Since the book is yours by dedication you ought to have your say in choosing the name for it.

I'm working again for films,[1] but the intervening period has left me a debt of £35 which I must clear very soon or else. I need fifty really. The only way I can get this is by writing a lot more stories, which I don't want to do, because not only am I totally barren of ideas for any; but writing stories will hold up more work on my novel, called either *Company of*

Shadows or *Conspiracy of Silence*, I can't decide which. It's a bore. On the other hand I've got to get fifty quid within the next fortnight. High-ho.

By the way, can you think of any way I could get hold of the two parts of *The Salesman*. I might be able to knock the material into shorter form.

Well, do drop me a line soon. Or ring up any morning.

All the very best,

Yours ever,

Julian

1   He'd obtained another scriptwriting job, this time working from home. His brief appears to have consisted of providing an adaptation of Graham Greene's novel *The Confidential Agent*, minus any potentially controversial allusions to the Spanish Civil War.

to DANIEL GEORGE[1]

Swan Court/Dachet/Buckinghamshire

2-8-44

Dear Mr George,

Thank you so much for a very kind and understanding review in last week's *Tribune*.[2]

I've often meant to write to you with reference to other kind mentions of me in your column; incidentally, the title of my collection was suggested by your own review of my story in *Modern Reading* No 6. I wanted at first to call it *They Can't Give You a Baby*, but Cape said people asking for it would get given Marie Stopes instead.

About my future work, whilst I entirely agree with your advice, I fear I haven't said quite all I want to about inefficient officers: the training period of 1940–44 remains a disgrace which has never been fully exposed.

My first novel, which I call a melodrama, *Company of Shadows*, includes scenes in a military psychiatric hospital and in the glass house and is the story of an army deserter versus a crypto-fascist gang and will be humorous only in spots.

I've also a second collection of 25 stories (not about the army) coming out from Hutchinson's.

I hope that one of these books, at any rate, will bear out your encouraging view of my writing.

Sincerely,

J. Maclaren-Ross

1 'Daniel George' was the pseudonym of D.G. Bunting (1890–1967), an author and literary critic who worked as an editor for Jonathan Cape. Following Rupert Hart-Davis's induction into the army, George played an increasingly significant role within the firm.

2 George had reviewed *The Stuff to Give the Troops*. 'What among many things distinguishes J. Maclaren-Ross from other recorders of life in the army,' wrote George, 'is his knowledge of the language. Having an almost infallible ear for word and phrase, he practises the fine art of selection: he neither invents a special jargon of his own nor concocts an unspeakable mixture of author's English and apprehended vernacular...The stories in *The Stuff to Give the Troops* are of civilians in the army rather than of soldiers, and active service is far away. That period when men under training in England were going stale is economically and amusingly depicted, criticism of the authorities and their methods being implied. The war has moved on since that time, but this record will retain its value. Now it is for the author to exercise his talent in a larger field. He must leave browned-off soldiers and inefficient officers behind him.'

to THE ROYAL LITERARY FUND

c/o E. Du Cros[1]/185c Cromwell Road/London SW5

6-12-44

Dear Sir,

May I be supplied with a form of application for one of the Grants administered by the Royal Literary Fund?

Yours faithfully,

J. Maclaren-Ross

1 Du Cros was a friend from Northfield Military Hospital. Like Maclaren-Ross, his writing had appeared in the first issue of the patients' magazine, *Psyche*.

to THE SECRETARY, THE ROYAL LITERARY FUND

c/o E. Du Cros/185c Cromwell Road/London SW5

22-1-45

Dear Sir,

Thank you for your letter and for the application form duly received.

In accordance with your regulations I enclose herewith a copy of my book for examination; the application form duly completed and the letters you require will follow shortly.

Yours faithfully,

J. Maclaren-Ross

to THE ROYAL LITERARY FUND

c/o E. Du Cros / 185c Cromwell Road / London SW5

30-1-45

Dear Sir,

In accordance with your regulations, I have already despatched to you a copy of my book, and am enclosing herewith two letters authenticating my case, the circumstances of which are as follows:

In July 1943 I was discharged medically unfit from the army after 3 years service. I had by then written over 50 short stories, most of which had already been printed in reviews and magazines. 25 of these, on army themes, were accepted by Messrs Jonathan Cape to form a collected volume shortly after my discharge.

I was paid £100 on account of royalties and subsequently a further sum of £50. When the book was eventually published a year later, a number of copies insufficient to cover the advance were printed,[1] as you will see from the enclosed statement. A reprint is announced for February, but I shall be unable to draw further royalties until October.

I also sold, last June, a further volume of stories to Messrs Hutchinson for an outright payment of £150; but no date has been given me for publication, nor has the volume been sent to the printers.[2] I am at work upon a novel but do not anticipate its completion until next winter, at the earliest.

The employment which I had obtained as a film-scenario-writer terminated early in 1944; since then I have attempted to support myself by submitting to various magazines; but, as I'm sure you are aware, the rates of payment for short stories in this country are extremely low.

My total earnings last year amounted to under £300, including the outright payment of £150; out of this, furthermore, I was obliged to settle debts incurred in peace-time, when, for a period of many months, I was on the dole.

There is not very much hope that my earnings this year will amount to anything approaching this sum; advances on the Swedish and French translations of my collection permitted me to eke out a while longer, but these sums are now exhausted and further royalties will not accrue until the translations actually appear: according to my contracts, in 2 years' time.

At the moment I am urgently in need of money; in not too good a state of health, which is aggravated by the winter, and moreover faced with an income-tax demand (enclosed herewith) for income earned over the past 3 years, whilst I was serving in the army.

Trusting, therefore, that this application will meet with your sympathetic consideration,[3]

I am,

Yours faithfully,

J. Maclaren-Ross

1 The original print-run of the first edition had been set at 4,000, but Maclaren-Ross's publisher had dramatically reduced this.

2 The volume was shelved by Hutchinson, which deemed the material too racy. The book's constituent stories have never resurfaced.

3 His application was rejected on the recommendation of Sir John Murray, the publisher, who had been asked by the Committee of the Royal Literary Fund to read *The Stuff to Give the Troops*. In a letter, dated 31 January 1945, Murray condemned the book for being 'vulgar'.

to JOHN LEHMANN

Imperial Hotel[1]/Russell Square/London WC1

17-5-45

My dear John,

Thank you for your letter and the enclosed cheque for £25. Of course the film article[2] cancels out the former advance of £10.

Regarding the article itself, and *Henry V*,[3] I felt that a more detailed examination of this film did not belong there; for despite its undoubted success, the magnificence of the production and the acting, I feel that it is an experiment not to be repeated; I would rather British films kept away from historical pageant (even Shakespearian), and from colour and spectacle, altogether: if Shakespeare is to be filmed by us, I would prefer *Hamlet* or *Macbeth* in black and white, concentrating in the latter on the drama of guilt and destroying ambition, with the battle sequences cut to a minimum. On the whole, however, I should like the British to concentrate on material not already written for the stage: stories conceived wholly in cinematic terms such as the French have given us (*Le Jour se Lève*[4] is an example). But this, I fear, would mean the employment of imaginative and creative writers to do the scripts and the wholesale sacking of hack 'story-editors' who see films purely as commercial merchandise.

If you like, I will add something to this effect on the proof; I do think the article should be as constructive as possible, while also pointing out the danger of complacence to the new directors and producers whose heads may have swelled with the unstinted praise given them up to now for their as yet incomplete achievements. I hope we shall be able to let the remark about Mr Rank stand:[5] one might add, if you like, 'detrimental in so far as one's hopes are concerned that British films of the future may favourably compare with the best Hollywood and Continental productions'.

There may have to be one or two alterations, once again, in the first and last paragraphs of the Hitchcock article[6] after I have seen *Spellbound*[7] on Sunday, as the story seems to be radically different from my idea of it.

Yours ever,

J.M.R.

1 He had moved here from his friend Edward Du Cros's flat. The Imperial Hotel was a grand, 350-room establishment overlooking Russell Square. It incorporated a Turkish bath, a winter garden, a restaurant and a dance hall. It also boasted a lift which, Maclaren-Ross claimed, was essential for him, as his injured knee hurt when he walked up flights of stairs.
2 'A Brief Survey of British Feature Films', published in *Penguin New Writing* 29.
3 *Henry V* (1944) was directed by Laurence Olivier, who also took the title role.
4 *Le Jour se Lève* (1939), directed by Marcel Carné, starred Jean Gabin and Arletty.
5 Agreeing to Maclaren-Ross's request, Lehmann resisted the temptation to cut the following remark in the published article: 'In talking of current British films, mention of Mr J. Arthur Rank also seems unavoidable. His determination to conquer the American market cannot fail to have a detrimental effect on film-making in this country…' (*Penguin New Writing* 29).
6 'The World of Alfred Hitchcock', published in *New Writing and Daylight*, September 1946.
7 *Spellbound* (1945), directed by Alfred Hitchcock, starred Ingrid Bergman and Gregory Peck.

to JOHN LEHMANN

3 Queen Street[1]/London WI

27-5-45

Dear Lehmann,

Here is the essay on Hitchcock as promised. I'm sorry I couldn't bring it round yesterday and it is a day late.

If you like it, will you do the same about a cheque as you did before, as unfortunately I am again hard-up? I will ring you on Tuesday or Wednesday.

Yours sincerely,

J. Maclaren-Ross

1   Maclaren-Ross had moved here from the Imperial Hotel. The building was located in Shepherd's Market, at that period a seedy district.

to JONATHAN CAPE[1]

3 Queen Street/London WI

4-6-45

Dear Mr Cape,

Since the 2nd impression of *The Stuff to Give the Troops* appears to be sold out in the bookshops and only obtainable direct from you, I wonder if you could see your way to advancing me whatever sum of money is due on this edition? I am aware that under the terms or our contract, the royalties are not due to be paid out until September, but the difference of 3 months would make all the difference to me at the present moment; and, I am sure, none to you.

I feel certain you will oblige me in this matter. Any cheque should be made payable to me personally and not to Messrs Curtis Brown, who are no longer acting as my agents.

Yours sincerely,

J. Maclaren-Ross

1   Jonathan Cape (1879–1960) was the founder of the company that bears his name. Maclaren-Ross's problems with the firm had already led to him looking for a publishing deal with another firm.

to JOHN LEHMANN

3 Queen Street/London WI

June 1945

Dear John,

Here is the Alun Lewis thing.[1] If you like it, will you do the usual? I'm sorry to be a curse. I'll ring you up sometime on Friday. Is lunchtime any good?

Overleaf you'll find a precis (rather long, I fear) of the whole damn situation.

J.

The present situation is this:

I sold 2 books to Messrs Allen Wingate:

Bitten by the Tarantula (a 40,000 word novel) and

The Weeping and the Laughter (stories: 40,000 words)

On each book I received an advance of £100.

It was agreed verbally that the 40,000 word novel would be published in August 1945. Later this verbal date was changed to November.

The plan for future work was that I was to deliver a novel of 80,000 words (call it for argument's sake *The Lunatic Fringe*)[2] by August; this was to be published in March 1946 (verbal agreement).

This novel, if acceptable, was to be sold on the following terms:

10% on the first 2,500

12 1/2% up to 5,000

15% up to 7,500

and an advance payable on acceptance.

Then terms were to be agreed upon for the very long novel (*The Trick Cyclist*)[3] which was to be published in 1946 (December).

The stories, *The Weeping and the Laughter*,[4] were to appear early in 1947.

It was made clear to me that a reprint of the short novel *Bitten by the Tarantula* was unlikely, for some time to come, as all available paper was to be used for printing 10,000 copies of the 80,000 word novel *The Lunatic Fringe* next March.

I agreed to that, although in the contract all rights revert to me if the book is not reprinted within 9 months.

Now the situation has altered: owing to difficulties with paper, they are no longer anxious to receive *The Lunatic Fringe* so soon; also, I suspect, because they are not keen to pay an advance of £200 on a book which has, now, no hope of being published by March.

Last night it was admitted to me that even if I were to deliver the novel within a fortnight, the earliest publication date would be July 1946. *The Trick Cyclist* would then appear in 1947, by which time they expect the paper situation to have eased up.

I made it quite clear that I would give no further terms for any work after *The Lunatic Fringe*, and it seems unlikely that they will even buy this with the position as it is – certainly not if I continue to refuse terms.

Even if they buy *The Lunatic Fringe*, I will still be free to offer *The Trick Cyclist* elsewhere, unless terms are agreed upon.

My plan is to complete and deliver *The Lunatic Fringe* as soon as possible, providing I can raise £200 to live on while I am completing it.

Then, either draw an advance from Allen Wingate, write *The Trick Cyclist* this autumn and offer it elsewhere; or if they do not take *The*

Lunatic Fringe, then offer that elsewhere with an option on *The Trick Cyclist*.

It all depends on my being able to raise, now, £200 on guarantee of repayment in 1946 when some of these books will have appeared and be selling. There will also be other rights and further royalties on *The Stuff to Give the Troops* by that time.

I do not feel that I am acting unfairly; I am extremely sorry about the paper situation, but I cannot afford to jeopardise *The Trick Cyclist* by turning it over to a firm so uncertainly placed.

As it is, I am risking the fate of 2 books: *Bitten by the Tarantula* and *The Weeping and the Laughter* – and maybe the novel *The Lunatic Fringe*.

I cannot risk any more than that by giving further options.

Furthermore, several verbal promises have already been broken: first the date was August; then November, now even that seems uncertain; I understood that enough paper was already guaranteed for a first edition of 5,000 copies; then again it was agreed that if I got into financial difficulties while writing the 80,000 word novel, I would be helped out; but when I asked for an extra £50 to help me complete it, I was refused on the grounds that they'd already paid out £200 on books for which they would see no return for some time to come – as though I were responsible for the delay in publication.

I was definitely told that money was no object; paper the only difficulty; then, directly the contract was signed, that they did not feel happy about receiving yet another book this year because of having to pay out another advance.

The whole affair is becoming too worrying for me; it seems that this uncertainty and procrastination will continue until 1947, as they've admitted, and that is far too long.

After my disappointment over the Cape book, and having to sell a volume of stories outright because I needed money, it seems I may have to sacrifice 3 more books: but I'm willing to do anything if I can safeguard *The Trick Cyclist*, which is very important to me.

In any case, next year will surely see my situation eased. The position should then be:

The Stuff to Give the Troops (stories)	1944
Better Than a Kick in the Pants (stories: outright sale)	1945
Bitten by the Tarantula (short novel)	1945
The Lunatic Fringe (novel)	1946
The Trick Cyclist (novel)	1946

So that I should be able to repay a loan by then, and surely there is some way by which the transaction could be made business-like and foolproof.

I'm sorry to bore you with all this; but if you are able to suggest some way out, I should be most grateful.

Yours ever,

Julian

1 'Second Lieutenant Lewis', a memoir of Maclaren-Ross's friendship with Lewis. The memoir appeared in *Penguin New Writing* 26.
2 *The Lunatic Fringe* was never written.
3 Like *The Lunatic Fringe* and other projects, *The Trick Cyclist* failed to make the transition from idea to reality. In 1940s slang, a 'trick cyclist' was a psychiatrist. The book would probably have been based on Maclaren-Ross's experiences at Northfield Military Psychiatric Hospital.
4 Not to be confused with his 1953 childhood memoir of the same title, this was the original title for the collection of short stories published as *The Nine Men of Soho*.

to JOHN LEHMANN

3 Queen Street / London WI

24-8-45

Dear John,

Thank you for your card; I didn't think you were coming back till the 25th. I hope we can meet soon, as I am very anxious to hear how you got on in France. I rang your place today but couldn't get any answer.

As for French rights, I'm uncertain how I stand until I look up the contract I have with Fontaine Editions, who are reading *The Stuff*. I think they've an option on my next but I'm not sure. There's not much I can do, either, until the books actually appear, as the MSS are out of my hands and presumably at the printer. Bonnier, however, rejected the short novel; so my Swedish rights are free, and if only the books would appear, I could do something about them. These delays are absolutely maddening; however I should know how I stand with Cape on October 1st when the statement of sales is due – and also, I hope, a cheque.

Talking of that, I wonder if you could possibly let me have that second cheque as soon as you can; I know it's not due yet, but I'm having a spot of bother with my landlady and want to give her a sub to keep her quiet. I hope you'll drop me a line and let me know when it's convenient for us to meet and have a talk; as there's a lot of things I'd like to consult you about.

Yours ever,

Julian

PS If you send the cheque, would you mind opening it?[1] Terribly sorry to fuss. I've sold that story 'My Father Was Born In Havana'[2] to Russell,[3] which means £20 but I don't know when I'll get it, so am hard up again.

1 'Open' cheques could not only be deposited but also cashed. A 'closed' cheque featured parallel lines drawn across them.
2 A short, gleeful account of his colourful antecedents.
3 Leonard Russell.

to JOHN LEHMANN

3 Queen Street/London WI

22-9-45

Dear Lehmann,

In reply to your secretary's letter dated 19th September, my story 'The Swag, the Spy and the Soldier'[1] is not in any way libellous; as to the paragraphs which the solicitors have mentioned, I do not consider that the words used[2] could possibly lead to a prosecution for obscenity. These words have all been used before in magazines and periodicals and in my own book about the army without any such result. In my opinion it would be a pity to alter them to euphemisms or to delete them altogether. While I fully realise the difficulties with which the solicitors are faced, I feel, personally, that one should do nothing to encourage a similar kind of puritanism to that which prevailed after the last war, and which caused a fine book like *Death of a Hero*[3] to be presented to the public in a mutilated form.

Yours sincerely,

J. Maclaren-Ross

1 Published in *Penguin New Writing* 26.
2 The controversial words included 'fuck it' and 'bugger'. 'Fuck it' ended up being amended to 'fog it', just the type of euphemism Maclaren-Ross deplored.
3 *Death of a Hero*, Richard Aldington (William Heineman, 1929).

PART II
(1946–54)

CENTRAL POSITION 175 ROOMS

COUNTY HOTEL

UPPER WOBURN PLACE
NEAR EUSTON STATION
LONDON, W.C.1

Telegrams: Countotel, London
Telephone: Euston 5544

Friday morning

Dear Tony,

I've hesitated a long time before writing this letter to you, but the fact is things are absolutely desperate with us; in fact we've been living for the last few days selling books, pawning clothes, and only getting a limited number of shillings from the proceeds of these activities. Now my laundry has been impounded because I couldn't raise the requisite number of shillings, and the hotel bill itself impends.

I know things aren't so hot with you either, but I wonder if you could help us out. Monica could give you a postdated cheque (March 1st) for her next month's salary (£30) if you could manage to advance us this sum; in the meantime I have several irons in the fire which will have been withdrawn red-hot by then. At the moment I can't raise a penny by any other means than the mortgaging of her salary — this month's is already mortgaged, I fear, and the money gone long ago. I enclose the cheque herewith in case you can. If so, will you draw cash and send it to me so I get it Saturday morning; these people are just about to make our lives unpleasanter than they are already.

If you can't, never mind. You know I would not attempt to borrow from a fellow-writer unless there was absolutely no other way.

Meanwhile I hope your own troubles clear up and Violet gets well again rapidly. Please give her our very best wishes.

Yours ever
JB

Abrasive though his personality had become, Maclaren-Ross demon-strated a surprising ability to sustain long-running friendships. The beginning of 1946 saw him briefly ensconced in Bognor Regis with C.K. Jaeger and family, their home providing a congenial bolt-hole. His return to London coincided with the publication of his novella *Bitten by the Tarantula*. Due to the earlier falling out with Jonathan Cape, publishers of his debut short-story collection, this latest book was released by a rival firm, run by the Hungarian émigré André Deutsch.

Back in the capital, Maclaren-Ross resumed the rootless, spend-thrift way of life destined to undermine his nascent literary career. At first he – and probably his current girlfriend Monica Foster too – stayed with Edward Du Cros, a friend from Northfield Military Hospital. Using the proceeds from the sale of magazine articles to *Penguin New Writing* and two radio plays to the BBC, he and his girlfriend installed themselves in the pricey Imperial Hotel, overlooking Russell Square. To cover his exorbitant expenses, prominent among them being his continued heavy drinking, he obtained an advance for a novel about his experiences as a door-to-door salesman. That novel was initially called *The Salesman Only Rings Once*, its title providing a clue to its hardboiled American inspiration. In October 1946, he delivered the finished manuscript to André Deutsch. Not long afterwards, Deutsch, with whom he had inevitably ended up feuding, published *The Nine Men of Soho*, Maclaren-Ross's third collection of short stories. It led the novelist Elizabeth Bowen, reviewing for *The Tatler*, to declare him 'a writer due for the first rank'.

He had, in the meantime, met the novelist and critic Anthony Powell, who would soon be installed as one of his staunch allies. Another such stalwart friend, John Lehmann, helped to alleviate his mounting finan-cial problems by commissioning him to write more articles for *Penguin New Writing*. Lehmann, who had just founded a small publishing house, also paid him to translate Raymond Queneau's colloquial novel *Pierrot mon ami*. Maclaren-Ross and girlfriend were nevertheless forced to decamp from the Imperial Hotel to a less exalted address, from where he made the next of several successful applications to the Royal Literary Fund for hardship grants.

During the run-up to the publication of *The Salesman Only Rings Once*, subsequently retitled *Of Love and Hunger*, Maclaren-Ross obtained a substantial advance for a new novel. The advance – for a thriller that went under the titles *Death and His Sweetheart* and later *The Dark*

Diceman – was sanctioned by Graham Greene, the novelist and Managing Director of Eyre and Spottiswoode, a well-established publishing firm. Like so many of Maclaren-Ross's mooted novels, the book was never completed, the constant need for ready cash compelling him to neglect it in favour of the short-term rewards of journalism. Through Anthony Powell, who greatly admired his work, he landed a series of commissions for the *TLS* (*Times Literary Supplement*), for which Powell had been appointed part-time fiction editor. To fulfil his obligations as a writer while sustaining his daily ritual, which involved lunchtimes and evenings in his favourite pubs and drinking clubs, he tended to work at night, large doses of amphetamines fending off sleep.

A combination of financial problems and an obsession with the cinema led Maclaren-Ross into his first screenwriting assignment for a feature-length movie. In the summer of 1948, he was hired as part of a team of writers adapting *Maria Chapdelaine*, a French novel about nineteenth-century settlers in the Canadian wilderness. His discouraging experiences as a novice screenwriter pushed him towards a crisis that culminated in him splitting up with his girlfriend. After a miserable interlude, Monica Foster's place was taken by Barbara Wimble. In common with her predecessor, Wimble was much younger than Maclaren-Ross, yet exerted a steadying influence.

Despite the myriad frustrations of working on *Maria Chapdelaine*, eventually filmed as *The Naked Heart*, he accepted further screenwriting work, first from a low-budget company, then from Alexander Korda's powerful British Lion/London Film Productions conglomerate. Neither of these assignments proved any more fulfilling than his employment on *The Naked Heart*.

His latest screenwriting and journalistic commitments completed, Maclaren-Ross turned his attention to writing *The Weeping and the Laughter*, its gentle tone and expansive prose contrasting sharply with his previous work. Maclaren-Ross's old friend Rupert Hart-Davis, who had recently set up a publishing company, bought the rights to *The Weeping and the Laughter*. When the book was released in 1953, it attracted a spate of flattering reviews, but its commercial failure brought about yet another rift between publisher and author, long-term amphetamine use contributing to his burgeoning paranoia.

Since the early part of 1950, Maclaren-Ross had been sharing a flat near Paddington Station with Barbara Wimble. By November 1953, their relationship appears to have temporarily collapsed, forcing him to move out. The two of them were, however, reunited in their flat a few months later. But Wimble's sudden departure during August 1954 threw his life back into disarray. Just as he had sought refuge with the Jaegers after the break-up of his marriage, the unexpectedly vulnerable Maclaren-Ross reacted by going to stay with friends, in this case the New Zealand writer Dan Davin and his family.

Maclaren-Ross had first met Davin in the Wheatsheaf over a decade earlier. The Davins now lived in Oxford, where Dan worked for the Clarendon Press, part of Oxford University Press. Seeking to escape from the scene of his recent woes, Maclaren-Ross set up home in a rented basement flat just down the road from the Davins. They soon found themselves cast as reluctant co-stars in the Maclaren-Ross drama which, as ever, lurched between comedy and tragedy.

to THE BBC

The Bedford Hotel[1]/Bognor Regis/Sussex

19-1-46

Dear Sir,

In reply to yours of 17th January.

It seems to me that a considerable mistake, to put it politely, has been made. It was 'mistakes' of this sort that caused me to tell Mr David Thomson when he first approached me to write a radio-play about Captain Kidd, that I was unwilling to undertake further work for the BBC owing to their slipshod methods of payment.[2]

This script was only undertaken on the understanding that payment for my work would be prompt and expeditious. I returned your form to you only on completion and delivery of the script. No money was forthcoming under the terms of the contract.

On Friday last I made a special journey to Rothwell House[3] to see the producer, who wanted some alterations made and one scene added. He assured me that if this was done the play would be definitely accepted. Mr David Thomson was present throughout the interview and will corroborate my statement.

But in view of the manner in which the matter of payment has been handled, I must be firm in requesting full payment (30 guineas) by Thursday next, or my permission to broadcast will be withheld. Of course half the fee will be forthcoming as repayment for my time and trouble. Please do not worry me with further correspondence – except a cheque for the sum stated – as I'm a busy man and detest writing letters.

Why, by the way, was your letter addressed to Bayswater Road[4] when my telegram explicitly specified above address? Please rectify this additional error when replying to me, by cheque, this time.

Yours very truly,

J. Maclaren-Ross

---

1 Maclaren-Ross and Monica Foster had registered here just before Christmas. They spent much of the holiday period with the Jaegers, who were living in the Bognor Regis suburb of Elmer.

2 David Thomson, a producer in the BBC's Features Department, had commissioned the script on 25 November 1945. Maclaren-Ross's script, forming the first instalment in a series called *Rogues and Vagabonds*, ended up being broadcast on the BBC Home Service on 2 May 1946.

3 A block of flats used as BBC offices.

4 From the second week of October 1945 until late December 1945, he'd been living at 59 Bayswater Road.

to JONATHAN CAPE

c/o E. Du Cros/185c Cromwell Road/London SW5

8-2-46

Dear Mr Cape,

Since my book *The Stuff to Give the Troops* now appears to be out of print, I must formally remind you that if another edition is not printed within the next 3 months, the copyright of the volume reverts to me.

I should also be glad if my royalty statements, when due, could be forwarded to above address.

Yours sincerely,

J. Maclaren-Ross

to DANIEL GEORGE

Imperial Hotel/Russell Square/London WC1

15-2-46

Dear Mr George,

Thank you for the very nice reviews lately.[1] I caught a glimpse of you at John Lehmann's house-warming recently but you didn't see me.

You may find Walter Deckert, the hero of my new long novel,[2] more uncommon even than Michel.[3] He is a mass murderer who kills for money and he is *not* a psychopath. Perhaps the book (based on the Weidmann case 1938–1939)[4] will this time be a best seller. It isn't existentialist, though. Alas.

Yours sincerely,

J. Maclaren-Ross

1 George had reviewed Maclaren-Ross's novella *Bitten by the Tarantula* and his short story collection *The Nine Men of Soho* in the 15 February 1946 and 22 November 1946 issues of *Tribune*. Assessing *Bitten by the Tarantula*, George wrote, 'If he had written it in French and deleted all humour from it, he might, bless his Sartre, have stood a chance of ranking with Albert Camus as one of the exponents of existentialism. However, one of these days someone will erect a philosophy on the basis of pure fun, and he [Maclaren-Ross] may be its chief prophet.'

2 The novel was *Death and His Sweetheart*, subsequently retitled *The Dark Diceman*. The surviving chapters are included in the posthumous collection *Bitten by the Tarantula and Other Writing* (Black Spring Press, 2005).

3 Michel, a character in Maclaren-Ross's *Bitten by the Tarantula*, was a 19-year-old drug-trafficker, thief and homosexual gigolo.

4 The German-born Eugen Weidmann was a debonair, softly spoken poetry lover. Along with four accomplices, he'd robbed and murdered half a dozen people in Paris, where he had also been plotting a series of kidnappings. Fluent in English, French and German, he was also adept at disguising himself. For Maclaren-Ross,

Weidmann was a real-life counterpart to the master criminals who featured in the silent movie adventure serials which had fascinated him as a child. During the summer of 1940, Weidmann's seventeen-day trial, culminating in the death sentence, had made the front-pages of many British newspapers. Years later, when Maclaren-Ross was holding forth to fellow drinkers in the saloon bar of the Wheatsheaf on Rathbone Place, Weidmann formed a recurrent subject.

to JOHN LEHMANN

Imperial Hotel / Russell Square / London WC1

28-4-46

Dear John,

Thank you for the copy of *PNW* 27; I like its new dress.[1] When I've finished this letter, I shall read the article by Hampson,[2] which looks most interesting.

I'm most terribly sorry about this affair of the £10.[3] I'd been definitely promised help by that Tuesday, but instead of help I only got rudeness and abuse; and consequently I've been going through the worst time I've had for seven years.

Now there is another very doubtful chance; I shall know on Monday, but if it doesn't come off I shall really be on my uppers and quite finished, because there's no chance of help anywhere. I've got to get through until I finish this novel for Wingate,[4] and as things stand I simply can't do it.

The ten pounds I will see are paid whatever happens. Please don't write and say it doesn't matter, because that I can raise anyway and I mean to. I will let you know what happens during the next few days.

As ever,

J.M.R.

I'm sending back the corrected proofs of Hitchcock. *Spellbound* will be showing in London next week.

1   Issue 27 of *Penguin New Writing* marked a change in the magazine's design. It retained its pocket-sized format, but the front cover became less spartan and the typesetting less compressed. The magazine also began to use colour illustrations, predominantly reproductions of paintings.

2   Written by John Hampson (1901–55), best known for his novel *Saturday Night at the Greyhound* (1931), the article was entitled 'Movements in the Underground'. It was the first instalment in a survey of English fiction over the previous 45 years. The article focused on fictional portraits of working-class life, among them Patrick Hamilton's *Twenty Thousand Streets Under the Sky*, James Curtis's *You're in the Racket, Too* and A.J. La Bern's *It Always Rains on Sunday*.

3 The £10 he had borrowed from Lehmann.

4 Allan Wingate was an imprint set up by the Hungarian émigré André Deutsch. Understandably reluctant to use his own German-sounding name, which would have aroused antipathy in post-war England, Deutsch had given the company a name chosen at random from the telephone directory. The novel mentioned by Maclaren-Ross was *Death and His Sweetheart*.

to JOHN LEHMANN

County Hotel¹/Upper Woburn Place/London WC1

21-1-47

Dear John,

I am enclosing herewith a formal acknowledgement of the 15 guineas advance on a story, which you kindly let me have last week.

Now I will outline to you a scheme which I have been thinking over and which may or may not recommend itself to you. Briefly it is this: as you know, I am anxious to start concentrated work on the long novel for you as soon as possible. For its completion, without other work intervening, money is necessary; this is what I would propose; I have now material for a book of stories and essays totalling 35,000 words, as outlined below:

Second Lieutenant Lewis	3,000
Mrs Pettigrew²	7,000
Monsieur Félix	3,500
Black³	2,000
Triple Life of Major Trask	1,500
Warning to OCTU Wallahs	1,500
A Mirror to Darkness	4,000
The World of Alfred Hitchcock	4,000
In Memory of Laird Cregar⁴	1,500
British Feature Films	4,000
Parade of Violence	4,000
	35,000

I would like to add to this material two long stories: 'One' and 'The Irving' (10,000 words apiece),⁵ making a volume of 55,000 words – longer than *Nine Men of Soho*.

I naturally offer you first refusal of this; it being understood that the book will not be published until after publication of the long novel agreed upon.

The terms I suggest are these:

An advance of £120, whereof £60 shall be payable immediately, and a further £60 on delivery of the two long stories themselves; the £120 which you have already paid me to count as part advance on the novel.

Perhaps we could meet very soon to discuss this scheme?

If, however, you don't care for it at all, please let me know quickly, as I have to get money from somewhere and go to work without interruption on the novel; that is, if you want it by mid-April.

Yours sincerely,

J. Maclaren-Ross

1 Maclaren-Ross and Monica Foster had been living here from November 1946, their tenure only broken by a visit to Bognor Regis to spend Christmas with the Jaegers.

2 The manuscript of this story, rejected in 1946 for inclusion in *Penguin New Writing*, has been lost.

3 In late 1946 Maclaren-Ross had tried to sell 'Black' to John Lehmann, but its theme – an attack on racial prejudice against black people – had scared off Lehmann, who was concerned it might antagonise *Penguin New Writing*'s white readership in the southern states of America. The manuscript of the story has since been lost.

4 Along with Sydney Greenstreet, Laird Cregar (1916–44) was one of Maclaren-Ross's favourite Hollywood character actors. Cregar, whose last film was released in 1944, died in his twenties. Maclaren-Ross's essay on him was either uncompleted or else the manuscript has disappeared.

5 These stories were either never written or the manuscripts have been lost.

to THE ROYAL LITERARY FUND

c/o D.M. Davin / 103 Southmoor Rd¹/Oxford

7-2-47

Dear Sir,

I am enclosing herewith 3 of my published books, the form of application duly completed, and two letters from responsible literary critics to substantiate my claim.

Briefly, my circumstances are these:

Demobilised from the army August 1943 after 3 years service in the ranks (infantry); no private or other income; worked for 9 months in the documentary film industry as a scriptwriter for Strand Films until the wind-up of the company in 1944; since then, have existed from hand to mouth on literary work: mainly the fees derived from short stories which I have afterwards collected and published in volume form.

Now this source is curtailed owing to the fact that I am engaged in a long novel which demands an immense amount of concentration and leaves little time for outside work. Consequently the small amount of money I had managed to save has dwindled rapidly away and I am now left all but destitute. Statements of sales on my last book are not due until next May; the money in any case is mortgaged on loans which I was forced to raise from friends; in one case I was forced by financial necessity to sell a book outright, so no more proceeds are due therefrom.

My health, aggravated by army service and the English climate, is bad, and I really have no idea how I am going to get through the next week or so. I wonder, therefore, if there is any possibility of making an especially quick decision in my case?

To say that my need is urgent would, I can assure you, be a master-piece of understatement.

Yours faithfully,

J. Maclaren-Ross

1 Leaving Monica Foster – who may have been unable to get any time off work – in London, Maclaren-Ross had gone to stay with the New Zealand writer Dan Davin and his family, who lived in a large semi-detached Victorian house at 103 Southmoor Road.

to JOHN LEHMANN

County Hotel/Upper Woburn Place/London WC1

16-2-47

Dear John,

Thank you for your letter to the Royal Literary Fund, which should land it this time all right, in case I don't get the Atlantic.[1] (Hope to God I do, as the Literary Fund won't do anything for another 4 weeks.)

On a separate sheet I have done the blurb for the novel I'm working on. I hope you'll like the idea behind it. My work-plan for my novels is this: they are all based on the individual in revolt, and battling with, various forces in the contemporary social system from 1930 to 1943. The struggle in each case illustrates some aspect of the system and illumines some particular scene typical of the situation under examination. Thus:

(1) *Of Love and Hunger* (Wingate)

Fanshawe, the public-school type of adventurer, selling vacuum-cleaners in a South Coast town during the summer of 1939. He ends up on the dole, but declaration of war providentially rehabilitates him as a Captain in the army. Conclusion in his own words: 'It's a pretty odd world when there has to be a war to give a fellow his second chance'.

(2) *Threnody on a Gramophone*

Anton Chernikov,[2] the dispossessed Russian exile, living by his wits in the South of France 1931–32. The struggles and stratagems of Anton and the other exiles of the Russian Quarter offer a contrast to the cosmopolitan pleasure-seekers, on whom they prey for a livelihood in a world which has now been destroyed: both parties being the product of a corrupt system.

(3) *Night's Black Agents*[3]

A symbolical melodrama. Rickard, the revolutionary intellectual, finds himself in revolt against the stupidity of army-routine and a crypto-fascist organisation in wartime London (1943). His desertion in order to defeat the organisation leads to his being hunted by both the army authorities and the fascists. Scenes include an army psychiatric hospital and a military detention barrack, where red-tape of disciplinary actions delays the defeat of the fifth-column.

(4) *Death and His Sweetheart*[4]

Deckert, the mass-murderer, outlawed by the society in which he wished to move, for class reasons, solves the problem of his sinister loneliness by killing for a living, until his arrest provides another unexpected solution. Scene: Soho and Southend, 1936.

You will see, therefore, that the Russian novel has its definite place in the schedule, as the South of France scene, with its corrupt iridescence, like the bodies of those flies which buzz round carrion, is in a sense a symbolical setting analogous to the village and aerodrome of Rex Warner.[5] But it is with its underworld that I am chiefly concerned; with the blow-flies themselves, who hasten the corruption of the carcass while at the same time feeding upon it.

Please let me know what you think.

Yours sincerely,

Julian

1 A grant for which Maclaren Ross had just submitted an application.
2 A fragment from this uncompleted novel is reproduced in Appendix 4.
3 The novel was never completed.
4 Later retitled *The Dark Diceman*, the manuscript was abandoned after about a quarter of it had been completed. The surviving section was published posthumously in *Bitten by the Tarantula and Other Writing* (Black Spring Press, 2005).

5 Rex Warner's 1941 novel, *The Aerodrome*, presents an allegorical story in which a village is taken over by the authoritarian forces that control the nearby airfield.

to THE ROYAL LITERARY FUND
c/o Allan Wingate Ltd/64 Great Cumberland Place/London W1
3-3-47

Dear Sir,

Reference my recent application for one of your grants, I would be grateful if you would forward your decision, after the Committee Meeting, to above address, as I am uncertain of my exact whereabouts from tomorrow onwards.

Yours faithfully,
J. Maclaren-Ross

to JOHN BROADBENT, HONORARY SECRETARY, THE ROYAL LITERARY FUND
c/o D.M. Davin/103 Southmoor Rd/Oxford
3-3-47

Dear Sir,

Many thanks for your letter of February 21st.

I was up in London on business over that weekend, and had I known of your kind invitation, would certainly have come to see you, but unfortunately your letter and my visit crossed. It is unlikely now that I shall be in London again before March 12th, but if I am able to come I shall certainly give you a few days' notice. Anyhow, I hope we may meet one day.

Yours faithfully,
J. Maclaren-Ross

to ANTHONY POWELL[1]
County Hotel/Upper Woburn Place/London WC1
Early March 1947

Dear Tony,

I've hesitated a long time before writing this letter to you, but the fact is things are absolutely desperate with us: in fact we've been living for the last few days selling books, pawning clothes, and only getting a limited number of shillings in the process of these activities. Now my laundry has been impounded because I couldn't raise the requisite number of shillings, and the hotel bill itself impends.

I know things aren't so hot with you either, but I wonder if you could help us out. Monica[2] could give you a postdated cheque (March 1st) for her next month's salary (£30) if you could manage to advance us this sum; in the meantime I have several irons in the fire which will have been withdrawn red-hot by then. At the moment I can't raise a penny by any other means than the mortgaging of her salary[3] – this month's is already mortgaged, I fear, and the money gone long ago. I enclose the cheque herewith in case you can. If so, will you draw the cash out and send it to me so I get it Saturday morning: these people are just about to make our lives unpleasanter than they are already.

If you can't, never mind. You know I would not attempt to borrow from a fellow writer unless there was absolutely no other way.

Meanwhile I hope your own troubles clear up and Violet[4] gets well again rapidly. Please give her our very best wishes.

Yours ever,

J.M.R.

1 A mutual friend had introduced Maclaren-Ross to the novelist Anthony Powell (1905–2000) and his wife, Lady Violet Powell (1912–2002), who also pursued a literary career.
2 Monica Foster (1923–c.95), Maclaren-Ross's girlfriend.
3 She worked at the Ministry of Information.
4 Anthony Powell's wife, Lady Violet.

to JOHN BROADBENT

c/o Allan Wingate Ltd/64 Great Cumberland Place/London W1

16-3-47

Dear Mr Broadbent,

Very many thanks to you for your letter and the cheque enclosed; I am returning the signed receipt herewith.

This cheque will indeed keep me going until the novel on which I'm working is finished, and I am more than grateful to you and the members of the Committee who awarded it to me.

I am in London now, and hope during the coming week to make an appointment with you, so that I may have the opportunity of thanking you in person for the unfailing kindness and courtesy with which you have treated me throughout.

Yours sincerely,

J. Maclaren-Ross

to JONATHAN CAPE

County Hotel/Upper Woburn Place/London WC1

23-3-47

Dear Mr Cape,

As the 2nd edition of *The Stuff to Give the Troops* must surely be exhausted by now, I write to give you the formal 3 months notice in writing: after which, should you fail to reprint the book within the period stipulated, the copyright returns to me. Please note above change of address for next statement of sales.

Yours sincerely,

J. Maclaren-Ross

to JOHN LEHMANN

County Hotel/Upper Woburn Place/London WC1

18-5-47

My dear John,

I am writing to you as promised with regard to the novel, its blurb, and all that entails. It is certainly true, replying to your letter of the 15th, that, though our original agreement was for a book of short stories and the option to see a novel, we have only talked about a novel for the past year. It is also true that we agreed that one of the books was to be ready by March 1st, 1946; however, I could not have delivered any manuscript to you by the date, since I was not by that time free from my contract with Allan Wingate. The novel which I wrote to fulfil the Wingate contract was not completed until October, 1946,[1] and the contract containing the rejected option clause was not signed until the November of that year.

Since November I have been attempting to get a book completed for you, but unfortunately I have never been able to raise enough money in a lump sum to concentrate on writing the book that I would have liked. I did, however, do all I could by raising £100 on the Wingate contract, for which I am obliged to return the sum of one hundred and *fifty* pounds when the total royalties of *Of Love and Hunger* become due.

In mid-January, as the sum which I had thus raised at an eventual loss of £50 to myself was exhausted, I wrote to you putting up the scheme of the book of stories and essays, which I hoped you would accept in settlement of the £120 advanced by you. I suggested, if you will recall, that you should put this book aside until after completion and publication of the novel, and, the original advance having been covered, that you should advance a further £100 for me to finish the novel in progress.[2] The purpose of this scheme was never, and is not now, to break away from our original agreement, but merely to secure the money on which I might have completed the work; had you accepted and given me the advance I asked for, I am confident that the book upon which I was then working would have been finished and delivered as per schedule. As it was, I was then obliged for financial reasons to embark on the translation of *Pierrot Mon Ami,*[3] which I had not contracted to finish until much later. This was a false move on my part, since, though it provided me with ready cash, it broke into the absolutely concentrated effort on which I have to embark in order to finish any one book. When I came to take the novel up again it just would not do, however hard I tried. This is my way of working, and if it is interfered with the result is always the same.

I am sorry to go into all this again: I think I have already explained it before. But I feel it is better for both of us to face up to the fact that I am utterly unable to complete a novel of any sort in these conditions. For the past three weeks I have done my utmost to raise the necessary capital: my schemes, among others, included the translation of *Loin de Rueil*[4] and the tentative John Chapter plan[5] on which I suggested you should pay me an advance.

I do see your point of view, why you refused, but at the same time what am I to do? It seems fairly certain to me that until I raise sufficient capital I shall be unable to complete a novel, and unless a miracle turns up, shall not be able to do so for many months to come. What I really need now is a complete rest and *not* more work; however, we'll let that pass.

Today in the writing game many difficulties arise which one can claim to be unforeseen: I do not think that the only difficulties really admitted in a relationship between publisher and author should be those experienced by the publisher. The position for an author today is far more difficult, since advances have not risen appreciably when the enormously higher cost of living is taken into consideration, and nowadays books take far longer to produce.

We come now to the question of a blurb for your catalogue. It seems to me futile to give you a blurb for a novel the delivery of which may be delayed far beyond the date desired by both of us. I had hoped against hope that I might be able to give you want you wanted, but financially things have reached such a new low with me that I must confess myself for the time being at any rate unable to do so. I could suggest that I submit to you the provisional blurb for a book about films which you proposed that I should write; this is a book which is bound to be eventually delivered to you, and its inclusion in your catalogue would not in any way entail your accepting it if you should not like it when it is completed.

The only other plan I can think of at the moment is that I should attempt to raise all the cash I can, which will not be very much, and finish quickly the first John Chapter novel, which I have in mind. Since the amount of capital which I may raise will be extraordinarily limited, this is the only type of book which I feel can possibly be embarked upon. When I have completed it – I hope it will not take too long (it depends on how quickly the money comes in) – I will submit it to you, and if you accept it I propose that you should pay me an advance royalty of £160, of which £100 will be payable on acceptance and £60 deducted from the advance previously paid to me by you.

Even in these days of small editions a book of this nature should surely sell enough copies to cover this sum in royalties, so I don't think I am asking for very much. With the £100 which is paid to me by you on this book I propose to finish the novel under my own name, the further £60 owing to you to be deducted from the advance royalties payable on the book, if you accept it. I hope that you will consider this a workable and reasonable scheme. If you do not, I don't see what more I can do at the present. I am simply not rich enough to embark on the writing of novels otherwise: my experiences with *Of Love and Hunger* have taught me that, whilst everybody is in favour of my writing novels, I might point out that a book of short stories like *The Nine Men of Soho* brought in on its first edition (including separate publication of the stories) something in the nature of £600, although this sum, owing to the serial publication of the stories, was spaced over a period far too long to be of any use to me; while *Of Love and Hunger*, a novel, has brought in on its first edition a total of £300 odd, out of which I lose £50 interest in raising money to enable me to write another novel, at a loss! I would quite like to write novels, but one has to be better off than I am to stand the losses entailed. Some other scheme, therefore, such as the John Chapter novels, has to be brought into being in order to balance the books; a loss of time and energy, no doubt, but I am constantly losing time and energy doing odd pieces of work here and there, such as writing this letter to you in order to put the position once and for all before you when I should be occupied doing a very different sort of writing.

Please let me know if you agree or not to the advance on terms I have suggested, if you accept the John Chapter novel when it is submitted to you; and whether or not you would like a blurb for the film book. I am afraid I cannot suggest anything further at the moment.

I shall be sending you along the revised Queneau article[6] to cover the ten pounds which you advanced me on Saturday.

Hoping to hear from you very shortly,

Yours ever,

Julian

1 That novel was *Of Love and Hunger*.
2 Maclaren-Ross was working on *The Dark Diceman*, formerly titled *Death and His Sweetheart*.
3 His translation of Raymond Queneau's *Pierrot mon ami* was published as *Pierrot* (John Lehmann Ltd, 1950).
4 A novel by Raymond Queneau, published in France during 1944.
5 Maclaren-Ross had considered writing a series of thrillers, under the pseudonym 'John Chapter'.
6 Lehmann turned down the article.

to JOHN BROADBENT

County Hotel/Upper Woburn Place/London WC1

25-6-47

Dear Captain Broadbent,

Thank you for sending back the copies of the books I submitted to you.

If it's possible I'd like to have a talk with you as soon as possible: this week if you can: my stay at above address is very limited. Any afternoon will do.

Hoping to hear from you soon,

Yours sincerely,

J. Maclaren-Ross

to ANTHONY POWELL

County Hotel/Upper Woburn Place/London WC1

5 or 12-2-48

Dear Tony,

I came across 3 books (review copies) which looked interesting, the other day. I wonder if they've gone to the *TLS*[1] and, if so, whether I could have them, or any of them? They were:

Sleep Has His House Anna Kavan (Cassell)

The Mountain of the Upas Tree Richard March (PL), and

Pursuit in Daylight Alan Wykes (Duckworth)

But probably you're doing them yourself. Do give me a ring when you're up. How's everything?

Julian

Jaeger's novel about me, *The Man in the Top Hat*, has just been accepted by the Falcon Press;[2] also some film boys are buying an option on it; if it comes off, I'm to do the script of *The Dark Diceman*: only £50, but £6,000 to come if they decide to take it up.[3]

Also Pierre Chevalier,[4] the French director, has written me; he seems to want to do the Tarantula. I suggest *Piqué par l'Araignée*[5] as a title. Unfortunately he can't read English and wants me to do a synopsis. Not so good: I don't think I can do that.

1   *Times Literary Supplement.*
2   C.K. Jaeger's novel, in which Maclaren-Ross appears under the guise of 'Uncle Julian', was eventually published by Grey Walls Press in 1949.
3   The film company was Everest Pictures. Within a matter of weeks, Maclaren-Ross had – along with C.K. Jaeger and Roger Vadim (1928–2000) – been employed to work on a film adaptation of Louis Hémon's 1923 novel *Maria Chapdelaine: A Story of Canada*. The film, starring Michèle Morgan and Keiron Moore, was released under the title of *The Naked Heart* (1950).
4   Pierre Chevalier (1915–?), French film director who often used Anglo-Saxon pseudonyms, among them 'Peter Knight'.
5   'Bitten by the Spider'.

to DAN DAVIN[1]

County Hotel/Upper Woburn Place/London WC1

19-2-48

Dear Dan,

Look I'm in a mess. Can't pay the bill, danger of being kicked out, clothes etc. seized.[2] No possibility of dough till next Thursday. But BBC

(Campbell)[3] is taking story,[4] reading it myself; fee (£20) payable after broadcast (Feb. 23).

Can you lend me 15. If you can, will save life. Will repay without fail from BBC cheque. More money in by then. Will you wire money order Euston PO[5] – and phone wire MUS 2897 telling me when it's there. Hope you liked my review of you in *TLS*.[6] Got book specially. Walter[7] doing you good one too. No more now: pen running out.

Love to all,
Julian

When are you coming up? Make it soon.

1 After an unpromising encounter in a London pub during December 1943, Maclaren-Ross had formed a close friendship with Dan Davin (1913–90), who had subsequently settled in Oxford. There Davin worked for the Clarendon Press, an academic imprint run by Oxford University Press.
2 Hoteliers were in the habit of seizing a guest's laundry until his or her bill was settled.
3 The South African poet and BBC radio producer Roy Campbell (1901–57).
4 The story was the bizarrely titled 'Two Fish Spivs and the King of the Goldfish Called Garth'.
5 Post Office.
6 Maclaren-Ross's review of Davin's *The Gorse Blooms* had appeared in the *Times Literary Supplement* on 17 January 1948.
7 Maclaren-Ross's friend, the novelist and literary critic Walter Allen (1911–95), whom he'd met while he was at Northfield Military Hospital.

to JOHN BROADBENT

County Hotel / Upper Woburn Place / London WC1

4-3-48

Dear Captain Broadbent,

I have been informed that the Prime Minister has authorised a grant of £200 on my behalf[1] and that you have consented to act as trustee. I should like to see you as soon as possible to discuss this matter; as you can guess, I am not in funds.

Yours sincerely,
J. Maclaren-Ross

1 The grant was a confidential one, made from the so-called Royal Bounty. Its purpose was to enable Maclaren-Ross to complete *The Dark Diceman*, his serial-killer novel. Not that Prime Minister Clement Attlee's staff were likely to have been aware of the book's subject matter. On the advice of the poet John Betjeman, who declared that it was 'no use expecting Maclaren-Ross to be practical about his affairs' (letter from Anthony Bever to Captain Broadbent, 17 February 1948, archive of the Royal Literary Fund), the money was paid in instalments.

to JOHN BROADBENT

The Mandrake Social and Chess Club[1]/4 Meard Street/London W1

5-3-48

Dear Captain Broadbent,

Thank you for your letter and the enclosed cheque for £50.

Unfortunately, having no bank-account of my own, I attempted to put the cheque through a friend's account; the bank-manager rang up Messrs Coutts, who said that they could not pay the £50 as the cheque was not drawn on the Royal Literary Fund, but was merely signed by you as a personal cheque.

In the circumstances I am returning the cheque herewith, and would request that you draw cash and send it per registered post to me at the County Hotel, or an *open* cheque[2] drawn on the Fund. Cash would be preferable and the earliest possible would oblige: by Monday if you can. I will certainly come & see you on Monday 15 at 4p.m.: I look forward to our meeting.

Yours sincerely,

J. Maclaren-Ross

1   The Mandrake was run by Maclaren-Ross's Bulgarian friend Boris Watson, born Boris Protopopov, who had previously operated another London club – the notoriously seedy Coffee An' on St Giles High Street. Like the Coffee An', the Mandrake occupied a spacious basement. In the days when the law insisted on London pubs closing between 3.00 p.m. and 6.00 p.m. and from either 10.30 p.m. or 11.00 p.m. onwards, clubs such as the Mandrake thrived. Even so, the licensing laws prohibited customers from buying alcoholic drinks without also ordering food. To get round this regulation, the Mandrake and other similar establishments would serve a sandwich with each drink. These sandwiches were dry and unappetising specimens. Pointing at one of them, Boris Watson would often declare, 'This is a sandwich for drinking with, not for eating.' Further information about the Mandrake and the Coffee An' can be found in the expanded version of the Maclaren-Ross biography *Fear and Loathing in Fitzrovia* by Paul Willetts (Dewi Lewis Publishing, 2005).

2   Opened, or uncrossed, cheques didn't feature two parallel lines drawn across them. By adding these to a cheque, the sender ensured that the cheque could only be paid into the recipient's bank account.

to JOHN BROADBENT

c/o Allan Wingate Ltd/64 Great Cumberland Place/London W1

11-3-48.

Dear Capt. Broadbent,

Thank you very much for your letter and the enclosed cheque, which I cashed this time without any difficulty.

I look forward to seeing you on Monday 15th, at 4p.m.

Yours sincerely,

J. Maclaren-Ross

to JOHN BROADBENT

County Hotel/Upper Woburn Place/London WC1

19-3-48

Dear Captain Broadbent,

Many thanks for the cheque received and duly cashed. Receipt of this will certainly facilitate my task.

With reference to the August instalment of the Grant, I have spoken to my friend Mr F.S. Fisher,[1] a chartered accountant (without, of course, telling him the source of the money) and he consented to handle various affairs for me. Therefore, I wonder if you would make the cheque payable to him when the time comes? I would, of course, sign the receipt for it. Fisher is the man I was telling you about who has a villa in the South of France where I should, later on, be able to stay. He also has other connections and property in France, and if this money is made payable to him in August, it would enable me, perhaps, to remain there much longer than I thought possible. Also, both as an old friend and in his professional capacity, he may be able to help me in business, and look after my interests whilst I am away.

His address is:

Old Pond Cottage

Cookham Dean

Berkshire

I hope you will have no objection to this arrangement? I am going down to the country now, but a letter forwarded to the above will reach me.

With, again, many thanks for the helpful way you have behaved in this matter,

Yours sincerely,

J. Maclaren-Ross

1   Maclaren-Ross's friendship with Gerry Fisher may have dated back to his youth on the French Riviera.

to ANTHONY POWELL

County Hotel/Upper Woburn Place/London WC1 (in haste)

20-4-48

Dear Tony,

Here's the elaborated review you asked for. But Tennyson's book[1] is bad and vulgar: best ignored. Croft-Cooke[2] and Walter Allen have both refused to do it.

Other reviews follow.

Do give me a ring when you're in town; we must meet. Kindest regards to Violet and yourself.

from

Julian

1   *Concordance to the Devil and a Lady*, by Charles Tennyson, grandson of the Victorian poet.
2   'Rupert Croft-Cooke' was the pseudonym of Leo Bruce (1903–79), a poet, playwright and crime novelist.

to JOHN BROADBENT

17 Holland Park Gardens[1]/London W14

29-11-48

Dear Captain Broadbent,

I have now settled permanently into a home in London, the address of which I give above. Perhaps you may wish to make a note of it, as I believe the final instalment of my Government grant falls due at the beginning of this December.

With many thanks for your kind attention in the past,

Yours sincerely,

J. Maclaren-Ross

1   Maclaren-Ross and Monica Foster had recently moved into a seedy flat here. The furniture was upholstered in red and all the walls had been painted the same colour, creating a hellish glow.

to JOHN BROADBENT

17 Holland Park Gardens / London W14

3-12-48

Dear Captain Broadbent,

Thank you for your letter, which I received yesterday.

I note what you say about the final payment of my grant not being formally due until January. I understood, however that we had agreed that, as the purpose of the grant was to make existence rather easier for me, I was to be paid the final instalment before Christmas. On this assumption, therefore, I have budgeted for the close of this year and the beginning of next.

I am sure you will understand my position in this matter.

Yours sincerely,

J. Maclaren-Ross

to JOHN BROADBENT

17 Holland Park Gardens / London W14

16-12-48

Dear Captain Broadbent,

Thank you very much for the cheque, which I received safely. You will by now have received my wife's note, so you will have seen that we did in fact agree on mid-December as the payment date.

Thank you again for all you have done in connection with this Grant. I am indeed extremely grateful, for your attention to my needs has made life and work much easier in this past year.

With every good wish for Christmas and New Year from my wife[1] and myself,

Yours sincerely,

J. Maclaren-Ross

1 At this time co-habiting couples were regarded as being unconventional. To avoid upsetting his more conservative friends and acquaintances, and to appease hoteliers and landlords, who tended to discriminate against such couples, Maclaren-Ross often referred to Monica Foster as his wife.

to JOHN BROADBENT

17 Holland Park Gardens / London W14

4-9-49

Dear Captain Broadbent,

I wonder if it would be completely useless for me to apply for a further Grant to the Royal Literary Fund? I am aware that one is not supposed to apply until a minimum of three years has elapsed; but my novel is now nearing its final phase[1] and a Grant would help enormously, circumstances being very desperate at the moment.

The book should have been completed early this year, but for personal trouble of an unforeseen nature which brought me to the verge of a nervous breakdown.[2] I'm sorry to bother you; but if my case could be brought before the Committee at their next Meeting, I should be very grateful.

Yours sincerely,

J. Maclaren-Ross

My last Grant was received on March 13, 1947.

1 For the purposes of obtaining additional money, Maclaren-Ross was exaggerating the progress he'd made.
2 The cause of his trauma was his separation from Monica Foster.

to JOHN BROADBENT

29 Lee Court, Lee High Road[1] / London SE13

9-10-49

Dear Captain Broadbent,

I had no reply to my letter of September 5th, so am writing to inform you of temporary change of address, as above. I have, unfortunately, been ejected from my flat at 24 hours' notice, owing to arrears of rent, and now have to look for somewhere else to live; as I am almost penniless at the moment, this will not be easy to find.

If the Committee would consider my case, at their next meeting, as one of extreme hardship, I would be very grateful.

Yours very truly,

J. Maclaren-Ross

1 Following his break-up with Monica Foster, Maclaren-Ross had met another young woman who would become his next long-term girlfriend: Barbara Wimble. He ended up moving into her top-floor flat in a modern block on Lee High Road. In a diary entry for 24 January 1950, Malcolm Muggeridge wrote, 'We [he and Anthony Powell] talked, inevitably, about... Maclaren Ross [sic]. Tony said that his present address was c/o Miss Wimble, and I said that this would provide an admirable title for a biographical study of him.'

to REGGIE SMITH[1]

29 Norfolk Square[2]/London W2

16-3-50

Dear Reggie,

Enclosed herewith is a play by an Indian friend of mine, which I myself found most interesting; it occurred to me that, though not written in radio-play-form, little alteration would be needed to make it suitable for broadcasting – or, perhaps, for television.

I promised Nasir Shamsi that I would forward it to you, and ask you if you would pass it on to the right quarter, after which it's out of my hands and any correspondence should be addressed to the author at the address given on the script. I'm sure you won't mind doing this.[3] How are you? We must have a drink one day – perhaps soon?

Yours as ever,

J. Maclaren-Ross

1 R.D. 'Reggie' Smith (1914–85), a producer in the Features Department of BBC Radio, was a generous-spirited working-class Brummie who became a close friend of Maclaren-Ross's. Smith was married to the novelist Olivia Manning, who used him as the model for the character Guy Pringle in her *Balkan Trilogy* (1960–65), and later the *Levant Trilogy* (1977–80).

2 Maclaren-Ross and new girlfriend Barbara Wimble had moved into this comfortably furnished three-bedroom flat at the beginning of 1950.

3 The play, entitled *The Slave*, was considered but swiftly rejected.

to JOHN BROADBENT

29 Norfolk Square/London W2

21-6-50

Dear Sir,

Would you be kind enough to forward me a form of application for a grant from the Royal Literary Fund?

I received a grant of £100 in March 1947, but I believe after an interval of 3 years that an author is once again considered eligible for application.

Yours very truly,

J. Maclaren-Ross

to JOHN BROADBENT

29 Norfolk Square/London W2

26-6-50

Dear Captain Broadbent,

I'm awfully sorry I didn't come to the phone when you rang me yesterday, but lately I've been working most nights until 3 and 4 in the morning, and I was trying to get some much overdue sleep. Also I didn't know it was you, and only heard quite by chance this morning – they are not very good at giving messages here.

I take the opportunity of appending some details, overleaf, about my circumstances during the past two years; I'm also available any afternoon you'd like me to call.

Yours sincerely,

J. Maclaren-Ross

When I received the Royal Bounty in 1948, I had intended to settle down and complete *The Dark Diceman*, a novel based on the life of Eugen Weidmann, the mass-murderer. The researches which I made into the life of this character soon convinced me, however, that this would be a much longer and much harder job than I had anticipated; I was also forced, owing to the facts which I unearthed, to scrap and rewrite much of the novel which I had already completed.

It was at this moment that a film company[1] appeared on the scene, became interested in the story, and wanted to screen it when completed; the only snag was that this company hadn't enough money to buy the story rights from me, as the company had only just been formed and was looking around for backing. The directors suggested that, if I worked on the adaptation and screen-play of a book the rights of which they'd previously acquired,[2] they would pay me £800, plus money for *The Dark Diceman* etc.; the total sum amounted to £1600. I brought in C.K. Jaeger to work with me on the script, and this was duly completed and accepted for distribution[3] when the film was made. We were now told that the sums owing could not be paid until the first shooting day, when the backing of the film would be released. I need not, I think, go into the promises, suspense, and final disillusions of the next few months: the alterations etc. (I worked on 3 different shooting scripts of the same film, for each of which I was promised separate payment, plus the initial fee.) In March 1949, I was paid £100, and it was explained that the film had been taken over by the distribution company which declined to pay more; and as, being of a foolishly trusting nature, I had no written contract, I had no redress either. It is, I believe, by all accounts, a fairly common experience, but that does not make it more palatable.

Disaster in my personal life, of a nature which I need not particularise here, now overtook me, and as a result of the psychological repercussions, left me incapable of taking up work on my novel until the autumn of 1949, when I started once again to rewrite it. Meanwhile, methods of earning a living have not been made easier by the collapse of most reviews and magazines which previously constituted markets. I cannot obtain further advances from publishers until existing contracts are fulfilled, and the financial crisis in the British film industry precludes the possibility of any further script work.

Earlier this year I had no money and nowhere to stay; I even spent two nights in a station waiting-room.[4] All the cash I have earned this year has come from reviewing for the *Times Literary Supplement* and writing middle articles[5] for the same market. What I need is a lump sum of money which would enable me to get something done, and also to rest from my present hand-to-mouth existence. I would like also to have a change of scene from London; a few weeks in France, without financial worry, would I think do me, psychologically, the world of good. I need not say that a grant from the Royal Literary Fund would be of inestimable value to me at the moment.

J.M.R.

1 Everest Pictures.

2 The book was Louis Hémon's *Maria Chapdelaine: A Story of Canada*.

3 A distribution deal was struck with the prominent firm British Lion.

4 This was an experience that he would repeat several years later. He wrote about it in his posthumously published memoir, 'Some Time I Shall Sleep Out', which is included in the *Collected Memoirs* (Black Spring Press, 2004).

5 So-called 'middles' in the *Times Literary Supplement* were extended essays about individual writers or literary movements.

to JOHN BROADBENT

29 Norfolk Square/London W2

5-7-50

Dear Captain Broadbent,

Enclosed herewith the letter from Evelyn Waugh recommending me to the Committee,[1] also a personal letter which he has written to the Earl of Ilchester, which I trust you will either forward to Lord Ilchester at his home address or give to him at the Meeting, whichever you think best.

I was most interested in the pamphlet 'David Williams', and particularly in the remarks of Disraeli in his speech, 'that they (authors) shall not sacrifice the labours that they have accomplished for a nominal return, in order to satisfy the requirements of the hour; and above all, that for the exigency of the moment they shall not be required to mortgage the future exertions of their intellect and the coming creations of their minds'.

As an author who, like many today, has too often found himself forced into such a position, I think the great man showed not only the uncanny astuteness which one would have expected of him, but an understanding of the writer's central problem that has never been so clearly stated.

Yours sincerely,

J. Maclaren-Ross

1 'I have followed Mr Maclaren-Ross's work since the first publication of a sketch of military life which I read in *Horizon*,' Waugh wrote. 'I thought that it showed genuine literary promise and accomplishment of a rare kind, and I think now that he has developed his talent well and that, given proper opportunities, he shall develop into a first-class writer. I believe that one of the things he needs most is financial support during this crucial stage of his career. I therefore greatly hope that you will be able to give him the freedom from immediate anxiety which is needed to mature his undoubted talent' (4 July 1950).

to THE BBC TALKS DEPARTMENT

29 Norfolk Square / London W2

12-7-50

Dear Sir,

With reference to the series of talks which are being given on the Contemporary Novel, I have recently written a middle-page article on the novels of Edward Sackville-West for the *Times Literary Supplement*[1] (where I have also examined the work of Henry Green,[2] Joyce Cary,[3] Stevenson,[4] and Edgar Wallace[5]), and it occurred to me that I might give a talk on Sackville-West in your programme. Failing this, I propose another very interesting writer, Anthony Powell, whose new novel is due to appear later this year; Eric Ambler is a name, too, which occurs to me.

In the case of Sackville-West, I would concentrate on *The Sun in Capricorn*; in the case of Powell, *From a View to a Death*, and I consider *The Mask of Dimitrios* to be Ambler's most representative novel to date.

Yours faithfully,

J. Maclaren-Ross

1 Maclaren-Ross's middle on the aristocratic writer Edward Sackville-West (1901–65), the Fifth Baron Sackville, was never published.
2 Pen-name of Henry Yorke (1905–73), author of *Caught* (1943) and other novels.
3 Joyce Cary (1888–1957), novelist probably best known for *The Horse's Mouth* (1944).
4 Robert Louis Stevenson (1850–94), poet, playwright and novelist whose books include *The Strange Case of Dr Jekyll and Mr Hyde* (1886).
5 Edgar Wallace (1875–1935), author of *The Four Just Men* and numerous other novels.

to JOHN BROADBENT

29 Norfolk Square / London W2

15-7-50

Dear Captain Broadbent,

I'm extremely sorry to bother you, but you will realise that, in my present position, I am anxious to know the decision of the Committee in regard to my case; if you could possibly telephone me at above address and let me know the result, I should be greatly obliged.[1]

Yours sincerely,

J. Maclaren-Ross

1 Probably swayed by Evelyn Waugh's intervention, the Committee of the Royal Literary Fund granted Maclaren-Ross £100.

to C.K. JAEGER

29 Norfolk Square / London W2

March 1951

My dear Jaeger,

So sorry I haven't answered your letter until now, but I've been so buggered and bewitched with my own troubles that I've not had time to look around. Besides, I'd hoped to be able to give a date when I could come down to Bognor – if indeed you're ever returning there – and now that looks like being some time after March 25th.

Are you likely to be there about that date – or at any rate for Easter? I'd rather come about the beginning of April and remain on until Barbara[1] could join me for the holiday; in the meantime I could get us a place to stay in case you've people coming down. I imagine this job of yours is not permanent – so tell me when you'll be available. There's no point in my coming if you're not likely to be there, and I have to lay my plans well in advance.

Your job sounds a bastard, though it should certainly give you unusual material.[2] You still ought to break away from it as soon as you can; London's a desert as far as I'm concerned, but there *is* one thing I've heard of: a new Government-sponsored film unit, run by the documentary-man John Grierson,[3] for making low-budgeted features. They may need scriptwriters and ideas: so if I were you I'd write for an interview to the address I've listed overleaf.[4] I went down to Ealing myself for a long interview with Sidney Cole,[5] but there's fuck all down there as their films for this year are already scripted.

What's happened to your book?[6] No reviews in weeklies or London newspapers; only one advert in the *TLS*; and no copies in the shops, except for one that Boris[7] saw in Better Books.[8] Nor have I received any copy here. If I were you, I'd come and kick up hell at the Grey Balls.[9] If you do, give me a ring. And let me know soon about coming down. That address, as I say, is overleaf.

Barbara sends love; mine to Lydia and the kids.[10]

Yours ever,

Julian

1 Barbara Wimble.
2 Jaeger had been employed as part of a team of labourers who, despite the intense cold, were constructing a runway at Maidstone Aerodrome in Kent. He slept in a Nissen hut, shared with 12 Irishmen. Although one of them – a huge man nicknamed 'Little Titch' – tried to make him feel welcome, Jaeger remembered the experience as being 'hellish'.

3 John Grierson (1898–1972) worked on numerous classic documentaries, including *Night Mail* (1936), for which he received a producer's credit.

4 'Miss Stella Jonchene, 3rd Group Ltd, Southall Studios, Southall 3281. Low-budgeted feature films; chief producer: John Grierson.'

5 Cole was an Associate Producer at Ealing Studios, the company responsible for such classics as *Kind Hearts and Coronets* (1949).

6 This was *Men of Fine Parts* (1950), C.K. Jaeger's first published children's book, using the pen-name 'Karel Jaeger'.

7 Boris Watson, formerly Boris Protopopov, a Bulgarian émigré who ran the Mandrake Club, a chess and drinking club in Soho.

8 A well-known bookshop on Charing Cross Road, run by Tony Godwin and John Clarke, the latter destined to find fame – under the pseudonym of 'Bryan Forbes' – as an actor, film director and novelist.

9 Maclaren-Ross's nickname for Jaeger's publisher, the Essex-based Grey Walls Press, owned by Charles Wrey Gardiner.

10 By then C.K. Jaeger and his wife Lydia had two children: Karel and Nicholas.

to HAMISH HAMILTON[1]

29 Norfolk Square / London W2
3-10-51

Dear Mr Hamilton,

Enclosed please find the books which you asked me to send you. I've added *The 9 Men of Soho* because I think perhaps the stories mentioned by Elizabeth Bowen in her review[2] (enclosed in the volume itself) might be worth your attention. I've also enclosed reviews by Betjeman[3] and George.[4]

I hope you will like the books and will come to a favourable decision shortly.

Yours sincerely,

J. Maclaren-Ross

1 Jamie 'Hamish' Hamilton (1900–88) was the founder of the publishing firm Hamish Hamilton.

2 In her column for *The Tatler and Bystander* magazine, Bowen wrote, 'The *Nine Men of Soho* is a collection of short stories by J. Maclaren-Ross – another writer due for the front rank. We are, we are told, to take the "I" of the stories to be the author himself – if so, he is working under chaotic conditions. Better, and more dire, pictures of the Bohemian extremity – in pubs and the Soho purlieus, in dun-beleaguered bungalows along half-made roads, in and out of bookshops and under the duress of the Army – are not, I should imagine, to be found.

'There is an at once savage and fatalistic tolerance in Mr Maclaren-Ross's approach to human beings: he has also often the merit of being extremely funny. The first and last stories – "Welsh Rabbit of Soap" and "My Father Was Born in Havana" respectively – seem to be the best; though "The Swag, the Spy and the Soldier" makes a good halfway, and there is something obliquely touching about "Lulu".'

3 John Betjeman (1906–84).

4 Daniel George, pseudonym of D.G. Bunting.

to RUPERT HART-DAVIS

29 Norfolk Square/London W2
7-10-51

Dear Rupert,

I've been trying to get you on the phone for weeks but you don't seem very accessible.

What I wanted to talk about was this: I've seen you're publishing Calder-Marshall's autobiography;[1] and if I like this I would put up a *TLS* middle on his work.

I have not, however, got any of his old novels; perhaps *you* have, or could arrange for Cape to send me copies at the above address. If they are file-copies they could be returned although I don't like to return them as they are part of my prerequisites as a critic.[2]

Perhaps you'd tell me how the position would stand about the books, and also send me a proof of the autobiography. The important thing is, if I'm going to do it, is speed in receiving the books: trade-departments are usually slow in dispatch, and I want to do the article next week, if it is to be done at all.

Yours ever,
Julian

1   The Rupert Hart-Davis imprint was publishing Arthur Calder-Marshall's *The Magic of My Youth* (Rupert Hart-Davis, 1951), an idiosyncratic memoir structured around its author's numerous near-meetings with the satanist Aleister Crowley.
2   He was alluding to the extra income available to critics, who could sell so-called 'review copies' to secondhand book dealers.

to RUPERT HART-DAVIS

29 Norfolk Square/London W2
22-8-52

Dear Rupert,

Wrong. I'm not asking for any money now. I thought we agreed at our initial talk that there was to be no advance until delivery of MS; besides, I've learnt by this time the folly of getting advances this way and consequently lower terms generally than I would be able to command with a MS in my hand. This was partly the cause of the poverty-period I've been through: and in the case of this book, which so far is the best thing I've done – and you know I don't boast about my work – I intend, for a change, to accept only the sort of terms I feel I ought to have, without haggling.

But I thought a drink and a talk – without necessarily mentioning money – would be nice: That, however, is up to you.

Yours ever,

Julian

to RUPERT HART-DAVIS

29 Norfolk Square / London W2

Early September 1952

Dear Rupert,

I called today on the off chance of seeing you: I have about 30,000 words of that autobiographical book done,[1] the start of which I showed you about a year ago, and I thought we might have a drink one evening soon and talk about it. My phone number is above if you'd like to ring me in the morning before noon: if you don't ring I shall know you're no longer interested, and will offer it elsewhere; but since you were the first publisher to see it, I thought you should have first refusal when it's completed.

Yours ever,

Julian

1 The autobiographical book was his childhood memoir, *The Weeping and the Laughter* (Rupert Hart-Davis, 1953).

to JOHN LEHMANN

29 Norfolk Square / London W2

19-9-52

My dear John,

Thank you so much for your letter and the cheque enclosed.

This was more than kind of you, for a fiver makes all the difference at times like this. About *New Soundings*[1] I rang you up yesterday, but you were in conference, to say that as soon as the MS is typed, I would be sending you along some extracts:[2] one in particular I think you might like, I'd like to read this over to you, as of course I should like to tell it myself on the air and you could then hear how it sounds. I'll ring you up next week when I shall have a copy and we could perhaps get together for an hour or so at your flat if you have the time free.

Yours ever,

Julian

1 *New Soundings* was a literary magazine programme, first broadcast on the BBC's Third Programme in January 1952. Its presenter was John Lehmann.
2 These were from *The Weeping and the Laughter*.

to RUPERT HART-DAVIS

29 Norfolk Square/London W2
23-9-52

My dear Rupert,

Here's *The Weeping and the Laughter*.

It has been suggested to me yesterday that I am not well-known enough yet for an account of my first 10 years to be interesting. If you have any grave doubts of this sort I don't think it's worthwhile considering the MS at all, since it's vital to me for urgent personal reasons[1] that this book be placed and the advance paid over by the 30th at latest if not, as I hope, before. Therefore I don't want to run any risk of waiting a week then getting a rejection, except of course the risk that you don't consider the book well enough written.

It would make a book at least as long as Calder-Marshall's, therefore could be sold at 12s 6d though I am rotten at figures, with a 12 1/2% royalty to start with, it works out at over £400 on a printing of 6,000, so I don't think two fifty's too big of an advance to ask.

I need not stress further the urgent need, to me, of your quickest possible decision.

Yours ever,

Julian

1 Those 'personal reasons' were the rent arrears he owed to his landlady, Mrs Lyle, who was, luckily for Maclaren-Ross and Barbara Wimble, very understanding.

to RUPERT HART-DAVIS

29 Norfolk Square/London W2
25-9-52

My dear Rupert,

There is no pistol: I am quite unarmed. I fear you mistook the pardonable impatience of a man who has worked without a break for 6 weeks, with very little food and sleep, for the presence of this imaginary weapon. I had scarcely eaten anything for nearly 2 days when I called on you, and I am certainly eager to put a stop to this existence by placing the book, but not to the extent of your feeling you should return the MS unread.

When we talked you said you would not take many days in reading the book; but if on the reflection you feel you require a long time, you are welcome; if you can give me some idea how long. If, however, you feel the advance I asked is too high, that's another matter. I don't think you would regret taking the book on the score of financial loss – I have never sold fewer than 4,000 copies and mostly far more.

I am altogether most distressed that this should have happened, as I've always felt you were the best publisher to do it: so you in reality hold the pistol.

The book is now with Leonard Russell; he is reading it purely as a friend who is good enough to advise me; and if you want to consider it again it's up to you: my phone number is above.

Yours ever,
Julian

to DAN DAVIN

29 Norfolk Square/London W2
28-9-52

My dear Dan,

Would it be possible for you to put me up[1] for 10 days or a fort-night? I've just finished a book and, having worked solidly for nearly 2 months without a break, am in urgent need of relaxation and congenial company. I do hope you'll be able to manage it; but if you can't, perhaps you could arrange somewhere inexpensive for me to stay at? I shan't be penniless but on the other hand, until the contract for this book is signed, I shan't be able to afford much for rent as this place costs me 4 gns[2] a week and I have to keep it on.

I should arrive either Thursday evening or Friday lunchtime, so if you can let me know soon I should be grateful.

Love,
Julian

1   Dan Davin still lived with his wife, Winnie, and their three young daughters, Anna, Brigid and Delia, at 103 Southmoor Road, Oxford.
2   A guinea was worth 21 shillings. In pre-decimal British currency, a pound comprised 20 shillings.

to ALAN PRYCE-JONES[1]

c/o The George[2]/Great Portland Street/London W1

4-10-52

Dear Alan,

If you are back from your holiday, I'd like to talk some possible business with you.

I can be found or phoned at lunchtime (until 2.30) tomorrow (Friday) at above address; or on Saturday morning (one-thirtyish) I will be in Berlemont's French House,[3] where we met last time. I may be going away myself soon, so hope to see you before I do.

Yours sincerely,

J. Maclaren-Ross

1 Alan Pryce-Jones (1908–2000) was, at that stage, editor of the *Times Literary Supplement*.
2 Situated at the intersection between Great Portland and Mortimer Streets, the George is a pub that was popular with BBC employees, many of whom spent more time there than at their desks. The conductor Sir Thomas Beacham nicknamed it 'the Gluepot' because its comparable popularity with musicians led them to become stuck there.
3 Under the tenancy of the Frenchman Victor Berlemont, the York Minster pub on Dean Street in Soho had become known as 'the French House'. During the Second World War, it had been a haunt of the exiled Free French forces. In peacetime it attracted a cross-section of visiting French celebrities. Many of them presented Berlemont with signed photos of themselves which were later displayed on the walls.

to DAN DAVIN

18-10-52

My dear Dan,

Arrived back yesterday to find Barbara awaiting me at the station, so I had quite a happy homecoming. *The Times* sent me the enclosed corrected proof of my article on Faulkner;[1] I'm therefore forwarding it on so that you can add it to the lot you already have.

Please remember me to all the people I met in Oxford, who did so much to make my stay there such an enjoyable one.

Give my love to Winnie:[2] Rashomon[3] sends his to Anna and the kids,[4] also to his contemporaries of the Southmoor[5] cat-world.

Yours ever,

Julian

1   Maclaren-Ross had written a middle on the novelist William Faulkner (1897–1962). It was published in the 13 February 1953 edition of the *Times Literary Supplement*.

2   Winnie Davin (1909–95).

3   Named after Akira Kurosawa's 1950 samurai film, Rashomon was a white Persian cat.

4   Dan and Winnie Davin had three daughters: Anna, the eldest, Delia and Brigid.

5   A reference to Davin's address: 103 Southmoor Road.

to RUPERT HART-DAVIS

29 Norfolk Square / London W2

28-10-52

Dear Rupert,

By now you will have received Leonard Russell's verdict on my book; in the meantime I sent it down to Walter Allen, who had already looked over the MS. Now he has read it fully, he writes that he likes it enormously and is sending a longer opinion which I hope to receive in time to include it here.

Now I had a long talk with Russell last night, and he confirms my own opinion that you are the best publisher I could possibly get. If, as I suspect, you should find my terms too stiff, I'm willing to exchange money for speed: in other words, if you haven't time to read the MS yourself, will you take Allen's opinion and Russell's that the book's good, make a reasonable offer of an advance and pay up this week? If so I'll drop my price.

In case you mistake this offer for a concealed firearm, I may say that I consulted Russell thoroughly before writing this letter. I can't really afford to go lower than the figure I named, but not only do I require ready money urgently but I feel I will not be making any sacrifice in the long run if this results in your publishing me. If you would ring me up in reply I should be obliged, as an extra day means a lot to me whereas 2 minutes on the phone cannot mean so much to you.

Yours ever,

Julian

to RUPERT HART-DAVIS

29 Norfolk Square / London W2

31-10-52

My dear Rupert,

I hasten to enclose my notes on the MS. I'm afraid they're rather rough, but you'll understand what I mean. I don't think we need say any more about 'Monsieur Félix';[1] I re-read the story this morning and think it'll fit in all right: anyway let's wait till we see the proofs.

Looking forward to seeing you on the 12th,

As ever,

Julian

1 Originally published in *Penguin New Writing* 30, 'Monsieur Félix' was a short childhood memoir, a revised version of which Maclaren-Ross dovetailed into *The Weeping and the Laughter*.

to RUPERT HART-DAVIS

13-12-52

My dear Rupert,

Could you find out for me – as soon as possible – how the television rights of Walpole's *Above the Dark Circus* stand?[1] There might be a chance of my doing a TV adaptation of the filmscript I showed you once, only it wouldn't be worth my while financially unless (a) they were prepared to be reasonable about the fee, taking, say, a 25% share; (b) they give a quick reply (I mean the executors). The script is completely altered from the book; I have had to add dialogue and new situations; so that it's really a play by me based on Walpole's book. And to do another edition for television on top means more work than I'd like to undertake for the small TV fee, if this is made even smaller.

On the other hand, a TV version might lead to new publicity for the book; also the possibility of selling this version to a film company. *If* you could find out for me what they think about this, I should be very grateful. I'm seeing the TV man, so far as I know, on Tuesday.

Looking forward to seeing proofs of *WATL*.[2]

Yours ever,

Julian

1 A novel by Hugh Walpole (1884–1941). As the author of *Hugh Walpole: A Biography* (1952), Hart-Davis would have had contacts with the Hugh Walpole literary estate.

2 *The Weeping and the Laughter*.

to HAMISH HAMILTON

29 Norfolk Square/London W2

13-12-52

Dear Hamilton,

Thank you for your letter.

Unfortunately I have been ill and for part of the time confined to my bed; new reviewing commitments[1] incurred to meet the consequent expenses will not make it easier to work single-mindedly on the novel as I would like.

Also proofs of my autobiographical book are due to arrive any time now, further distracting me from the task in hand.

However, I will let you have another report in due course.

Yours sincerely,

J. Maclaren-Ross

1 Leonard Russell, the Literary Editor of the *Sunday Times*, had hired him to cover the two-week absence of the novelist C.P. Snow (1905–80) during the last week of January and the first week of February 1953.

to RUPERT HART-DAVIS

29 Norfolk Square/London W2

20-12-52

My dear Rupert,

Thank you for your letter, the proofs, and returned MS of *WATL*.

I think it's beautifully printed, and personally I've no objection to the squiggly things.[1] At any rate I hope you'll leave the ones round the dedication and the numerals: I feel the chapter-headings need some decoration too, even if you think the ones you already have won't do.

Now for some points you raise:

(1) Punctuation: It's mainly the colons and semi-colons that I feel may sometimes be misplaced; where the dialogue is unpunctuated (as on page 44) or a longish sentence runs on without becoming obscure owing to lack of commas, I'd like it left, as I tried to achieve in such passages a special sort of syncopated rhythm which I think on the whole comes off. I'm sure you'll know what I mean.

Anyhow, meanwhile I'll make my own corrections and alterations in the text, and wait until I hear from you again.

(2) Banting:[2] I'll willingly approach him, but can you find out for me where he is? He's sold his old house and I've not seen him about

for years. If he's unobtainable, I'll try to get Henri Jonas[3] (this would be a great scoop, as he's never done a book jacket yet), or John Minton.[4] All these will want to read the book first, I expect.

(3) Photographs: No. I hate being photographed,[5] and the only one I have is so sinister it would be unsuitable for present purposes. Michael Pete or Douglas Glass[6] – both of whom I know – are probably the best chaps. What'd you think?

(4) *Above the Dark Circus*: Thanks for making enquiries. The movie rights acquired by Huston[7] have surely run out by now: the period is ten years copyright. Besides, in 1948, Curtis Brown[8] was offering Nelson Scott[9] the film rights for £2,000. Perhaps you could find out from them how things stand? I'm not on the best of terms with C.B.,[10] or I'd ring him myself. Anyway, I'm seeing Basil Bartlett[11] at TV on Monday and I'll put the idea up.

Yours ever,
Julian

1 He was referring to the embellishments around each of the chapter numbers.
2 The surrealist painter John Banting (1902–72).
3 Henri 'Harry' Jonas (1878–?), Dutch painter.
4 John Minton (1917–57), English illustrator and painter.
5 For that reason there are only a few known photographs of him.
6 Douglas Glass (1901–78) was an expatriate New Zealand photographer who took many well-known portrait shots.
7 The film director John Huston's (1906–87) credits include *The Maltese Falcon* (1941) and *The African Queen* (1952).
8 The Curtis Brown literary agency, founded by the American-born Albert Curtis Brown in 1899.
9 Canadian film producer who employed Maclaren-Ross as a screenwriter in 1949.
10 Spencer Curtis Brown (1906–80) who ran the Curtis Brown literary agency, founded by his father.
11 Sir Basil Bartlett (1905–85), a playwright and former lieutenant colonel in the Intelligence Corps, was employed as a Drama Script Supervisor for BBC Television between 1952 and 1955.

to DAN DAVIN

29 Norfolk Square / London W2

18-1-53

My dear Dan,

Thank you for your letter; I didn't answer it immediately because I felt instinctively you would call on me Friday – and sure enough you did. I only got your note at 12.35, and at once ran to the Wheatsheaf:[1]

only to be told that you'd just that minute left. I have a message asking you to ring me if you should come back; ten minutes later the phone went, but instead of you, at the other end there was Dick Scott. Broke but full of new plans: I spent an hour or two with him in the Wheatsheaf later.

Never mind about the essays, though I'd like to have something done by the Press. It was never, by the way, my intention to make that book[2] a comprehensive survey of the novel today and yesterday, but to pick out a few authors who've either not been mentioned enough or, in my opinion, not examined in the way they should be – the connecting link being the fact that they show their characters in action rather than through introspection or psychological analysis.

As for my news: I had to accept a £150 advance for *The Weeping and the Laughter* in the finish, in order to get it out quickly. Having paid £75 to my landlady, I was stricken with piles, which was expensive and very very painful: a fortnight in bed and the doctor every day. An operation impends, but I'm putting if off as long as I can.

Hart-Davis kept his word re speed: I had proofs (page) by Dec. 20th; they're all corrected and Harry Jonas is now finishing the jacket. Publication: April 17th if not sooner; there's talk of it being the *Evening Standard* Book of the Month, but of course that'll turn out to be balls. You'll get an advance copy as soon as they're ready.

For the rest, I'm doing – as you may have seen last week – the novels for *The Sunday Times* in place of Snow;[3] but they'll probably only keep me on for a fortnight. I've just prepared my copy for January 25th. Then there's a new Television Firm set-up run by Norman Collins,[4] who writes me very friendly letters: it's possible there's quite a good job there – I shall know next week.

I've no money, as *The [Sunday] Times* only pays monthly. But early in February I shall touch,[5] so I might come to Oxford again if you can put up with me in a somewhat lighter mood!

All love and love to all,
Julian

1   A pub on Rathbone Place, just off Oxford Street. Maclaren-Ross had been a regular there since his discharge from the army. During the 1930s and 1940s, it was a favourite haunt of writers and artists.
2   Maclaren-Ross and Davin had discussed the possibility of expanding his essays for the *Times Literary Supplement* into a book about contemporary novelists. This idea had been rejected by Davin's employers.

3   The novelist C.P. Snow (1905–80), who was a regular reviewer for the *Sunday Times*.

4   The novelist Norman Collins (1907–82) had become the Deputy Chairman of the Associated Television Company, which was preparing to make its first transmission. Prior to that, the BBC had had a monopoly over television broadcasting in Britain.

5   'Touching' was slang for obtaining money, in this case the money owed by *The Times*.

to RUPERT HART-DAVIS

29 Norfolk Square/London W2

19-2-53

My dear Rupert,

As you see, they've given me the G.P. Fund.[1]

Could you advance me any of it until the cheque comes through? I should be asking you to cash this for me in any case, as I've no banking account.

Sorry to be a nuisance again, but it's bloody to be a broke when one knows there's money due a week ahead.

Yours ever,

Julian

1   The Society of Authors had awarded him £30 from the Gertrude Page Fund.

to RUPERT HART-DAVIS

29 Norfolk Square/London W2

22-2-53

My dear Rupert,

On Thursday last I handed a letter to one of your secretaries, who assured me that it would be given to you, and advised me to ring you at 9.30 the following morning for an answer.

When I did so, however, I was informed that you were in conference and that, though you had received my note, no message had been left for me; nor have I heard anything from you since.

I am anxious that our relationship should proceed smoothly, and I have had experience enough of publishers to realise that this result is more easily achieved if one does not ask favours; at the same time, in a case like this, one's publisher seems the natural person to turn to, and there is no reason why you should not do what I asked you, since you would be covered against loss in any events.

I can only conclude that, as you would scarcely ignore my letter, you cannot have received it after all: a thought which disturbs me.

Perhaps you'd phone me on Monday morning and let me know what has happened?

Yours ever,

Julian

to RUPERT HART-DAVIS

29 Norfolk Square / London W2

26-2-53

My dear Rupert,

Thank you for your letter.

I have thought over what you said from all points of view, but with all possible allowance I cannot pretend to understand your attitude. I would like to make it clear, however, that it was as a publisher and *not* as a friend that I was asking you to help me out; the view which I hold, that one's publisher is the proper person to approach in such circumstances, seems to be held also by everyone I know: *especially* bankers, who always say, 'Why don't you go to your publisher?' It's at this very moment in my career that I need all the help I can get in surmounting the little irritating hurdles placed in my way not so much by shortage of money, but by the difficulty of obtaining money which I've earned or is due to me by reason of literary work in the past. Delays in paying up even small sums result in periods of forced creative inactivity, plus unnecessary hardship and discomfort: all of which could be avoided, in the first instance, by some consideration on the part of those from whom the money's due, but who are easily antagonised by any attempt to obtain prompt payment: while being, at the same time, only too eager to get their hands on the work in the first instance.

It's just this disgust for their whole attitude which has prevented me from writing all these years, and the patent inequality displayed in the relations between publisher or editor and author which led to my hostile attitude in the past, and must inevitably again unless some alteration occurs. However, it seems hopeless to write all this, because – let's face it and friendship apart – we're on opposite sides of the fence and however much you may understand my difficulties you cannot afford, in your professional capacity, to ameliorate them.

I'll say this, though, that your letter is scarcely encouraging (because of what it epitomises), or conducive to writing more books in conditions similar to the present ones.

Let's hope these may change with publication of the first one: I enclose, meantime, a plan of the second volume and its successors, which may give you an idea of the scope and purpose of the total work.

We might meet to discuss this soon if you've any time to spare: discussion of work in progress often helps me at a moment like this when I've the whole thing more or less mapped out in mind.

As for the rest, we must agree to differ, and it seems, misunderstand one another.

Yours ever,
Julian

to RUPERT HART-DAVIS

29 Norfolk Square/London W2
6-3-53

My dear Rupert,

Thank you for your letter: it looks, however, as if I still haven't made my point-of-view clear, so, tiresome though it may be for both of us, I'd better have another shot.

Let me put it this way: you were once in contact with more than 100 soldiers in the ranks, all of whom were being messed about just as I was, but I was the only one who wrote a book about it which expresses their point-of-view.[1]

Many an officer told me I was difficult or impossible because I wouldn't accept a ready-made conception of 'that's the way things are and you can't alter them'. *You* liked the book I wrote; but the War Office didn't, but there they couldn't afford to since they were on the other side of the fence which *I* didn't build.

It's easy to laugh at, and sympathise with, my viewpoint when you're not directly concerned with what I'm attacking; I don't suppose directors of vacuum-cleaner firms laughed much over *Of Love and Hunger*, but you, among other publishers, did. Now when I write *Business and Desire*,[2] you'll say that I'm prejudiced and imagining antagonisms that don't exist: in fact that I suffer from persecution-mania.

So I'm right about the army and about vacuum-cleaners, and clear-sighted about my childhood, but totally and wilfully wrong-headed about publishers and editors? How come?

I don't suppose my parents would like *The Weeping and the Laughter* much: they were, being parents, on 'the other side of the fence'. When I use this expression, it doesn't imply the antagonism but merely a different way of looking at things. A publisher, however friendly, simply *can't* see things as an author who depends on money from his books for a living; nor can an editor.

It's not a question of antagonism at all. An editor asks for an article by a certain date. I deliver it. Then I want to be paid. But he has his own system of payment, just as a publisher has, and if I want cash on delivery I become 'a bloody nuisance'. I've been told so. Yet I don't think the editor's requirements are a bloody nuisance because he names a date for delivery. Therefore I think his attitude's unfair.

I wrote a short piece on Pritchett[3] for *The Sunday Times*, which was printed on Feb. 1. It's only a couple of guineas but I still haven't had a cheque. Yet you see, Rupert, I can't get any tradesman to give *me* 2 guineas credit: and why should I ask when there's money owing for work done?

You speak about writing a book in 6 weeks. What do I live on while I'm writing it? One meal and 10 cigarettes a day, like with the last one?

Or an advance from a publisher before the book's written? Then I deliver the MS; the money's been spent writing it and I wait a year before I see any return – *if* the book sells. Is that any good to me?

You talk of working hard: on Wednesday I was working at 5 a.m., and from 2 p.m. till 7 p.m. on Thursday – doing what? A middle-article on Simenon[4] for the *TLS* to get myself some money.[5]

I'd like to spend all my time writing books and not doing these odd jobs, but I'm afraid until a lucky break comes and I get the Book Society & Literary Guild choices, I'll have to regard them as a pure luxury – with criticism, film jobs etc. for daily bread.

What's the alternative: a regular reviewing column; BBC criticism; publisher's reader? Walter Allen, for once, will tell you these jobs take every moment of your time and energy and leave nothing saved in the bank. He's just told me so!

Nobody can do anything without capital. You could not be a pub-lisher without it. I have none. If I could write a novel and get someone to buy me out of my other contracts plus a large advance (all of which could be recovered by publishing my other books plus the new novel etc.) this would be the way out – but who will? That would give the capital I need, but to the publisher it would be a gamble which I've given up asking anyone to undertake. So it looks as if I'll just have to hope and pray.

Now Rupert I assure you I hate writing letters, and I only do so in an effort to make you see how I feel. Do try to examine the points I make and don't just pick out some bit you choose to take as personal – because I am not – repeat *not* – antagonistic to you at all.

I'm trying to make a go of it because this time I want a publisher that I can stay with as long as my difficult situation (which, by the way, I *don't* enjoy or regard as inevitable) permits me to write an occasional book.

We might meet for a drink sometime and discuss those plans I sent you but which you didn't comment on.

Yours ever,

Julian

1 The book was *The Stuff to Give the Troops*.
2 A never-to-be-completed autobiographical novel in which he planned to vent his anger at the publishing world.
3 The novelist, critic, memoirist and short-story writer V.S. Pritchett (1900–97).
4 Georges Simenon (1905–89), Belgian crime writer who created the popular 'Inspector Maigret' novels.
5 Maclaren-Ross's essay on Simenon was published in the 20 March 1953 issue.

to DAN DAVIN

29 Norfolk Square/London W2

15-3-53

Dear Dan,

How would it suit you if I came down next Friday (20th)? The next week leads us a bit too near to Easter, by which time I should have to come back here; also, having just written a short television film[1] and been promptly paid, I'd feel better if I came while I've still got some of the cash in hand. However it's up to you: don't let me upset any household arrangements.

By now you should have been sent a copy of my book (publication date March 27); I had my advance copies on the 10th. I hope you may find it of interest. Incidentally, Lusty[2] turned it down because he thought it 'too short'; yet it still makes a book of 229 pages and is 70,000 words in length.

Love to all,

from

Julian

1 No record of the script, which was never filmed, has survived.
2 Dan Davin's far from respectful nickname for John Lehmann.

to KENDAL B. HARRIES[1]

29 Norfolk Square/London W2

17-4-53

Dear Mr Harries,

Thank you for your letter; I am glad you liked my book and sorry you can't enlighten me about the Hooded Terror.[2] Odd you should mention Bognor since that is the 'winter town' mentioned in the latter part of the book,[3] and where the love affair later takes place.

Regarding your query, I am 40 years old. As stated on page 70 I 'saw' *Quo Vadis* (first Italian version)[4] as a babe in arms.

Yours very truly,

J. Maclaren-Ross

1 A London-based literary admirer who had contacted Maclaren-Ross.
2 A villain from silent movie serials, about whom Maclaren-Ross had written in *The Weeping and the Laughter*.
3 In *The Weeping and the Laughter*, his memoir of his childhood, Maclaren-Ross describes the autumn of 1922, when he and his parents moved from France back to England. 'The town in which we stayed on our return was not Bournemouth,' he wrote, '... but it too was at the seaside and had an arcade, though on a smaller scale than the one at Boscombe and there were fewer cinemas; in fact, as I remember, in those days only two. It was a winter town: that is to say winter is the season with which I principally associate it.' (*Collected Memoirs*, Black Spring Press, 2004, p. 125) A second reference to the 'winter town' occurs near to the climax of *The Weeping and the Laughter*, which sees Maclaren-Ross and his parents leave Bognor Regis and return to France in the summer of 1923. 'We embarked on what turned out to be a rough crossing ... via Boulogne, leaving, as I thought, the winter town behind for ever,' he recollected (*Collected Memoirs*, p. 132).
4 *Quo Vadis* (1912) was directed by Enzo Guzzoni.

to RUPERT HART-DAVIS

29 Norfolk Square/London W2

12-5-53

My dear Rupert,

I have received a note from Jocelyn Brooke,[1] who says he was asked to review *The Weeping and the Laughter* for *The Sunday Times* but could not owing his absence in Sicily. This still does not explain why Russell didn't ask someone else to review the book, for he must have realised that nearly 2 months have elapsed since the advance copies went out, and that something must therefore have gone wrong as far as Brooke was concerned. Have you rung him again?

Another matter which requires explanation is Brooke's letter, forwarded from your office, should be dated 28 April and bear 3 post-marks: (1) Canterbury, 29 April (2) London, W1, 6 May (3) London, W1, 7 May. Surely letters addressed to your care, which might contain important news from me, are not allowed to lie around for over a week before they are re-addressed, and then wrongly, hence the 3rd postmark.

There are also some other questions I'd like to ask:

(1) Why, in view of the good notices my book received, has no advertisement of it appeared since publication, apart from a small one sandwiched – in among other titles and bearing only a tiny note from *The Times*? Doesn't it deserve a decent column to itself?

(2) Why have friends of mine in Maidenhead and in Bognor – where I lived for years where there would have been a big demand for the book – been unable to obtain it except (and only very recently) from libraries?

(3) Why should my landlady, who attempted to buy a copy for someone, be told at Whiteley's in Queensway a fortnight ago that they'd never heard of the book, and at Smith's in Kensington that they were sold out and had received no further copies?

Such incidents – by no means isolated – do not bear out your claim that 'you'd do your damnedest' to sell the book. Certainly, unless the book is properly publicised and pushed by your travellers both in, and outside, London, it will be a dead loss; I trust you won't quote the example of Calder-Marshall's book again in replying to this – what I'm concerned about is the promotion of my own slender volume which seems to me, is being allowed to die a natural death.

Yours as ever,

Julian

1   A novelist and memoirist whose genre-bending books include *The Orchid Trilogy* (1948–50).

to H.R. TOWNSHEND[1]

29 Norfolk Square/London W2
15-5-53

Dear Mr Townshend,

Thank you for your reply to my letter, which was intended for Mr Hart-Davis and *not* undated, if you will look under the signature, which is where I date all my correspondence. Your answers to my queries are of course unsatisfactory, as you must realise. Nobody in an office ever admits to a mistake in re-forwarding letters, but if this duty were allocated to one particular person, it would be easier to attach responsibility in the case of delays.

With regard to advertising, I have seen all those you mention: seven of which appeared before the book was published; the remaining four are the very small ones I refer to in my letter of the 12th instance. My query referred to *separate* and *post* publication, with quotes from the reviews it has received, as is customary when the book has been well noticed. In my opinion, too, it was a mistake to label the book 'an autobiography of childhood' in the advance publicity, instead of using the sub-title which I myself had chosen.[2] To emphasise the childhood angle was not a good selling point.

I do not think the Smiths, or any other bookseller, has a prejudice against my work: nor, in the past, has it been necessary to force copies upon them; but considering the good reviews it might be advantageous to re-approach such firms as have not re-ordered.

I hope Mr Hart-Davis will be able to satisfy my curiosity a little more fully on his return.

Yours very truly,

J. Maclaren-Ross

1   A senior employee at Rupert Hart-Davis Ltd.
2   Maclaren-Ross had chosen the subtitle 'A Chapter of Autobiography'.

to RUPERT HART-DAVIS

29 Norfolk Square/London W2

16-5-53

My dear Rupert,

I'm sorry that my letter dated 12 May should have been passed to Mr Townshend; it was addressed to you by name and intended for you alone.

Since writing it, I've had another letter from Brooke, who says that Lambert[1] (he thinks) has got someone else to review the book; so perhaps by Sunday that query will have been disposed of.

As you'll see from my reply to Mr Townshend, I was not satisfied with his answers, because they had little relevance to the questions I asked: nor is it much use trying to put someone initially in the wrong with the 'undated' gambit, when a simple glance at the signature would have shown the date underneath, as is my invariable habit.

Don't think that I'm trying to tell you how to run your own business or how to sell books, but I must be allowed my own opinion that an advert quoting a number of favourable reviews attracts more public notice than the bare announcement that a book is to appear (unless the author's Priestley[2] or Shute[3]). Reviews are all very fine, but most people haven't time to read them thoroughly, except in the case of writers such as those I've named; when, however, they are boiled down to a brief chorus of praise, they *do* catch the eye – I can vouch for that as an average reader and, alas, ex-book buyer.

Mr Townshend may be right in saying that most booksellers, having once subscribed, do not re-order when sold out; but if so, then surely some attempt should be made to re-arouse their interest and not to leave it apathetically at that. Besides, I'm a pretty constant bookshop visitor, and as you know a pretty keen observer, and I've always noticed that a crop of good notices produces a resultant increase in the number of copies on display – in many cases, a second impression, except when the subject is impossibly highbrow. Remember, Rupert, that though I'm not a publisher, I have a fair of knowledge of what goes on when a book comes out; I didn't have to be a professional soldier to know what happened in army depots: personal experience and some intelligence were all I required – and I haven't lived by writing for 10 years without knowing a bit about the book trade, though I see it from a totally different angle – the CO, confronted with a squad of recruits and the results of their training, also saw things differently; and so, however sympathetic he may be, must a publisher.

What has gone wrong with my book and how can it be remedied? I suggest that we meet and talk this – and other things – over on your return; letter-writing, in my opinion, only clouds the issue where a few words face to face could clarify it. My previous suggestion, that we should meet to discuss the plan of future volumes which on that occasion I enclosed, was met with silence; but I hope that this time you once arrange a meeting in an effort to get things straightened out between us.

Yours as ever,

Julian

1 Jack Walter Lambert (1917–86) was the Assistant Literary Editor of the *Sunday Times*.
2 J.B. Priestley (1894–1984) was an extremely successful novelist, playwright and critic. His novels include *The Good Companions* (1929).
3 Nevil Shute (1899–1960) was a popular English novelist whose best-known novel was probably *A Town Like Alice* (1949).

to DAN DAVIN

29 Norfolk Square / London W2
19-5-53

My Dear Dan,

Being as usual in straitened circumstances, I am applying to the Royal Literary Fund for a grant, and I wonder if you'd like to write a short letter about my work etc. (with special reference to *The Weeping and the Laughter*), to support my application? I think that, as secretary to the Press Delegates, you'd be just the man to impress them. I'm writing also to David Cecil[1] asking him to do the same: he wrote me a very nice note about my book.

The letter, headed 'To Whom it May Concern', should be sent to me here and I will forward it on, in time for their meeting early next month. I hope it won't be too much bother; as I say, it need not be anything very long.

I hope all goes well with you, and that you'll drop in on me when you're next in town. My love to Winnie, Anna, and the kids.

Yours in haste,

Julian

By the way, they're doing *TWHTL* on the radio on Sunday: John Raymond *Talking of Books* at 4.45.

1 Besides holding an English Literature professorship at the University of Oxford, Lord David Cecil (1902–86) wrote biographies of Jane Austen, Sir Walter Scott and others.

to JOHN BROADBENT

29 Norfolk Square / London W2

19-6-53

Dear Captain Broadbent,

I would like to apply for a grant to the Royal Literary Fund. As you may remember, I was last awarded one three years ago. Since then, this March, I published the first volume of my autobiography, *The Weeping and the Laughter* (Hart-Davis, 12s 6d); but this, though exceptionally well received by the press, does not seem so far to have cleared the advance of £150 which I drew last October (incidentally it is being done on the radio in John Raymond's *Talking of Books* programme on Sunday June 21).[1]

I have an enormous debt for rent mounting up here (about £250); I gave my landlady £75 out of the £150 in October; but since then, as I have no steady income coming in, of course it has mounted up again. These circumstances make it very difficult for me to concentrate as I would like, on writing the second volume of autobiography which the critics say they are waiting for, and I would also like to pay off as much as I can to my landlady who has been so good to me.

If you would send me the form of application I will fill it in forthwith, and apply to Lord David Cecil and D.M. Davin (Secretary to the Delegates of the Clarendon Press) for letters of recommendation to support my claim, together with a copy of my new book.

Yours sincerely,

J. Maclaren-Ross

1 The item on *The Weeping and the Laughter* was postponed until the following month. At 4.45 p.m. on Sunday 21 June 1953, Maclaren-Ross appeared alongside the humorist Arthur Marshall and the novelist Angus Wilson as a guest on this BBC Home Service radio programme.

to DAN DAVIN

29 Norfolk Square / London W2
27-6-53

Dear Dan,

Thank you for your letter; I'm sorry to be giving you trouble, especially as I've unwittingly misled you: for, according to the instructions on the form of application, the letter I need should confirm, not so much the literary status of the applicant (anyway, the Committee members know all about me), but the fact that he is 'in want or distress'.

So if you mention that you know me to be hard-up and that I was still so when I stayed with you after I'd just finished my book and after it came out, and again when you visited me in London, I'm sure it'll do the trick. Your official status will be known to the Committee already; the form demands two or more letters from 'respectable persons', 'authenticating the merits of the case'.

I've sent off most of the stuff already and the application comes up on July 8th; so if you wouldn't mind sending your letter direct to the secretary, he'll include it in my file.

His address is:

The Secretary

The Royal Literary Fund

Stationers Hall

London EC4

The envelope should be marked 'Ref – J. Maclaren-Ross', which, by the way, is how my name is spelled.

I've had a filthy time recently, with Barbara ill and in the hospital,[1] so I could do with a lucky break. Do let's meet when you're next in town.

Love to Winnie, Anna & kids,

from

Julian

1 During the middle of that month, Barbara Wimble had been rushed into St Mary's Hospital on Praed Street in London, probably suffering from some form of gynaecological condition.

to DAN DAVIN

29 Norfolk Square/London W2
14-7-53

My dear Dan,

A belated note to thank you for writing to the RLF[1] on my behalf, and also to apologise for the trouble you were put to.

The fund – though Hart-Davis was on the Committee – wouldn't give me any actual cash to continue working on, but it did send a cheque for £100 to my landlady, in part payment of the debt I owe her – which helps a bit, although it leaves me in the red, still, to the extent of £200! Meanwhile, however, something else has turned up: *Punch*, now edited by Malcolm Muggeridge, with Tony Powell as a literary editor, has taken four of my things at one go: a parody of Eric Ambler; a parody of the *New Statesmen*; and two short stories, one of which will be printed next week. Before this, I'd done a parody of P.G. Wodehouse and one of Launder and Gilliat, the British film-producing team,[2] with special reference to Gilbert and Sullivan[3] (this was in the form of a filmscript). Wodehouse by the way wrote me two charming letters: I'd also done a *TLS* article about him, and he said that in consequence Penguin Books had decided to print another five of his books. Such is the power of the press – except when a book of mine is praised!

Now look: why don't you do something for *Punch*? It's a quick ten or fifteen guineas. Here's the dope: between 800 and 1,000 words, any form you like if it's funny, but I'd advise you to look at an issue of the paper first. 'How Frogs Saved Daddy's Life' strikes me as the gimmick. They were also talking of doing something of Cary's[4] at one time.

Despite this windfall – though I've not had the cheque yet – I'm not feeling so bright really: Barbara had a relapse tonight (a bad haemorrhage) and is now back in St Mary's Hospital, though the doctors say she's in no danger. When she's out of the wood, she'll be going on holiday – end of this month – and I thought that then I might pop down and see you for a weekend or something unless you yourselves are going Sisam-wards[5] at that time.

I wish you'd look in on me when you're next in town: I've had a lot to tell you about, including my drinking-session with C.P. Snow at the Saville Club.

Did you see my letter in the *Statesman* (last issue July 11) about Rayner Heppenstall's book[6] – incidentally I think the novel might interest you: it's about that hospital Rayner was in, and I appear as a character, having been there at the same time. He's done a portrait of me as a MONSTER: which should please you! I'll send you my copy if you like.

Do try something for *Punch* – the shorter the better they like it. 3 typed pages the max.

Love to Winnie, Anna, and kids,

from

Julian

1   Royal Literary Fund.

2   Frank Launder (1907–97) and Sidney Gilliat (1908–94) were the producers of a string of popular British movies, many of them comedies. Both men also worked as directors and screenwriters. Maclaren-Ross's send-up of them, entitled 'Lansdowne and Grosvenor', was published in *Punch* on 24 June 1953.

3   The librettist W.S. Gilbert (1836–1911) and the composer Arthur Sullivan (1842–1900), creators of *The Mikado* (1885) and other operettas.

4   Dan Davin's friend, the novelist Joyce Cary (1888–1957).

5   A reference to Dan Davin's friend, Kenneth Sisam (1887–1971), the former Secretary to the Delegates of the Oxford University Press. Sisam had retired in 1948, then moved to a house on St Mary's, one of the Scilly Isles. From 1952 onwards, Davin had got into the habit of staying with him for the final two weeks of the university's summer holiday.

6   The writer and BBC producer Rayner Heppenstall's autobiographical novel *The Lesser Infortune* (1953) featured a substantial section set in Northfield Military Hospital, renamed 'Wroth Hall'. Maclaren-Ross's alter ego was 'Dorian Scott-Crichton'. Maclaren-Ross's letter referred to the 'stupid malice to which [the protagonist] is subjected' by the higher ranks; the uncomfortable living conditions in the hospital; and 'the indiscriminate waving of white feathers at men of intelligence who, through no fault of their own, spent the recent war struggling to free themselves from the nightmare fly-trap of a Kafkan bureaucracy'.

to DAN DAVIN

29 Norfolk Square/London W2

19-7-53

My dear Dan,

Terribly sorry about Friday: I didn't think you'd be up so soon, and 3 days before I'd arranged to go down to Maidenhead for the day to see Gerry Fisher (remember him?) starting on the 11.20 from Paddington, so no time to wait for you and let you know. I left a card in the hall explaining, asking you to leave a phone number where I could contact you in the evening if you were staying: I could have put you up for the night. But as there's no resident housekeeper and nobody to answer the door, I suppose you didn't get it: the card was there untouched when I returned. Too bad: hope we may get together soon. Barbara's now out of hospital and back home in, I trust, improved health. Don't forget my suggestion about *Punch*. Book that might interest you: novel in New Zealand slang. Title: *She's Right.*[1] Publisher: Collins. Can't remember author's name.

Yours ever,

J.M.R.

1   1953 novel by Dairmid Cameron Cathie.

to JOHN DAVENPORT[1]

29 Norfolk Square / London W2

23-8-53

Dear Davenport,

Having heard nothing from you with regard to the BBC meeting last Monday, at which my proposed contributions to the Third Programme were to be discussed,[2] I wonder if you could ring me about one p.m. and let me know what decision, if any, was reached in this connexion?[3]

I have been asked by Stephen Spender[4] to submit a fairly long piece for his new magazine *Encounter*; and, though a definite subject has not yet been decided-upon, it will certainly be one of the episodes to be incorporated later in my next volume of autobiography *The Rites of Spring*.[5] It would help me to avoid any possibility of duplication if I knew, as soon as possible, whether the particular material we talked about should still be reserved for broadcasting purposes.

Sincerely,

J. Maclaren-Ross

1   John Davenport (c.1910–66) was a literary critic and BBC producer.
2   Maclaren-Ross had interested Davenport in the possibility of providing two reminiscences, both of which were destined to form part of *The Rites of Spring*, the never-to-be-completed sequel to his memoir *The Weeping and the Laughter*. One of these reminiscences, earmarked for a 30-minute reading, concerned the seventeen-year-old Maclaren-Ross's visit to the Riviera home of the writer Frank Harris (1856–1931). Davenport was planning to hire Maclaren-Ross to read both pieces.
3   Davenport wrote to him on 25 August 1953, reiterating the BBC's interest in broadcasting extracts from *The Rites of Spring*. To placate Maclaren-Ross, Davenport mentioned that he'd recommended that the poet Stephen Spender (1909–95) should commission the piece for *Encounter*, the magazine co-edited by Spender.
4   See previous note.

5 The piece, entitled 'Monsieur L'Abbé', appeared in the December 1953 issue of *Encounter*. It focused on Maclaren-Ross's time at an idiosyncratic French secondary school, run by a Catholic priest.

to RUPERT HART-DAVIS

29 Norfolk Square/London W2

24-8-53

Dear Rupert,

As I see no new stocks of my autobiography *The Weeping and the Laughter* in the bookshops, despite the notice John Raymond gave it in his Sunday book-talk on the radio (commonly acknowledged as the most influential programme with regard to increasing sales), and all the other favourable reviews it has received, I can only conclude, in the absence of any information pertaining to the book's progress, that the first printing must be exhausted and that you do not intend to reprint.

I assume, furthermore, that if such were not the case, you would have advertised the book further: instead of which my last two letters to you on the subject have remained unanswered and all mention of my book has been excluded from your recent advertisements.

Therefore I offer the customary three months notice in writing, after which, should no second edition be issued, the copyright of the work, as per contract, reverts to me.

In the circumstances, and especially since my letters asking you to discuss the plan of the total autobiography with me have also remained unanswered, I feel that you will release me from the option to consider the second volume *The Rites of Spring*;[1] and should I receive no reply to this letter within the next ten days, I shall feel at liberty to offer the aforementioned book to another publisher: together with *The Weeping and the Laughter* copyright when three calendar months from the date appended below shall have elapsed.

Yours as ever,

J. Maclaren-Ross

1 Though this volume was never published, substantial chunks of it *did* appear in print. These comprise 'Monsieur L'Abbé', 'The Bird Man', 'The Gondolier of Death' and 'A Visit to the Villa Edouard Sept', all of which were reprinted in the posthumously published *Collected Memoirs* (Black Spring Press, 2004).

to JOHN DAVENPORT

29 Norfolk Square / London W2

28-8-53

Dear Davenport,

After due consideration I have decided against doing any stories or talks for the BBC 3rd Programme. The conditions of acceptance and the dates of payment are really so problematical and uncertain, that I fear the whole project, as has happened to me so often in my past dealings with the BBC, might result in a waste of time which at the moment I can ill afford.

I'm sorry, but I think you'll appreciate my point of view. I rang you at your office yesterday, but you were not in; and when I called in at the Stag¹ to tell you this morning, you were occupied, so I didn't interrupt.

Sincerely,

J. Maclaren-Ross

1 The Stag's Head was a small pub near Broadcasting House. It functioned as an alternative office for many BBC producers. A a result, numerous writers, actors and musicians were drawn there in search of work.

to RUPERT HART-DAVIS

29 Norfolk Square / London W2

3-9-53

Dear Rupert,

In your letter of Sept. 2nd, you expressed the wish to avoid quarrelling with me, but in the same sentence refer to previous, unanswered letters of mine as being petty and antagonistic: scarcely words, one would have thought, designed to keep the peace, especially when, in fact, the letters in question (copies of which lie before me now) are merely concerned with queries to which every author has a right to expect an answer, concluding in each case, with a request that we should meet to discuss the total plan of my autobiography, the second volume of which you now seem anxious to publish.

On the other hand, your letters have been, to say the least, outspoken with reference to your opinion of my personality, and of the attitude which you persist in attributing to me; and I feel that the time has come for me to reply in kind.

First of all, who are these booksellers who accuse me of 'being a nuisance in their shops', and refuse, in consequence, to order my books? They cannot, even if their allegations were true, be very good men of affairs to allow personal prejudices against an author to interfere with business: and therefore the absence of my book on their shelves could not have much effect on its total sales; but unfortunately the book-sellers whom I know personally are all on friendly terms with me, and I can recall only once having a dispute in a bookshop and that was in Victoria 10 years ago: nor am I the sort of person who goes around announcing his identity when about to make a purchase. So I'm at a total loss to know what you're talking about, though I do note your complete readiness to accept without question the statement that I am guilty of disorderly or unbecoming conduct in public, and even warn me that if I 'go on in this way' every bookseller and *publisher* will be against me – which contradicts curiously your denial, in a letter dated March 2nd, that any such state of antagonism exists. I must here and now deny the accusation of misbehaviour alluded to above, and warn you furthermore that it must go no farther than the secretary who typed your letter to me. If you will give me the names of these booksellers, I will take prompt legal steps to suppress any repetition of such malicious gossip: if, however, the names are not forthcoming I shall be forced to believe it a fabrication on someone's part (the story must have passed between at least two persons before reaching you, and I cannot help feeling that you have made a great mistake in retailing it to me).

If you think I am dogmatic and feel I 'know best about everything', I certainly prefer to follow my own convictions where the welfare of my work is concerned: regarding the sales of this particular book I am indeed, having no alternative, forced to leave matters in your hands, but I feel that the brusque commanding tone in which you insist on such a policy would be more becoming from a publisher who had been triumphantly successful in selling my book – instead of which, the figures you quote imply (from those already quoted in your letters dated 30th March and 8th April respectively) that you have managed to sell only 900 copies of a well-reviewed book in the last 5 months: including libraries etc.

The next volume, however, is a different thing altogether; I have no intention of watching it follow the fate of the first, nor can I under-stand your wish to perpetuate a relationship which you seem to have found neither congenial nor profitable.

If you were so keen to see the next MS, you should not have ignored my two requests for a discussion of the proposed work after a plan of this had been sent to you, thus treating me with a contempt to which I am unaccustomed; and it will do you no good whatever to exercise your 'option': since what you actually have is an option not on the book itself, but to have first refusal of the MS on terms to be arranged. I need hardly tell you that, in view of the tone of this last letter alone, I will come to no arrangement with you, and that it will be futile to insist: unless what you want is to hold onto the MS for the two prescribed months and prevent me from obtaining an advance elsewhere during that length of time – a practice for which 'petty' would be too mild an epithet.

No, Rupert, if I were indeed the temperamental, self-willed, wrongheaded fool you like to pretend I am, then you should have employed more tact in handling me if you wished to continue publishing my books; I am not that type of person, but nonetheless there are limits to my patience, and I have submitted to your uncalled-for outbursts of asperity long enough.

I consider the tone which you have adopted to be arrogant and presumptuous, and where you express sorrow for appearing 'censorious', you should, in my opinion, apologise for being impudent. Unlike yourself, I am *not* sorry to express my displeasure, and please spare me the protestations of friendship at the end of your next letter, which I trust will be couched in a more courteous form: displays of irritability are better reserved for those authors to whom, as a publisher, you have proved yourself indispensable.

Yours,
Julian

to JOHN DAVENPORT

29 Norfolk Square/London W2
27-9-53

Dear Davenport,

Most awfully sorry, but after working day and night on this piece for you (not the Frank Harris one but a schooldays story).[1] I find, on finishing it today, that it works out at over 17 pages of my handwriting (normal BBC length 8 or 9pp.) and at 35 minutes reading time.

Now while I'm always willing to cut, and indeed I told you I would, one simply can't cut 6,000 words into half; at least not when one's taken some pains over the writing of it and there's not much padding.

So I'll just have to try again to fit something else into your length, which (at my reading pace) would be about 3,000 words. This is a bore, because it upsets the schedule I'd planned out for the series of three, but still.

Next week I hope to be about again (I have been at work so hard I've sat up 2 nights without sleep), and when I've recovered I'll hope to see you in the Head[2] and bring along something we can discuss.

Sorry once again,

As ever,

J. Maclaren-Ross

1 The 'schooldays story' was 'The Gondolier of Death', which was later included in his miscellany *The Funny Bone* (1956).

2 The Stag's Head pub, where John Davenport was a regular.

to WINNIE DAVIN[1]

29 Norfolk Square/London W2

6-10-53

My dear Winnie,

Really I must apologise for not writing to you before, and for neither receiving you when you called nor meeting you, as you suggested, in the Wheatsheaf later on. Taking the latter case first, I must have been dead to the world, having gone to bed at 7 a.m. that particular morning, and I didn't wake or find your note pushed under my door until 5.30 that afternoon, when it was of course too late to meet you.

And the cause of this was simply solid work. I've been at it without respite for about 5 weeks and I have neither been downtown during that time nor had a moment to write a letter, except a business one now and then. The weekend before last I worked 62 hours solidly without going to bed at all; last weekend for 48 hours without sleep.

Nature of work? A lot of short stuff for *Punch*;[2] two very long extracts from my 2nd volume of autobiography, for Spender's magazine *Encounter*;[3] and the outlines for 3 reminiscences when I'm supposed to do for the Third Programme.[4] The object of this? To collect as much money in a lump as possible and then be free to settle down to a longer piece of work: i.e. a novel. Nor will those pieces be wasted; for they are mostly autobiographical, and though they'll have to be radically recast, they're useful studies for Part One of my next volume (which I shan't write until all the stuff has been printed or broadcast).

However, I've finished at last (except for *The Sunday Times* book reviews (novels) which I've undertaken to do on Oct. 18 and Nov. 1), and sometime this week the work should pay off, when I'll be free to look around. I hope that all of you enjoyed your holiday this summer; I keep on trying to get sent to Turkey but no one is biting so far.

When I have collected the dough, I'd like very much to come down and see you all, Friday to Monday, if you've any weekends free? It'd have to be pretty soon, though, before most of the money gets paid out one way and another. Perhaps you or Dan will write when it would be convenient, or maybe he'll call if he's coming to town? Give him my love: and love to you all, though I never have much to go round.

As ever,

Julian

1 Winnie Davin, wife of the novelist Dan Davin.
2 At that time Maclaren-Ross was writing short memoirs and stories for *Punch*, among them 'The Almighty Dollar' and 'Bop'.
3 The extracts were 'Monsieur L'Abbé', published in the December 1953 issue, and 'The Bird Man', which featured in the January 1956 issue.
4 One of these was 'The Gondolier of Death', later included in Maclaren-Ross's miscellany *The Funny Bone* (1956). None of the mooted programmes was commissioned.

to MR ARNOLD[1]

29 Norfolk Square/London W2
17-10-53

Dear Mr Arnold,

Thank you for your letter of the 15th inst.

The book arrived at my address on Thursday morning and must have been despatched after my telephone call to you, so it could not have conceivably reached me Wednesday afternoon.[2]

As for the way it was addressed, I enclose the label herewith so that you may judge for yourself. However, it was forwarded under my correct name to Oxford[3] and I am now reading it. Though in my review I may disagree with some of Mr Usborne's opinions, this makes no difference to the pleasure I am deriving from the book itself, and I hope you will convey to the author my congratulations on it.

Since the review will be 2,000 words in length and I especially asked Mr Spender to let me do it,[4] I thought it might be worth your taking some trouble over getting the book to me promptly; I am sorry you should have thought me unduly fussy.

Sincerely,

J. Maclaren-Ross

1 Presumably an employee of Constable, publisher of *Clubland Heroes*.
2 Mr Arnold or one of his colleagues had pencilled in a note on the letter, stating that the promised review copy of Richard Usborne's *Clubland Heroes* had been posted the day before Maclaren-Ross's phone call.
3 Maclaren-Ross was staying with Dan Davin and family at their house on Southmoor Road.
4 The review had been commissioned for *Encounter*.

to DAN DAVIN

29 Norfolk Square/London W2
21-10-53

My dear Dan,

I'm enclosing the typescript of 'Monsieur l'Abbé', which I'd like you to look over for faults in the very short section dealing with actual religious education (pp. 17 to 20). I know you're busy, but if you'd just mark down (on a separate sheet of paper) any changes you think should be made in the vocabulary etc. (i.e. 'Our Lady' for 'The Holy Virgin') I'd be very grateful: I expect they'll want to go to press very shortly.

As always I enjoyed my stay in Oxford very much, and hope to see you very soon in London. Perhaps we could have lunch?

Love to all at 103,[1]

from

Julian

1 Refers to the Davins' address: 103 Southmoor Road, Oxford.

to MR ARNOLD

29 Norfolk Square / London W2
23-10-53

Dear Mr Arnold,

Thank you for your letter of October 21st.

As for the review, I enjoyed Mr Usborne's book immensely, though I disagree with him on several points, notably about Dornford Yates and John Buchan;[1] originally I was going to write a long essay on the latter myself, and when *Clubland Heroes* appeared, asked specially to review it as an opportunity to express my own views on the subject of these writers. One day I mean to do a book myself tracing the development of the thriller (as distinct from the detective story) from *Treasure Island*, through the novels of Buchan and the films of Fritz Lang[2] and Alfred Hitchcock, to Graham Greene and the contemporary manner (Ambler,[3] Household[4] etc.), not forgetting Conrad and the Americans such as Hammett.[5]

I'd be very pleased indeed to meet Mr Usborne and yourself for lunch, if you don't mind waiting until I have completed and delivered my essay on his book:[6] as I don't like reviewing anyone I know personally, unless I've been following the author's work for so long before a meeting that a social contact can no longer in any way influence my opinion. Sometime next week, however, I will ring you with pleasure to arrange a date.

Sincerely,

J. Maclaren-Ross

1 Usborne had expressed admiration for Yates's work, praising his 'diamanté prose' and 'ageless wit'. Maclaren-Ross found this stance 'preposterous', even going so far as to state that he could find little evidence of the latter. He also disagreed with Usborne's assertion that Buchan had 'failed in character-drawing'.

2 The German film-maker Fritz Lang (1890–1976) directed numerous thrillers, notably *Fury* (1936), *The Woman in the Window* (1944) and *The Big Heat* (1953).

3 The novelist and screenwriter Eric Ambler (1909–98), whose 1939 novel *The Mask of Dimitrios*, provided the basis for one of Maclaren-Ross's favourite films.

4 The novelist and playwright Geoffrey Household (1900–88), best known for his 1939 novel *Rogue Male*.

5 Dashiell Hammett (1894–1961), author of *The Maltese Falcon* and other novels.

6 Entitled 'A Totem of the 1920s', the essay appeared in the March 1954 issue of *Encounter*.

to JOHN DAVENPORT

29 Norfolk Square / London W2

23-10-53

Dear Davenport,

If, at your meeting on Monday, no decision has yet been reached regarding my story 'The Gondolier of Death', I think it would be better if you returned the MS to me straightaway so that I can send it elsewhere.

When I gave it to you a fortnight ago, I did not anticipate a delay of 2 weeks, but understood you would inform me of the meeting's decision on the following Tuesday.

If it's only a question of length, 6,000 words, at my speed of narration, would not take more than 30 minutes, especially with the cuts I intend to make; and since the 3rd Programme includes a talk of this length by Dr Fraser Darling on Sunday and Thursday, and a 25-minute broadcast by Walter Allen on Friday, I frankly fail to see what all the indecision is all about.

Hoping to hear from you on Tuesday,

Sincerely,

J. Maclaren-Ross

to DAN DAVIN

29 Norfolk Square / London W2

8-11-53

Dear Dan,

Apologies: I should have written earlier thanking you for reading 'M. L'Abbé' so promptly. I'm glad there aren't any errors except for the query you raise about the order of ceremonies: I don't think that matters, since the Catholics will know and the non-Catholics won't care; also, since the MS was already in proof by the time I got the copy back from you, it would have meant the printers being given added work had I changed anything more than the alterations I had already made.

New: I do *The Sunday Times* novels again on Nov. 29, and am lunching with Lambert[1] on Tuesday: so will hear then if there's any chance of an eventual permanency. 2 more pieces accepted by *Punch* (one satirising the possibilities conjured up by Rupert H.D.'s remark about booksellers not taking my book because of personal dislike etc.);[2] the article on Bulldog Drummond,[3] Buchan[4] and Co. finished and paid-for by Spender – very promptly.[5]

I'm sending *Maria Cross*[6] back to you: I think it's a good book, except that it's unfair to draw inferences about Evelyn Waugh's psychological make-up from what his father said about him as a child; but to go into all the questions involved would land me with too much reading (Claudel[7] etc.) so instead I've agreed to review the new Chandler for *Encounter* and do a general article on this type of American thriller, using *The Long Goodbye* as a basis.

We're leaving here on Wednesday the 11th, and I don't quite know where were shall go yet: so anyway don't write or call after that day, and I'll let you know the new address as soon as possible.

Love to all,

As ever,

Julian

PS Davenport[8] made a resounding muck-up of the 3rd Programme story for me; as for the new editor of *First Reading*,[9] Mr Moira Shearer,[10] well...

1 Jack Walter Lambert was the Assistant Literary Editor of the *Sunday Times*.
2 The piece in question was 'In Their Black Books', published in the 25 November 1953 issue.
3 The character created by Herman Cyril McNeile (1888–1937), who had, under the pseudonym 'Sapper', written *Bulldog Drummond* (Hodder & Stoughton, 1920) and other popular novels.
4 John Buchan (1875–1940), author of the thriller *The Thirty-Nine Steps*.
5 Under the title of 'A Totem of the 1920s', the article appeared in March 1954.
6 Novel by Conor Cruise O'Brien (Chatto & Windus, 1954).
7 The French poet Paul Claudel (1868–1955).
8 The literary critic and BBC producer John Davenport (c.1910–66).
9 *First Reading* was a BBC radio programme, edited by Ludovic Kennedy from 1953–54.
10 Moira Shearer (1926–2006), the dancer and actress, best known for her performance in the film *The Red Shoes*, was married to the journalist Ludovic Kennedy (1919–).

to DAN DAVIN

5d Hyde Park Mansions[1]/London NW1

24-11-53

Dear Dan,

Above is my new address. Don't be put off by the postal number: it's the second turning on the left off the Marylebone Road, just past the side of the Blue Hall cinema Edgware Road.

Should you call, Flat d is the first door on the right as you enter No 5; but if you could let me know when you're likely to be in London, we could arrange to lunch somewhere.

Hoping to hear from you soon.

Love to all,

from

Julian

1 Though Maclaren-Ross's relationship with Barbara Wimble had not yet ended, they appear to have agreed to live apart. Maclaren-Ross had then moved into this block of flats. One of his fellow tenants was the gangster Jacob Comacho, better-known as 'Jack Spot' (1916–96).

to DAN DAVIN

5d Hyde Park Mansions/London NW1

29-11-53

Dear Dan,

Thank you for your letter.

It's kind of you to have recommended me to Cumberlege.[1] I don't suppose for a moment he will want me for the job,[2] but if he does – and the fee isn't too impossibly low – I will certainly take it on. The difficulty will be to decide which writers can be classed as English; I would say Scots, Irish, Welsh, New Zealand, Australian, Canadian, yes; Americans, no. Then, also, I would try to find a story by each author which has not been anthologised too often: for instance, I know one by Pritchett (called 'The Goldfish') which appeared in *The Statesman* in 1942, but has never been included in any of his collections. Then what about Indians? At the time Mulk[3] and Subra[4] were writing their stories, India was still part of the Empire, so I suppose they could go in. Anyway, let's wait and see.

About Dylan.[5] His death was a terrible shock to me; for in an odd way, which Dylan himself understood well enough, he was my friend. I'm also happy to say that I had a drink and quite a long talk with him on the day before he went to America. I was the only person to ring up *Encounter* after his death and offer to do a personal memoir of him (the fee, of course, to go to his wife and children). Spender agreed straightaway, asked me to come down to the office for a special talk about it; then he went to Rome and while he was away, everyone sent in their solemn tributes and they went to press without me.

So now I'm doing a much longer piece, about the summer of 1943 when we worked together on scripts for Strand Films, and I shall try to show Dylan alive again, as he was 10 years ago. It is all I can do for him now, who did nothing for him when he was actually living.

As ever,

Julian

1 Geoffrey Cumberlege (1891–1979) was a colleague of Dan Davin's boss at Oxford University Press.
2 The project was an anthology of English short stories which Oxford University was planning to publish. Davin had suggested that the book should be edited by Maclaren-Ross.
3 The Indian writer Mulk Raj Anand (1905–2004), author of *Untouchable* (1935).
4 The Singhalese short-story writer, Alagu Subramaniam.
5 The poet Dylan Thomas (1914–53).

to JOHN LEHMANN
    12 Regents Park Terrace[1]/London NW1 (please note change of address)
                                                            6-1-54

Dear John,

Congratulations on No 1 of the *London Magazine*: particularly on MacNeice, Plomer, and the Elizabeth Bowen extract:[2] although this latter is so scintillating that it almost blinds and one requires dark glasses to read it.

I renew my offer of a contribution of some sort – and of a drink – when we can discuss possibilities of what shape this might take, other than that portion of autobiography on which you were not keen.

The best of luck anyway, for 1954.

As ever,

Julian

1 Maclaren-Ross had just moved to this tall, stucco-fronted building on the Camden Town side of Regent's Park.
2 The magazine, which had been launched under Lehmann's editorship, included an extract entitled 'The Dinner Party'. It appeared alongside work by the poet Louis MacNeice and the novelist William Plomer.

to DAN DAVIN

30-1-54

Dear Dan,

Sorry to hear you're in dock.[1]

Will certainly come and have a natter. Afternoon (3–6) always the most likely; will try to come Monday (four or fiveish) but will ring up if I can't manage that day. Books for *Times* (*Sunday*) just finished, but obituary of Sydney Greenstreet still impends (for *Punch*) and may delay visit for day or two.

All the best meantime,

from

Julian

1 Davin was a patient at Guy's Hospital in London, where he had, on 29 January 1954, undergone an operation to remove gallstones.

to RUPERT HART-DAVIS

29 Norfolk Square[1]/London W2

28-2-54

My dear Rupert,

Having printed two novel reviews by me (Jan. 11 and Jan. 25),[2] *The Sunday Times* now owes me something over £30. Their complicated system of payment, however, does not allow them to pay until a week following the end of the month in which the reviews appear.

Meanwhile I, the poor bloody critic, have to go without eating, and yesterday stayed in bed all day because I simply hadn't got the money to come out with or the six penny fare downtown. In no other walk of life could this possibly happen, and in the novel I'm writing I am doing my best to show up such abuses.[3]

Now, if I phone up the Accounts Dept. in your presence and instruct them to make out the cheque to your firm, could you advance me the money? The date for payment (which should be February 7th – 10 days time) can be definitely ascertained, also the exact sum; I can write a letter confirming the phone conversation and leave it in your office to post, so everything's covered.

Please help in this way; I'm really feeling half-faint with hunger and fury, and I've just twopence in my pocket. No use asking Russell[4] to do anything; he has made it quite clear that he disapproves of my habit of 'dunning editors', as he calls it: by which he means asking for prompt payment on acceptance: not, as in the present case, weeks after publication.

Yours ever,

Julian

1 Since Maclaren-Ross had resumed his old itinerant way of life, Barbara Wimble had probably agreed to let him use this as a postal address.

2 These included a rare hostile review of Kingsley Amis's novel *Lucky Jim*. 'Mr Amis,' Maclaren-Ross wrote, '...is not the only débutant to confuse farce with comedy, schoolboy grubbiness with wit.'

3 As he envisaged it, *Death and Business* – the alternative title for *Business and Desire* – would chronicle his experiences between 1944 and 1949. Late the previous year, the publishing company Hamish Hamilton had paid him an advance for the book, which was, however, never completed.

4 Leonard Russell, Literary Editor of the *Sunday Times*.

to JOHN LEHMANN

c/o Sunday Times/Kemsley House/London WC1

8-4-54

My dear John,

Thank you for your letter and for the cheque, which arrived with great promptitude (and open, to boot) this morning.

I'm glad you liked the review, though there are probably one or two slight alterations I'd like to make on the proof.[1] Perhaps you'd better send the proofs, and letters in future, to above address; as, after Easter, I hope to be leaving here[2] and have not yet been able to find a suitable flat.

Perhaps on my return from Bognor (about the 20th)[3] we might meet and have a drink together? I want to get on with a novel, also my 2nd vol. of autobiography; so am rather against doing any more criticism for a bit, with the exception of a fairly long essay on Patrick Hamilton which I've been thinking about for some time.[4] If this interests you at all, we might talk about it when we meet.

As ever,

Julian

1 The piece was published in the July 1954 edition of the *London Magazine*. It focused on three now forgotten novels, together with Brian Moore's *Judith Hearne*. Whilst praising Moore's 'considerable narrative gift' and 'genuine talent for characterisation', he criticised the Joycean influence which, he felt, 'often lands an air of pastiche to the novel'.

2 Probably 52 Norfolk Square, London.

3 He had, most likely, arranged to stay with C.K. and Lydia Jaeger, who still lived in Bognor Regis.

4   John Lehmann commissioned the essay. Entitled 'Mr Hamilton and Mr Gorse', it examined the novels about the villainous 'Ernest Ralph Gorse'. It was eventually published in the January 1956 edition of the *London Magazine*.

to DAN DAVIN

6-6-54

Dear Dan,

My new address, as promised and hope you come up soon. But let me know a day or two before so we can arrange a proper meeting.

Have just had the push from *The Sunday Times*. Your (Oxford's) Miss Murdoch[1] seems to have scored a winner, though I haven't read her novel yet. Paddy?![2]

Love to all,

from

Julian

1   Iris Murdoch was a graduate of the University of Oxford. Her picaresque novel *Under the Net* had just been published.
2   Maclaren-Ross was suggesting that the hard-living protagonist of her novel bore a resemblance to Dan Davin's boisterous New Zealand army friend Paddy Costello.

to JOHN LEHMANN

52 Norfolk Square / London W2

17-7-54

My dear John,

I thought you might like to see the enclosed memoir of Frank Harris in his last year.[1]

Sorry about the cut-about on pp. 4 and 5, but I'd included a story about Queensbury,[2] told me by my father, which on 2nd thoughts should perhaps not go in after all. The whole thing's just too long (nearer 7000 than 6) but I know exactly where to cut, should you want to print it.

As for the repetition of 'Bugger' (pp. 21–22) it should be cut and 'Sodomite' (a Harris expression, though the other was what he actually said) substituted: 'Bugger' need only be used once (the second time, emphasis).

If you could let me have a decision as soon as you can, I'd appreciate it, though I know you've tons of MSS to get through.

As ever,

Julian

1 The memoir 'A Visit to the Villa Edouard Sept' was published in the June 1955 edition of the *London Magazine*.
2 John Sholto Douglas (1844–1900), Marquis of Queensbury, father of Oscar Wilde's lover, Lord Alfred Douglas.

to JOHN LEHMANN

c/o D.M. Davin/103 Southmoor Rd/Oxford
27-8-54

My dear John,

Just a line to put above address in writing, in case I wasn't too clever over the phone the other day.

I have just lost girl, home, and everything else at a moment's notice,[1] so I need hardly stress the urgent need for the Frank Harris fee:[2] also, should you hear of any work that anybody wants done, that would be in my line, I hope you'll remember me.

Also, the Frank Harris proofs are ready, letters addressed to above will be forwarded to me immediately: so if I haven't given you a new address by then, please send them here.

As ever,

Julian

1 His long-term girlfriend, Barbara Wimble, had just left him, the break up of their relationship bringing about the end of their tenancy at 29 Norfolk Square.
2 The payment for 'A Visit to the Villa Edouard Sept', his memoir of meeting Frank Harris.

to ANTHONY POWELL

213 Woodstock Road/Oxford
29-8-54

My dear Tony,

Barbara left me last week, which means, as you'll appreciate, the complete disruption of a way of life that I've lived for the past 5 years, and the necessity to re-cast one's existence entirely: not so easy at the age of 42.

Apart from the emotional wrench, there is also an economic side to be considered: by pooling our earnings, life was made a little easier, and it was possible for me to settle down to write a book with an occasional excursion into short stuff to keep the boat afloat. Now my expenses will be doubled, and financial pressure also.

I have taken up a room at above address for at any rate a week, and plan to get down to work in Oxford for as long as the small sum of money lasts out.

Meanwhile, I propose – in order to supplement my income – a series of topical pieces on Oxford in the vacation for *Punch*.[1] Examples: St Giles' Fair (6–7 Sept.).[2]

Summer schools and foreign students etc.

Perhaps also a documentary/funny piece on the British Association (scientific congress) (general treatment), which opens tomorrow, might yield something: though here I'd need a press-card to get in.

There's no real need for a direct commission: if the *idea* appeals to you, I'm pretty sure the pieces would, and am perfectly prepared to go to work on them right away.

Perhaps you'd show this to M.M.[3] and talk it over with him, letting me know as soon as possible. I'm sorry to bother you, but the need is really urgent and transcends by far the ordinary one for money; the possession of 60 or 70 quid extra would at the moment make all the difference to my future and that of my work. So, though I don't want to belabour this point or invoke the Old Pal's Act, I do hope you'll be able to suggest some other work if the above idea fails to appeal: though I believe Oxford seen with a fresh eye might result in some of my best pieces.

Anyway, I'm sure I can rely on you to try your best.

As ever,

Julian

1 Anthony Powell didn't commission the proposed articles.
2 Though this article wasn't commissioned, Maclaren-Ross later featured St Giles' Fair as a backdrop to his novel *Until the Day She Dies* (1960).
3 Malcolm Muggeridge, editor of *Punch*.

PART III
(1954–56)

59 Southmoor Road
OXFORD

My Dear John, Thank you so much for your letter and the card:
yes, I do need the cash. This will mainly go in covering small
debts; but if some pieces I've sent to _Punch_ prove acceptable,
I will be in London again this week (Wed. or Thurs.) and hope
to see you then.

I've thought out a new plan for approaching
the Girl (or at anyrate producing a _rapprochement_), in
which you might play an impersonal intermediary rôle:
at anyrate I'd welcome your advice on it; and things
ought not to be left too long like this.

I agree with you about _Chariot of the Sun_:
it is not quite satisfactory in its present form, but that
was written some weeks ago, before I acquired some
startling new information that changes my whole
approach to the subject. (The presentation, however,
should still be, on the whole, apparently unemotional
and ironical: the narrator realizing — with the reader —
only at the end, the true meaning of the whole experience.)

I'll set to work on a piece on Hamilton (confining
myself mainly to the three Gorse novels, though I don't
think it should be printed as a review), and I think
you'll like it. 1500-2000 words? The title — following
that of one of the books concerned — would be:

Mr Hamilton and Mr Gorse.

As ever,

Julian

16·10·55

Despite all the kindness lavished on Maclaren-Ross by Dan and Winnie Davin, Oxford was an odd choice of refuge for him. Over the years he'd never made any secret of his dislike of the city and many of its inhabitants. Dressed in his flamboyant, increasingly threadbare get-up, he cut an incongruous figure outside his natural metropolitan habitat.

Invariably he seemed to approach each fresh situation, whether it involved a new publisher or girlfriend or novel, with optimism untarnished by more than a smidgen of self-knowledge. Sure enough, the optimism about his move to Oxford would prove groundless, his letters testifying to the developing friction between himself and the long-suffering Dan Davin.

Even though he'd left London, he continued to derive an irregular and paltry income from journalism commissioned by publications based in the capital. Besides writing for the *TLS* and *The Listener*, he produced reviews and parodies for the weekly humorous magazine *Punch*, to which Anthony Powell had just been appointed Literary Editor. In search of additional income, he took on a screenwriting job for Britain's first, soon-to-be-launched independent television channel. Once again exploiting his fluency in French, he also obtained a commission from the publishing firm Hamish Hamilton to translate *Maigret et la grande perche*, a detective novel by Georges Simenon.

Within only a few weeks of accepting the translation assignment, tension between him and the publisher was apparent. Worse still, on a work-related trip to London, he encountered the woman who would become the focal point of a damaging obsession. That woman was Sonia Orwell, widow of George Orwell, author of *Animal Farm* and *Nineteen Eighty-Four*. Unluckily for Maclaren-Ross, she had what appears to have been a well-earned reputation for giving admirers the runaround. From his initial encounter with her in the Wheatsheaf, he developed a fixation which swept him to the brink of madness. As well as compelling Dan and Winnie Davin to endure interminable monologues analysing his dealings with Sonia Orwell in painstaking detail, he decanted his thoughts about her into numerous letters to them and other friends. He even made plans to translate his operatic passion for her into a novel and a screenplay entitled *The Girl in the Spotlight*.

By the summer of 1955, his infatuation with her had yielded only a single lunch date, yet that was sufficient to encourage him to return to London so he could be close to her. First he had to raise the money to finance his relocation. He did this by hawking round a collection of miscellaneous writing – literary parodies, short stories and memoirs, many of them previously published in *Punch*. The volume, released under the title *The Funny Bone*, was bought by Elek Books, a small, newly founded publishing firm. With the advance from Elek, he set up home in the Park Court Hotel in Lancaster Gate. Shuttling between there and the West End pubs and drinking clubs, he plotted to win over the object of his fixation.

to HAMISH HAMILTON

59 Southmoor Road[1]/Oxford

13-10-54

Dear Mr Hamilton,

As per enclosed plan, I am engaged in collecting my short humorous and satirical pieces which appeared in *Punch* and elsewhere, but not so far in volume form.

These should make a book of 60–65,000 words (at the least), approximately the same size and genre as Arthur Marshall's *Nineteen to the Dozen* (which, by the way, I greatly enjoyed).

55,000 words of the proposed material will be ready in about a week or before; for the copies of the remainder, I am applying to editors of the magazines in which the pieces originally appeared.

To save time (which, to me, is always of the essence), I am circularising several publishers with this proposal; but, should you be interested, I will gladly give you first refusal.

All I would require would be:

(a) £120 advance, on acceptance.

(b) A decision within 7 days of receipt of the material amounting to 55,000 words.

The remainder would be delivered as soon as I have obtained the necessary copies (14 days?): a letter from *Punch* would of course be obtained giving permission to reprint; the other copyrights are mine.

I hope you will both be interested in this proposal, and that you may accept the book; for the advance would greatly help me to complete the novel *Business and Desire*, on which I hope to resume work when funds enable me to be independent of piece-work & literary journalism.

Yours sincerely,

J. Maclaren-Ross

Please return enclosed plan if project does not interest you.

1 Without informing Dan and Winnie Davin, Maclaren-Ross had rented a basement flat near to their house.

to RUPERT HART-DAVIS

Please note change of address: 59 Southmoor Road/Oxford

19-10-54

My dear Rupert,

With regard to my second volume of autobiography, I would like, now, to be free to offer this, when completed, to another publisher.

I regret, as I daresay you do, that various factors have made it impossible for us to continue a business relationship; but at the same time there can be little point in retaining an option to consider a book 'on terms to be arranged' when no chance exists of our coming to terms.

Therefore I ask you for a formal letter freeing me of the option, so that I may begin my negotiations well in advance, without loss of time.

Yours sincerely,

Julian

to RUPERT HART-DAVIS

59 Southmoor Road/Oxford

22-10-54

My dear Rupert,

Thank you for your letter of October 21st.

I appreciate the points you raise; at the same time our relations in the past have not been notable for their smoothness, and it is hard for me to forget an exchange of correspondence whose acrimony – not initiated by me, as the letters themselves prove – is unique in the history of my business relationships.

I am sorry you should have lost money on *The Weeping and the Laughter*: all the more since I have, myself, not made any. But I believe that with publication of the 2nd volume (irrespective of whose imprint it appears under), you will find a demand for Vol. 1 will arise, and be able, by re-issuing it, to recoup your losses and mine.

For the past year I have been obliged to plunge into literary journalism etc.; working at such unrelieved pressure that my health has been impaired and my private life, finally, wrecked; moreover, except for the extracts from my 2nd vol. which have appeared, or are due to appear, in magazines, I had no time left to get my own work done.

Now I have evolved a scheme which will bring in enough money to enable me to finish the book in comfort; this entails the collection in volume form (60–70,000 words) of 30 humorous and satirical pieces (parodies, short stories, sketches, etc.), many of which have appeared in *Punch* (whose proprietors have given me permission to reprint).

I have approached publishers, several of whom have expressed interest, providing I could give them an option on my 2nd vol. of autobiography; and since this is my only chance of obtaining enough money to complete the said volume in peace, it is not one I can afford to neglect.

It occurs to me, however, that I might offer this collection to you as a solution to our joint difficulties; it is not an unattractive proposition, and by publishing it you would be helping me: to, I trust, our mutual advantage in the future. Then, with goodwill on both sides, it would surely, as old friends, be possible to start afresh, since I concede that it would be preferable for the autobiographies to appear under the same colophon.

I enclose, therefore, a plan of contents; and, should you express interest, the material itself would follow directly I receive it from London, where it is at present stored.

£120 advance.

Decision within 7 days of receipt of MS.

Should you accept the collection, I would then propose an advance of £200 on the 2nd autobiographical volume, same royalty terms; and an appropriate clause could be inserted into the new contract.

Should you, however, not be interested, then I will have done all I can, and would ask you again to release me from your option, since by retaining it you would be preventing me from obtaining a means of financial support and continuing my work, which I feel sure you would not want to do.

Yours ever,

Julian

Not Good Enough For Punch

I. Burlesque[1]

'Good Lord, Jeeves'	(P.G. Wodehouse)
'Lansdowne and Grosvenor'	(Biographical Films)
'Planetoid 2003'	(Science Fiction)
'I am a Chimera'	(Christopher Isherwood)
'The Pursuit of Fame'	(Nancy Milford)
'Reading'	(Henry Green)

'Obituary for Ambrose'   (Eric Ambler)
'Maigret at Oxford'   (Georges Simenon)
'Weekend Competitions'   (*New Statesman*)
'Food for Thought'   (Culinary Books)

II. Plots, Ten and Six[2]
'The Episcopal Seal'   Strand[3]
The Gold Fish (originally broadcast as
'The Two Fish Spivs')   BBC
'The Almighty Dollar'[4]

1 These were all literary parodies.
2 A section devoted to short stories.
3 The short story 'The Episcopal Seal' was originally published in *Strand* magazine.
4 A short story, published in the 14 October 1953 issue of *Punch*.

to HAMISH HAMILTON

59 Southmoor Road/Oxford
25-10-54

Dear Hamilton,

Thank you for your letter of 15th October.

I'm sorry you couldn't see your way to doing the Miscellany (the middle section of which did actually contain 10 stories, 3 of which were 5,000, 3,500, and 7,000 words respectively).

With regard to *Business and Desire* it is kind of you to consider making me another advance, but I've decided never to accept again an advance on an unwritten work. I would not have done so then, or got into the tangle with Wingate, had I not believed that substantial sums of money were to be paid to me by film-producers who subsequently broke their words and cheated me.

Secondly, the portions of this novel which are written need drastic revision and rewriting in the light of later developments in the film-world which is its background; and the purpose of selling the collection I proposed to you was to obtain money enough to undertake this revision in peace and push on, therefore, to the book's conclusion.

However, now that you've taken over Simenon,[1] perhaps you might consider the possibility of my translating a short Maigret (which I would undertake for about £100). I don't know if you saw the translation

I did, for Lehmann, of Raymond Queneau's *Pierrot mon ami* in 1950, but it got pretty good notices.

> With kindest regards,
> Yours sincerely,
> J. Maclaren-Ross

1 The British rights to the work of Georges Simenon.

to RUPERT HART-DAVIS

59 Southmoor Road/Oxford
26-10-54

My dear Rupert,

Many thanks for yours of October 25th.

I enclose forthwith the pieces in my possession down here, as marked on the plan (20,000 words approx.), which may give you some idea of the general form; and directly my cases, containing the remainder, are sent to me from London, I will dispatch the other MSS to you. (Any day now – I hope!)

I'm very glad indeed that you're prepared to consider my suggestion, and will do all I can to co-operate if you decide to accept the collection.

> With best regards,
> As ever,
> Julian

Please keep the enclosed safely, as they're the only copies I have.

to HAMISH HAMILTON

59 Southmoor Road/Oxford
28-10-54

Dear Hamilton,

Thank you for your letter of October 27th.

I don't blame Mme Simenon at all for wanting to vet a translation; for, though Simenon on the face of it looks easy, many translators get an off-beat feeling into the rhythms that prevent the work from reading naturally: it is precisely this fault that I have underlined in my parody *Maigret at Oxford* (shortly to appear in *Punch*).[1]

I agree to the terms you proposed and would be prepared to translate a dozen pages of *Maigret et la grande perche* as a sample, at the appropriate fee; the only snag is condition 3.

I have no typewriter and have typed none of my stuff since 1943; all editors and publishers have the stuff set up from my MSS (indeed Hart-Davis' printers not only set my autobiography from the MS, but returned the holograph copy to me without a blemish on it, and still bound). This applies to all my work, novels as well as articles, stories, etc.

To employ a typist would, I fear, render the work of translating uncommercial by reason of the cost; besides, if I were to break my rule in one case I would have to break it in others, thus giving myself either extra work or added expense: to say nothing of the time factor.

However, I hope that you may reconsider this condition, or think of some way round the difficulty.

With kind regards,

Yours sincerely,

J. Maclaren-Ross

1 'Maigret at Oxford' appeared in the 8 December 1954 issue of *Punch*. The piece consistently parodies what Maclaren-Ross regarded as the 'offbeat' and unnatural rhythms imposed on Simenon's writing by previous translators. A good example of this occurs in the following extract: 'The street they were walking down was certainly dark, and very long. Called Merton, if Maigret properly understood.'

to HAMISH HAMILTON

59 Southmoor Road/Oxford

2-11-54

Dear Hamilton,

Thank you for your letter and the copy of *Maigret et la grande perche*, just received.[1]

I'm glad you agree that a MS version is possible, and I'll have something ready for Mme Simenon very shortly.

By the way, you might tell them that it was I who wrote the article on Simenon in the special French number of the *TLS*, just after *The Stain on the Snow* was published.[2]

With kind regards,

Yours sincerely,

J. Maclaren-Ross

1   Writing on 1 November 1954, Hamish Hamilton had given the go-ahead for Maclaren-Ross to translate a sample section of the beginning of *Maigret et la grande perche*. Hamilton agreed to let Maclaren-Ross submit a handwritten extract which the company would then pay to turn into a typescript.

2   Maclaren-Ross's essay, 'The Simenon Cycle', appeared in the 13 March 1953 issue of the *Times Literary Supplement*. Simenon's *The Stain on the Snow* was published by Routledge and Kegan Paul.

to HAMISH HAMILTON

59 Southmoor Road/Oxford

3-11-54

Dear Hamilton,

I enclose 20 translated pages from *Maigret et la grande perche* (approx. 5,000 words).

This is a very rough, quickly done version, but it will perhaps give Mme Simenon an idea of what abilities I possess; and having a lot of work on hand I thought the sooner it was done, the better.

I have been guided throughout by the principle of making text read as naturally in English as I could in such as short space of time.

I have rendered 'La Grande Perche' as 'Long Tina', because this has the correct underworld sound for England (I know of a 'Long Flora'), whereas 'The Beanpole' sounds all wrong. Another title would, in any case, have to be found for the book itself.

I would also advise against using, for this country, the sort of chapter titles ('In which Maigret' etc.) to be found in the original.

I apologise for the few erasures and insertions; speed must be my excuse. There will be none in the final version.

I would be greatly obliged if you could send me a cheque for the enclosed, to be deducted from the final payment should I do the complete translation; then, if Mme Simenon does not approve, we're all square and no harm done.[1]

Yours sincerely,

J. Maclaren-Ross

1   Hamilton complied with Maclaren-Ross's request, and sent him a cheque on 4 November 1954.

to HAMISH HAMILTON

59 Southmoor Road / Oxford
11-11-54

Dear Hamilton,

Thank you for your letter.

I see Mme Simenon's points, though of course trying to render the 'rhythm' of the original is what makes most translations read unnaturally. The whole point of Simenon's style is its colloquial ease, and this is apt to get lost if one sticks to the order of the French sentences when translating.

Another difficulty is slang. This book is full of it, and all the pungency will be lost if the treatment's too polite and the English equivalents are not given. Then again, French lower-class people don't necessarily use bad grammar, while the English ones do. This tends to make a translation seem unreal.

However, I am returning the 5,000 words with corrections; more than these, I cannot do.

I'd like to know definitely by next week whether I'm commissioned to do the whole book or not, as this isn't clear from your last letter; and I'd rather put the idea aside altogether if I can't get to work on it at once, as I've a lot of stuff on hand.

I may say that I don't like 'Lanky Liz' at all: it sounds like an old comic film and would not like to take the blame for affixing this nickname, however.

Looking forward to hearing from you,

Yours ever,

J. Maclaren-Ross

to HAMISH HAMILTON

59 Southmoor Road / Oxford
15-11-54

Dear Hamilton,

I've received a letter this morning from Mr Richard Brain[1] re the Simenon translation, and am writing him separately on several points.

I am now ready to embark on *Maigret et la grande perche* at 2 guineas per 1000 wds, and would welcome a cheque for £40 down as per your letter of October 27th.

The 10 guineas you have already paid me might be deducted from the final payment, on delivery of complete MS.

A copy of *Maigret Right and Wrong*, which I understand is now on sale, might also not come amiss, if you can spare one.

As ever,

J. Maclaren-Ross

1   One of the editors at Hamish Hamilton.

to RICHARD BRAIN

59 Southmoor Road/Oxford

16-11-54

Dear Mr Brain,

Thank you for your letter of November 15th.

I still have a copy of the French and will now proceed with the work. I think that between us we might be able to manage Mme Simenon in the last analysis; while attempting to keep as much as possible to the order of the French sentences, it is important to avoid an unnatural ring in English, and sometimes concessions will have to be made with regard to this: otherwise Simenon's easy style will become distorted by his wife's well-meant insistence on following the original. I will mark examples of what I mean on a future copy.

I think what you say about the initial conversation is right, but the gentility must be 'genteel' and not genuine. As to underworld slang, it's important to use the current English equivalents and not either Americanisms or terms current in the late 18th century, as appear frequently in translations from the French.

I still don't like to be associated with 'Lanky Liz'; after all, it's I who am going to get the blame for anything of the sort, and I think Mme S. would be wise to leave such choices to me, as an acknowledged expert in the vernacular style. Why won't she have 'Lofty', which would be correct? And why 'Liz' when the girl's name is Ernestine?

However, we'll see. Also about a generic title: *Maigret and Lanky Liz* would be inconceivably awful.

Sincerely,

J. Maclaren-Ross

to RICHARD BRAIN

59 Southmoor Road/Oxford

18-11-54

Dear Mr Brain,

Herewith the missing links, also end of Chapter 4.

Chapter 5 is almost complete, but needs a bit of revision.

Wherever there's an asterisk, I'd like you to look at the French and advise me; we can go over the typescript together later.

Sorry I could not get up to town after all this week; hope to be up next Tues. or Wed. and will ring you then.

Sincerely,

J. Maclaren-Ross

to HAMISH HAMILTON

59 Southmoor Road/Oxford

18-11-54

Dear Hamilton,

Thank you for your letter of 17th Nov. and the cheque enclosed under separate cover.

I can find no mention, however, in your initial letter of 28th October, of the translation having to go to Mme Simenon for a final OK; it says that her approval would be given (or the reverse) on 'a dozen pages or so of a Maigret novel'. (I did 20 pp.)

Nor did it mention that she would make extensive corrections as she did, and that I would therefore have to revise these initial pages in such as way that they are well-nigh unreadable and will have to be copied out again. My letter of 11th Nov. made it clear that I expected definite approval on the revised version of these 5,000 words.

In Mr Brain's letter there is a mention that Mme Simenon will wish to have a 'quick check' on the final translation, but nothing about more revision etc.

However, with good will on all sides, I've no doubt that we'll be able to arrange matters satisfactorily: my point is that while I shall of course want to revise the script myself on *minor points*, I am not prepared for extensive corrections by Mme Simenon (as in the first 5,000 words) which will mean my having, virtually, to do the whole translation twice.

If this is to be the case, it is not anywhere in the terms of my commission and would have to be done at her own expense. I hope too that all of the corrections will not be as silly as 'she wore a decent frock' for 'elle portait une robe correcte', or we shall all look fools – particularly me.

I think, too, that in view of all this, a note should be included: 'Translation revised and presented under the supervision of Mme Georges Simenon,' because I don't want to take back the can for anything she insists on that I might disagree with – such as 'Lanky Liz'.

Meantime I hope to have some more ready soon. How about *The Wife of Sad Freddie* for a title? It's in the Simenon tradition.

Yours ever,

J. Maclaren-Ross

PS I haven't had a copy of *Maigret Right or Wrong* yet.

to ANTHONY POWELL

59 Southmoor Road / Oxford

19-11-54

My dear Tony,

Many thanks for your letter of the 16th Nov.

I am writing you in reply this very detailed letter, and I would like you to *take up the points one by one with the Editor,*[1] *and let me know the decision in your next.*

(1) Sexton Blake.[2] Yes: I'll get this done v. soon[3] and, on arrival, will you arrange for payment, because – although, as you will see later, I am no longer, at least temporarily, on the rocks – I do need some new clothes, and every little helps, as the Old Woman said as she wee-wee-wee'd into the sea.

I'm having, however, some difficulty in getting Blakes: only two a month come out now, but I've sent the children of friends[4] out to look, and hope to have a batch in over the weekend. You'll be glad to hear that the sex-angle has been taken up, so your original point is covered. The only one I managed to get begins: 'It was a girl's shapely legs and a girl's curly head that really started the whole thing'; it also contains this gem: 'The cork flew off with a pleasing pop and Tinker expertly filled the four glasses already placed in readiness. It was not often that the Baker Street pair celebrated in champagne at their own home, but this was a very special occasion...' As you see there'll be plenty of material: including satire directly aimed at people like myself, who evaluate seriously in the *TLS* thriller-writers like Hammett, Wallace etc.

(2) Perhaps in the other *TLS* number you would like to print my 'Lit. Slug Books Four',[5] as the theme of this seems to connect up, and my 'Middle' will of course be anonymous.[6]

(3) Simenon parody. The new Maigret (published by Hamilton) came out last week, so perhaps – coinciding with the Simenons' London visit – this might be the next of my pieces to come out.

A propos: I am going to do the next Maigret translation; and I now see that the off-beat note that I have caricatured is due to the influence of Mme Simenon (apparently an American) who insists on supervising and correcting all English versions. (Example: 'Elle portait une robe correcte' – of a reformed prostitute. My version: 'She was respectfully dressed'. Mme S.'s correction: 'She wore a decent frock'.) She also insists on the 'rhythm' of the original being followed implicitly, and that the order of the French sentences must be strictly adhered to.

Possibly, publication of the parody within the next week or two would make her see her own folly, and you'd be helping me in this way.

(4) Two ideas for future special parody-numbers of *Punch*: which, if they are adopted, I being a business-man, would expect some emolument:

A *Saturday Book* number[7] (which speaks for itself).

A *Punch* number: in which we all parody each other (I'd better do Carson[8] though, as he'll be furious but I can handle him. I've a pip of an idea for this, too. You know he changed his writing-name from Peter Brooke to A.C. but there were two other people called the former: the theatrical producer and another author. Well I'd have 3 people called Carson – not including the narrator – meeting at the Cannes Film Festival or somewhere...) I think this whole idea would be a Wow – or Gimmick, to use a more hateful and modern expression.

(5) Parodies for the future (to be written and delivered, of course, when you like).

a) Evelyn Waugh. I was very interested in what you wrote me, though it seems goodness knows how sad. I think however a parody called 'Waugh Among the Ruins' (remember *Waugh in Abyssinia*):[9] Guy[10] watching entranced as the mushroom-shapes blossom in the ambient air above Grosvenor House etc.; with Grimes[11] etc. appearing reproachfully before their creator during the Atom War, and the heroine – a strong woman, called Helena,[12] of the new Amazon Race, nostalgically showing photographs of the Royal Family and her mother dressed as a deb, to the hero in an underground cave... (or something).

(a) The Scarlet Pimpernel:[13] helping refugee aristocrats to escape from the Welfare State to the New World. Sir Percy would of course be an English film-star, knighted, naturalised American; and his henchmen would be the cast from a Pimpernel film... Title: 'That D****d Elusive Pimp-er-nel'.

(a) The Saint.[14] Not only did Leslie Charteris, the author, contribute a pompous preface to the Saint Omnibus, saying that he was under-valuated as a writer etc.; but the Saint himself has become a real figure so to speak: there are Saint clubs in the USA and the Saint himself is supposed to edit a Crime Magazine, the first English Number of which came out last month over here...

And that is all as far as business is concerned; but overleaf please find some personal notes. If you could let me know about above suggestions etc. I'd be obliged, as I'm likely to be snowed-under soon. I'm trying to budget work to be done, however much in the future.

Oh, and one more idea:

(a) A quasi-serious article on literary page, about distinguished lit-erary figures who've done *Punch* parodies (Thackeray[15] etc.) – unless this has already been covered.

I was very amused about the letter from Gerald Hamilton,[16] whom I know, in this week's *Punch* (there's also – unless I'm much mistaken – a portrait of him, when younger, in Cockburn's[17] novel *Beat the Devil*, as the muddling master-criminal Petersen: played by Robert Morley in the film-version). I liked also Price's parody of the *London Mag*:[18] which contained a crack at me; all the more enjoyable because unintentional, for he couldn't have known that Lehmann was doing an extract from my autobiography concerning a visit to Frank Harris in 1930![19]

Norman Collins kept his promise[20] and has engaged me at £20 a week, for 3 months to start with; but it's unlikely I shall get the sack then, because I've just done a script for them and am starting on another:[21] so by next week I shall have more than cleared a month's money. I know you'll be pleased to hear about this: that's why I'm telling you, but I don't have to say it's *confidential* – for reasons you may guess. Outstanding debts, to people too close for comfort, have already reduced this income, recently, by half...

Incidentally, it's been on my conscience for years that I owe you a tenner which you kindly lent me at a terrible, snow-bound moment;

and I would like – if I may – to settle this when I've made my final arrangements for this new collection of bits and pieces (including the outstanding *Punch* material).

I would also like – with your permission – to dedicated this book to you personally, in acknowledgement of friendship and the help you've always given me;[22] and I'd like – in the Author's Note – to include a special note of thanks to Muggeridge for being so kind during a very tense period, which I would not like to (but doubtless shall) live through again. Would you ask him if he has any objection?

I hope soon to be in London again and am fixing up a new flat in Baker St (the Blake country), and hope that you will come and stay a night or two when you are also up; we can then crack a bottle (of bubbly, of course) and have a bloody good natter.

I really do apologise for the length of this, but I don't expect to be able to write a letter of more than 10 lines for the next six months, so thought I'd get all this off my chest.

I'm doing the Lustgarten Trial Series (recently parodied in *Punch*) for Collins's company, oddly enough!

As ever,

Julian

1 Malcolm Muggeridge.

2 The Sherlock Holmes-inspired hero of a long-running series of detective stories, written by numerous authors. Like Holmes, Sexton Blake was based in Baker Street in central London.

3 The Sexton Blake parody was either rejected by *Punch*, or else it was never completed.

4 Dan and Winnie Davin's daughters.

5 'Lit. Slug Books Four', a fictionalised account of his time as a book reviewer, was published in *Punch* on 27 August 1955.

6 During that period, contributions to the *Times Literary Supplement* were anonymous.

7 *The Saturday Book* was an annual hardback miscellany, edited by Leonard Russell. Three of Maclaren-Ross's stories had appeared in it. The third issue, published in October 1943, had featured 'Are You Happy in Your Work'; the fourth issue, published in October 1944, had featured 'The Two Retired Chess Champions and the Girl Who Preferred to Play Draughts'; and the fifth issue, published in October 1945, had featured 'Welsh Rabbit of Soap'.

8 Anthony Carson, the pseudonymous humorist and travel writer whose work appeared in *Punch*. Maclaren-Ross had first got to know Carson over twenty years earlier.

9 Published in 1936, *Waugh in Abyssinia* was one of its author's seven travel books.

10 Guy Crouchback, protagonist of the *Sword of Honour* trilogy of novels (1952–61).

11 Captain Grimes, a roguish character from Waugh's first novel, *Decline and Fall*.

12 A reference to *Helena*, Waugh's novel about St Helena, published in 1950.

13 The 1905 historical novel by Baroness Orczy. A popular film adaptation of it, starring Leslie Howard and produced by Alexander Korda, was released in 1934.

14 The hero of a series of adventure novels, written by Leslie Charteris (1907–93).

15 William Thackeray (1811–63), author of *Vanity Fair*.

16 The confidence trickster Gerald Hamilton (188?–1970), is widely acknowledged as the model for the character 'Mr Norris' in Christopher Isherwood's *Mr Norris Changes Trains*. Yet the 17 November 1954 edition of *Punch* carried a long letter from him, headlined 'The Importance of Not Being Norris'. 'Sir,' the letter begins, 'The rumour that I am the Mr Norris who changed trains is again given currency, this time in an article by Mr Claud Cockburn. I do not know how the rumour got around. Christopher Isherwood always said that it was a composite character...' Hamilton would, of course, undermine his claims by publishing a memoir called *Mr Norris and I* (Allan Wingate, 1956). The article to which Hamilton refers had featured in the 27 October 1954 issue of the magazine. Entitled 'The Belated Oscar Award', it described the unveiling ceremony for a plaque in honour of Oscar Wilde's residence in Tite Street, London. Hamilton was one of many well-known people present.

17 Under the pseudonym 'James Helvick', the Irish writer Claud Cockburn (1904–81) wrote *Beat the Devil*, which was turned into a successful film, starring Humphrey Bogart.

18 Maclaren-Ross is referring to a humorous article by the regular *Punch* contributor R.G.G. Price. Under the title 'Cast List', Price wrote that 'The *London Magazine*, with that horrible coyness that spread from copywriting to culture in the days of *Horizon*, heads its notes on contributors: "In Case You Don't Know". Well, I didn't know that Richard Drain is starting his third year reading English at Sidney Sussex, that Sofronis Sofroniou is reading for an MA or that David Collinson has sold only one poem and this is it. Nor do I care...'

19 After a mildly amusing sequence of spoof biographies, parodying the *London Magazine*'s 'In Case You Don't Know' section, R.G.G. Price went on to lampoon the type of writing featured in the publication. 'As I assemble my team,' he wrote, 'I begin to see their works, the translations from more Greek poets who have not yet learned English, the pages torn from a book of forthcoming reminiscences describing a visit to Norman Douglas or André Gide, the very straightforward story of the hot, childhood day when the other little goatherd fell down a crevasse and left the narrator unable to forget how he turned away to eat a handful of dates (the very same handful of dates that provides the title of the story)...' Maclaren-Ross's forthcoming contribution to the *London Magazine* only served to underline the accuracy of Price's humour. The article was, after all, an excerpt from the second volume of its author's reminiscences – an excerpt focusing on the day when the young Maclaren-Ross had visited not Norman Douglas nor André Gide but the comparably decadent Frank Harris.

20 In his role as Managing Director of the Associated Television Company, Collins had promised to hire Maclaren-Ross as a screenwriter.

21 Maclaren-Ross was adapting Edgar Lustgarten's books about famous English trials. His scripts were never filmed.

22 Anthony Powell gave permission for the book to be dedicated to him.

to RICHARD BRAIN

59 Southmoor Road/Oxford
20-11-54

Dear Mr Brain,

Thank you for your letter of 19th November, and the contract enclosed, which I am returning (signed) herewith.

2 business points first of all:

(1) The date for completion (Clause 2).

In Mr Hamilton's initial letter, & subsequent correspondence, there was no mention of a stipulated time for completion; I have no reason to think that the translation *won't* be finished by 31st Dec. and (while I realise that delays are covered in a bracketed clause) I'll do my best to let you have it either then or before. On the other hand I don't want to feel pursued by time's winged bloody chariot, before the translation (film-work), but which I didn't think would descend upon me yet.

I may add that I'm quite as anxious to get it done quickly as you are to have it, for the money I shall receive on completion is budgeted for a special personal purpose,[1] apart from anything else.

(2) Apropos of the final payment: the word 'approved' (clause 3).

I repeat that I did *not* accept originally the idea that Mme Simenon would have to approve the *complete* script, and I don't now. That is to say that, while I'm prepared to make any (sensible) minor amendments that she will want me to make and to be as sympathetic to her point-of-view as is consistent with my views on what a translation should be like (trenchantly expressed, fortnightly, during my 8 months tenure on *The Sunday Times* book-page), I'm not prepared to wait until she has given her approval before being paid, and my signature on the contract must be taken to agree to normal publishers' agreement and approval *only*. (A matter of form, since I'm not going to send in a lot of non-sense and expect to be paid for it.)

I would be glad to hear from you that my views on these points are fully understood.

Indeed, I would like to meet you next weekend in Oxford very much. Please let me know where and when we can meet, but preferably over drinks, as I hate talking dry.

I think your letter received yesterday was very sensible, and I'm sure that, between us, a satisfactory conclusion may be reached. I have now adopted 'Lofty' instead of 'Lanky Liz'.

It had not been clear to me that Mme Simenon's comments were only suggestions, and it was perhaps the touch of the royal command which I (perhaps erroneously) detected, that put my back up.

I was brought up in France, read Simenon years before he was known in England, was one of the first people to recommend his books when they came out here, and would not have been chosen by the *TLS* to do a middle on him had they not thought I understood the spirit of his work. It is that spirit that I want to put over, and it would be a pity if his easy style were made to look awkward by Mme S.'s over-zealous insistence on retaining the construction of the French sentences throughout. That is what we will have to make her understand.

About the MS. I don't like writing on wide-spaced lines; in any case, I've decided to do the MS (with my corrections) in order to save time, and have it typed quickly in London for me if I can't find a satisfactory typist here (if you don't mind doing this). Then the typed portions could be returned to me, as they are done for my minor alterations; and very soon a complete typescript would be ready first for Mme S., and then the printer. Naturally, if you were to have it done for me, the cost of typing would be deducted from the final payment and it would be at my expense. Let me know, please, what you think of this.

Looking forward to our meeting,

Yours sincerely,

J. Maclaren-Ross

PS Yes, thanks; I've now received the new Maigret & am reading it; we'll talk about it when we meet.

1   Maclaren-Ross was anxious to move to London in order to be close to Sonia Orwell (1918–80), widow of George Orwell, who lived on Percy Street. After encountering her in the Wheatsheaf earlier that month, he had developed an obsession with her.

to RUPERT HART-DAVIS

59 Southmoor Road/Oxford

20-11-54

My dear Rupert,

I'm sorry not to have written to you until now about the *Punch* book, but I've been trying to collect my things – containing the rest of the material and a lot of effects, which I can't afford to lose – from London.

When my girl Barbara and I agreed to part, she stayed behind in the flat and promised to send my things on when I needed them. By the time I'd been able to give her a definite address in Oxford, she had moved but had left the cases behind, having given British Railways instructions to call, fetch them, and forward them to me here. BR told her they had called repeatedly and got no answer at the house, which seemed to be empty: the proprietor has apparently gone away.

Barbara then phoned me at a friend's house, knowing that I still had the keys to the house and flat, and asked me to send them to her, when she would arrange everything with B.R. and have the cases forwarded immediately.

I sent the keys by registered post on November 4th and have heard nothing since. I wrote to her last Saturday and have had no reply.

I don't know what she can be doing, but I wonder if this would work: this is if you wouldn't mind doing it.

If *you* rang her up in her office, as my publisher and said you were awaiting these MSS, that you understood she was forwarding them to me and when could you expect receipt, it would stir her into action as nothing else seems to. Relations between us, by the way, are perfectly friendly, and there's no reason why she should not have kept her promise: but just in case she means to let the matter slide, she wouldn't like to think that somebody else – particularly my publisher – was aware of her remissness: and at any rate she'll let you know what she means to do.

Her name is Barbara Wimble, and she's secretary to the managing director of Films de France Ltd,[1] 78 Dover Street: Tel. Hyde Park 8866. She's always alone in the office between 2 and 3.

If you *could* ring her, I'd be much obliged to you as a friend, apart from the business angle, because these cases contain things very precious to me and I'm getting terribly worried about them.

As ever,
Julian

PS Quite agree about using another title for the book, by the way.

1   A Mayfair-based film distribution company.

to DAN DAVIN

59 Southmoor Road/Oxford

21-11-54

My dear Davin,

The purpose of this letter is to make you acquainted with my reactions (aroused at last) to certain conversations which we have had, the subject of which (initiated by you) dealt with the shortcomings of my character, attitude to life etc. These reactions are set out in a letter because our meetings usually take place either in your home, and I was taught never to be rude to my host, or in the Victoria[1] where (to quote your own words) you feel that you are more or less the maître de céans.[2]

I sympathise with this latter assumption; although, when I was in the same position in the Wheatsheaf, I was too polite (no self-complacency implied: just a question of upbringing) to show my irritation when, as an unknown Colonial writer, you would barge in – only too frequently – on the assembled company and glowering, ignoring introductions – started, having had too many pints elsewhere, to talk about bloody pommies etc. There was a particularly embarrassing morning when you brought in your ill-behaved drunken chum Costello,[3] who started to bang his fist on the counter and talked, at the top of his voice, about the fucking English. The proprietor (Red[4] or it might have been, at this time, Arthur[5]) wanted to have him thrown out, and I had to go round quietly and explain that, since you were a friend of mine, and he was a friend of yours, this must not happen. Of course you'll say that you've no recollection of this, because you claim that you've such a bad memory (odd, however, that you remember so well any bad behaviour on the part of a friend of *mine*, whose guilt really consists in that he may have expressed opinions which you disagreed with – or, sorry, I expect you'd rather I wrote: 'opinions with which you disagreed').

Of course, in a way, it's odd, too, that I should have been such a fool as to put myself in a position where, being down, I could be kicked by you. (An old pommie custom forbids the kicking of a man who's down.) But, though I'm grateful for your initial, magnificent welcome on Aug. 21st and for your frequent generous outbursts of genuine sympathy with my plight (restrained, immediately afterwards, by your uncontrollable desire to be regarded as, in your own words of highest praise, 'a wily New Zealander'), I cannot forget that these were soon qualified by your frank statement that it had been a bore to put up with me, and to put me up (though this was at your own invitation): also that you described 'my stupid troubles with my girlfriend' as too puerile, really, to be taken seriously – when you must have known, as an intelligent man, that they represented a difficult turning point in my life.

Last night, coupled with this evening, was the last straw. Again – though refusing to cite a particular example – you accused me of consistent bad manners towards the people you've introduced me to down here: when pressed, you were pleased to state, only, that my main solecism consisted of 'talking too bloody much' in their presence. It naturally didn't occur to you – since *you* are the colossal egoist you accuse me of being – that I might find the Oxford manner towards myself, as a stranger, intolerably casual and devoid of the conventional social graces which I've been led to take for granted in any polite milieu (not really surprising, I realise now, since most of the existent luminaries have worked their way up from some grimy provincial town by their ability to specialise in a particular subject). You could not understand that to hear childish sensitivity expressed towards London criticism – by people whose one distinction it is to have written an academic study of some creative writer or poet (long dead, of course) – might be distasteful to me, since no professional author would dare to voice such sentiments, as this is contrary to metropolitan etiquette.

I used to believe that anyone should be entitled to express his opinion of a person newly introduced, without being sharply reprimanded in a pompous and lordly tone by his old friends – particularly when the author of the reprimand is host at the time. Perhaps – contrary to this belief – I should have checked you from expressing *your* opinion in the old days: it might have made you into a better, less conceited man – though, doubtless, a less successful one in the sphere you now occupy.

I could go on much longer with reminders of your own bad behaviour and thoughtlessness, but will cite only one example: how you, about a year ago, got Boris[6] to phone up my flat (instead of phoning yourself), and convey a sort of Royal Command that I must immediately, at 6 p.m., come to the Mandrake Club, because the Great Man had arrived in London at a moment's notice and hadn't much longer to wait; how I, having worked night and day, and gone to bed at 4 p.m., got up as a matter of course and phoned Barbara (who'd also worked all day in an office) to go down and try to keep you entertained until I got ready and found a cab downtown; how you at once ran me down to Barbara in the presence of an Oxford stranger, censoring my stupidity in dealing with publishers, and this in a place where anyone might overhear and where your drunken pronouncements might injure my professional character; how, when I arrived, I was greeted several times with 'Hullo Monster'[7] – a term (doubtless) of affection, which is all right in Oxford but misplaced in London, where I had to keep up a position of rather more importance (as a creative, professional writer and critic) than that which you hold here; how you were going to phone us (which you didn't do) at home to say where you'd be later, and how we had to go back to the flat and wait for a call that never came, instead of enjoying ourselves at a restaurant or club – etc. etc.

I would never have cited such petty instances (annoying though they were) had you not brought up everything you could think of against me at a time when I was practically defenceless, desperate, and in need of bolstering up instead of taking down.

I will say 3 things in conclusion:

(1) That, instead of writing an article which could have been profitable and must be done tomorrow instead, I have sat up writing this stupidity because your cumulative attitude has made me too angry, at last, to concentrate on anything else (and, incidentally, your protestations of tiredness induced by work, staying up late etc., make me feel, considering the strain of my own life and the hours I keep, rather like Roger Bannister[8] listening to the complaints of someone who's had to run to catch a bus.)

(2) I shall be in the Victoria, I dare say, since I've made an arrangement with George (unsponsored by you) to cash the cheques I receive; so that, if there's anything you'd like to say to me à propos this letter, you will have the opportunity of doing so.

(3) In view of your insistence last night that Cary[9] should be paid £5 which I owe him, I will do so at once instead of buying myself a pair of shoes; I'd hate you to be held responsible for introducing a Bohemian scrounger to the sacrosanct city of Oxford, but you may be sure that I won't tell Cary that you had to prod me into repayment, because I don't think, somehow, that he'd like you for doing that, and I know how much you value his opinion.

As ever,
Sincerely,
J. Maclaren-Ross

1 The Victoria Arms, the Davins' favourite local pub, situated conveniently near to their home.
2 'Master of the house.'

3   Paddy Costello.
4   Redvers 'Red' Glendenning, manager of the Wheatsheaf during the Second World War.
5   Arthur Harrodine took over the managership of the Wheatsheaf from Redvers Glendenning.
6   Boris Watson, owner of the Mandrake Club (see note 1, p. 121).
7   An in-joke, referring to Maclaren-Ross's 14 July 1953 letter to Davin in which he had complained that he'd been portrayed as a 'monster' in Rayner Heppenstall's autobiographical novel *The Lesser Infortune*.
8   Roger Bannister (1929–) was famous for being the first runner to cover a mile in less than four minutes.
9   The novelist Joyce Cary, a friend of the Davins. They introduced him to Maclaren-Ross, who was an ardent admirer of his work. Maclaren-Ross quickly antagonised Cary.

to DAN AND WINNIE DAVIN

59 Southmoor Road/Oxford
21-11-54

Mr J. Maclaren-Ross regrets that, owing to immediate pressure of work, he finds himself unable to accept your kind invitation for Wednesday November 24th.

to RICHARD BRAIN

59 Southmoor Road/Oxford
24-11-54

Dear Mr Brain,

Thank you for yesterday's date & the signed contract enclosed.[1]

For our meeting in Oxford,[2] I would suggest the Turl St bar of the Mitre Hotel at 11.30. You will know me because I carry, invariably, a malacca cane with a silver top.

Looking forward to seeing you,

Yours sincerely,

J. Maclaren-Ross

1   Brain had notified him that the translation had to be delivered by the end of the year, and that payment would be issued on delivery. Mme Simenon's approval would not have to be secured first.
2   Brain, who was due to stay at Lincoln College, Oxford, had suggested that they meet for a drink.

59 Southmoor Road/Oxford
1-12-54

My dear Rupert,

At last my box has arrived from London, and I find that Barbara has not enclosed one single copy of *Punch* containing my contributions!

However, I've written to *Punch* today, sending money to cover price and postage on these back numbers and asking them to send the copies *directly to you*: so with any luck you should receive them on Friday. (These contain the nine items marked 'V' on the enclosed plans).

Meanwhile I enclose herewith:

(1) 'The Gondolier of Death' (typescript)
(2) '35 Years of Cinema Going' (typescript)[1]
(3) 'The Ancient Captain' (published proof)[2]
(4) 'The Gold Fish' (2 versions – original and broadcast – for your choice)
(5) 'The Shoestring Budget' (MSS)[3]
(6) 'But and Bon with Burke or Hare' (MSS)[4]
(7) 'Lit. Slug Books Four' (galley proof)
(8) *'2nd Lieutenant Lewis' (galley proof)[5]
(9) *'The Triple Life of Major Trask' (contained in 2 copies of Pie)[6] (under separate cover)
(10) *'Warning to OCTU Wallahs'[7]
(11) Letter from Bradbury or Agnew[8] (giving permission to reprint)

With the items published in the *Punches* which you'll receive, this is all except for 'The Episcopal Seal' (5,000 wds) and 'I Liked the Army',[9] both of which I'm trying to get from her. However, as I said in an earlier letter, I would ask you to make a decision on the present material – to include, of course, those in the *Punches*.

The army stuff marked with an asterisk is included because people are always asking why I don't reprint these particular items.

As ever,
Julian

1 The piece was never published and has since been lost.
2 A spoof essay about a fictitious writer of boys' adventure stories, published in the 31 May 1954 edition of *Punch*.
3 A thinly disguised account of a brief period Maclaren-Ross spent working for the Vandyke Picture Corporation, a low-budget British film company. 'The Shoestring Budget' was eventually published in *The Funny Bone*.

4   This piece, evidently about the early-nineteenth-century graverobbers William
Burke and William Hare, was never published and has since been lost.

5   A memoir of Maclaren-Ross's friendship with the Welsh poet Alun Lewis,
previously published in *Penguin New Writing* 27, April 1946.

6   In Spring 1944 this short story appeared in *Spring Pie*, a quarterly magazine
produced in aid of a bookbinders' charity.

7   Under the overall title of 'No Laughing Matter', 'Warning to OCTU Wallahs'
was one of two sketches that appeared in *Summer Pie*, published during the summer
of 1944.

8   The owners of *Punch*.

9   Using the amended title 'I Like it in the Army', the story was published in the
second issue of *Bugle Blast: An Anthology from the Services*, released in the summer
of July 1943.

to RUPERT HART-DAVIS

59 Southmoor Road/Oxford

4-12-54

My dear Rupert,

Many thanks for your letter of December 2nd.

I've just this morning received one from the publisher of *Punch*,
stating that, in accordance with my request, the nine issues containing
contributions of mine have now been sent to you, so that you're now
in possession of the complete material, except for 'The Episcopal Seal'
(5,000 wds) and 'I Liked the Army' (2,000 wds), which I will obtain for
you should you decide to publish the book.

I think it's terribly good of you to spend your weekend reading the
stuff, and to give me such a quick decision, especially since I've taken
so long to send it in (though this was through no fault of my own).

I do hope that you accept the book, as this will solve a lot of problems
for us both. In any case, whatever your decision, I'll be in London next
week Tuesday or Wednesday and hope you'll be able to spare a few
minutes for a talk (and, I hope, a quick drink), as we'll have a chat in
either case.

Yours ever,

Julian

to RUPERT HART-DAVIS

59 Southmoor Road/Oxford
8-12-54

My dear Rupert,

Thank you for your letter.

I'm sorry you have decided not to do the book.[1] I shall be in London tomorrow (Thursday) from 11.30 a.m. to 6.30 p.m.; and I thought that, if you happen to be free sometime between those hours, we might be able to have a word or two. Anyhow I'll ring you on arrival at the station.

As ever,

Julian

1 The volume, which Hart-Davis had rejected, was subsequently published by Elek Books – another small London-based firm – under the title *The Funny Bone*.

to DAN AND WINNIE DAVIN

59 Southmoor Road/Oxford
2 a.m. 12-12-54

Dear Dan & Winnie,

Sitting here thinking things over in silence, I simply had to write you this note to thank you properly for your kindness to me tonight.[1]

I don't think you can possibly know what this meant to me: to see the very real interest you are taking in something that I myself might be inclined to dismiss (though not overtly) with a shrug & a smile, had some friend of mine put the same case to me.

I suppose that something like this was bound to happen to me, at my dangerous age; but at any rate, even if it comes to nothing, it has given me a new reason for living and for making the bid for position and power which perhaps I should make at this stage of my career.

Whatever happens re Collins,[2] don't worry about me, my dears: and if you feel like laughing at me sometimes as a romantic fool in the grip of an impossibly lyrical attachment, don't think I'll be offended. God knows I'm amused enough at my own antics, though not in the least bitterly – nor am I at all ashamed.

If I come back tomorrow night in time, I'll ring on arrival at the pub, and hope to see you, Winnie, at any rate.

As ever,

Bloody old Julian

1 Dan and Winnie Davin had listened to his account of how he had become infatuated by Sonia Orwell.

2 His employment with Norman Collins's firm, the Associated Television Company, was precarious.

to DAN AND WINNIE DAVIN[1]

2.45 a.m., 12-12-54

(I suppose, as far as I can make out, because all dates for me nowadays originate from the day – as distinct from Dec. 10 – on which I met HER.)

Dears,

I'm back.

The outcome of course was totally different in every way from what anybody could have thought or expected. I don't understand what *did* go on myself, except that I seem to have been very unwise.

If you're interested to hear what went on, come round: the doctor, having been phoned by me from London, has instantly condemned me to bed again when he heard my new symptoms.

1 An indication of Maclaren-Ross's state of mind is provided by his handwriting. On this occasion, his obsessively neat lettering was replaced by an atypical scrawl. His burgeoning obsession with Sonia Orwell had left him so distracted that he didn't even remember to sign the letter.

to HAMISH HAMILTON

59 Southmoor Road/Oxford

14-12-54

Dear Mr Hamilton,

Thank you very much for your letter re 'Maigret at Oxford'. Please accept my apologies for not answering it before now, but I have been having a very difficult time lately. Don't think that I have not appreciated the compliment that this letter was in your own handwriting when it could, quite easily, have been typewritten by a secretary. I hope that, if you can spare the time when I'm in London (within, possibly, the next few days), we might have a drink together somewhere and talk things over.

Sincerely,

J. Maclaren-Ross

to RICHARD BRAIN

59 Southmoor Road/Oxford
14-12-54

Dear Mr Brain,

Thank you for yours of 13th Dec.

I'd no idea – nor did you tell me when I rang you up last Friday – that you'd actually gone down to wait for me in the Freelance Club[1] on Thursday last, until Anna (coming late on duty on Friday night) informed me of the fact. Actually, what I said on the phone was that, if you were to ring the Freelance, they would give you some indication of my movements and that, if you happened to be free at the appropriate time, I would phone you back on arrival and we could then arrange something.

I'm sorry if you were inconvenienced, but you will realise that, as when you come to Oxford, on my rare visits to London all sorts of things are arranged for me in the meantime.

I'm expecting to be summoned to town again by Norman Collins this week: probably on either Thursday or Friday, and I hope that we may meet then. I will ring you on arrival (11.40 a.m.) and, should you not be free in the morning or afternoon, we might get together in the evening of the particular day, as there's a 12.15 from Paddington at night and I could catch that, as I have done before.

I'll do my best about the latter half of Chapter 2, but I do wish you'd send the material already submitted to the typist right away, as there seems no point otherwise in my breaking my back getting it ready for typing. As for the page numbering, surely this could be left out; either this could be done in ink – which I would do personally if necessary – or passed back to the typewriter later.

The whole point of my submitting the material piecemeal is that I should not have to correct a huge batch in one go, but do it bit by bit: as I explained earlier. Speed is the main object, is it not?

Sincerely,

J. Maclaren-Ross

1   A small Soho drinking club at 26 Romilly Street, London.

to RICHARD BRAIN

59 Southmoor Road/Oxford
2-1-55

My dear Brain,

Here's the last 2 chapters of *Maigret et la grande perche*.

If you can expedite a cheque for the remainder of the fee, less what the typing will come to, I'd be most grateful; since I'm having a row with my firm[1] because they stopped a week's payment for the time whilst I was ill.

As the festivities accounted for the last advance I had from you – and lucky I got it, because the letter stopping payment arrived Xmas Eve – you can guess that I'm not in a prosperous state.

Give me a week or so, if you can, before bunging in the relays of typescript for correction, because it always helps to have a breather in between: one can then see the thing with a fresh eye.

In any case, I shall probably take a day in town when I've settled this little bit of nonsense, and will hope to see you then.

With best wishes for 1955,

from

J. Maclaren-Ross

1   The Associated Television Company.

to RICHARD BRAIN

59 Southmoor Road/Oxford
3-1-55 (3 a.m.)

My dear Brain,

Typescript received this morning: our letters must have crossed. By now you'll have Chaps 8 & 9.

Here is the copy (100 pp.) duly corrected; I'm keeping the carbon for us to play about with later.

I'm not as displeased with this as I thought I would be: it does read like English.

Your title won't do, though.[1] Obvious reasons.

I suggest (though neither is too good):

Maigret and the Sad Safe-Breaker.
Maigret and the Lofty Girl.

Better send me those comments of yours, so that I'll have them in time for the next batch.

As ever,

J.M.R.

1 *Maigret and Lanky Liz.*

---

to RICHARD BRAIN

59 Southmoor Road / Oxford

6-1-55

Dear Brain,

Here are Chaps. 5, 6 and 7 corrected, and by now you should have received the first four.

I hope the typing-charge is moderate, because in places it's shockingly careless: I thought 'Were you wearing green shoes as today' (addressed to the dentist) was rather nice. I also enclosed some lines (p. 168) which had been left out altogether.

Yes, I do hope, too, that Mrs S. will take my parody to heart, for *Maigret's Mistake*[1] is terribly stilted and unreal: 'introduced' for 'shown'; 'office' for 'study' and 'that has happened to me' for 'sometimes I do' etc.

If you're calling the book *Maigret and the Two Girls*, then how about *Maigret and the Burglar's Wife*? or *Maigret and the Tall Girl*, plus *Maigret and the Dead Girl*? This would probably be the best.

I now await 8 and 9.

Sincerely,

J.M.R.

1 Published by Hamish Hamilton in 1954.

---

to RICHARD BRAIN

59 Southmoor Road / Oxford

7-1-55

Your letter of 6th just received.

I must dissociate myself from 'Lanky Liz',* and have some kind of prefatory note, saying that the title – and the nickname – are the choices of Mme S., as I simply cannot have reviewers pouncing on me for this, when the book comes out.**

I hope, too, that – since we agreed long ago that 'L.L.' was only a suggestion of Mme S.'s and that 'Lofty' should be substituted – this isn't the thin edge of the wedge, and that all the stilted nonsense I referred to above isn't going to be imposed on the translation.

In any case I think a note saying 'This trans. has been made under Mme S.'s supervision' is essential for my protection, and – in view of my parody – she might pipe down when she hears that I insist on such a note.

* If the girl's name were 'Elizabeth' it would be OK. As it is, she couldn't possibly be nicknamed that. Even 'Lanky' on its own, would be better.

** They're bound to, if only *because* of the parody, which most of them will have seen.

    J.M.R.

to RICHARD BRAIN

59 Southmoor Road / Oxford

12-1-55

Dear Brain,

Thank you for your letter of 11 Jan.

Good for you about Lanky Liz: but why not *Maigret and the Tall Girl*?[1]

Herewith the last chapters corrected, and omission (my fault this time!) rectified.

Please send the cheque, expressed if possible, or at any rate by return, because I need it v. v. urgently.

If I get it in time, I might come up on Friday; if so, will ring you on arrival: 11.40 a.m. We might have a drink.

Yours sincerely,

J. Maclaren-Ross

1 Maclaren-Ross's translation was ultimately released using one of the titles he'd suggested: *Maigret and the Burglar's Wife* (1955).

to ANTHONY POWELL

59 Southmoor Road/Oxford
15-1-55

My dear Tony,

Alas, not a good start to the New Year.

Flat in London proved complete frost on inspection. (Bathroom outside; 'independent' Scots housekeeper, plus drunken husband – ex-Commando – with habit of locking her in lavatory after nightly beating.) Might be good enough for *Punch* (sometime),[1] but not my cup of tea.

TV job also a frost. (Super-Olympian attitude on part of production-director – 'if you care to wait 30 minutes or so, he *may* see you, but I can give no guarantee that an interview will be granted' – followed by cutting-off of payments on Christmas Eve because I had been painfully ill for a week and had omitted to send medical certificate. Subsequent letters of surpassing insolence, with accusations of malingering, despite certificate and presence of 2 doctors at bedside. Amount of work delivered – 3 scripts in 25 days[2] – deemed insufficient. Non-intervention policy on part of Big Boss.[3] Production-director beaten finally on all counts; payment duly resumed etc.; but of course job ends Jan. 24th.)

Would therefore welcome a bit of reviewing, if possible, to eke out following weeks.

Hope all is well with you.

All good wishes for 1955.

Yours ever,

Julian

PS Thanks for printing Maigret parody so promptly. Might teach Mrs S. a lesson: she says she enjoyed it, but we all doubt that chez Hamish Hamilton. My translation duly finished and corrected (typescript: Mrs S.'s 'revision' and proofs yet to come).

1 Inspired by his visit to the flat, Maclaren-Ross wrote a short piece called 'The Gem'. It must have been rejected by *Punch*, but it was eventually published in *The Funny Bone*, his collection of miscellaneous writing.
2 The scripts were probably for the *Colonel March of Scotland Yard* series, starring Boris Karloff.
3 Norman Collins.

to DAN DAVIN[1]

59 Southmoor Road/Oxford
7-2-55

Dear Dan,

It's becoming more difficult to obtain an Interview with you than with the editors of the *TLS* or *Punch*.

I arrived at the Victoria last night at 9, having bolted my dinner in order to be in time, only to be told by Winnie – at 9.30 – that you had 'retired to bed': an explanation which seemed not only inadequate but ironical to a man who'd been nearly 2 days without sleep. I can't help feeling that it might have been more thoughtful to have telephoned either Royal Oxford[2] or the Victoria and told me that a subsequent appointment with Morpheus prevented you from being there.[3]

Yrs,
Julian

1   The letter was marked 'PRIVATE & PERSONAL: BY HAND'.
2   When Maclaren-Ross received a large cheque, he liked to treat himself to a blow-out meal at the swanky Royal Oxford Hotel, in the centre of the city.
3   Dan Davin quoted from this letter in his memoir of Maclaren-Ross, featured in *Closing Times*.

to ANTHONY POWELL

59 Southmoor Road/Oxford
19-2-55

My dear Tony,

Herewith the Dutourd[1] review as requested.

Please expedite a cheque by return, if possible; things are really rough with me, and I've been living on biscuits and cheese for the last 3 days.

Some pieces for *Punch* follow, which I hope may prove acceptable to you.

Yours ever,
Julian

1   Jean Dutourd, author of *The Milky Way* (Museum Press, 1955).

to ANTHONY POWELL

59 Southmoor Road / Oxford
22-2-55

My dear Tony,

Thank you very much for arranging payment for the review so quickly, and in cash. This looks like being a very bad-luck period, and just when I hoped to get on with my novel at last.

Rupert has decided not to publish the collection of short pieces after all: as being, I suppose, too slight a book; but he's freed me from his option on the second volume of my autobiography, so I'm in a position to offer this to anyone who will take on the collection without delay.

I have sounded Hamilton,[1] Gollancz,[2] Deutsch:[3] no dice. I wonder if you know of anyone who would like to do it? Of course there are some new little firms, but I daren't try them because the autobiographical series is involved.

I'm only asking an advance of £120 on the collection (to enable me to start on a novel in reasonable piece of mind), though of course I should want much higher terms on the autobiography.

I'm sure the collection would sell reasonably, if browsers have some idea of the contents. (About 65–70,000 words.)

If you can think of anybody likely to be interested, please let me know; it's difficult for me now, not being on the spot.

Yours ever,
Julian

1 Hamish Hamilton.
2 The publisher Victor Gollancz.
3 The publisher André Deutsch, who had by then left Allan Wingate Ltd and founded another company – André Deutsch Ltd.

to ANTHONY POWELL

59 Southmoor Road / Oxford
8-3-55

My dear Tony,

Glad you liked 'Sfumato';[1] hope you may also approve of the enclosed,[2] which is modelled on the latest Elizabeth Bowen that I've just read. What I've done is to forecast a future for the characters in *The Death of the Heart* (my own favourite and, after all, her best known book); but the situation in the new one – though set in Ireland – is basically the same (letters stolen and read instead of a diary). I thought I'd provide in this way some commentary on her work to date, which seems to me the purpose of parody rather than to just pick out some particular book. Otherwise, as you'll realise if you've occasion to glance at *A World of Love*[3] (which God forbid!), all the elements are included; it's not nearly as long as it looks, because of spacing etc., though it can if necessary be cut in proof.

I hope to be sending in an Agatha Christie 'Poirot' parody[4] ('The Eeny Meeny Miny Mo Murders'), which has a rather amusing idea; and possibly, I thought, a Nevil Shute[5] (a new book of his is being serialised in some magazine, though they're all the same anyway). My ambition is to place 4 pieces with you altogether (including 'Sfumato'), as I've an irksome debt hanging over me here and next week will be particularly difficult.

Thanks for sending in the review-books – I can do with them, though unfortunately none so far have been much good.

Yours as ever,
Julian

1 Maclaren-Ross's parody of Augustus John's memoir *Chiaroscuro* (1952). The parody was published in the 13 April 1955 issue of *Punch*.
2 Maclaren-Ross had enclosed his Elizabeth Bowen parody, 'A World of Women'. Powell must have approved of it, because it was published in the 23 March 1955 issue of *Punch*.
3 Elizabeth Bowen's 1955 novel.
4 The Agatha Christie parody was either never written or, perhaps, rejected by Powell.
5 Maclaren-Ross's Nevil Shute parody featured in the 8 June 1955 issue of *Punch*.

to DAN DAVIN

59 Southmoor Road/Oxford
2-4-55 (3.20 a.m)

Dan,

Please come & see me today when you're free.
Julian

I'm having Dr Spence[1] as soon as Mr Goodman[2] *can get him for me.*[3]

1 The Davins' doctor.
2 Maclaren-Ross's landlord, Oscar Goodman, lived directly above Maclaren-Ross's basement flat at 59 Southmoor Road.
3 Maclaren-Ross was convinced that he was suffering from blood-poisoning.

to JOHN LEHMANN

59 Southmoor Road/Oxford

15-5-55

My dear John,

Thank you for the June *London Magazine* received yesterday. I was very surprised and very pleased to see you'd printed the Frank Harris; also the choice of review was very appropriate at the moment.[1] This is most kind of you and should – with the note in 'In Case You Don't Know'[2] – create just the right kind of effect.

I hope to be financially able to come up this week and start my little siege: I've managed to hold everything at bay until now. Then I hope to see you and discuss some future ideas.

By the way, I wonder if you could have a passage from an article of yours in *New Writing and Daylight* copied for me? It is from 'The Armoured Writer' (Part 1, I think), Autumn & Winter 1942, and refers to 'that world of the thriller... in which the individual stands as little chance of survival as a sparrow striking a high-tension cable'. (I quote from memory.) I'd like to use it as an epigraph for a novel I'm preparing, and I haven't all my books by me in Oxford.

Looking forward to seeing you soon,

As ever,

Julian

1 Of the book reviews that Maclaren-Ross had already delivered to the *London Magazine*, Lehmann chose to print one that focused on Nigel Dennis's satirical novel *Cards of Identity*. For Maclaren-Ross, its portrayal of people whose identities can be effaced by another person must have reminded him of how his obsession with Sonia Orwell had affected *him*.

2 The 'In Case You Don't Know' section of *London Magazine* comprised brief notes on the contributors. Maclaren-Ross's memoir was accompanied by the following note: "'A Visit To The Villa Edouard Sept", in an expanded version, will form part of J. Maclaren-Ross's second volume of autobiography, entitled *Threnody on a Gramophone* and now in preparation.' This second volume, also advertised at the front of *The Weeping and the Laughter*, was never published. The surviving sections of the book, later retitled *The Rites of Spring*, feature in *Bitten by the Tarantula and Other Writing* (Black Spring Press, 2005).

to WINNIE DAVIN

May 1955 (10 a.m.)

Dear Winnie,

I have no more money left.

But a letter from *Punch* this morning says they are going to do my parody of Marquand.[1]

Will you be an angel and do the following for me, or I'm sunk – as today is Friday and it's the only way of getting money before weekend.

Please ring Mr Caudery at *Punch* (Central 9161) as early as is convenient: explain that I have blood-poisoning; cannot get up; have no money coming in owing to the strike;[2] and ask him to send the fee to me by Telegram Money Order at this address *today* (as letters are taking 3 to 4 days even *Expressed*).[3] Tell him this fact.

I will then try to get Mr Goodman to collect it for me.

Name of parody (John P. Marquand) is 'Fifty Years' (Caudrey will want to know this).

Thank you!

1 His parody of the work of the American novelist John P. Marquand (1893–1960) appeared in the 20 July 1955 issue of *Punch*.
2 There was a railway strike in progress.
3 He was referring to the Express Postal Service.

to WINNIE DAVIN

Late May 1955

Dear Winnie,

Would Mr Jago cash a cheque (*from Gaston, the bookseller* of Chancery Lane)[1] for me, d'you think? On your recommendation? The other night you said, if you remember, that he would. I have to catch 11 o.c.[2] bus to go over to Gerry's,[3] and I have left myself short of ready cash (!!!), otherwise I wouldn't disturb you with this.

So sorry,

In haste (*taxi waiting*)

Love,

Julian

GOOD LUCK to you both – till Sunday!

GOOD LUCK!

GOOD LUCK!

(You really shouldn't have laughed at my Terror Machine – remember that I'm a vurry vurry sensitive guy!) *HA. HA.*

1 Maclaren-Ross sold regular consignments of his review copies to this shop. Provided a book was in mint condition, Gaston paid half the cover price for it.
2 O'clock.
3 Gerry Fisher's cottage at Cookham Dean near Maidenhead.

to WINNIE DAVIN

28-5-55

My dear Winnie,

I do apologise for not rolling up. But having been awake from 6 a.m. until 1.30 p.m. yesterday, I must have dozed off and woke, to my horror, at 9.20. I could still have reached you, but for the fact that *my kettle takes half an hour to boil*; so I'd given up the idea. Pity, because I'd also intended to have a meal somewhere, and there was nothing to eat in the house. So I went without both food and drink.

As I predicted, that issue of *London Mag.* has begun to show results. Letter from Ackerley,[1] editor of *Listener*, offering me the novel page for 3 months, starting in June, 1,500 words fortnightly, 15 guineas per article, a free hand, and *all* the novels that come in (about £4 or £5 a week extra, when they're sold at half-price). This, with my one review book a week from *Punch* (6 guineas) would bring me up to about £18–£20 a week again. I have written accepting: it shouldn't be nearly as hard as *The Sunday Times* chore.

Still no decision from *Punch*.

See you perhaps in Lamb & Flag[2] this morning.

Love,
Julian

1 The writer and editor J.R. Ackerley (1896–1967).
2 Located at 12 St Giles Street, Oxford, this pub was within walking distance of where both Maclaren-Ross and the Davins were living.

to DAN AND WINNIE DAVIN

Early June 1955

PLEASE READ CAREFULLY AT YOUR LEISURE.

Dear Dan and Winnie,

It's now 8.45 a.m. and I've had no sleep all night (or all day yesterday) trying to work out what to do, without success. The state I've got myself into shows that I'm bound to crack if subjected to any more unnecessary strain. I just can't face it.

The only way I can free myself of my obsession is to settle down and concentrate on a book to the exclusion of all else. But where? The food situation renders it impossible to work here in a concentrated effort: I would only alternate between biscuits and cheese and bouts of eating and drinking at Royal Oxford which would wipe up the little money at my disposal.

I'd high hopes (like yourselves) of Gerry's as a refuge, but my weekend there proved conclusively that this won't do. Where then? London? Too expensive and too much temptation to kill loneliness by rushing out on an occasional disastrous. binge! Barnstable? God knows there seems nowhere.

Please help with advice. Don't write: I'll hope – if well enough – to drop in and catch you when you're free. I wouldn't bother you but as you know I've nobody else to talk to who knows the whole gen.

I've suddenly realised that – in my folly – I've fallen into a trap and that this girl, having spotted the whole thing, meant to try and hurt me as much as she can.

I've no intention of giving her the opportunity, as I don't want to get so badly mauled that I shan't be able to get on with my work – and this she is able to do.

Therefore I won't ring her this week or any other week or day and will destroy all letters from her unopened.

I might, in the early stages, have given your phone number for messages: so please, I beg of you, *don't* pass any on, *whatever they may say*, or tell me if there have been any: I daren't risk any upset in my state of nerves. I'd rather not mention her again.

All I can ask of you is, sometime when you can, discuss together where I should to go to start writing, bearing in mind the sort of income I shall have.

And will you please keep this letter carefully where nobody can see it inadvertently?

With apologies for fuss and my scrawl... J.

to DAN AND WINNIE DAVIN

59 Southmoor Road/Oxford
Early June 1955

Dear Dan & Winnie,

Perhaps one of you might care to drop in here for a chat sometime. I can't come out myself, because (a) I've no money (b) have eaten nothing but biscuits & cheese for past 3 days (c) am suffering from severe dihoerrea – or however you spell it (d) am consequently in bed, and have been since Sat. night.

As ever,

J.M.R.

to DAN DAVIN

First week of June 1955

Dear Dan,

Immobilised and in awful pain: I only had one hour's sleep.

Would you ask Dr Spence to come & see me? I can't get up and anyhow I doubt if he'd come on a Sunday to see a stranger, unless asked to do so by one of his regular patients. It was a Sunday when I had my last go, and had dreadful difficulty getting a Doc.

Please ask him to bring some pain-killer: I can't go on like this. Last time I had to have a shot of Morphia.

And would you please come round yourself, *before* the Doctor because there're some practical things I have to talk over before & after his verdict. I daren't have the operation: nor go into a hospital at this critical time. However, we'll see.

I'm sorry to bother you – especially on your day of rest – but who else have I got?

Also have you got a towel you could lend me? Mine is very dirty: meant to buy one yesterday & forgot.

J.

to DAN AND WINNIE DAVIN

3-6-55 (5.45 p.m.)

Dear Dan & Winnie,

Couldn't go to town today.

Boil hurt so during night, I didn't get any sleep at all. My neck is stiff & swollen like an angry cobra's hood, and I don't know whether to have Doctor or not. The pain continues without let up, & I can't lie down to sleep properly.

Please pop in sometime tonight, if either or both of you have a moment; I've nothing to read, having finished *Acceptance World*:[1] but wouldn't mind discussing this.

I have de Polnay's book for you: have you anything else?

As ever,

J.M.R.

1 *The Acceptance World* (1955) was the third volume in Anthony Powell's 12-volume series *A Dance to the Music of Time*. Even before becoming a friend of Anthony Powell's, Maclaren-Ross was a fan of his fiction. On 16 February 1951, the *Times Literary Supplement* had published 'From a Chase to a View', Maclaren-Ross's essay about Powell's writing.

to WINNIE DAVIN

First week of June 1955

My dear Winnie,

Dr Hewitt has been, and says this is a carbuncle & not blood poisoning; all the same I have had a penicillin injection and am to have others daily: also penicillin tablets to take.

I won't be fit for another week, which is terrible because there's absolutely no money coming in; no books can be sent (postcard to that effect from *Listener* this morning); and letters are now taking *four days* to arrive.

The Doctor is coming every day until I'm well.

But the carbuncle has burst and I have to wash it & treat it with cottonwool and keep a pad of this in position on my neck to avoid further infection.

This latter is difficult because I've nothing to hold the pad in position. Have you an old *scarf* or something you could lend me to tie round?

Sorry to be a bother; I've also nothing to *read* again.

As ever,

Julian

to DAN AND WINNIE DAVIN

First week of June 1955

Dear Winnie & Dan,

I had to have the Doctor about that boil on my face on Tuesday: the boil has now burst leaving a colossal hole in my jaw, making shaving unwise if not impossible for today anyway, so I can't come out.

Besides, I have a hangover of death, owing to having fallen in with a local businessman yesterday; and, though I've unfortunately nothing here to drink, I'd welcome some company sometime today if one of you (or both) is/are not too busy.

I'm in bed where I mean to stay short of an earthquake, and feel shocking; but have to read & review a damned book.

Anyhow, if you do feel like dropping in and cheering me up a little, it would be a kindness to a sick old gentleman. And if you come, will you please bring me *London Magazine* (Spring Number) and I'll lend you the new one if you haven't already got it? Just tap on the side window whether the light's on or off.

Love,

Julian

PS I won't really be expecting you, so there's no need to send an excuse for not coming or anything like that.

to DAN DAVIN

59 Southmoor Road/Oxford

Summer 1955

My dear Dan,

Thank you for the drink last night.

I'm sorry I was taken queer before the end & had to go; but truth is I haven't had anything solid to eat for some days and have had to stay in and work nonetheless: also my little illness[1] is troubling me a bit.

Until the holiday is over & the editors get back & get to work, I shan't have any money at all – which means Wed. or Thurs. at earliest.

Have you any money?

I do not have any.

I do not have cigarettes either.

Tonight I could go down to Royal Oxford and get tick, but I can't get cigarettes on the bill – or cigars. Then there are 2 or 3 days to get over before what's owing to me comes in; and meantime I must do more work. On empty belly & no fags, not easy.

If you have any money please let me have some. I will pay.

I will look in on you at home about 7.15 p.m. (when you've had dinner) and hope for best. Unless you've a moment to look in here sometime before.

Don't want to come over to pub, because crossing road makes me dizzy in this state; also am not fit company just now in big crowd.

This letter written v. simply because I expect you've a hangover; & I can never take anything in, myself, when I have.

Letter from USA enclosed. Good prospect for future?

I want to ask advice about something; but won't while you've guests to attend to.

Will go to sleep now. Nothing else to do.

As ever,

Julian

1 The illness to which he referred so coyly was piles.

to RUPERT HART-DAVIS

59 Southmoor Road / Oxford
Summer 1955

Enc. contents plan of *Threnody on a Gramophone*[1]

My dear Rupert,

Although I have much amplified and altered the contents of the *Punch* collection which I showed you in December, bringing this up to over 80,000 words and adding new material, short stories, etc., I now see, from attempted negotiations, that publishers are unlikely to (a) take it on as an 'isolated' book (without an option on the autobiographies also); (b) that the sort of publishers that would do the *Punch* book are not, in my opinion, capable to handling the autobiographies in the way they should be handled.

Therefore, I'm faced with having to set aside the collection at the present moment; but since I require the sum of £125, which will bring me back to London in October, I will have instead to ask publishers for this sum as a part-advance on the second volume, which I hope to complete by the New Year, if not before (provided I can work solely on it).

I therefore make you the offer before setting out on a round tour, as it would be nice if the other 3 vols could be brought out by the same publisher that did the first (all are planned out).

My suggestion would be £120 immediate cash, £80 on delivery of MS; royalty terms same as on Vol. I, also same agreement in general. You have seen 'Monsieur L'Abbé' and 'The Gondolier of Death'? Also the memoir of Frank Harris in *London Magazine*; there will be another extract printed in the next (I think) *Encounter*, called 'The Bird Man'. It seems to me reasonable to regard these 25,000 words or so as samples of what Vol. II will be like. (Complete plan enclosed herewith.)

If you agree to above suggestion, I will come up to London on receipt of your letter and sign contract etc. (I would take half-and-half advance,[2] but the extra £20 is required as a deposit on a flat; it is imperative for personal reasons that I should be re-established in London by October, when I've got a new job starting.)

You will recall that I have never asked you before to make an advance on an unfinished book, but I now have no alternative but to do so: since if *somebody* does not supply me with sufficient small capital to lick the 2nd vol. into shape, it will not be written at all.

I can always make a decent living by writing without writing books at all (which even if successful bring in nothing like the income I can earn by devoting my energies to freelance work alone); and though I may want to write books, I see no reason to do so for the benefit of publishers who are not willing to help me get the job done.

I threw up a £20 a week job with Norman Collins TV lot in March because I saw no future in it for me except hard plodding hack work; but now the work I did while I was with them will be coming out, and I have already been circuitously approached by other firms.

As a matter of fact, however, I want to keep out of TV altogether. I'm now working on a film-project[3] (my own original story, which means that I have control) with a producer and prefer the cinema medium, as you know; but this is just to show you that there is no need for me to draw advances on unwritten books in order to keep going (*Punch* and the amount of reviewing and critical work I do, attend to that fairly well, besides other jobs).

But after the starvation-period I went through while writing *The Weeping and the Laughter*, I returned gradually to the conclusion that publishers should help authors write their books by advancing a sum to cover expenses during period of writing (it's bad enough that this should come out of the *author's* pocket in the long run!); and otherwise I, for one, would say 'sod books for a game of tin writers'.

So please drop me a line: there's also a project of a short novel (the basis of my film) which we might discuss: same terms, except that you only get a synopsis first (Lehmann knows all about this).

If I don't hear by Thursday, I'll conclude you're away, like everybody else in London. Hope for the best, however.

As ever,

Julian.

1 Never someone prepared to waste what he regarded as a good title, this had, when *The Weeping and the Laughter* was published, been advertised as the second volume of a planned four-volume autobiography. Volume III was going to be titled *The Sea Coast of Bohemia*. He intended the final volume to be called *Khaki and Cockayne*.
2 Half (£100) on signature of the contract and the remaining half on publication, rather than the £120/£80 split he suggests earlier.
3 The project was *The Girl in the Spotlight*, a thriller based on his obsession with Sonia Orwell.

to JOHN LEHMANN

59 Southmoor Road/Oxford

25-7-55

My dear John,

I'll be up in London for the day tomorrow, Tuesday; and will ring you when I arrive in the morning.

If you could manage to make yourself free for half an hour or so in the evening, I would very much like you to hear the blind man play:[1] we could have a drink at the club where he is after 8 p.m., and there he would go over some of the tunes from *The Girl in the Spotlight*;[2] you could also tell me what you think when you've seen him.

I'm trying to arrange for him to come down to Oxford so that we could talk over the whole project more fully.

The Faulkner may take a few days more than I anticipated,[3] as there are a few complications involved; but as you know, I'll do it as quickly as possible.

As ever,

Julian

1 The 'blind man' was Stanley Hume, a pianist who, when not drifting round Europe, was a regular in the Soho clubs.

2   This planned screenplay about his obsession with Sonia Orwell subsequently metamorphosed into a BBC radio series and a novel, the latter retitled *My Name Is Love* (1964).

3   Lehmann had commissioned Maclaren-Ross to review *A Fable* and *Faulkner's Country: Tales of Yoknapatawpha County*, two newly released books by the American writer William Faulkner, whose work Maclaren-Ross admired. The review, in which Maclaren-Ross praised Faulkner's 'consummate narrative gift, his mastery of atmosphere and detail', was published in the November 1955 issue of the *London Magazine*.

to WINNIE DAVIN

26-7-55

Dear Winnie,

Going up to London today. Morning began rather well, with fan-mail – oddly enough from Charles Causley, author of the poem 'My Name Is Love' etc. which I quoted to you last night. Coincidence? Perhaps. And here's another:

Apropos dreams, and all that rot.

I called her[1] when I got back, between 3.30 and 3.45 a.m., just to see. She duly came, but in a very odd form: in the shape of a newspaper-cutting, with large vivid photograph, announcing her engagement to George Weidenfeld[2] – but dated, quite plainly, 1951. (Is *that* the relationship?)[3] This was accompanied by a Central European voice singing satirical verses about her, which angered me so much that I awoke – to find my watch pointing to 3.40 a.m.! Never mind: on my way. Wish me luck.

Excuse haste, love,

J.

1   Sonia Orwell.
2   The publisher George Weidenfeld (1919–) was Sonia Orwell's employer.
3   Maclaren-Ross had heard that she was romantically involved with someone else.

to C.K. JAEGER

59 Southmoor Road/Oxford

2-8-55

My dear Jaeger,

I see from the Autumn *Bookseller* that *The Bull that was Terrifico*[1] (which I presume to be *The Little Matador*) is due to come out from Putnam's soon: congratulations! What about *The Startled Saint*?[2] I suppose you won't get that out until I come down to stir you up once again: though this isn't likely, as I'm up to the eyes with more commissions than I've had for years – mostly critical stuff, as I've decided at long last to seize power, and that's always the way to do it in this benighted country where the actual creator is given less respect than the pompous asses who are paid to 'adjudicate' upon his work. (I chucked TV in March.)

Also I'm returning to London very shortly, where it looks as though I may be setting up a film at last. The secret of this is that it's my own story, and that for the first time it centres round a woman, instead of having women in merely as adjuncts – however important – to men. (Remember Rudolph's[3] words.)

From this, you will deduce that the final blow has fallen, and that I'm in love at the age of 43 – and you'd be right. And with – and this ought to please you, with your taste for fantasy – a girl whom hard-hearted, intelligent men say in all seriousness is a destroyer, and even *a witch*! How about that, eh? Better than selling one's soul to the devil. When the time comes, please send all appropriate wedding presents such as dried heads, wax dolls, voodoo drums, and a large cauldron to stew the children in (though I believe witches can't have any) c/o Satamax, London.

Enormous emotional drama reigns at the moment: with the girl fleeing madly across London and asking my friends to save her from me, on the grounds that (a) she is quite indifferent, and (b) terrified of becoming involved. Meanwhile I'm not pursuing at all, but have just had her special theme-song composed by *a blind pianist*, and will play it to her over the phone at 2 a.m. directly it's recorded. Drop me a line. By the way, this is all quite serious.

Love to all,
Julian

1 A children's book by C.K. Jaeger, published by Putnam & Co. in 1955, under the name 'Karel Jaeger'.
2 *The Startled Saint* was an unfinished novel, the manuscript of which was destroyed in a domestic fire. Inspired by the period when C.K. Jaeger had been a labourer helping to build a runway at Maidstone Aerodrome, the book borrowed its name from the local pub. In *The Startled Saint*, C.K. Jaeger poked fun at Maclaren-Ross's status as a lapsed Catholic. 'Julian took exception to it,' Jaeger's son Nick wrote. 'I think this was another example of the side-swipes that Father occasionally aimed at Julian – he was too good a target to miss and generally Julian enjoyed the literary arrows that were generously fired but religion was a no-no.'

3   Rudolph Cartier was one of the financial backers of *The Naked Heart* (1950), the ill-fated film on which Maclaren-Ross and C.K. Jaeger had been employed as screenwriters.

to ANTHONY POWELL

59 Southmoor Road/Oxford

10-8-55

My dear Tony,

Expressed to you herewith a little piece on Edgar Wallace's character, Bones:[1] in the manner of 'The Man Marlow'[2] and 'The Sporting Rabbit'.[3] If you like it, would you pass word on to Caudery:[4] there's a letter to him also enclosed, if you wouldn't mind sending it up to his office?

I thought of doing one or two more on these lines, combining a sort of literary 'profile' together with a defence of the underdogs of fiction. The next one I had in mind is Mr Ricardo, the retired tea-planter (or, sorry, merchant) of Mincing Lane, and 'Watson' to Hanaud, A.E.W. Mason's preposterous clown of a French detective.[5] Any use trying?

Also I saw, advertised at a quid in a bookseller's catalogue, what might prove a promising basis for a *general* piece. (By the way, I much enjoyed Stella Gibbons's *Dr Arnold of W–*, and in fact all her things: the Budding Secretaries are adorable.) The book in question is *The Tyro* Vol. I (1864), by Members of Harrow School – including, among the contents, 'The Spectral Sportsman'; 'The Supernatural', and 'Necromancy at Harrow'. Surely there would be something there? Will you tell me, when you write, your own view on these 2 ideas: this and the Mason?[6]

By the way, soon – if you haven't already – you may be hearing some gossip about me that's on its way round.[7] It's nothing to do with business or the literary life – just personal. I needn't, I know, ask you to laugh it away as ridiculous and – as indeed it is – not only unlikely but quite unfounded. You're pretty well bound, I'd say, to be next on the list for circulation: all my friends are being taken in turn.

As ever,

Julian

PS You may not be a Bones man, so perhaps I should explain that his spelling was highly individual (and he always tried out everything 3 times). In fact one might call the piece 'Again and Agen and Aggain Bones'.

1 Lieutenant Tibbits, nicknamed 'Bones', was a character who appeared in *Sanders of the River* (1911) and other novels by the thriller-writer Edgar Wallace (1875–1932). 'Again and Agen', Maclaren-Ross's piece about Bones, appeared in the 14 September 1955 issue of *Punch*.

2 'The Man Marlow' was a spoof article by Maclaren-Ross, published in the 29 June 1955 issue of *Punch*. The premise of the article was that 'Marlow', narrator of Joseph Conrad's *Heart of Darkness*, was a real person.

3 Following the template established by 'The Man Marlow' (see previous note), this provided a spoof biography of the gentleman burglar A.J. Raffles, hero of a series of novels by E.W. Hornung (1866–1921).

4 Caudery was a colleague of Anthony Powell's at *Punch*.

5 'Mr Ricardo' and the French detective 'Inspector Hanaud' appeared in novels such as *At the Villa Rose* (1910).

6 Of the two proposals, only the A.E.W. Mason spoof was commissioned by Anthony Powell.

7 The gossip probably concerned his ongoing dangerous infatuation with George Orwell's widow, Sonia, which led him to stalk her and contemplate her murder.

to JOHN LEHMANN

59 Southmoor Road / Oxford

14-8-55

My dear John,

Thank you very much for sending so promptly the Faulkner fee (formal receipt enclosed herewith); I hope that you were satisfied with the alterations I made.

I am now answering your letter of the 6th, rather belatedly I fear; but I'm in a slightly mixed-up state about the personal aspect of things and I wanted time to try and get it clear in my mind before making any further moves (though I haven't altogether succeeded.)

Firstly, let us see what has actually happened, viewed from the point of view of someone who *doesn't know* my feelings towards the girl concerned.[1] Any outsider would think her behaviour was silly and injudicious, if not actually insane and monstrous. For here is a girl whom I've always treated kindly, who has put herself out in the past to do me little services in return, so that there can be no cause for antagonism on either side. Now she's in a position to do business with me, although I've not seen her for 8 years (very important), *except that once for perhaps 10 mins last December*. She shows, when approached, every sign of wanting to do business if it can be done; and is pleased and even enthusiastic when I ask her out to lunch to discuss it. (All perfectly normal behaviour on both sides, since we'd always got on well before.) We have drinks and lunch, which, since it went on till 4.30, seems to indicate we got on well at this reunion, or she could easily have made an excuse to break it up (the office and so on). When I ring up from Oxford the following Tuesday for the discussion as arranged, she envelopes the whole thing in mystery, says it can't be done for a reason she'd rather tell me personally; when I come up to see her, she can't meet me owing to a sudden personal disaster (I would say absolutely genuine: she couldn't have faked all that on the phone, and why bother anyway – a straightforward letter turning the deal down would have sufficed); asks me to ring next day: again she isn't free (again, I'd say, genuine); this time I'm a bit annoyed (as I would be anyway, at all this cryptic buggering about; then I get a most odd (but very polite) letter (which I'll show you next time we meet) regretfully turning down the business angle (everything in it could have been said to me 3 days before when I phoned from Oxford, and the matter closed altogether); I reply with what I thought was a very nice note, offering help if she needed it in her personal trouble (people don't as a rule mention desperate calamities in their private lives unless they want help – and this again I'd have done had things been normal: especially as all during lunch she'd been asking my advice and opinion on various things); I received no reply, thought perhaps she hadn't had the letter (as a parcel of books sent off had gone astray – and still hasn't been traced – just about that time), so rang her up in London to ask her out for a drink, *as she'd asked me to do last time we spoke on the phone*; got the cold shoulder; made a few faintly derisive remarks (again quite in character, except that ordinarily I'd have torn her in strips for impudence, woolly-headedness, and general inability to conduct other business or social relationships in a normal manner) and rang off abruptly.

Then I find, 3 minutes later, that she's got Davenport[2] invited to a party (a man she is known to hate, who dislikes her and doesn't hide it, and whom she hadn't seen for two years: though I happened to mention at lunch that he was a buddy of mine), approached him immediately and gives him the routine just as she later gave it to you – exactly the same, all about me being keen on her and she doesn't know what to do etc. Davenport said, on being asked by me where she got that idea, that she said she got it from you: either a trick on her part to drive a wedge between us, or else Davenport himself (though he knows very little about my feelings on the subject: a possible affair was all he'd gathered) let something slip and tried to cover it up (I don't think so, though: because *she approached him first*).

Now, to an outsider, all this would seem frightful on her part – and indeed, I assure you, does. First she mucks up – apparently – a simple business deal (after she'd come to you for advice and been told to go through with it); and then goes round saying that some man's 'interested' in her who has seen her only once in 8 years and never made any sort of pass (verbal or otherwise), on the basis of one (business) lunch and 3 phone calls: all undertaken at *her* instigation! Then, to cap all, 14 days after the last phone-call (which on both sides might be deemed final) she approaches *you* (again, a friend of mine) with the same pack of rot: even though I've made not a single move to contact her!

What right has she to assume all this? If she got it from Davenport, why believe a man who dislikes her and whom she dislikes? Even if *you* (which we know didn't happen) warned her against me, it sounds a most unlikely story, for after all she knows me reasonably well: she knows that I am usually supposed to like very young girls (and almost never blondes); so if I wasn't attracted to her 10 years ago, why should I be, so suddenly, now? And why is she so scared? She has always trusted me and treated me with extreme deference: why try to make a dangerous enemy by (a) being rude when asked to come out perfectly politely – a thing that's *never* happened to me before; (b) spreading rumours which only make her look an ass all around the clock, for it only shows that she doesn't know how to cope with a situation which (if founded on fact) must arise, with a girl of her looks, about twice a week; but, since she's no evidence to go on except (possible, but dubious) hearsay or her own intuition, hints at the sort of sex-fantasy more appropriate to middle-aged unattractive maiden-ladies.

Monica's[3] opinion – and here we must listen to a contemporary of the one concerned and a woman who not only knows her way about but knows my technique backwards – was as follows:

(a) that any girl in the circumstances – and particularly this one – hearing or feeling that after all this time I had become emotionally or physically drawn towards her, would be vastly intrigued, *quite apart from anything she herself might think or feel*, and would definitely go on seeing me even if it was only – at its most bitchy – to get me to commit myself and so add a scalp before beating a retreat – and then, if she wanted to be malicious, spread the rumours.

I agreed, but said: 'What about pity, though? Not wanting me to get "hurt" and so on?'

She said: 'Darling, with the best will in the world, no girl has ever pitied you – I've known you say it rather irritably – or regarded you as other than iron-clad, if not actively indestructible.'

I said: 'Suppose she *is* frightened of me? That I'll leap on her and try a rape or something?'

She said: 'You have no reputation of that kind, and a woman of her experience must know you're not the sort to make the slightest pass without encouragement; besides which, passes can't be made in public places and you haven't asked her to go on any long moonlight drives or rides: if you do, she need only tactfully refuse. No girl would ever be frightened of you *unless you were made angry*, and she's going the best way about achieving the very situation in which she may have cause to fear you. She can't really be such a fool.'

I said: 'Then why?'

She said: 'It must be to draw you on. Or, if she's genuinely scared at this stage, then you must mean something to her and *she's* afraid of getting hurt.'

I asked: 'How can she feel anything? After one meeting?'

She said: 'Well, these things do communicate themselves, you know. Tell me exactly what went on when you met.'

(b) After she's heard it – and as you know I've an absolutely photographic memory – she said: 'Oh Jay,⁴ it was a *monstrous* flirtation, and she forced the pace throughout. If you say you gave very little ground, I believe you: for God knows you're impenetrable enough – even after we'd been seeing each other for weeks I'd no real idea what you felt about me, and you've much more control now.'

So much for Monica – but of course she couldn't prophesy what the next move might be.

The most important thing of all, to my mind, is the question of that December meeting in the pub. Her manner was hostile and abrupt: not at all what you'd expect from a girl who'd always been friendly towards me and now ran into me again after many years. Even the most casual acquaintance would have at least *pretended* to be glad to see me.

Yet, when I rang her up first about the business, she was just as usual, delighted to hear from me etc., yes she'd come to lunch, of course, whenever I liked, *hadn't seen me since the old days* etc. *No mention of that meeting* – but then I didn't mention it either. You could feel a tacit conspiracy between us to not bring it up – *why not*, on her side?

When at last she fell in beside me at the bar, there were no big social greetings – the false 'why, *darlings*' etc. – as one might expect, especially when business is supposed to be afoot: she came up behind (I heard her coming, don't worry) and put her bag on the counter, just as Monica or Barbara might have done when we met in the same places every evening, or like someone coming home. She wouldn't look at me at first, though (I couldn't have looked at her either, but for my dark glasses in which she could see nothing except the reflection of her own face: I'd come prepared, you see).

However, I'd so arranged things that she was forced to sit facing me while I stood at the bar with a fair distance in between. Then became animated, smiled, held her glass in both hands, and – taking my recent illness as an excuse – began to comment on my appearance: I was so much thinner than she'd expected, she remembered me so much heavier and about 18 feet high like Orson Welles and so on. I said that I hadn't grown any shorter and it was a good idea to lose weight in middle age etc.; this went on for ages while I began to feel persecuted and to glance around as if gunmen were creeping up on me: I couldn't understand where she wanted to get. Then, too late, I saw. I'd said: 'Well, I wore big teddy-bear coats in those days, and they always make you look enormous: besides I *was* about 2 stone heavier.'

She said: 'Oh no, you wore a dark overcoat. Like a business executive.'

I said: 'I've never had a dark overcoat. At least, not in 1947…'

She said: 'I'm not talking about 1947. I'm talking about last December.'

I was frozen. She did it well, suddenly becoming very casual, in contrast to the almost hypnotic stare she'd been using to get us to this point; but I knew we were there at last.

She said: 'Oh you wouldn't remember. You were busy talking, I don't think you even noticed me…'

I said: 'Oh, that's right. We…'

I was frozen. She did it well, suddenly becoming very casual, in contrast to the almost hypnotic stare she'd been using to get us to this point; but I knew we were there at last.

I said: 'Oh, that's right. We *did* meet. Why, I spoke to you.'

'Yes, but you hardly knew who I was, and you turned away at once.'

I said, in my Laird Cregar voice: 'You wore a short fur coat, you had your hair done like Laura,[5] you wore a green silk scarf. The time was 2.50 p.m. on Thursday 9th December.'

She said: 'Oh, then you *did* notice me!'

I said: 'Yes, I remember everything that happened that day, for it was the day the initial moves were made – not by me – that caused me to quit my job in TV.'

She said: '*Oh!*' For a moment I thought she was going to throw her glass at me, so I motioned to the barman to put some more champagne in it. Then I said: 'But I noticed, you see. Do you remember what I said to you?'

She should have said 'No,' but instead she said 'Yes.' There was a slight tinge of Cregar in her voice too.

I said: 'Then, if you do, you must know that I noticed you.' It was her turn to look hunted, so I got her quickly into James Mason and the Rochester myth[6] and she was all right again.

(On the 9th Dec. I had slid over to where she was standing slightly apart from us and said very softly: 'You're very beautiful. I'm sorry I didn't catch your name...'

She said with fury: 'Oh, you don't have to do that to me.'

I said: 'But honestly, I didn't catch it.'

She said: 'You know perfectly well who I am.' She was looking at the ground throughout.

I said: 'But I don't.' I didn't, but a dawning fear went through me, and I recognised her just as she muttered her name.

I said: 'My God. I'm awfully sorry. I really wouldn't have known you.'

She asked: 'I've changed so much?'

I said: 'Oh, for the better. Don't worry about that. For the better,' and as I turned back to the two men with her, I could feel her looking at me: she didn't speak afterwards, even to say goodbye. I believe she put a spell on me that day: I don't believe the thing came from me at all.)

It took me about an hour to get her away from the champagne-bar (no business got talked at all); at lunch she was quite warm, human, and friendly, even affectionate – certainly not frightened, and if she was bored, why stay? She made 3 big bids to turn it into a flirtation (but I turned off the 'I suppose you feel alone even now' stuff), and still no business was talked until I insisted (at 4.15). Most of it was hurriedly arranged in the taxi; but on the way out of the restaurant, I said airily, determined not to give anything away: 'Now the idea of all this stuff was to get to know you. I mean, if it does turn out you're going to handle my stuff, it's necessary that we should be able to get along personally. I always like to have *somebody* in a publisher's that I can deal with...' Then I looked down and saw the way she was smiling. I said: 'Oh dear, you don't believe any of this, do you?' She said: 'No. Do you?' I hailed a cab quick, and said: 'Well perhaps not, but all the same we'd better make *some* kind of arrangement...' She said: 'All right. I'll be good.'

At the end, I said: 'Now do your best, but if this goes wrong, I promise I won't blame you; either way I'll ring you up, and if you like – whether it's yes or no – we can meet, and if you don't want to, there's no need, and I won't hold that against you either.'

She said: 'But aren't we going to meet anyway? You were going to tell me all about films. Making them, I mean. Weren't you?'

I said: 'I don't know all about making films. But I daresay that I can tell you something about it.'

She leaned forward and did the hypnotic thing again and said: 'It *is* going to be pictures, isn't it? You *said* so. I mean you're not going to get involved with literary power-politics and just let the pictures slide?'

I said: 'No. I won't let them slide.'

She relaxed and said: 'Then that's all right.'

Soon after I drove away.

And then *what about this*? During lunch, I said casually, talking of the old days, 'Of course you were only a child then...'

Instantly she got terribly agitated; her hands shook; her cigarettes and matches spilt all over the place (she smokes after every course and asks permission every time, which I thought was carrying politeness a bit far). She said: 'No, no. I was much older than you thought. I'm not young now. If you think I'm young it won't be any use.'

I said: 'Your firm won't publish my books if I think you're young?'

She said: 'You know very well what I mean.'

I said: 'How old do you think *I* am?'

She hid her face in her hands, and then: 'You *look* in your early thirties, but you can't be because you *must* have been in your late twenties when I first met you... so now you'll be 37. Or 38.'

I said: 'I was 32 then. I'm 43 now.'

She said: 'Oh. Well. Perhaps it's because those were my first days and you were there, but you'll always...'

I said: 'Stop that. Don't say that. If anybody says it, I'll say it to you.'
She said: 'Say it, then.'
I said: 'Not now.'
She said: 'Yes. Now. Say it to me now.'
I said, in my toneless voice: 'All right. "You'll always be young to me".'
She said: 'Thank you. I hope I will.'

Now you see how odd the change of front is – eh?

Where was the fear then? Did she try to run? I could swear she was happy and content; and I was surprised because I hadn't expected it: I expected a lot of haughty, imperious stuff. I was watching all the time for the slightest warning to go slow, and never got it; still I was incredibly cautious (for me), I hardly drank any wine at all, but kept on filling her glass: yet she was steady as a rock, so it wasn't that on either side (nor have I ever been tight at any stage of this relationship, or when speaking to her on the phone: I wondered whether *she* was, once, but on the whole I'm inclined to doubt it.)

I've thought over your advice a great deal, but I'm sure it would be wrong to write to her again. It would merely confirm her story – or suspicions – that I'm after her; whereas, if I sit tight – she may come out in the open. I have 2 very strong feelings: (1) that she may quite simply approach me as though nothing had gone wrong, or (2) that she'll arrange for me to be somewhere where she is, and to pick a flaming row (this will certainly end in floods of tears and a recon-ciliation – probably in public, if she's not prevented. I know this one of old). I'm convinced – and do believe me when I say that I'm not deluding myself, when there is really nothing there – that it's not over yet. I can always feel – especially when it's important – if it's hopeless: there's simply either a barrier or an emptiness in the other person and you can do nothing to make contact. But I made contact with her all right: or why is she making such a fuss? People who're indifferent just don't bother, and that's that. If she didn't give a damn she could come out with me every night and never get involved, because I'd have no power over her at all.

As for the business, if as you say it was the wrong approach, how else could I have contacted her without arousing suspicion? My belief now, as I've said, was that she was never much interested in that: but then again, in that case, why go into it all? A firm 'No thank you' at the start would have been enough. However, let me know what you think now, in the light of all this. I'll try to get up Wed. or Thurs., and hope we can meet. If only I could come back altogether: but it depends on this damned *Punch* book and I've no idea where to place it (Deutsch & Methuen have both refused: the latter, even to consider it).

As ever,

Julian

News of *Girl in the Spotlight* soon: lots of new stuff about my witches. I've my last *Listener* article to do this week,[7] then I'll be free: but on the other hand, moneyless!

1 Sonia Orwell.

2 John Davenport.

3 His ex-girlfriend Monica Foster.

4 Monica Foster's nickname for him, based on his professional name, 'J. Maclaren-Ross'.

5 Gene Tierney played the title character in *Laura* (1944), one of Maclaren-Ross's favourite films.

6 This is a reference to the movie star James Mason (1909–84), whose good looks and sinister charm led him to become typecast. In numerous films, among them *The Seventh Veil* (1945) and *The Wicked Lady* (1946), he played suave scoundrels, many of whom are reminiscent of the character 'Mr Rochester' in Charlotte Brontë's novel *Jane Eyre* (1847). By referring to 'the Rochester myth', Maclaren-Ross is presumably suggesting that the character is an archetypal figure in romantic fiction.

7 His last set of reviews for the 'New Novels' section of *The Listener* was published on 8 September 1955. The four novels under consideration included Kingsley Amis's *That Uncertain Feeling*. Maclaren-Ross wrote that 'Mr Kingsley Amis's choice of title (perhaps a trifle unfortunate for a second novel) epitomises, nonetheless, not only the moral and psychological dilemma of the hero, but the author's own irresolution: since he was clearly undecided whether to write a satirical comedy of provincial manners or a basically serious study of marital relations – two literary genres extremely difficult to fuse, if not wholly incompatible... [Even so,] there is ample foretaste of excellent work to come when Mr Amis has, himself, shaken off *That Uncertain Feeling*.'

to JOHN LEHMANN

59 Southmoor Road/Oxford

21-8-55

My dear John,

Thank you for your letter, which certainly shakes me, for reasons that you will see. Let us try to get at the truth methodically. To do this I will have to answer your 2 questions inversely, because that's the way of it.

I made no attempt to get hold of her (since 9th December) before the 31st of March, when I came round to have a drink with you and told you my story. Until then, only 2 people knew about it: Dan Davin who lives in Oxford (who doesn't know either her or anybody who does and therefore couldn't help – and certainly wouldn't talk anyway; and my best friend in London, who does not know her either – *nor does she know him*, which is right now going to be useful; he *absolutely* wouldn't talk, not only because of loyalty to me but for a variety of other reasons which we won't go into: one of them being that he knows only too well what happens to those who let me down – an example of which I'll give you later).

The above was written *before* we met yesterday in London.

So: back to 6 p.m. on 31st March, you heard the story and instantly guessed the girl's identity: I don't know why, because I'm a good story-teller, and my whole object was to keep this secret until the pay-off.

Because why should she, hearing I'd rung up on April 1st (but had *not* rung back as half-arranged), come rushing round to you with enquiries about my work? And why *you*, when she'd no reason to believe, *then*, that you knew more about me than anyone else? Why didn't she ask Connolly? Remember she hadn't seen you for months, and that the Frank Harris piece hadn't come out then (*was not even in proof*). Why not go to Spender, who had published my autobiograph-ical piece, 'Monsieur L'Abbé', the previous year in *Encounter*? Which she told me she'd read?

(PLEASE REFER TO ABOVE PASSAGE AGAIN WHEN, LATER ON, I REPORT PHONE TALK WITH HER ON JUNE 20th.)

Then you said you'd not seen her for some months but told me where she worked. I mentioned *Punch* book and autobiographies and said I'd get in touch with her: thus killing two birds with one S.

So that when – as we now know – she came to see you *next day*, April 1st, you would naturally assume that I *had* got in touch with her; whereas I'd merely rung the firm in the morning, while she was out, and left my name, saying I *might* ring later.

But I did not actually ring her until 14th APRIL, from Oxford; spoke of *Punch* collection & possible option on autobiographies; she said indeed she was interested and would give me a decision within 7 days. (She didn't say she knew me personally, until after accepting an invitation to lunch the following week-day to be arranged later; then I pretended to suddenly tumble to who she was, and she admitted this – then saying *we hadn't met for 8 years*.) *So what about the meeting on 9th Dec.???* But I didn't mention this either: That's why I said, in my last letter to you, that some sort of tacit conspiracy existed between us from the start.

It's even plainer now that it was from the dialogue when we finally met (see my last letter: full report) that this brief encounter made an impression on her too, isn't it?

Meanwhile back to April 14th. (Series of dates, with comments on action, now follows).

MARCH 31st: I tell you about Dec. meeting for first time.

APRIL 1st: I ring firm and leave name.

She comes to you to talk about me.

APRIL 14th: I ring her from Oxford as outlined above.

I post off *Punch* book material with business letter, outlining terms I wanted (£120 advance), and mentioning title of *second* vol. of autobiog. (Please note that *second*.) Also say that the sequence is all planned out, and option would be given should *Punch* book prove acceptable. But would she please reserve judgement and give *no* decision either way until I was able to meet her for lunch in London, because I had a few points to discuss since we were acquainted personally?

Tone: very formal. Asking her, in conclusion, please not to trouble to answer, because I'd so much work on hand that to write letters was agony to me. (She *didn't* write: another tacit conspiracy.)

APRIL 20th: Wrote her brief note, enclosing a revised plan of *Punch*-book and saying I couldn't come to London that week but would she kindly wait until I did. (No reply from her – as arranged.)

APRIL 26th: Proofs of Frank Harris piece received from you and corrected by me.

APRIL 27th: Sent her duplicate, corrected, Frank Harris as a sample of 2nd autobiog. volume, with note saying I'd contact her when able to come to London. (No reply from her – as instructed before.)

MAY 15th: Frank Harris piece printed in *London Mag.*: also *Cards of Identity*[1] review, which she must have read.

I have made no further contact with her because I'd certain ideas on how to conduct our prospective meeting, and I wasn't ready yet.

JUNE 2nd: At last I am ready!

I ring her from Oxford accordingly. What about lunch next week? My tone: formal, business voice. Hers: very friendly and a little timid. Yes, certainly, Tuesday would be lovely. *But* she had to say they'd decided (or rather *he* had) against *Punch* book. She would have told me before in a letter, but I'd said not to write. Apologetic, but couldn't we still

discuss doing the autobiogs. Yes, I said; but I needed money and I
didn't want to ask for an advance on an unfinished book. She said why
not? She quite understood, and it could quite easily be arranged. I said
dubiously, well we might discuss it perhaps. She said: 'But aren't you
going to take me out then?' To my horror, it suddenly developed into
a murmuring intimate conversation of the sort that one has with
girlfriends of long standing (I mean the tone of voice): the sort of phone
talk that usually ends with 'I love you'. In this I was forced unwillingly
to participate, until it was being conducted in whispers.

('Where are we going to meet?'
'This railway strike's on. Times of trains from Oxford are so
uncertain.'
'But you'll come in the morning?'
'I'll do my best.'
'I'll wait for you. When will you ring?'
'When I get there.'
'*As soon* as you get there? Your very first call?'
'Yes.'
'Promise?'
'Yes. Good-bye.'
'Bye.')

This so horrified me that I told Davin that I'd a good mind to send
a note saying I'd decided against meeting because they wouldn't do
Punch book – that she'd eventually guessed by some devilish intuition
what I wanted and was forcing the pace in order to get me to admit it
and then turn me down. Davin said grimly that I was going even if he
had to knock me out and put me on the bloody train himself.

But I *didn't* go – because that night blood-poisoning struck; I was in
frightful pain; doctor called in; M & B;[2] codeine; penicillin; travelling,
and even getting up, out of question for 14 days at least.

JUNE 5th: (Sunday): Wrote her saying I couldn't make it because of
illness (repeated Doctor's orders as above). I'd get in touch when well
again, but please don't write me.

JUNE 12th: Better sooner than expected. Doctor says I can go to
London following week, but advises convalescence at friend's house near
Maidenhead at weekend (17th–19th). Wrote her accordingly, asking
her to phone me at latter (giving her my host's number) if she *wasn't*
going to be free to meet with me on Monday or Tuesday (20–21st). She
did not phone.

JUNE 20th: Phoned her from host's house to say I couldn't come until Tuesday or Wednesday because there were no vacancies in London hotels until then. She and I then had the following astounding conversation.

She: 'Oh hullo, it's you.' (Bright and happy.)

'How d'you do?'

'Your voice.'

'I see. Well what about this lunch?'

'Wednesday? I *could* make Tuesday, but ...'

'No, Wednesday's fine.'

'Where?'

'Anywhere you like.'

'No, you choose.'

'Well, meet for a drink in Hatchett's[3] first and decide? That's near you.'

'Yes, lovely. One o'clock?'

'One o'clock. Oh – by the way, I asked you in my last letter whether you'd thought over the autobiography business carefully meanwhile. Have you?'

'Well it depends on whether you can get free, doesn't it?'

'Free from what?'

'The publisher who did the first volume.'

'Hart-Davis?'

'Is that who did it?'

'Of course. Don't you know?'

'Well no I didn't actually. You see, I didn't know until I looked over your first letter again that there *had* been a first volume after all.'

'Are you attempting to joke with me, Miss Thing? If so, I assure you that it's singularly ill-advised.'

'*Of course* I'm not joking.'

'You have never read *The Weeping and the Laughter*?'

'I'm afraid not.'

'Or, apparently, heard of it even? Don't you read any reviews?'

'Well, you see I was away when it came out. I was in America. I was away for two years. I missed all the reviews of everything.'

I swallowed. I was so angry I could scarcely speak, but I said: 'Miss Thing. I first contacted you in mid-April. It is now mid-June. *Do you mean that in 2 months you haven't made any enquiries about the latest work of someone you – presumably – thought of doing business with?*'

'No. I ... I'm afraid I didn't.'

'You once had a reputation for efficiency. Didn't you ask *anyone about me at all*?'

'No. No, I didn't.' She now sounded desperate.

'May I ask you *why* you didn't?'

'I...I can't tell you.'

'Can't or won't?'

'I can't.'

'You mean you just don't know?'

'No. I mean I *can't* tell you.'

'Well, I don't get that; but perhaps when you have read the first volume and decided whether or not you're really interested in this project, you'll get in touch with me again – what?'

'But Wednesday.'

'Wednesday?'

'The date on Wednesday.'

I said: 'Miss Thing. What the devil would be the good of meeting on Wednesday? What would we talk about? Unless you've read my first volume, we can't possibly talk business, and I'm afraid I just have not got the time to rush up to London in order to take young women to lunch.'

'Oh, so this date was just business?'

'Well, what did you suppose?'

'I thought you wanted to take me out?'

'Miss Thing, I'm so sorry, but this is my host's phone and I really can't use it for 10 minutes at a time in order to talk nonsense. Up to now, 2 months of my time have been wasted, so please don't waste anymore.'

'I'm sorry. I've ordered a copy of the book and it should arrive tomorrow...'

'Another thing,' I interrupted. 'I am naturally free from Hart-Davis, otherwise how could I offer you an option at all? And yet you asked me whether I'm free.'

'I'm sorry,' she said again.

I said: 'Well, just write me when you've read that book. Goodbye.'

I'd quite forgotten that I was in love with her, for nothing makes me quite so angry as (a) people who waste my time in business and (b) people who are inefficient, especially when they're career-girls.' Also my recent illness made me more irascible that ever. But after about a couple of hours I remembered I'd had a date with her and thrown it away; so I rang the firm back and got put through to her at once.

'Oh hullo. I thought you'd ring.'

'Did you? Why?'

We were now suddenly back on the murmuring plane, whereas most girls in her place would have been aloof, angry, hurt, or triumphant. She was just glad (and not put on either.) This removed all anger from me, naturally, at once.

She said: 'You can't expect me to tell you that,' and laughed – but again not triumphantly at all, nor coyly.

I said: 'No. But listen. I've been thinking things over.'

'You'd like that date to be on again?'

'Now's your chance to deliver a shattering snub.'

'Of course I won't. I'd set that day aside to be free for you.'

'So you'll come?'

'Yes of course.'

'Well, thanks,' I said, completely disconcerted. 'See you at one on Wednesday then.'

'There's something you're supposed to say first.'

'An apology? But look, you have been a bit silly, haven't you?'

'Yes, I have, and I didn't mean for you to apologise.'

'Then what?'

'You know.'

I did. I said: 'I'm taking *you* out. Is that it?' She laughed. 'Of course. After all, we can get a lot of preliminary stuff out of the way as well, can't we?'

'Yes. Then I'll see you.'

'You will. I won't ring or send a wire cancelling it, or just not turn up, in case that crossed your mind.'

'It did.'

She said: 'Of course. But it'll be all right. You'll see.'

I said in my Ned Beaumont[4] voice: 'Well, thanks for reassuring me.'

She said: 'Still, if I didn't come, wouldn't you be disappointed?'

'Yes. Bye-bye.'

That was the prelude to our meeting on 22 JUNE.

But we know this parade of not knowing the facts of my autobiography etc. to have been a pack of lies, for she was talking to you about me as early as APRIL 1st – and no doubt to others as well. So she *must* have known I was free to contract for autobiographies, and she must surely have found out about *The Weeping and the Laughter*, and almost certainly have read it as well. So why pretend to be a fool? To trick me into believing she was one, and then do me down on terms later? No, because she never tried to. Besides, until on 22nd June I showed her the plans of 2 novels, as well as the autobiographies, at the very end of our meeting, I never got the impression that she was interested in the business end at all. But the plans of my whole future work *did* impress her very much. I made it plain that the novels involved getting out of contracts with other firms and that she was not to mention them at all to her boss. Later, I said, if they took on the autobiographical, *she and I* together might work out some way to manage about the novels but this was between ourselves and *not* to be publicised yet. She agreed, and also to ask for only £120 part-advance to enable me to finish the 2nd autobiographical volume; then, if that was OK when I rang up the following Tuesday, she and I were to meet and work out actual contract-details before any money changed hands. (All *my* suggestion.)

Why the novel-plans were there at all was because I'd brought them along to impress her *as a girl*, thinking then that she'd only be interested in a serious writer whose work was planned out for years ahead (as indeed it is). It hadn't occurred to me that my film ambitions would impress her far more; by the time I realised this, it was too late to remove the novel-plans from the envelope containing autobiographical stuff, for she'd already got hold of this in the taxi and was reading through the outline of *Business & Desire* which (as I explained to her) no one else has ever seen (my novel about the film business).[5]

Now, over to JUNE 28th (see my last letter):

When I rang up, she couldn't say what she wanted, because there were people in her room, and it was very confidential. Could she ring me back at Oxford? On the second call, she still wanted to explain things personally; it had gone wrong, but it was all so difficult to say unless she could see me; I said (in my kindest and most reassuring voice – never known to fail, because heard so rarely) that she wasn't to worry, nor was I angry with her; of course we'd meet, and we made a date for 6 p.m. on JUNE 29th (see my last 2 letters). Then we had hysteria over the phone & her personal troubles, etc.; she'd ring me first thing next morning at my hotel.

JUNE 30th: She didn't ring me.

Meanwhile all my *Punch* collection stuff was still at her office; they hadn't been able to send it back before because of the rail-strike (by now over). I thought I might collect this personally, viz approaching another firm; so I rang her office: 4 p.m. she'd gone out. Wasn't coming back that day. Nobody knew where she was. Her secretary said all the material concerning me had been sent back to Oxford with a letter written the day before. (She'd never mentioned any letter to me.) I said, what was in the letter? Nobody knew; there was no carbon; no file, because she handled everything to do with me herself and never discussed it except with the boss (presumably, as there'd been 'a lot of conferences'). The secretary was never present even when I rang up (she said this so tartly, having obviously been waved out of the room whenever this happened). I got annoyed during this conversation and showed it. I said I was sure no letter had been written, and that no material had been sent back. The girl went and made a search; then came back and said there was nothing in the office, but that she'd been told perhaps Miss Thing kept all my stuff at home. I rang off.

You and I had a date that evening between 5 & 6. Then I heard for the first time that she'd been to see you about me (but this was *after* we'd had lunch, because you said 'a week ago'). I told you what had happened when I saw her etc. and you remarked on her odd state when she called on you. Your advice was to ring her from home that evening.

I did (see my last letter). She said that she'd written me *that day* and had the material sent back with it from the office (received on my return to Oxford).

But the letter as you see is postmarked 8.15 *that night*: posted *after I'd rung her* and obviously one she'd typed herself, and if you look at it carefully, taken a great deal of trouble over the phrasing and even the typing. And it's dated, for some reason, *Tuesday*: when on the two previous days she'd not spoken of a letter at all! Why bring me up to London, why all the secrecy, when the letter would have served? And why mention *fiction*?

I think I know: because she showed the boss those novel-plans (against my wishes) and suggested they should buy me out of all contracts & give me some large sum of money as well. Of course I wouldn't do this: whereas if she'd just asked for the £120 I wanted, it would have been okay. (She'd never anticipated much difficulty herself.) She wouldn't be the first girl to bugger things up by trying to pull off some big stroke on my behalf without consulting me first. So much, I fancy, for the business end.

The *Punch* collection, and other material, by the way was not sent off *until the following Monday*, after she'd had a nice letter from me in answer to hers of '28th June', offering any help I could give if she were in trouble and asking her to let me know when she was free. No reply.

JULY 19th: I ring her for the last time when next in London. We know the result. Meantime she's contacted Davenport with the story that I'm keen on her.

JULY 26th: Letter from you saying she'd approached you with same story two days before (July 24th).

Which brings us up to date, and now I don't know what to think. But I've been told that, so far as anyone knows, there's no other man. Now I'll keep in the background myself, and shortly somebody else will be dealing with her for me. All this is a pity, because when we met I did genuinely *like* her, contrary to expectation. I'd look after her (not my usual role), and God knows she seems to need it. I think she's afraid of becoming involved in an *affair* with me, and that if I could persuade her that it wasn't like that, it would be all right – sometime, anyway; and I'm willing to be patient. So far as I know, she's never really told anybody that *I'm in love with her*, because she can't possibly know.

She could of course be mixed up in the diabolism that's going around just now: this would explain her panic, and it's in character. But her approaching you on the day after I first spoke to you about it is *really* uncanny, so is her resemblance to my sister Carol[6] (a girl who used to share all her mental traits, as of course I do to a great extent).

Tell me sometime what you think of all this. I'll be up again week after next, when we must have – if possible – a longer talk about *The Girl in the Spotlight*. I'll write you separately about that meantime. I'm posting the *Punch* collection material off to Sadleir[7] over weekend, and it all really depends on my getting that money. So let us pray.

As ever,
Julian

PS I consulted Barbara[8] (without mentioning girl's name or anything) briefly over lunch, as I did Monica, and she said no woman would go round telling my friends I was 'interested' in her but that she was not interested in me, unless it meant the contrary. She said bluntly that it was bloody silly, boring behaviour anyway, Barbara was with me for 5 years; is 26; bright; and very (now) sophisticated. She is no longer in love with me herself. J.

1   Satirical novel by Nigel Dennis, published in 1955. Maclaren-Ross's review of it appeared in the June 1955 issue of the *London Magazine*. His sympathetic assessment of it was accompanied by his thoughts on the art of satire: 'While the great satirists of the past directed their shafts of ridicule at faults and follies inherent in human nature itself, rather than at any manifestations characteristic of their particular time, twentieth-century satire almost always depends for effect upon topicality – the castigation of trends and institutions necessarily impermanent in a rapidly changing world, thus accounting for both the exaggerated acclaim with which it is often greeted, and the evanescence of its popular appeal.'

2   M&B tablets were a kind of antibiotic.

3   An expensive West End restaurant.

4   The main character – a gang boss's laconic sidekick – in Dashiell Hammett's *The Glass Key* (1931). Maclaren-Ross first read the novel, which he greatly admired, during the summer of 1931.

5   The focus of the planned novel had shifted from the book world to the British film industry.

6   Carol Cheavin (1898–1970), who had been born Caroline Mary Ida Ross, was living in New Zealand.

7   Michael Sadleir (1888–1968), novelist and director of Constable, the company that published the novels of his protégé Patrick Hamilton (1904–62).

8   His ex-girlfriend Barbara Wimble.

to WINNIE DAVIN

27-8-55 (2.30 a.m.)

My dear Winnie,

Looking through my papers on getting home, I found rough copy of the note to you about which we were talking tonight, which I have copied again (remember that I'm a canny Scot!)[1] and now enclose.

Please, next time we meet, tell me *exact date* when you first heard the rumour concerned. If nobody tells me the truth – and of course she herself never tells it, nor do I tell it to her – it merely complicates a situation which, if it would end in my destruction, would not matter terribly, but which *will* matter should it end in hers. I really must know if you heard this between 29 June and 19–26 July. *Try* to remember.

Apropos J.D.:[2] on 19 July he told me that he went to a party where he didn't expect to see her, and then she started to say that I was interested in her, but she was indifferent etc. – quoting, according to *him*, J.L.[3] as her source of information. I could tell, however, that he was not only spinning a yarn about this but about everything. If she phoned him, it's much more significant. I never asked or told him to phone her about anything: indeed he said at one time (on July 1st) that she must never know (thinking then I'd had a mere affair in mind) and he would if possible secure information in an indirect way. But it was on

19 July that her attitude towards me crystallised into antagonism; I phoned him directly afterwards and received roundabout (but very hedging) information. J.L. – phoned by me later – said he hoped I wouldn't expect him to deny that *he'd* given the show away; but he believed this came, not from her in an attempt to set us at loggerheads, but from J.D. who not only dislikes him, but probably (remember what he is, according to him, *supposed to have said*) – out of some confused loyalty to me – made some remark to her which naturally caused her to strike out against me: because people like herself and myself will hit out straightaway if there's the slightest suggesting that one or the other is not interested (or only out of self-interest). So I'm sure you were right when you said J.D. (who's always made a mess of everything – business until now – which I've had the misfortune to deal with him) received a phone call from *her*. Otherwise how did it come into your mind? I *never* asked him to get in touch with her (see overleaf); in fact he said he couldn't, because she hated him and anyway he hadn't seen her for some months. So, if it didn't come from me, you didn't imagine it (why should you?) and *she must* have phoned *him*. This would be in character with everything she's done so far (especially with J.L.). There were only the following names mentioned by me as friends of mine (and I could see her making a mental note of each one, as plainly as if she'd written them down in a notebook): Dan – impossible to get at; J.L. – approached as early as April 1st and lunched-with on the 24 June (two days after her lunch with me); and J.D. himself (approached, either way, at earliest opportunity). The latter is the weak link, because (a) he's the reverse of tactful – though he gave me some information without which there'd be no *GIS*[4] (b) he didn't realise how important the thing was to me until he started to tell me that he'd talked about me to her, and then at once his story because confused and scarcely credible (though containing a germ of truth, because she approached J.L. in the same way 10 days later – having chosen her version she was sticking to it, and I (out of pride) would have done the same.

So please try to remember about these 2 points. Read this at your leisure; excuse scrawl, but I'm in terrible haste and my cut hand doesn't help (incidentally – another superstition – you have to shed your own blood by accident before you can do certain things); and let me know when you can. Please keep this until you've got dates as straight as you can remember them, and *then destroy it*. Try to help this poor unhappy tormented child whose only real fault was to get mixed up with someone like me, and who – if I may make an appeal to sentiment – is after all a woman like yourself. I may still be able to save her from what is coming: I wish I could, but things get out of control sometimes.

Excuse long scrawl; must work now.

Love,

J. (3.15 a.m.)

1 Maclaren-Ross had Scottish ancestry on his father's side of the family. His grandfather, William Ross, was a very successful businessman who ran a shipping company called the Thistle Line, a name calculated to emphasise these roots north of the border.
2 John Davenport.
3 John Lehmann.
4 *The Girl in the Spotlight.*

to WINNIE DAVIN

Early September 1955

Dear Winnie,

Trapped. Slight piles. And no money at all. *No* review-books from *Punch* until Tony returns (another 2 weeks) so *no* money available from *Punch* until Caudery returns (2 weeks). *TLS* editor away (2 weeks). Spender away (until Mid-Sept. – 8 or 9 days).

No other sources, though suggestions welcome.

Punch book seeks publisher.

Am working on long story £60 for *Encounter* against Spender's return,[1] but have nothing to smoke since noon yesterday, would welcome some fags, bread, and books (*Witch Wood* by Buchan[2] – Anna[3] has it). Very boring and miserable this enforced wait. Come & see me if you have a moment.

J.

1 This may well have been 'Astrid: A Long Story', which never appeared in *Encounter*. Only fragments of the piece have survived. One of these was post-humously published in *Bitten by the Tarantula and Other Writing* (Black Spring Press, 2005).
2 John Buchan (1875–1940).
3 Anna Davin, teenage daughter of Dan and Winnie Davin.

to HAMISH HAMILTON

59 Southmoor Road/Oxford
25-9-55

Dear Hamilton,

Your advertisement of *Maigret and the Burglar's Wife* in the current *London Magazine* reminds me that I have not, regrettably, dealt with the proofs of this translation.

Two other matters that occur to me:

(1) My new collection[1] (Plan of contents enclosed herewith) now totals 80,000 words and includes 12 stories of various lengths (I hope to include also a 10,000 word story which I'm engaged in completing),[2] some of which have not been previously printed; in view of this, and the considerable success which my *Punch* pieces have had (viz letter from Malcolm Muggeridge, also enclosed, which please return), it might be worth your while to consider the volume after all; and by paying the £125 advance that I require in order to return to London, help me to defray expenses while completing my novel: on which I must abandon work for some time unless financial support is forthcoming from somewhere.

(2) I have recently read Pierre MacOrlan's novel *Quai des Brumes*, from which the famous French film was derived,[3] though the book bears little resemblance to it. I was enormously impressed: it antedates in its general attitude the existentialists such as Sartre and Camus (it was first published in 1927) and, although tragic in essence, is also at times extremely funny.

No English translation exists, to my knowledge, and I'd be pleased to undertake one at the same rates as the Maigret and deliver it within 16 days or so (the volume is about the same length; unfortunately I have no copy of my own, but one would be attainable at Hatchette's).

Yours sincerely,
J. Maclaren-Ross

Enc.: Contents plan of *Funny Things Happen*.
Personal letter from Malcolm Muggeridge (*contents confidential*)[4]

1 At this stage the collection was called *Funny Things Happen*. The title of the published book was *The Funny Bone* (1956).
2 This unidentified piece, probably 'Astrid: A Long Story', wasn't included in the finished book.
3 Directed by Marcel Carné, *Quai des Brumes* (1938) starred Jean Gabin.

4 Muggeridge's letter contained a declaration that Maclaren-Ross was 'the best living parodist', a claim later quoted on the dustjacket of *The Funny Bone*.

to DAN DAVIN

September 1955

Dear Dan,

Enclosed letter from Tony speaks for itself.

I received a review-book from *Punch* yesterday and posted off the review, so there's a faint chance that money will arrive tomorrow (£6.6 cash.)

At the moment I've exactly nothing; had nothing to eat all yesterday; and my last shilling has just gone into the meter.

If you've got a moment sometime today I wish you'd pop up; there seems no point in my getting out of bed (besides I feel too ill) and I've no one else to discuss the position with.

I haven't been so worried for a long time, as all avenues seem to be closing down.

Yours ever,

J.

Still no supplementary cheque from *TLS*, as promised (twice) by A.P.J.[1]

1 Alan Pryce-Jones, editor of the *Times Literary Supplement*.

to RUPERT HART-DAVIS

22 or 29-9-55 (2.30p.m.)

Dear Rupert,

My book is now finished.[1] If you're still interested, perhaps you could spare 5 minutes' talk, as there's a point or two I'd like to settle first. You'll appreciate that now it's done. I don't want to waste any time in placing it, so I don't think there's any point in beating about the bush. If you'd rather not handle it I would much rather you said so right out. I will call back later today in the hope of seeing you. If not and I haven't had a ring from you by 12 noon tomorrow – as they don't seem certain whether you're coming in today or not – I shall know you're not interested and it's useless to contact you further.[2]

Yours ever,

Julian

1 He was referring to *Funny Things Happen*.
2 Probably swayed by his previous dealings with Maclaren-Ross, not to mention the poor sales of *The Weeping and the Laughter*, Hart-Davis decided against publishing the book.

to JOHN LEHMANN[1]

59 Southmoor Road/Oxford
26-9-55

Sir,

Both your editorial and Lawrence Lipton's article 'The World Behind the Billboards', in the September *London Magazine*, raised many points of interest to all who are concerned with contemporary trends in literature, though I would like to 'take issue' (as his compatriots put it) with the stance adopted by Mr Lipton as a whole. (It seems curious, by the way, that Nelson Algren[2] should be quoted as the spokesman for the younger generation, since he can scarcely belong to it himself: surely a novel of his was published in this country and highly praised by the late James Agate[3] during the Nineteen-Thirties?)

Mr Lipton cited with approval Mr Robert Graves' dictum that writers, in order to keep going, should accept odd, menial jobs rather than semi-literary ones: but they have always done so, or been forced into doing so faute de mieux;[4] I can assure both Mssrs Graves and Lipton, from personal experience, that attempting to sell vacuum-cleaners on commission, when not queueing up for the dole, is no more conducive to 'independence of judgement' or the maintenance of personal integrity, than would be any of the proposed substitutes – which, while far from desirable, might offer a degree of comfort and time in which to concentrate on some form of literary activity.

Moreover, 'disaffiliation' for young writers is nothing new, nor is going to the slums rather than the suburbs for material (can George Orwell's *Down and Out in London and Paris* have been so soon forgotten?), and the sort of 'disaffiliation' Mr Lipton describes seems uncomfortably close to that juvenile romanticism which has perennially found its inspiration in the sordid. There is no reason why 'the secret hearts' of the destitute and the disgruntled should be more worth 'plumbing' than those – to quote an English example – of the envious psuedo-artistic Soho bums in Roland Camberton's *Scamp*;[5] drug-addiction among 'bright teenagers', jive, juvenile delinquents, 'Greenwich Village junkies', would appear, as subjects, no more rewarding than Scott

Fitzgerald's portrayal of their Jazz Age equivalents, while *The Great Gatsby* and *Tender is the Night*, by examining the last strongholds of the feudal system and analysing the corrupt values of the hollow capitalist heart, seem likely to prove of more significance as social documents than anything produced so far by the 'disaffiliated' school, for corruption does not spread from below but from above: the focal points of infection 'are more likely to be found among the higher income-groups than at the lower levels where the disease is already rife. The respective views from the window of a Chicago slum saloon and that of a fashionable yacht club are different, that is all: the canker exists in human nature itself rather than in any special environment.'

We are told that some 'disaffiliated' authors have already seen four and five figure royalty cheques: a sight denied to the most 'serious' novelists in England (despite the moans about art not paying enough in the USA), and as for 'high-paying slicks',[6] they simply do not exist over here. Surely, too, Mr Ralph Ellison[7] spends a great deal of time lecturing at American universities, and Mr J.D. Salinger[8] in writing for the *New Yorker*: hardly 'disaffiliated' activities commensurate with 'dedicated independent poverty' or 'the long lean view'. When Mr Salinger's adolescent narrator[9] says, 'If there's another war they better stick me in front of a firing-squad,' it remains to be seen whether he, and other members of his generation, will not after all 'object' to such a fate: such arrogant and idealistic pronouncements were made in 1933 by Mr William Saroyan (an early example of 'disaffiliation', who also found his material among the Dickensian and Dostoevskian figures 'Behind the tote-boards'), but when war broke out he joined the army and wrote, in *The Human Comedy*, one of the most nauseatingly sentimental pieces of jingoist propaganda to appear during the recent conflict.

From Diana Lattimer's statement that 'only poverty is holy',[10] it is but a step to the saintly paupers inhabiting Saroyan's later underworld (sanctified and softened once the author, by achieving prosperity, had managed to escape from such surroundings himself), or the romanticised tramps from *Tortilla Flat*:[11] poverty is a humiliating and degrading state which should never be accepted as 'holy' by anyone, while to 'dedicate' oneself to it is pure adolescent idiocy.

You are right in saying that the Ministry of Fear[12] is more likely to be housed graciously 'at the end of a long tree-shadowed drive' (as the late John Buchan seems instinctively to have known); but the lack of violent protest and passion in this country, of which you rightly complain, is due not only to the English writer's latent snobbery and desire to conform with society directly society shows willing to accept him, but also to a sinister encroachment foreshadowed by Mr Simon Raven in his letter in your October issue.[13]

It is the stealthy onset of the state-aided young men 'who cannot afford a claret', the under-privileged, high-necked-sweater-wearing cocoa drinkers, that we over here have to beware-of, rather than Mr Raven's flippant and irreverent 'squires' or 'the priests of *Kitsch*' denounced by Mr Lipton: these, together with the ex-Soho, back-scratching and back-biting, talentless survivors from *Scamp*, the bitter-sipping contingent in duffle-coats who have contrived to obtain small 'critical' platforms and subterranean positions as publishers' 'advisors' etc., who will suck all colour, all vitality, from the literary life: their sole desire being to live like rats among the ruins which they have helped to honeycomb.[14]

J. Maclaren-Ross

1   Perhaps due to its embittered tone, the letter, intended for publication, never featured in the *London Magazine*.
2   Nelson Algren (1909–81), author of *The Man with the Golden Arm* and other novels.
3   James Agate (1877–1947) was generally regarded as one of the leading British critics of his generation. Most of his writing focused on the theatre.
4   'For want of anything better'.
5   The pseudonymous Camberton's 1950 novel featured a scathing portrait of Maclaren-Ross, whose alter ego was 'Angus Steerforth-Sims', former travelling salesman, author of *Gotcher Mate* and ubiquitous patron of 'the Corney Arms', an obvious stand-in for the Wheatsheaf.
6   American glossy magazines, among them the *Saturday Evening Post*, which paid high fees for short stories.
7   Ralph Ellison (1913–94), author of *The Invisible Man* (1952).
8   J.D. Salinger (1919–), author of *The Catcher in the Rye* (1951).
9   Holden Caulfield in *The Catcher in the Rye*.
10   'Diana Lattimer' was a character in *The Human Comedy* (1945).
11   John's Steinbeck's 1935 novel.
12   A reference to Graham Greene's 1943 thriller.
13   Simon Raven's letter, published in the October 1955 issue of the *London Magazine* offered a snooty and disdainful commentary on the debate about the critical writings of F.R. Leavis. 'Dr Leavis's adherents,' Raven proclaimed, 'are largely state-aided young men who cannot afford a claret and Peacock approach to literature. They come from poor homes where books are a luxury and must be taken seriously. They come from a naturally Puritanical caste ...'
14   Maclaren-Ross painted a disapproving portrait of this new brand of London bohemianism in his short memoir 'Bop'. First published in the 23 September 1953 issue of *Punch*, it was later reprinted in *The Funny Bone*. The piece described a visit to a bebop club, located 'beyond a no-man's land of bomb-craters and blitzed buildings somewhere north of Tottenham Court Road.'

to JOHN LEHMANN

59 Southmoor Road / Oxford

12-10-55 (6 a.m.)

My dear John,

Herewith the novel-review: I've done the four best (that girl's book, contrary to expectation, is very good).[1]

If you can expedite the cash, I'd be very grateful; I'm terribly short (masterpiece of understatement).

John Guest[2] returns on 24th Oct. I phoned his secretary from London and checked. Will write him and get off all the stuff to await his arrival.

I've had a very amusing letter from William Faulkner (apparently staying at Brown's Hotel) re my *Punch* parody. I replied (I hope) in kind.

Look, I've had a proof-copy from Sadleir of Patrick Hamilton's latest, *Unknown Assailant* (out Oct. 24th). How about 1,500–2,000 words on the Ernest Ralph Gorse novels (about the murderer, you know), of which this is the third?[3]

I think Hamilton's one of the best living novelists, and I'm very keen to do an article on these books now that I've all the material. Let me know what you feel!

As ever,

Julian

Excuse waste paper: have no other at moment.

1 Perhaps due to lack of space, the review didn't appear in the *London Magazine*.
2 John Guest (1911–77) worked as a Literary Advisor at the London-based publishing firm Longmans. Maclaren-Ross must have hoped to secure a book deal with the company.
3 *The West Pier* (1951) was the first. It was followed in 1953 by *Mr Stimpson and Mr Gorse*. The three are now known as the Gorse Trilogy, although it was Hamilton's intention to write further instalments.

to ANTHONY POWELL

59 Southmoor Road / Oxford

13-10-55

My dear Tony,

Further to my last letter, I'm enclosing herewith, as I suggested, a parody of Faulkner based on *A Fable*. As I'm sending this off by Express Post, I hope it may reach you before Thursday.

The Listener, last Saturday, managed to get a parcel of books to me by the Oxford train, and the parcel contained not only the Faulkner but the new Evelyn Waugh.

I'm therefore going to do a parody of the Waugh also this week, modelled on *Officers and Gentlemen*,[1] and hope it may be more successful than the last one I submitted, which was actually based on an extract from the new novel printed in the *London Magazine*.

My doctor hopes I'll be fit by Wednesday; I'm spending the weekend with a friend at Maidenhead[2] and coming up to London for 3 days or so on Monday 20th, when I hope to see you and have a chat, among other things, about *The Acceptance World*, which I've read and enjoyed: though pp. 62–64 gave me the cold shivers, as I'm at the moment afflicted by the same secret disease as your narrator.[3]

As ever,

Julian

1 Evelyn Waugh's 1955 novel, which formed part of the *Sword of Honour* trilogy.
2 Gerry Fisher.
3 The passage culminates in the moment when the narrator is driven through the snowy streets of London by his friend, Peter Templer. They share the car with two women. Though one of the women nods off, that doesn't stop the narrator from falling in love with her. 'Although not always simultaneous in taking effect, nor necessarily at all equal in voltage, the process of love is rarely unilateral,' the narrator muses. 'When the moment comes, a secret attachment is often returned with interest. Some know this by instinct; others learn in a hard school.' For Maclaren-Ross, the scene had particular resonance, thanks to his obsession with Sonia Orwell.

to JOHN LEHMANN

59 Southmoor Road/Oxford
16-10-55

My dear John,

Thank you so much for your letter and the card: yes, I do need the cash. This will mainly go in covering small debts; but if some pieces I've sent to *Punch* prove acceptable, I will be in London again this week (Wed. or Thurs.) and hope to see you then.

I've thought out a new plan for approaching the Girl[1] (or at any rate producing a *rapprochement*), in which you might play an impersonal intermediary role: I'd welcome your advice on it; and things ought not to be left too long like this.

I agree with you about 'Chariot of the Sun':[2] it is not quite satisfactory in its present form, but that was written some weeks ago, before I acquired some startling new information that changes my whole approach to the subject. (The presentation, however, should still be, on the whole, apparently unemotional and ironical: the narrator realising – with the reader – *only at the end*, the true meaning of the whole experience.)

I'll set to work on a piece on Hamilton (confining myself mainly to the three Gorse novels, though I don't think it should be printed as a review), and I think you'll like it. 1,500–2,000 words? The title – following that of one of the books concerned – would be: 'Mr Hamilton and Mr Gorse'.

As ever,
Julian

1 Sonia Orwell.
2 Probably a short story based on Maclaren-Ross's unrequited passion for Sonia Orwell. The manuscript has been lost.

to JOHN LEHMANN

59 Southmoor Road/Oxford
26-10-55

My dear John,

Thank you for your letter.

I'm glad you liked the Hamilton article. Of course, publish any time that fits your schedule, but I would be grateful if you could arrange for the fee to be sent to me: as you know, this is being a difficult time for me, and extra finance helps to prevent the death of my private dream (which must on no accounts be allowed to take place).

If it helps, you *could* print it as a long review of the 3 Gorse books, since the 3rd volume is due out any day; but I'd rather it came out as a critical article. However, you as editor must decide.

By the way, I don't know if I mentioned that I sent John Guest all the *Punch* book material, portions and plan of future autobiographies etc., last week, with a letter saying you had advised me to do so; so he may be ringing you up about it.

As ever,
Julian

to DAN DAVIN

59 Southmoor Road/Oxford
8-11-55

My dear Dan,

Allow me to write you a letter which, I hope, may cancel out that one I wrote to you on Nov. 21 '54.

I was not drunk when I approached you in the Victoria last night, only very tired, strung-up, and certainly not happy: though none of these states, in my opinion, is an excuse for anything; I have always believed, between men who are friends, in Jowett's advice to the young[1] which, as a Balliol man, you know much better than I do.

I merely felt that if, as might well be, you felt (though I did not) that our association should end, it was better to have a showdown and get it over quickly and quietly rather than prolong any agony which you, as resident here, would have to endure more than I would.

I saw, however, that I was apparently mistaken and that such did not seem to be the case. I'm very glad and do let's try to avoid such quarrels in future. I have never pretended to be easy to deal with, but you must realise that things are far from easy for me, on the other hand, and that a lot of people during the past year have taken up an attitude toward me which I fear they will have cause to regret in the future. Of course I realise also that you work extraordinarily hard and also get very tired and consequently more irritable than you are by nature; but don't forget that you have something to work for and so it isn't all in vain, I must work only for myself and therefore I don't pity you, for you're in the happier position; but don't think that I feel that you should pity me or that I am envious of you: I am sincerely glad that you have a pleasant life surrounding you; but on the other hand I chose my way of living, and so must accept it (while reserving the right to complain of minor annoyances which are not my fault). I don't wish to put myself up as a martyr: indeed I hope one day that I will be happy too; I don't see myself as a man with wife and children like yourself, Nelson Scott, Jaeger etc.: yet if the children of all of you, at times (though I don't like to admit it), can touch my Beaumont-hard heart, perhaps this might be a good thing – who knows, least of all myself.

Anyway, I thought you took this evening awfully well; and I shall not forget last Christmas when you gave me a very happy time (one of the terrors that obsesses me at the moment is the thought of the next).

I wouldn't like you to think that I bear malice for some of the arguments we had last year; if I seemed sometimes to be annoyed when you indicated some faults you have found in me it was because (a) in some cases you were wrong (b) to paraphrase yourself, when I was railing against Oxford: 'I know all this myself, so why should I have to hear it from you' (c) I spend a great deal of time making fun of myself in print much more viciously than anyone else can do, so feel that I should be spared it by others in private life! On the other hand, when I first came down here, I was at a very low ebb; and if you sometimes seemed antagonistic, it spurred me into resisting you: whether you intended this as remedial treatment or not, I don't know, but anyhow on the whole it did me good. So thanks, anyway.

Now, I have, as you know, another interest in life; and however that turns out, it has done me good too. Of course I'm an egoist, but not (I hope) a selfish beast; I haven't tried deliberately to make my girls unhappy, and Monica, I'm happy to say, gives me now a very good reference. All the same, this is the first time in my life when I have found a young woman whom I know I can live with always; and, given the chance, I will devote all my time, apart from work, to making her happy (as distinct from seeing that she is not actively *un*happy.)

Never mind that. I'll drop in tonight at D. Towers[2] about half-eight and pick you up if (as I hope) you're both free for a drink. I'd be obliged if you wouldn't tell Winnie what's in this letter, because I think she might be upset if she thought there was a final break imminent, though of course I may be wrong there – you know best.

So long,
Julian

1 Benjamin Jowett (1817–93), former Dean of Balliol College, Oxford. 'Young men make great mistakes in life,' he declared; 'for one thing, they idealise love too much.' Maclaren-Ross may also have been thinking of another of Jowett's pronouncements: 'Never retreat. Never explain. Get it done and let them howl.'
2 103 Southmoor Road, Dan and Winnie Davin's home.

to DAN AND WINNIE DAVIN

Dear Dan and Winnie,

Hughes[1] has fixed things about the *Punch* book and autobiographies with Elek on terms which I think aren't bad: I am writing provisionally accepting, but would like to consult you about the contract if possible tonight on your return from the sherry party or sometime tomorrow: also we ought to drink to my future trip, don't you think?

All will be settled with George etc. next week, after I've been up to town to sign contracts, draw advance etc.

As ever,

Julian

If it isn't too much bother you could get me some sliced bread today, I'd be awfully grateful as I haven't slept all night, and don't want to go out till this evening.

1 Maclaren-Ross's new literary agent, Edmund Hughes, who was based near Colchester.

to C.K. JAEGER

59 Southmoor Road/Oxford

18-11-55

My dear Jaeger,

How very nice to hear from you. I'd begun to get very worried, and was just about to ring up your home. I'm sorry to hear you've been ill and glad to hear you've recovered. I myself nearly died this summer. Blood poisoning: 6 tablets of M&B per day, plus 6 codeine to kill the pain; then a penicillin injection every day for a fortnight. I'm more or less alone here and was delirious for two days: moreover, against doctors' orders, I drank a half-bottle of brandy and started to roar with laughter at the thought that the great dream might end like this, as a bad joke which was on me. I hope that when the end does come, I may feel as happy as I did then.

However, the dream didn't end; and Monica (now happily married), whom I met recently, said that I looked exactly the same as when she first saw me in 1943. I have had grey in my hair, but it just combs out. A young man said in 1949: 'I say Julian you're getting awfully grey.' I said, 'Who the hell cares?' I saw him last year and he was almost *completely* grey, though ten years younger – or more – than I am. I said: 'Why, my dear boy, you really must start dyeing your hair.' He said: 'Why don't *you* look any older, damn you. Are you Dorian Gray?' He didn't realise he'd made a bad pun (*'grey'* – see?) Ha ha. Joke over. Strike a light. Buy a lantern: as Chris *Grey* used to say. Ha ha ha – eh?

Jordan's news is terrifying, but very very funny as you wrote it.[1] Bloody good dialogue. However, I don't think his kids will suffer much, as they surely must be growing up by now, and he'll damn well have to provide for them or lose his job in the Civil Service (if he's still got it).

I don't like the sound of 'Mrs Zeus'[2] at all, but am very glad about the other books: hope *The Bull*[3] is a great success. Have seen no reviews yet, for I read no newspapers or weeklies unless some critical piece of mine appears therein. (My article on Jean Cocteau is on the 'Front' in this week's *TLS*, and my piece on Raffles' biographer 'Bunny' is in this week's *Punch* – you better get hold of the latter: it partly concerns *cricket*).[4] There's very vague talk of making me into an editor, but I don't believe it. (Very strictly confidential, and I am going into no details because I really don't know them.)

What I can't understand about your letter is why it doesn't even *mention* MY news. The most important thing in his life happens to your oldest friend, and you don't comment at all. Think of it – love comes at last to Julian, as it must to all men (and as death came to Charles Foster Kane).[5] *At first sight*, my dear boy. How about that, eh? No details about that, either, yet. The girl is still running fast. She must have reached Tibet by now. I haven't rung her up for 4 months. *Patience* – see?

I think that, as a novelist, you'll find the story fascinating when you hear it in full. It's not at all like Jordan's, but full of irony and fate. The toughest and wisest blokes in London are speculating about the outcome. The betting's on me so far – though this is the most formidable girl I've ever met. She can hold her own with me on any ground (including drinking) and has thus far anticipated my every move and outwitted me. Also the most beautiful thing I've seen. No sex comes into it: I haven't even touched her hand, though we've had one lunch meeting lasting from 1 p.m. until 5 p.m. with champagne, wine, and brandy. I thought I'd got her under my spell, but she slid away laughing. However, just wait.

I'm still here, and hating every moment of it. Putting through a deal (I've just come back from a couple of days' business talks in London) and when it comes off, am returning to town for good.

I'd love a weekend, but I don't know when. *What about Christmas?* I'll have plenty of dough then, and otherwise will be completely alone. Why don't you come over here for the day, or weekend? Only trouble is digs. They're terribly full up and hotels are expensive. The Davins might put you up but I've just had a row with them. Davin (d'you remember Dan Davin, New Zealand novelist, Wheatsheaf and Imperial Hotel '45–46?), now that he's a big shot at the Oxford University Press, has a way of being pompous at times and telling me off. I've kept my temper for nearly a year but suddenly I let it out last week.

Write to me quick. May be up in town. Wed. and Thurs. next. What publisher's Karel with?[6] I'll ring her up and take her out (unless you object).

Excuse odd handwriting. Am in bed recovering from London hangover, but must get up now (it's 3 p.m. and I must post some letters).

Love to Lydia, Nicholas[7] *et al,*

from

Julian

1 The nature of the news is unknown. It concerned their old friend Martin Jordan.

2 A character in *Dr Zeus,* an unpublished children's book by Jaeger.

3 *The Bull was Terrifico* (1955), Jaeger's latest children's book.

4 Unlike Maclaren-Ross, who had no interest in sport, Jaeger was a keen cricketer.

5 A jokey paraphrase of the voiceover from the film *Citizen Kane* (1941), starring Orson Welles in the role of 'Charles Foster Kane'.

6 C.K. and Lydia Jaeger's daughter Karel had found a job with Lomax, Erskine and Co, a central-London-based company that published trade magazines such as *Timber Technology.*

7 The Jaegers' son.

to RICHARD BRAIN

59 Southmoor Road/Oxford

2-12-55

Dear Brain,

If possible, I would appreciate a complimentary copy of *Maigret and the Burglar's Wife.* I haven't seen any reviews of it yet, but then I almost never read the papers nowadays.

Maurice Richardson, however, has apparently reviewed it in *The Observer* and told me on the telephone yesterday that he thought my translation the best one to be done of Simenon so far: which shows that I was right to insist on not too much interference from Mme S.

Sincerely,

J. Maclaren-Ross

to ANTHONY POWELL

59 Southmoor Road/Oxford

3-12-55

My dear Tony,

Thank you for your letter accepting the Collins parody[1] and also for printing 'So Long My Buddy'[2] so promptly and without cuts. I tried to contact you last Wednesday in London but you were not available that day.

I hope you'll find the Innes parody acceptable if I am able to finish it this weekend.[3] I've sent you one of the new Kersh short-story collection.* (Enclosed herewith.)[4]

On second thoughts, perhaps I'd better not do Cary just now, as he is not well at the moment and his admirers down here would certainly take the view that I was launching an unfair attack.

You'll be glad to hear that my new collection, mainly composed of the *Punch* pieces is – unless some monstrous last-minute misfortune intervenes – going to be published by Elek Books: I should be signing the contract new week, afterwards returning to London for good.

The dedication, with your permission which you gave me last year, will be to you; and I am also mentioning Malcolm Muggeridge's kindness to me in a special note of thanks.[5]

As ever,

Julian

* 'Men Without Bones'.

1   His parody of the novels of Wilkie Collins (1824–89) appeared in the 7 March 1956 issue of *Punch*.

2   A parody of Raymond Chandler's novels, published in the 30 November 1955 issue of *Punch*.

3   Maclaren-Ross's parody of the novels of either the thriller writer Hammond Innes (1914–98) or, far more likely, the crime writer Michael Innes, pseudonym of

J.I.M. Stewart (1906–94) may have been rejected by Powell. On the other hand it may never have been completed.

4   The parody based on Gerald Kersh's collection *Men Without Bones* (1955) never appeared in print.

5   At the beginning of the book, Maclaren-Ross registered his 'especial gratitude to Mr Malcolm Muggeridge, Mr John Lehmann, and Mr Leonard Russell, whose sympathetic understanding of a writer's problems enabled me to survive many a difficult crisis'.

to KAREL JAEGER

Royal Oxford Hotel/Oxford[1]

12-12-55

My dear Karel,

I'm coming, unexpectedly, to London tomorrow (Tuesday), arriving Paddington at about 11.35 a.m. when I will ring you at the office, on arrival.

I hope you will ask your boss to give you a longer lunch-hour than usual, as I'd like to take you out at least for a drink. If you say your uncle is coming up, I'm sure they will let you off.[2] At any rate, have a go.[3]

In great haste,

with love from

your Uncle Julian

1   Though Maclaren-Ross used the headed notepaper of the Royal Oxford Hotel, he was still living in a dingy basement flat at 59 Southmoor Road. He most likely obtained the notepaper during one of his trips to the hotel to treat himself to occasional, solitary blow-out meals, usually prompted by the arrival of a cheque from a publisher.

2   From a young age, Karel and her brother Nick had been encouraged to call Maclaren-Ross 'Uncle Julian'. When their father wrote *The Man in the Top Hat* (1949), Maclaren-Ross featured in the central role under that name.

3   The suggested ruse worked. 'Unfortunately,' wrote Karel Bartholomew (née Jaeger), 'though I have racked my brains, I can't remember where Julian and I went for lunch. It's bound to have been pretty liquid wherever it was!'

to JOHN LEHMANN

59 Southmoor Road/Oxford
29-12-55

My dear John,

Many thanks for your letter, which arrived bang on Xmas morning and cheered me up a bit.

Enclosed is what I consider one of my best pieces: I've been at work on it for days. It's 5,000 words: probably too long for a *Coming to London*,[1] also I'm possibly not eminent enough for inclusion in that series. But I think one should get a glimpse of more recent, and different, literary figures.

If you like – and I hope you may – and can't include it in the series, then call it 'From Highbury to Horizon'[2] and print it as a separate autobiographical piece.

But if it's acceptable, please arrange for a quick fee: I've now paid all my debts in Oxford and with the holiday I shall be sunk soon if I don't refuel. Still waiting for BBC news – the dilatory bastards.[3]

Another thing: I have to make another descent (personal reasons) on London next week or week after, or my prey may escape.

Can't explain now: have been working all night, it's now 9 a.m. and I'm dead tired.

Please excuse haste and let me know about this piece soon as you can.

As ever,

Julian

PS Another, more explicit letter will follow, about *GIS*[4] etc.

1* A series of articles featured in the *London Magazine*.
2 The memoir, rejected by Lehmann and subsequently lost, covered his life between 1935 and 1940.
3 Maclaren-Ross must have approached the BBC with a programme idea, but there's no record of the proposal in the BBC Written Archives.
4 *The Girl in the Spotlight.*

to JOHN LEHMANN

59 Southmoor Road/Oxford
10-1-56

My dear John,

It occurs to me that it would be a good idea to have a 2,000–3,000 words on Samuel Beckett, now that *Molloy* will come out in English (reviewed in *The Listener* 5th Jan.; brought out by some new publisher whose name I've never heard before).[1]

Nobody in England has done an article on his novels yet: though there's a very bad one in *New World Writing* No 5 (the same issue that contains instalment I of your autobiography); and it would be nice for the first one to appear in *London Magazine*.

I was reading Beckett in the 1930s and recommending his early books to people when nobody else took any notice and most of the reviews were lukewarm; and was delighted to see him reappear in his present guise, especially since I'd been told he was dead.

Among my books stored in London, I have *More Pricks than Kicks* (1936), the early volume of linked stories, and can remember enough (having read it again 2 years ago) to write about it; but I would need:

The French *Murphy* (to refresh my memory)

The French *L'Innommable*[2]

The French *En Attendant Godot*[3]

The English *Molloy*

I'm reading the French *Malone Meurt*,[4] which Davin has lent me, but had better have a copy of that too, as he'll be wanting his back. Hachette's will have the French ones of course, if you haven't them yourself. My article would be about the novels; but *Godot* would have to be mentioned, and I have not yet seen it.

Drop me a line if you'd like me to do this.

I've sent off the 2 French collections, with another note on *The Forge* inside.

In haste,

As ever,

Julian

1 John Calder.
2 English version: *The Unnamable* (1953).
3 English version: *Waiting for Godot* (1955).
4 English version (not in print at the time Maclaren-Ross was writing): *Malone Dies* (1958).

to WINNIE DAVIN

11-1-56 (7.39 a.m.)

Please excuse haste etc.

Dear Winnie,

I've probably got to go to London today to see the literary editor of the *Standard* who has asked me to do a story for their 'Did it Happen?' series.[1] D'you remember, when I wanted desperately last spring some money to go up and see Yolande, I sent in 'The Bird Man' for this very series and got it back, plainly unread, within a few days? Well, now I'd be ready to bet that it's the appearance of this story in the January *Encounter* that has led to the very polite letter I received yesterday!

(IRONY AND PITY COLUMN) The fee by the way is 40 guineas for 1,500 words, and 50% of the world syndication rights in the future!

Just shows that, whenever I have trouble placing anything, it always turns out to be one of my most influential things in the end! (Let's hope that goes for the *Punch* book too.)

Post has just come with *another* commission to write for *Nimbus*.[2] and *one* guinea per 1,000, rather different eh? The editor (or one of them) is David Wright.[3]

I was so glad to see Dan's proofs and know the novel is underway at last:[4] perhaps it may be a good year for us all.

I've not slept at all (various things bashing at my mind), so I'm probably a bit light-headed; but, though I'm the world's *last* giver-away of MSS (and none of mine will ever have any intrinsic value), it occurred to me you might like to have the first transcripts of my 2 lyrics for *The Girl in the Spotlight* tunes.

You may think they're absolutely puerile, but 'Break of Dawn' is actually a sympathetic parody of the Cole Porter–Ted Lewis[5] school, and also has some slightly sinister overtones of my own. One day I might play the tune and sing it for you (as Errol Barrow[6] has cured me of self-consciousness in this direction); but only if you ask me to, so you can easily escape the worst! Ha ha ha – some mad, monster-like mirth here!

As ever,

Julian

1   The 'Did it Happen?' feature, consisting of a supposedly true story, appeared in each night's issue of the *London Evening Standard*. Readers were invited to vote 'Yes' or 'No', depending on whether or not they believed the story was true. Instead of writing a new piece, Maclaren-Ross submitted an old short story to Harold Harris, the paper's Literary Editor. The story, retitled 'Old Ginger Says Goodbye', was included in the 31 January 1956 issue.

2   A shortlived literary magazine. Maclaren-Ross never fulfilled the commission.

3   David Wright (1920–94), poet and regular on the Soho pub and club circuit.

4   The novel was *The Sullen Bell*, published in 1957.

5   Ted Lewis (1890–1971), flamboyant American band-leader.

6   A Barbadian ex-RAF serviceman (1920–87).

PART IV
(1956–64)

CONCLUDING our thrilling serial story of heartache & intrigue —

"JULIAN
LOVES
SONIA!"

"The greatest love
story since Tristan
and Isolde."
(JOHN LEHMANN)

"Made for each other."
ANTHONY POWELL
in Punch (office).

POSITIVELY
LAST
INSTALMENT!

THE STORY SO FAR

JULIAN, hurriedly entering El Vino's, a Fleet-street bar, late for an
appointment with an editor, encounters instead an old acquaintance,
the Welsh poet KEIDRYCH RHYS. They start to drink together. (NOW READ ON.)

KEIDRYCH: Yes, life's sad. Think of all the people we used to know who've
died since those days — Alun Lewis, Anna Sebastian, Shirley Cocks,
Barry & Mara, Dylan … all of em dead and gone, eh?

JULIAN: Death's sad too. Everybody dies except Sonia Brownell.

KEIDRYCH: A helping hand mightn't come amiss in that direction, eh? (giggles)

JULIAN (softly) Sorry, old boy. Perhaps you misunderstood — it doesn't actually do
to talk against Sonia to me.

KEIDRYCH (taking a step back) No no. of course not. Look have another drink.
I've nothing at all against the poor old girl, anyway.

CABLES : PARCOHOTEL LONDON.   INLAND TELEGRAMS : PARCOHOTEL PADD, LONDON.

For several years Maclaren-Ross had been reliant on journalism to provide a precarious living. His move back to London coincided with a sudden decline in the number of journalistic assignments offered to him. He temporarily plugged the gap by persuading the BBC to commission him to write a radio dramatisation of one of his short memoirs. Nevertheless he soon had to switch hotels, leaving behind the latest in a series of unpaid bills. These included rent owed to his former landlord in Oxford, who had impounded his luggage until the debt was settled.

Via a chance encounter with Anthony Cronin, the young editor of the weekly magazine *Time and Tide*, Maclaren-Ross obtained a reviewing job. Cronin ended up taking pity on this once celebrated writer and offering him somewhere to stay. Still fixated by Sonia Orwell, every facet of whose behaviour he subjected to obsessive scrutiny, Maclaren-Ross proved a wearisome guest for Cronin and his wife. After several weeks spent with them in suburban Wembley, he returned to his wandering, boozy routine.

Towards the end of April 1956, a welcome distraction from Sonia Orwell was provided by a young divorcée named Diane Bromley, formerly Mollie Sturgeon, niece of the publisher Leonard Woolf. She and Maclaren-Ross, who had met in a Soho club, embarked on a fraught romance, their hotel-hopping existence punctuated by heated rows and recurrent separations. As if that wasn't unsettling enough, Maclaren-Ross also had to contend with a brief spell of imprisonment, a libel action brought against him by the writer H.E. Bates, and spells of homelessness during which he was reduced to sleeping on a park bench and in a Turkish bath. Against this chaotic backdrop, Maclaren-Ross enjoyed a surprisingly productive period as a writer. He wrote for *Punch*, the *Times Literary Supplement*, and the *Sunday Times*; he worked on three scripts for low-budget films, and, fuelled by his interest in pulp fiction and Hollywood crime movies, he launched a successful career as a writer of radio thrillers.

Early in 1957, he began work on *Until the Day She Dies*, a radio series drawing on his fixation with Sonia Orwell. By the time it was broadcast the following year, Diane Bromley had given birth to their son, Alex. The couple subsequently married in a hasty ceremony at the local register office. To support his family, Maclaren-Ross wrote more radio scripts for the BBC, scripts that led one critic to hail him as 'radio's Alfred Hitchcock'. He also used *Until the Day She Dies*, together with two other serials he'd written, as the basis for novels.

Just over three years after his marriage, he and his wife moved to Brighton, where his mother-in-law was recuperating from a serious illness. During their ill-fated south-coast sojourn, his wife began an affair that ushered them towards their final separation. Leaving her and his son in Brighton, Maclaren-Ross decamped to London, only to find that his increasingly sour relationship with the BBC was as irretrievable as his marriage.

Another period of poverty and homelessness ensued. In the wake of at least two failed romances, he met Eleanor Brill, a Northern Irish woman who worked for Reuters news agency. The two of them were soon living together in her Notting Hill flat. Meanwhile, he started writing reviews and essays for the *London Magazine*, founded by John Lehmann but now edited by the poet Alan Ross, whom he'd first got to know almost twenty years previously. Appreciative of his work yet wary of him, Ross agreed to serialise his proposed *Memoirs of the Forties*. Among the first episodes to feature in the magazine were reminiscences of Dylan Thomas and Graham Greene. Less than half of the planned chapters had, however, been completed when, in November 1964, the fifty-two-year-old Maclaren-Ross suffered a fatal heart attack.

Despite being unfinished, *Memoirs of the Forties* was published in hardcover format the next year, bolstered by a selection of his other writing. The book received a string of enthusiastic reviews, one of which acclaimed its 'unrivalled picture of those almost mythical Forties'.

to WINNIE DAVIN

4-2-56

My dear Winnie,

Enclosed herewith my *Evening Standard* story, with a photo[1] giving you, perhaps, some idea of how I will look as the Terror in *Until the Day She Dies!*[2] Incidentally, 'Ginger'[3] is one of the stories rejected by *Punch* during that odd period when I was trying so hard to raise money for a new suit and also for the wherewithal to entertain S.[4] in the manner to which I thought she'd be accustomed. So I won finally by selling it for double-fee. No news of her yet, and all my pipelines cut off: incidentally Gordon Watkins of *Picture Post* turns out to know Margot Walmsley[5] quite well, and says she has ambitions socially and has a special conception of herself as a social butterfly of the cocktail-party class. Funny how they're all connected, isn't it? So it won't be long before S. knows of the new developments: but meantime she hasn't replied at all to Hughes's letter asking permission to use the epigraphs,[6] which should have been forwarded to her by the mysterious friend, Mrs Bagnall (or Bagnold) who lives below.[7] I heard roundabout rumours that she has a crush or attachment to Roland Penrose the painter (50 to 60 years of age), maybe abroad with the Penroses at the moment and *might* be preparing to step down the epigraph proposal sharply: so I got in first by getting Hughes to send another letter saying that after all I'd decided not to use the quotation concerned. However, the news of the serial and the film may bring her out of hiding and into my web, if she's really keen to go into movies.

Meanwhile I have started something else and may, when I come back to Oxford, be bringing it down as my personal assistant. It is tall, Austrian and blonde; smart, works as a club hostess, has been on the stage, and had initial quarrel with me last night and went home courageously holding back tears: as per schedule. It really conducted the quarrel awfully well.

Rang it today and patched things up; but it sounded still a bit dubious; my swift changes of front may have shaken confidence. But we shall see: it's not nearly as unsuitable as it sounds, though I know really that S. is the only one who will do. I have the conviction that if we could meet face to face all this nonsense could be tidied up in a moment: though not if she meets me late at night, when the personality of the Terror tends of recent weeks to take over and is apt even to break out in violence if provoked – as when I suddenly took hold of a rude man in a club and half-throttled him with his own scarf: also stamping several times at intervals on the ankle of an outrageous scrounger (which made the Austrian girl give a merry peal of laughter), but this man, undeterred, waiting until we'd all gone over to listen to a coloured pianist, drank up all the drinks on the bar and limped out into the night unseen by anyone.

If you happen to go into 59[8] to pick up the waiting English text of *Godot*, please – if it's not too much bother – pick up some pyjamas from laundry parcels (I've only one pair up here) and send them to me (stamps enclosed); also any letters (except Income Tax). But there's no special hurry if you're very busy. Old Mr G.[9] I think ought to forward things to me: he can't be as ill as all that. I haven't sent him any money last week because I've none to spare;[10] but will send some this coming week; though I do expect him to forward letters etc. and try to help a little. It's damned annoying having to do about ten peoples' work without assistance when I don't feel at all fit and have to keep up this terrible pitch all the time, with even my voice beginning to fail. Now that it seems to be coming at last: I often feel secretly frightened and very much alone; but must not show this to anyone or my power over them would go and I'd be back where I was before (and may be yet!), like flounder in the sea. I miss you very much, as there is nobody to laugh at me anymore. Hope you will on my return, though not in front of Thea (that's her name).

Love to all,

from

Julian

Hope to finalise everything during coming week: then return, to write the full story, for about a fortnight; but am still uncertain of exact date.

1   The photo depicted him staring at the camera, his right hand holding a cigarette-holder to his lips. A print of this much-reproduced image is held in the Hulton-Getty Archive, London.

2   A planned filmscript in which Sonia Orwell was recast as 'Linda', a girl stalked by the menacing figure of 'the Terror', a role he intended to play himself. He even devised a publicity slogan for the film: 'The picture with a starless cast, whose cast is terror itself!'

3   The original title of the story published in the *Evening Standard*'s 'Did it Happen?' section.

4   Sonia Orwell.

5   Margot Walmsley (1914–97) worked for the literary magazine *Encounter*. She and her journalist husband held regular parties at their Kensington home, where

journalists and fiction writers mingled. She was the dedicatee of Maclaren-Ross's short boyhood memoir 'The Bird Man'.

6   Via his agent, Edmund Hughes, Maclaren-Ross had contacted Sonia Orwell, requesting permission to use a quotation from her late husband's work as the epigraph to both his filmscript and a planned radio adaptation of it.

7   She lived in the flat below Sonia Orwell's on Percy Street in central London.

8   Maclaren-Ross's previous address: 59 Southmoor Road, Oxford.

9   Mr Goodman, Maclaren-Ross's former landlord at 59 Southmoor Road.

10 Maclaren-Ross owed rent arrears to Mr Goodman. On leaving Oxford, Maclaren-Ross had agreed to pay off the debt in weekly instalments.

to WINNIE DAVIN

11-2-56

My dear Winnie,

Thank you so much for the packet, which arrived this morning, and for all the trouble you've taken.

I've written to Mr G., but sent no money: for one thing I've scarcely any until next week when I'll have tied all the loose ends together; and for another, one of the letters (dated 2nd Feb.) contained a commission for an 18 guinea article from Pryce-Jones, which – not having heard from me – he'll have given someone else by now: also there was a proof from *Punch* – among 5 others – for a parody scheduled for next week's issue and now too late for it. Tony's doing his best to get stuff out, because I've got about seven on the stocks and until some of these appear, I can't send any more in. So now I'll have to wait another week – and didn't get any review book last week because I'd not corrected my proofs, which also gives me an undeserved reputation for neglecting my work.

If there's a wife (and I have never seen one), *she* could quite easily have forwarded the letters. It's no good yelling for money and holding onto correspondence which would enable me to make some.

I thought the attached 'serial' might amuse you. So, as you'll see, my big dream dies – and for a personal life I shall have to look elsewhere. This by the way is strictly confidential, of course, until I decide how to use the information myself. Next week I'll let you know all about the real serial etc.

Love to all,

from

J.

CONCLUDING our thrilling serial story of heartache and intrigue
'The greatest love story since *Tristan and Isolde*.' – John Lehmann
'Made for each other.' – Anthony Powell in *Punch* (office)

JULIAN LOVES SONIA!
Positively last instalment!

The Story So Far
JULIAN, hurriedly entering El Vino's, a Fleet-street bar, late for an appointment with an editor, encounters instead an old acquaintance, the Welsh poet KEIDRYCH RHYS.[1] They start to drink together. (*Now read on.*)

KEIDRYCH: Yes, life's sad. Think of all the people we used to know who've died since those days – Alun Lewis, Anna Sebastian, Shirley Cocks, Barry O'Mara, Dylan... all of 'em dead and gone, eh?
JULIAN: Death's sad too. Everybody dies except Sonia Brownell.[2]
KEIDRYCH: A helping hand mightn't come amiss in that direction, eh? (giggles)
JULIAN: (*softly*) Sorry, old boy. Perhaps you misunderstood – it doesn't actually do to talk *against* Sonia to me.
KEIDRYCH: (*taking a step back*) No, no. Of course not. Look have another drink. I've got nothing at all against the poor old girl, anyway.
JULIAN: Old? We ourselves are scarcely young.
KEIDRYCH: Who's thirty-three?
JULIAN: Well, she is. Or thereabouts.
KEIDRYCH: Yes and the fucking rest. Why I remember in 1936...
JULIAN: Keidrych, *how old do you think this girl is*?
KEIDRYCH: About forty-seven, I suppose.
JULIAN: *Forty-seven*?
KEIDRYCH: Can't be much less. Oh, wait. Yes, maybe a bit less. Say forty-five. Now I come to think it was '38 not '36... I'd have been – now let me see...
JULIAN: I don't care how old *you* were, Keidrych. *How old was SHE*?
KEIDRYCH: Twenty-six, twenty-seven. Must have been, because when Lynette took her up...
JULIAN: Lynette?
KEIDRYCH: My ex-wife. Very well off then. Her papa. Argentine railroads. So of course poor little Sonia attached herself and clung on

desperately. Not that I blame her: she had to have *some* source of income. With the mother running this conspicuously unsuccessful boarding house at Margate...

JULIAN: *Is that what the mother does?*

KEIDRYCH: Sure. Mind you, I do think it's rather creditable of the girl to have educated herself as she has done, no schooling to speak of, even if part of it had to be done at Lynette's expense... Look I have to meet a chap at the Cock now.

JULIAN: I will come to the Cock. Listen you must tell me all about Sonia. Come on Keidrych – give.

KEIDRYCH: Well in those days her chief ambition was to perfect her French. Because, as she put it, good French was the mark of an 'educated person'...

JULIAN: She can't have put it in those words.

KEIDRYCH: Ready to swear it anywhere, old boy. Of course she'd a rather odd vocabulary at the time, you see. The highbrow, classy manner came later, she learns very quick. And so Lynette took her over to France one or twice and introduced her to a few others whom she could ponce on for a change.

JULIAN: Didn't she ever do any work?

KEIDRYCH: God no. All she wanted to do was to become famous.

JULIAN: She said so?

KEIDRYCH: Frequently. Sometimes in French – her accent having become a little less quaint by that time... Well here's the Cock. Chap I want to see must have gone...

JULIAN: What about the convent in Switzerland?

KEIDRYCH: There wasn't one so far's I know.

JULIAN: And the finishing school is also all balls?

KEIDRYCH: When would she have gone there? And who would have footed the bill? Not Ma, certainly – she was too busy dealing with the lodgers.

JULIAN: (*who has now begun to shrivel to half his size*) Ma from Margate?

KEIDRYCH: I say old boy, you don't look well at all. Better have some stiff kind of drink. Whisky?

JULIAN: Brandy. Brandy. Brandy.

KEIDRYCH: A treble brandy, please, and a Scotch... what's wrong, Julian? Did you take her for a *deb* or something? I must admit she does it awfully well, of course Connolly was quite taken in... his own French being so bloody indifferent, and besides by the time she'd wormed her way into *Horizon*, she really did speak almost perfectly...

JULIAN: Poor witch.

KEIDRYCH: Bitch?

JULIAN: Witch. The Gothic legend. The medusa. The fatal woman whose face stopped a thousand hearts.

KEIDRYCH: Oh well, she had to hide things up somehow. Pretty ashamed of her beginnings of course, being a truly colossal snob... And then having lived off Lynette all these years, she wrote long long criticisms of her poems, beginning 'Dear Miss Roberts' and signed with her full name, turning them all down and finally saying she was sorry, they just weren't good enough for *Horizon*.

Of course when the magazine showed signs of folding, she rushed back to Lynette in a panic and started a madly friendly campaign... that was before poor old George[3] came into the picture. *Then*, naturally, Lynette was thrown over again; and when she'd got her hands on the money,[4] oh, she went on a grand tour, having had a beauty treatment first...

JULIAN: You must agree that she *is* beautiful?

KEIDRYCH: Oh yes – though it must cost the earth to keep her looking so well preserved. I don't advise *you* to take it on, old boy; you'd never earn enough in a thousand years.

JULIAN: I'm not taking it on. I'm opting out.

KEIDRYCH: What? *Surely you're not a snob, old boy?* Ma too much for you?

JULIAN: Yes I am, by God. I *am* a snob. A truly colossal snob.

A YOUNG WOMAN: But how honest of you to admit it.

JULIAN: Are you a snob too?

YOUNG WOMAN: And proud of it.

KEIDRYCH: Oh hullo Diana. Julian this is Diana Houstoun-Boswall.

JULIAN: With a hyphen?

DIANA: Emphatically. Have you a hyphen also?

JULIAN: Def'.

DIANA: Goody-goody.

JULIAN: You've a very direct stare.

DIANA: I was wondering what you looked like without those glasses.

JULIAN: You want me to take them off?

DIANA: Please.

JULIAN: There. You find the outlook a trifle bleak?

DIANA: But interesting.

JULIAN: You don't come from Margate?

DIANA: I do not. Can I look at your glasses?

JULIAN: Yes.

DIANA: Can I try them on?

JULIAN: Yes.

DIANA: Now you can see your *own* face for a change.

JULIAN: Lorsque je me regarde dans la glace, je n'arrive meme pas à faire peur à moi-meme.[5]

DIANA: *Quai des Brumes*?

JULIAN: (*bowing*) So. You go to movies?

DIANA: I adore movies. You speak French very well.

JULIAN: My accent was a bit quaint when I went to a finishing school in Switzerland.

DIANA: I don't believe boys have them.

JULIAN: But I'm not a boy.

DIANA: Thirty-three?

JULIAN: No, forty-seven.

DIANA: You're making fun of me.

JULIAN: Not of you, darling.

DIANA: So you're not forty-seven?

JULIAN: No, but people of that age do exist. And sometimes they look younger. Will you have a brandy?

DIANA: My favourite drink.

KEIDRYCH: (*by now surrounded by the BOYS, who have appeared suddenly from nowhere*) Stop flirting, Julian, or I'll tell Sonia about you. And then she won't take you down to Margate for the hols, so there!

DIANA: Who's *Sonia*?

JULIAN: A girl I used to know.

DIANA: Don't you know her any longer?

JULIAN: Not now. She hasn't really enough prestige for me.

DIANA: Are you ambitious, really?

JULIAN: I'm going to be famous. When I've perfected my French. Look, this pub's about to shut. Come and drink all day in Soho. I'll show you a club where…

DIANA: My dear, I can't. I've got to go to the BM[6] and study law.

JULIAN: Then we'll get a cab and I'll drop you off.

DIANA: No I've a car outside. I'll drop *you*.

KEIDRYCH: You be careful. Julian's quite good at dropping people. He just dropped his great and only love, haven't you old boy?

JULIAN: *Picture Post* ought to give me *two* thousand for her.

DIANA: I see you *are* going to be famous, after all.

JULIAN: I owe it all to Mamma. That and my convent upbringing. (*The pub closes with a crash. They go out to the car.*)

THE END

1   The pseudonym of the Welsh poet William Donald Rhys (1915–87), a fellow regular in the Soho pubs and clubs.

2   Sonia Orwell's maiden name.

3   Orwell.

4   This refers to the money from the literary estate of George Orwell, which amounted to just under £10,000.

5   'When I look at myself in the mirror, I can't even manage to scare myself.'

6   The British Museum, London. In those days, the British Library Reading Room was housed there.

to WINNIE DAVIN[1]

85a Warwick Avenue / London W9
April 1956

My dear Winnie,

So sorry I haven't been able to write you before to thank you for your gallant efforts to recover my pen etc. from 59 Southmoor: I still am in a frightful financial mess; but will fight my way out somehow during the next fortnight, I hope, and then send enough money to Goodman to salvage my things, or come back to Oxford for long enough to settle up, look round the locations for my book and film, and move back again.

Meanwhile, would you do 2 things for me?

(a) Send the Beckett books – including the French ones, which I will faithfully return – to the *inserted* address,[2] that of John Gawsworth, who will know where I am and forward them to me: because Lehmann is crying out furiously for his promised article; and I've said I'll finish it this coming week.

(b) At the cleaners' down past the Victoria (you know the one) I left my crimson (or maroon) jacket to be done before Xmas; I paid for it just before my last but one trip to London and they promised to sent it to No 59: therefore I handed over the ticket, but it never came. In the general hurly-burly that ensued, I didn't go fetch it or find out what happened: they're not on the phone and were closed when I called on my way to the station, and London, last time.

Now my other things need cleaning urgently; I've nothing to change into, can't afford to buy a new jacket, so if you could collect the red one for me and forward it to Gawsworth's place[3] I'd be infinitely obliged.

All other news later: I'm just reviewing *Dylan in America*[4] for the *TLS* and see that at the moment I am leading (unlike me) a détraqué Dylan-like existence. I've also done a middle *TLS* article on the new Angus Wilson novel *Anglo Saxon Attitudes*, which will be published on May 14th and contains a full-length portrait (and attack) on Sonia under the name of Elvira Portway.

I got wind of this and in my article (entitled 'Mourning becomes Elvira') turned the attack into a means both of confounding Wilson and making love to Sonia in print; I've also organised the younger men (such as Anthony Cronin of *Time and Tide*)[5] into an anti-Wilson contingent, so am afraid he's been very unwise to attack her at all.*

Love to Dan and Anna and the children: hope all's well at home and abroad. If Dan's coming to town, ask him to look in the Caves de France,[6] where I usually hang out in the afternoons now.

Pray for me, for things which are by no means going well and the net tightens closer around me from day to day.

All love,

from

Julian

* This is of course strictly confidential.

PS I see that Neville Rogers has acted on my advice and sent a chunk of Shelley to the *London Magazine*:[7] I hope it tops the bill in the advert for next month's issue (why doesn't someone advise me on places in which to sell *my* stuff?).

1   Written on notepaper from the Celtic Hotel, 61–63 Guilford Street, London.
2   85a Warwick Avenue, London W9.
3   He was staying with the eccentric poet and editor John Gawsworth and his new wife Anna. Since there was no spare bed, Maclaren-Ross was sleeping on the sofa.
4   *Dylan Thomas in America* (1956) by John Malcolm Brinnin.
5   Cronin was the editor of this weekly magazine.
6   The Club des Caves de France was a notoriously sleazy Soho drinking club at 39 Dean Street.
7   Under the title 'Shelley and the West Wind', an extract from Neville Rogers's book on the poet had appeared in the latest issue of the *London Magazine*.

to ANTHONY POWELL

4-6-56

My dear Tony,

Having seen the Birthday Honours list,[1] I hasten to congratulate you.

Enclosed is a little piece which I hope you may like, as I am involved in a very boring situation which I would not trouble you with, except that I am desperate for dough and haven't even a proper pen to write with. If it is suitable, please let Mr Hillier[2] know, because the need is really urgent and the more I can get the better (at the moment I have 90).

I will ring you up at 3.30 to see if you have a review-book for me also.

Yours ever,

Julian

1 Anthony Powell had just been awarded a CBE in the Queen's Birthday Honours List.
2 In the Accounts Department at *Punch*.

to ANTHONY POWELL

19 Holland Park Avenue[1]/London W11

19-7-56

My dear Tony,

Thank you for your letter.

I have already delivered a copy for you, and hope you may enjoy some of the pieces that have not come your way editorially.

I understand about the difficulty of reviewing it in *Punch*, but think that personal recommendations (as distinct from denying that the stuff is absolute shit) may be equally tricky in view of the dedication.

As ever,

Julian

PS Although a crossword addict, I'm afraid the Lear/P.C. Wren[2] tie-up escaped me entirely.

1 After at least two weeks during which he had stayed with John Gawsworth, Maclaren-Ross had got back together with Diane Bromley. Together they'd rented a flat at the Notting Hill end of Holland Park Avenue.
2 Edward Lear (1812–88), artist, illustrator and writer; and P.C. Wren (1875–1941), author of *Beau Geste* (1924).

to ALEC C. SNOWDEN[1]

Sefton Lodge Hotel[2]/Lyon Street/Bognor Regis/Sussex

7-1-57

Dear Alec,

Since our telephone conversation last night, I have re-read your letter and notes, and have come to the conclusion that you had better get another writer to work on *The Key Man*.[3]

To begin with, I don't think we are likely to see eye to eye about the way it should be handled: I see it not as primarily an action picture but a human-interest drama centring around people who are characters in their own right, in an *English* setting.

These could never be turned arbitrarily into 'Canadians', for the sake of a possible American market,[4] and I could never write the kind of 'Sez you' dialogue that would be required. To my mind, the Americans themselves will always make this type of picture better than we can; and it is useless to imitate them. These 60-minute films should be peculiarly English, if they're to be interesting at all. Jelf for instance could be nothing but a Cockney (as decided-upon in the synopsis); and a credible one to boot, using the sort of slang that most members of a British audience would understand.

The trouble with these little films is always that the American influence is predominant, and that's universally successful because they stick to their own people and backgrounds: the Italians ditto. I'd no idea that we were going to have to curry favour with the US or I would never have agreed to work on any of the projects. In fact, at least twice I have said – without contradiction – to you that the reason for my interest was that here we at least *didn't* have to have American actors, whose reasons for being in English film-stories always seem so false. Just as years ago I refused to write stories using American idiom, created my own style of English colloquialism, and was more successful in consequence than any of the bogus tough-guys.

This a great disappointment to me in every way, because the £100 you advanced me has been spent entirely on living expenses while working on the script; and I have also incurred a debt at this hotel, believing that when I delivered the rest of it I would be paid within a short time. Now I am in a dreadful mess, without hope of setting up; and must do some of my own work (which yields quicker returns) instead, if I want to avoid considerable unpleasantness.

I am leaving you the further 10½pp. that I have done, and I hope you can get someone else to make the necessary alterations.

If you want to discuss anything, I shall be at GER 4444 (Mandrake Club) between 3 & 4 and you can leave a message; but I honestly think I've done all I possibly can: to try to see the story and characters another way would destroy all their reality for me.

I am returning also *The Long Night*[5] as I shall not be able after all to work on it, since I am abandoning *The Key Man* project,[6] with which we agreed it should be included.

Sincerely,

Julian

1 A film producer who held the post of General Production Manager at the Film Producers' Guild and sat on the Board of Directors at Merton Park Studios, which specialised in low-budget movies. Maclaren-Ross had met him in the Freelance Club.

2 Maclaren-Ross had arranged to stay here over Christmas. He and his girl-friend were due to spend some time with the Jaegers who were, by then, living in the suburb of Elmer Sands. Diane Bromley didn't, however, turn up at the station, leaving Maclaren-Ross to make his way to Bognor Regis by himself.

3 A low-budget crime movie about an investigative reporter who becomes embroiled in a Soho gangster's attempts to track down the hidden proceeds of the robbery that landed him in gaol.

4 The film eventually went into production starring the Canadian actor Lee Patterson.

5 Alec C. Snowden was planning a screen adaptation of Hartley Howard's novel *The Long Night* (1957).

6 Snowden persuaded Maclaren-Ross not to opt out of the project. Maclaren-Ross delivered the completed script on 14 January 1957. A few days later Snowden hired him to polish the script of a science-fiction thriller poised to go into production at Merton Park Studios. *The Key Man* was released in London during June 1957.

to JOHN GAWSWORTH

22-3-57

My dear John,

Got your new address, just recently.[1]

Hope you and Anna[2] may be at Bridge Hotel 7p.m. tomorrow (Saturday) to have some drinks.

If you can't make it, please phone at above in morning (name of HYDE,[3] please).

All the best to you both,

from

Julian

1 This new address was 16 Warrington Crescent, London W9.
2 Gawsworth's wife, a divorcée in her early fifties.
3 For a short period during 1957 Maclaren-Ross's mental state had so deteriorated that he'd became convinced his personality had been hijacked by the villainous character from Robert Louis Stevenson's novella, *Dr Jekyll and Mr Hyde*. Even after he'd regained his sanity, he liked to use the name.

to REGGIE SMITH

39 Kensington Square Gardens¹/London W2

15-8-57

My dear Reggie,

I'd very much like to talk over the radio serial² as soon as possible. Could you ring me at above to make date – for tomorrow lunchtime if you're free?³

As ever,

Julian

1 In the final days of April 1957, Maclaren-Ross and his girlfriend had moved into a furnished flat here.
2 *Until the Day She Dies* was a mooted drama series, inspired by his obsession with Sonia Orwell.
3 In a BBC memo, written only a few days later, Reggie Smith acknowledged that Maclaren-Ross 'live[d] as he earn[ed]', causing problems for himself. Yet Smith remained sympathetic towards him, partly because of his literary abilities. 'Maclaren-Ross has a special talent for making apparently trivial dialogue carry the weight of character,' Smith wrote in another memo, dated 29 January 1959.

to REGGIE SMITH

39 Kensington Square Gardens/London W2

17-8-57

My dear Reggie,

Herewith I am sending you my screen-play *The Key Man*, the film-version of which will be generally released on Sept. 9th.

With very little difficulty, this could be translated into an hour-length version for radio; and the fee for this would help me with my expenses while writing *Until the Day She Dies*, the serial on which I'm now engaged.¹ But in order to finish it requires complete concentration on the one subject, and a temporary cessation of the film-work which provides me with a living; therefore alternative sources of income must be found. It struck me that the above suggestions might solve the problem: I'd be interested to know what you think of the idea and whether, if the subject is likely to be acceptable, a quick deal could be arranged.

Perhaps we could meet Monday evening and talk about this: also the serial about which I'd like to consult you?

As ever,
Julian

I'm enclosing also the additional ending for the American film version (to be shown on TV in the States), which I propose to use for the radio-play.

1   On 15 October 1956 Barbara Bray had commissioned a 30-minute specimen instalment of the series. Satisfied with this, she paid Maclaren-Ross to write the next five episodes.

to REGGIE SMITH

99 West End Lane[1]/London NW6
16-9-57

My dear Reggie,

Herewith 3 episodes of the serial *You Have Been Warned.*[2] You will see that I have varied the technique from narrative in Ep. 1 to straight-forward dialogue in other episodes, where narrative is not necessary: it will be necessary again in Ep. 6, thus making it a pattern.

You will also see that I have devised various ways of getting through without synopses.

Now what about money? I have a flat here with Diane[3] but nothing to pay rent with (due Wednesday). I seem to remember you saying you could get me something through on 3 episodes, so I am sending them along by hand this morning: hope you like them.

I could definitely promise delivery of the remaining three on Friday morning, providing cash on delivery were guaranteed to me; only I wouldn't strain myself if delays were likely. Doubtless you could help to arrange this? But I'd also have to have something to keep me going meanwhile. (Until Friday.)

I'll be in the George[4] tomorrow (Tuesday morning) at 1 p.m., if we could have a word about what's doing; or ring me at above number tonight after 7 or tomorrow morning before 11.30.

All the best,
from
Julian

PS If you're not in, or likely to be, this morning, Diane will pass the script to Barbara Bray⁵ in the Script Dept. J.

1 After several rapid changes of address, Maclaren-Ross and his girlfriend briefly took up residence in this two-storey house in north London.
2 Adapted from the thriller *The Reader is Warned* (1939) by Carter Dickson, the pseudonym of John Dickson Carr (1905–77). Yet Reggie Smith would come to realise that Maclaren-Ross's value to the BBC was 'less as an adaptor than as an original writer who uses the book or story as a starting point for his very odd creations' (BBC memo, 26 January 1959).
3 Maclaren-Ross's girlfriend Diane Bromley (1926–78). Born Mollie Bella Sturgeon, she used the name 'Diane', which she pronounced 'Diana'. At the time she had become romantically involved with Maclaren-Ross, she was using her previous husband's surname, 'Bromley'.
4 The George pub, located at the junction between Great Portland and Mortimer Streets.
5 Barbara Bray (1924–), writer, critic, translator and broadcaster. At that time she was working as the BBC's Script Editor at Drama (Sound). She later collaborated with Samuel Beckett and Harold Pinter.

to BARBARA BRAY

37 Ladbroke Square¹/London W11

15-11-57

Dear Mrs Bray,

Enclosed herewith a copy of a Carter Dickson novel, originally published under the much more effective title *Lord of the Sorcerers*. If you approve, I would be glad to adapt it as a six-episode serial forthwith, as I agree with the author in thinking it the best of his books: for it manages to hold the attention throughout with no actual murder being committed.

I hope you liked my version of *The Reader Is Warned*. I expect Reggie Smith passed to you the letters which contained my comments on the characterisation & construction; but if there are any points you would like to discuss, my telephone number & new address are above.

Yours sincerely,

J. Maclaren-Ross

1 A crowded rooming-house in Notting Hill.

to BARBARA BRAY

37 Ladbroke Square/London W11

12-12-57

Dear Mrs Bray,

Herewith at last the first 3 Episodes of *Until the Day She Dies*.[1] At the last moment, the form of the Third Episode had to be changed to fit-in with those forthcoming, so it took longer than I thought.

If you could get in touch with Miss Dean[2] as soon as possible to arrange payment – if possible, even for this afternoon – I would be very grateful. I intend to finish the last 3 Episodes, if not before Xmas at any rate by the New Year; and if I'm to work constantly, as this would require, supplies of ready money are constantly required.

Hoping you will like the material appended,

With best wishes,

Yours sincerely,

J. Maclaren-Ross

1 The first episode of the radio series, broadcast on the BBC's Light Programme, was aired on 23 June 1957. Maclaren-Ross was given an uncredited acting role as the sinister 'Waiting One'.
2 Miss Heather Dean worked in the BBC's Copyright Department.

to BARBARA BRAY

25 Anson Road[1]/London NW2

2-10-58

Dear Mrs Bray,

Herewith Episode 8, and revised ending for Episode 7, of *The Girl in the Spotlight*.[2] All scenes are to be expanded and the total script revised after completion of the final episode, for which I would be glad if you could arrange payment now, as you have done with the last two.

I hope to complete final version of *The Doomsday Book* this week;[3] then revise the first half of *The Girl in the Spotlight* after the last Episode is delivered: for which I will have to have Episodes 5, 6 and 7, to make sure there are no loose ends and the story hangs together, but will collect them when I deliver *The Doomsday Book*.

Reggie Smith tells me that he sent in a favourable report on my story 'The Swag, the Spy and the Soldier', which he hoped would be done as a double bill of 30-minutes plays with 'I Had to Go Sick'.[4] If this has in fact been accepted, would you let my wife have the copy of *Penguin New Writing* containing the story so that I can plan out my radio-adaptation?

Yours sincerely,

J. Maclaren-Ross

1 Now the parents of a baby boy, Maclaren-Ross and Diane, whom he'd married nearly three months earlier, had rented an upstairs flat in a terraced house in suburban Cricklewood.

2 The first episode of Maclaren-Ross's drama series *The Girl in the Spotlight* was eventually broadcast on the BBC Light Programme on 25 September 1961.

3 *The Doomsday Book* was a radio thriller series, commissioned by the BBC.

4 An expanded sixty-minute adaptation of 'The Swag, the Spy and the Soldier' was commissioned by Reggie Smith on 4 March 1960. For both this play and the dramatisation of 'I Had to Go Sick', the BBC cast Maclaren-Ross as the narrator and recorded his performance. Neither play went into production, however. In the case of 'The Swag, the Spy and the Soldier', repeated delays led to the radio rights lapsing. Annoyed by the backlog of his unproduced plays that had built up, Maclaren-Ross refused to extend the period for which he'd granted those rights to the BBC.

to BARBARA BRAY

6 Courtfield Gardens[1]/London SW5

18-11-58

Dear Mrs Bray,

As you will see by the title, the enclosed is intended as a companion-piece to my *I Had to Go Sick*, the two to be broadcast in one programme.

If you approve of this idea, I would be grateful if you could ask Miss Dean to prepare a contract for my signature tomorrow afternoon, and I will telephone you at 4 p.m. tomorrow to see if this is possible. If you are at a meeting then, perhaps you would leave a message as to the result of above?

Yours sincerely,

J. Maclaren-Ross

1 The bitter rows that punctuated his second marriage appear to have led Maclaren-Ross to move to this address while his wife and child remained at 25 Anson Road.

to PHILIP WOOLF[1]

25 Anson Road/London NW2
Mid-December 1958

Dear Mr Woolf,

As the husband of your niece, Molly[2] [sic], I take the liberty of writing to you on the subject of my stepdaughter Sally[3] [sic].

The child and myself have not yet met; formerly, owing to the scarcity of suitable accommodation in London, we were living in a flat too small for her to visit; but now that we have at last been able to obtain a large flat with 2 spare bedrooms (where your sister stayed a fortnight ago), it would make us very happy if you would, as her legal guardian, allow her to stay with us for a day or two after Xmas.

We have a 5-month-old baby of our own, who Sally has seen only once; as you will appreciate, it is difficult for my wife to journey down to Taunton with so young a child, whereas your ward could be comfortably accommodated here; and we could take her to various pantomimes etc. before she returns to school.

You will understand also that my wife feels deeply the continued enforced separation from her daughter; and it would be pleasant for all concerned if Sally and her half-brother could become better acquainted.

Molly tells me that the ruling of the Court precludes Sally living permanently with her mother; but surely there would be no objection to a short stay: if my suggestion interferes with your Xmas arrangements, then perhaps she could come next Easter?[4]

With compliments of the Season.

Yours sincerely,

J. Maclaren-Ross

1 Philip Woolf (1913–61), brother of the publisher Leonard Woolf.
2 Shortly after the birth of their son, Alex, on 7 July 1958, Maclaren-Ross had married her.
3 Sallie Baker (1948–2005) was the child of a previous relationship between Maclaren-Ross's wife and Peter Baker, a war hero and member of parliament who had since been gaoled. Due to her mother's rackety way of life, she was the subject of a court order, placing her under the guardianship of her uncle, Philip Woolf, who lived at Golden Manor near Taunton, Somerset.
4 On 27 December 1958, Woolf wrote to Maclaren-Ross, refusing permission. Alex Maclaren-Ross and Sallie Baker didn't get to know one another until nearly four decades later. Their friendship was truncated by Baker's death.

to THE BBC

235 Victoria Road¹/London N22
16-4-59

Dear Sir,

Mr R.D. Smith informs me that he wishes me to act as narrator in my 30-minute radio-play *I Had to Go Sick*, which he is pre-recording during the week starting May 5th.

In order that a contract may be sent to me, I am notifying you of my change of address as above, which will be operative for the next fortnight.²

Yours very truly,

J. Maclaren-Ross

1 With what was then the considerable sum of £25 in unpaid rent owing to their landlord and landlady at 25 Anson Road, Maclaren-Ross had moved, together with his wife and baby, to this address in Alexandra Park.

2 Contrary to his prediction, Maclaren-Ross – not to mention his freshly acquired wife and baby son – was able to remain there until 11 July 1959. That day they moved into a one-bedroom flat at 108a Tollington Park, in the Finsbury Park district of London.

to THE BBC

235 Victoria Road/London N22
8-5-59

Dear Sir,

In reply to yours of 5th May, the BBC has indeed got my present address, since a contract for recording reached me a fortnight ago. I always notify the Drama Department of a change of address and ask the officials there to pass it on when necessary, as I have no secretarial staff of my own to deal with such eventualities.¹

In only two cases, when I was uncertain of where I would be staying, have I given Broadcasting House as a forwarding address: once to a German Broadcasting Company whose letters to me might otherwise have gone astray.

I cannot be responsible for private persons who read my name in *The Radio Times*² and attempt to contact me through the BBC; if I wished them to, they would be in possession of my address. Mr Ashbury³ has been notified of the above and had in any event no right to trouble you.

Yours faithfully,

J. Maclaren-Ross

1 On 5 May 1959 W.L. Stretton, Head of Programme Contracts, had written to Maclaren-Ross urging him to stop giving Broadcasting House as his postal address. Stretton claimed that Maclaren-Ross was inconveniencing BBC staff.

2 The BBC's television and radio listings magazine.

3 Leslie Ashberry, together with his wife Margaret, had rented the 25 Anson Road flat to the Maclaren-Rosses. In an effort to obtain the rent arrears owed to him by Maclaren-Ross, Leslie Ashberry had written to Maclaren-Ross care of the BBC.

to DONALD McWHINNIE[1]

Royal Hotel[2]/Woburn Place/London WC1

21-12-59

My dear Donald,

When I worked out a plan of my proposed subject,[3] I found it would work out at double the length which I had originally envisaged; so I was unable to produce a finished script as I'd intended, but hope that you will be able to commission it on the basis of this outline as a 60-Minute Play instead.[4]

I think you will find the finished product provides a really unexpected final twist and the portrait of the paralysed sadist, revelling in his melodramatic role, should be interesting to work on.

Hope to see you for a pre-Xmas drink on Tuesday morning; I have a new book of TV scripts which might be of interest to you.

As ever,

Julian

1 Donald McWhinnie (1920–87), stage and television director, who was, at that point, the BBC's Assistant Director Drama (Sound). Besides commissioning several scripts, McWhinnie had produced a radio adaptation of Maclaren-Ross's screenplay *The Key Man*. This was broadcast on the BBC Home Service on 6 August 1960.

2 With characteristic extravagance, Maclaren-Ross had moved his family into a suite of rooms here in early October 1959.

3 A 30-minute play entitled *The Dancing Master*.

4 Under the title *Mr Mephisto*, this new drama, for which Maclaren-Ross pocketed a scriptwriting fee, was never completed.

to HAMISH HAMILTON

Royal Hotel/Woburn Place/London WC1
2-1-60

Dear Hamilton,

When can I expect to receive my six presentation copies of *Until the Day She Dies*,[1] promised for publication in early January?

It seems a bad start to mislead booksellers by advertising it in their leading organ as a 'detective story', when it is specifically subtitled 'A Tale of Terror'. Actually, it might be called an Anti-Detective Story, in the sense that some plays are Anti-Plays.

Yours sincerely,

J. Maclaren-Ross

1 From its origins as an idea for a filmscript, *Until the Day She Dies* had been transformed into a BBC radio serial and then a novel, published by Hamish Hamilton.

to DONALD McWHINNIE

Royal Hotel/Woburn Place/London WC1
7-1-60

My dear Donald,

Here's the synopsis for the 30-Minute Play which I thought of but which somehow wouldn't organise itself before Xmas.

It's one of my attempts to reconcile a bizarre plot with realistic setting and characters, and from the 6 pages I've written of the script, it's working out very well: I hoped to get it all done last night, but now it won't be completed until tomorrow morning.

However, please put the contract through today, if you like the enclosed outline, and the finished script can be on your desk tomorrow at 11 a.m.[1]

We must in any case meet to have a talk soon about plans for 1960.

As ever,

Julian

1 The play, entitled *The Man in Aurora's Room*, was commissioned by Donald McWhinnie on 8 January 1960. Maclaren-Ross wasted no time in delivering the completed script. As part of a double-bill with a dramatisation of Maclaren-Ross's wartime short story 'They Put Me in Charge of a Squad', the play was broadcast on the BBC Home Service on 11 June 1960.

to RICHARD BRAIN

Royal Hotel/Woburn Place/London WC1
11-1-60

Dear Brain,

If you would leave my presentation copies of *Until the Day She Dies* downstairs at your office on Jan. 18th, either my wife or I will call in and fetch them, as I'm uncertain where we shall be staying at that time.

Yours sincerely,

J. Maclaren-Ross

to RICHARD BRAIN

Royal Hotel/Woburn Place/London WC1
14-1-60

Dear Brain,

Thank you for your letter of Jan. 13.

I'm glad the publication date is advanced to Feb. 11th. One of us will call in on Monday; and if copies aren't there, come back later on: we won't be far away, though I'm not sure yet of exact address.

Good about the German rights: I got DM 1050 for the total serial, so I think you were right to accept 800.[1]

Yours sincerely,

J. Maclaren-Ross

1 The payment, made in Deutschmarks, had been for the German rights to the novel *Until the Day She Dies*.

to RICHARD BRAIN

White Hall Hotel[1]/Montague Street/London WC1
22-1-60

Dear Brain,

Forgot to say this morning that I'll require 6 more copies[2] for personal use at author's rates, if you'll debit them to me?

I've been so busy promoting private campaigns that I forgot to reserve one for the woman to whom the book is dedicated:[3] the others are for the radio-producer[4] and various other people at the BBC[5] (copyright, accounts, etc.), who are always helping me by putting payments through promptly.

I'll be at the above hotel until next Friday at any rate.

Yours sincerely,

J. Maclaren-Ross

1 Around the second weekend of January 1960, Maclaren-Ross and his family had left the Royal Hotel and taken two rooms at the nearby White Hall Hotel, a smaller, less pricey establishment.

2 Copies of the novel *Until the Day She Dies*.

3 The dedication read 'Winifred Davin. Her book.'

4 The producer was, presumably, his close friend, R.D. 'Reggie' Smith.

5 They included Heather Dean from the Copyright Department. She was entrusted with issuing advance payments to writers who had been commissioned to supply scripts. In that role, she was frequently helpful to the impecunious Maclaren-Ross.

to MISS WAKEHAM[1]

White Hall Hotel/Montague Street/London WC1

14-2-60

Dear Miss Wakeham,

Thank you for your letter of 12th February, reference BBC Transcription approval of my 8-Episode Serial *The Doomsday Book*.[2]

My address is still as above, and if you could arrange payment of the fee (£268 16s). with minimum delay, I would be very grateful, since I have sundry accounts to settle during the early part of the coming week and am being pressed for payment.

Yours sincerely,

J. Maclaren-Ross

1 Miss Wakeham was an assistant in the BBC's Copyright Department.

2 The BBC's Transcription Department had received the manuscript of the serial, ready for it to be turned into a typescript.

to DONALD McWHINNIE

White Hall Hotel/Montague Street/London WC1

2-3-60

My dear Donald,

Since *Y List*;[1] *Dream Man*,[2] and *Master of Suspense*[3] are now all scheduled for production by Reggie Smith, and *The Doomsday Book* also is at last to be broadcast,[4] could I be commissioned for a new 60-minute Play?

I am enclosing herewith the first half of one on which I've been working,[5] and hope I could be contracted for half the fee on the strength of it: since, as you know, with the recent robbery I am in urgent financial straits. Could you inform Diane what you decide?[6]

Hope to see you sometime today, as I'm narrating in studio 36.[7]

As ever,

Julian

1 An adaptation of his wartime short story of the same title. Reggie Smith employed him to play the role of the story's narrator. Despite his narration being recorded by the BBC, the play didn't go into production.

2 *Dream Man* was broadcast on the BBC Light Programme on 12 April 1960.

3 Produced by Reggie Smith, *The Master of Suspense* was broadcast on the BBC Home Service on 5 May 1960.

4 *The Doomsday Book*, featuring specially composed music by Humphrey Searle, had its first of eight episodes broadcast on the BBC Light Programme on 4 April 1960. That week's edition of the *Radio Times* featured the following plug for the programme: 'J. Maclaren-Ross is a writer of thrillers that can really thrill... For Anthony Jacobs, who plays a leading role in it, association with Maclaren-Ross always has a happy connotation: "The first radio lead I ever played," he told us, "was in his *Captain Kidd*, back in 1946, which, incidentally, was also produced by the same man, Reggie Smith. This time he's given me a really original character: a radio journalist – tough, bad-tempered but efficient – who gets involved in criminal affairs. I modelled my performance on at least one BBC reporter I know, and he should seem very real."'

5 The play was a radio dramatisation of his 1940s short story 'The Swag, the Spy and the Soldier'.

6 Two days after writing this letter, Reggie Smith commissioned the play for production on the BBC Home Service.

7 Maclaren-Ross had been hired as the narrator of the dramatisation of his wartime short story, *Y List*, produced by Reggie Smith. After a half-hour rehearsal, his contribution was recorded between noon and 12.30 p.m. that day. Though the play appeared on the BBC's long-term schedule, it was never broadcast.

to RICHARD BRAIN

Bedford Hotel[1]/Southampton Row/London WC1

2-4-60

Dear Brain,

Above address and telephone number will find me at any rate until after Easter, should you wish to contact me.

Yours sincerely,

J. Maclaren-Ross

1 During his family's stay at the White Hall Hotel, they'd built up a sizeable debt to the management. Using a £47 fee from the BBC, Maclaren-Ross paid what he owed, then moved his family to the larger Bedford Hotel.

to RICHARD BRAIN

Bedford Hotel/Southampton Row/London WC1

8-4-60

Dear Brain,

My address until Friday 22nd April will be:

The Bonnington Hotel

Southampton Row

HOL 6525

I hope that you will be able to let me have my half-share of the Ace Books[1] advance on *Until the Day She Dies* before Easter, as I have many out-payments to meet during the coming week.

Yours sincerely,

J. Maclaren-Ross

1   Ace Books was a paperback imprint. On 5 April 1960, Brain had written to him at the Bedford Hotel, announcing that the company had bought the paperback rights to *Until the Day She Dies*. Maclaren-Ross was due to receive £200.

to RICHARD BRAIN

New Court Hotel/Inverness Terrace/London W2

13.6.60

My dear Brain,

Herewith, as promised, chapters one to six of *The Doomsday Book*:[1] 3 episodes of the radio version, out of 8 altogether.

Actually, Part One *The Man Who Cannot Die*, up to end Episode 4, Chapter 8 of the novel, is now finished but will overlap into the MS book containing Part Two, as I explained.

Please let me know your opinion when I've read this. I'll be at above address until Friday week. The novel, on present form, should be ready well in time for November publication.

Yours sincerely,

J. Maclaren-Ross

PS Mistakes in dates have been rectified and timings should be fairly accurate.

1   In the wake of turning *Until the Day She Dies* from a radio serial into a novel, Maclaren-Ross was doing the same to his other radio serial, a thriller entitled *The Doomsday Book*.

to HAMISH HAMILTON

11-8-60

Dear Mr Hamilton,

Reference the option which you hold to see the MS of my next novel, on terms to be arranged, I now propose that we should conclude a deal on *The Girl in the Spotlight*,[1] of which one quarter is completed and the MS already read by you, since it was completed last winter.

As I have already delivered 2 novels[2] to you on the terms decided upon between us 2 years ago, I suggest that they should now be doubled: i.e. and advance of £500 on *The Girl in the Spotlight*, of which £200 would become payable immediately on the quarter of the MS which you have seen.[3]

I will ring Richard Brain tomorrow (Friday) at 3.30p.m. to find whether these terms are acceptable to you; and, if not, will expect to collect a letter from your premises releasing me from the option in order that I may approach another publisher.[4]

Yours sincerely,

J. Maclaren-Ross

1 He was planning to turn the radio series *The Girl in the Spotlight* into a novel.
2 *Until the Day She Dies* and *The Doomsday Book*.
3 Maclaren-Ross was in the process of writing *The Girl in the Spotlight*, a novel based on his earlier idea for a filmscript.
4 The novel was rejected by Hamish Hamilton.

to RICHARD BRAIN

19-11-60

Dear Brain,

Herewith the proofs of *The Doomsday Book*, corrected as far as I am able.[1]

I think the details of the Gothic house are correct, though I am uncertain of the spelling of 'poinset' windows, also whether this is the correct architectural term. Could you verify it for me?

There is also the question of two songs, 'My Future Just Passed' and 'Maybe You'll Be There', from which quotations are made in the text. I sang them both myself in the radio version, but not the second stanza of 'My Future Just Passed' quoted on page 95, which should be verified.

I see no reason why permission shouldn't be granted to quote this tune, since 'My Future Just Passed' dates to 1930; however, there'll have to be the usual acknowledgements: Reggie Smith at the BBC Drama Dept. will put you onto whichever music publisher is concerned. It'll be damned awkward and necessitate re-writing dialogue if they *won't* grant permission for this one; if there's any trouble about 'Maybe You'll Be There', I can however knock up another lyric as I did over 'Darn that Dream'.

If you want to contact me at the above number during the coming week, I'm usually in until about midday.

Yours sincerely,

J. Maclaren-Ross

1 The book was published in 1961.

to MAX EDEN[1]

74 Little Albany Street / London NW1

Late March/early April 1961

Dear Max,

Maureen in hospital from midnight Monday when taken with the pains.[2] Your letter to the Council posted.

Sorry to hear about your cheque: still, you'll have it by now.

My bastards won't pay me for that adaptation of Wilshaw's[3] until the *broadcast*, which leaves me absolutely penniless over weekend. I do apologise for not sending £2 but I've had no money all week. Nor is there any food in the house; only Ratty[4] gets fed.

Next week promises to be better (it couldn't be worse) and I will send the two quid on directly I get them, unless (a) I am imprisoned for Neg. Maint., which is threatened,[5] or (b) I starve to death before Monday.

Hope all's well with you,

Love,

Julian

PS No news yet of Maureen; her brother called, but I couldn't tell him where she was because she refused to let me know.

1 Max Eden (1923–) was a painter who had become a close friend of Maclaren-Ross. Eden had just taken up a teaching job at Southport School of Art. During the week he was based in Liverpool. At weekends he'd return to London. Knowing that Maclaren-Ross was homeless, Eden had let Maclaren-Ross move into his studio. This was located in a Georgian house, part of a row of buildings due to be demolished. The buildings were on Little Albany Street, close to Regent's Park.

2   Maureen, an art-student friend of Max Eden's, was expecting a child.

3   The BBC had bought an option to broadcast Harold Wilshaw's adaptation of Maclaren-Ross's celebrated short story 'A Bit of a Smash in Madras'. The option was, however, allowed to lapse.

4   Maureen's cat.

5   Having separated from Diana, Maclaren-Ross was supposed to be paying maintenance for her and their son, Alex. He had, unsurprisingly, failed to make the required payments.

to   MAX EDEN

74 Little Albany Street / London NW1

16-4-61

Dear Max,

They *have* started: house at back, opposite the bog, is nearly down already. One has to shit in bucket owing to falling brick and slate overhead. But the Irishmen doing it say there's no danger to us and ours will be the last to go. Forge along the road has extension until October.

Meanwhile 2 Final Notices for Rates and Water. Can you stall them, because although I've no money at moment, there should be a big publishing deal with Hodder & Stoughton[1] coming off any day next week and then I can contribute.

Life's hell just now, no food not even for Rat, in fact you may find I've eaten him when you arrive.

Looking forward to seeing you,

Julian

Don't forget to bring plates, forks, knives etc. and sheets for big bed. It's impossible to clean dishes because I've no mop and only one dirty dishcloth, but I might have enough to buy some before Sunday. The one towel is filthy too.

Will of course get pictures out in last resort.[2]

1   Maclaren-Ross was, most likely, hoping that Hodder & Stoughton would buy the rights to his novel *The Girl in the Spotlight*. His hopes went unfulfilled. Instead, the book ended up being published in 1964 by Times Press, a small Isle of Man-based company. By then, the title had been changed to *My Name Is Love*.

2   Eden was using the studio to store dozens of his paintings.

to MAX EDEN

74 Little Albany Street/London NW1
21-6-61

Dear Max,

Maureen left weeks ago with baby, didn't she write you? All of a sudden, taking everything with her, forks, knives (including carving and bread), plates (all except your big one), coffee percolator etc., and leaving me only the saucepan she used to shit in. (Ratty, however, was left for me to look after.)

So bring tools, china, cutlery etc. also sheets for your bed, as those have gone too. I am going to gaol on Tuesday next for sure unless I raise £10 by Friday night to send to the court, but don't mind as I've been practically starving these last few weeks. No money at all at the moment.

Looking forward to seeing you.

Julian

No news from St Pancras¹ yet, but men digging up street this morning.

1 The local council, responsible for the impending demolition of 74 Little Albany Street.

to MAX EDEN

74 Little Albany Street/London NW1
7-7-61

Dear Max,

Am sending on the enclosed: opened it in case there was anything I could do; unfortunately, at the moment, there isn't. I'm 49 today and have exactly fuck-all: not even cigarettes.

However, all's not lost yet. Look forward to seeing you weekend after next.

Julian

Chap from Council (redheaded) just caught me at front door, asked me when we'd be out of here, said they were starting demolition 1st week in October. Told him to see you after next weekend, here.

to ROGER MACHELL[1]

74 Little Albany Street / London NW1

13-8-61

Dear Mr Machell,

With reference to the acceptance for publication of *The Doomsday Book* in the USA by Messrs Ivan Obolensky, I wonder if it would be possible for you to give me written confirmation of this, and of the terms and advance agreed-upon, if any?

Being at the moment in a very difficult position financially, I might then be able to raise through a solicitor the advance in question. Some indication of the time which may elapse before the money is actually paid-over to your firm would also be helpful in this connection.

Yours sincerely,

J. Maclaren-Ross

1   Roger Machell (1908–84) had taken over from Richard Brain as Maclaren-Ross's point of contact with the firm Hamish Hamilton.

to MAX EDEN

74 Little Albany Street / London NW1

24-9-61

Dear Max,

Have been all week rehearsing a recording of *The Girl in the Spotlight* (written and paid for 2 years ago), so sorry I couldn't write before.

News: Fritz has been and collected the panels. Ratty disappeared last Friday (18th) and is still, alas, missing.

Bastard kids threw stone through window, landed on your big plate on shelf below and broke it, but I will get you another one. Fire next door yesterday.

We've a peculiar young couple staying upstairs who never move or speak (I've never seen them, though Diane has:[1] I think she's imagined them, like the mother in *Psycho*).[2]

Money: I should have a small cheque soon to send to you, but haven't received my transcription fee yet; and as yet can't pay deposit on a flat.

Diane is madly home-hunting, hopes to find something by Friday; but I'm tied up until weekend (next) with this serial play and can't do much to help. Bad situation.

Gas company has sent card, saying they're coming to do something on Thursday: is it to collect the stove?

I'll of course send on the blankets etc.: have spoken to Sid re storing the other stuff and he's agreed. We'll have to do it on Sat. next however, as I have to leave house every morning to reach studio before 10.00 a.m.

Please listen to *Spotlight* on Monday:[3] if not to the other full-length play.

Love,

Julian

1   Maclaren-Ross and his wife had got back together.
2   The 1960 film, directed by Alfred Hitchcock. Norman Bates, the deranged motel owner at the centre of the movie, imagined that his dead mother was still alive.
3   The first episode of *The Girl in the Spotlight* was broadcast on the BBC Light Programme on 25 September 1961. Two evenings earlier the BBC Home Service had broadcast *The Man With a Background of Flames*, Maclaren-Ross's radio play, featuring his friend the actor and publisher Tony Van den Bergh. *The Girl in the Spotlight* incorporated the signature tune which Maclaren-Ross had, six years previously, commissioned Stanley Hume to compose in honour of Sonia Orwell.

to ROGER MACHELL

9-11-61

Dear Mr Machell,

After the very handsome way the firm has behaved to me since our breach last summer, and the amount of work you put in to produce, sell, and promote *The Doomsday Book*, I feel that I should offer you again my new novel, *The Girl in the Spotlight*.

As you know, 25,000 words of this are completed and have been read by you and the radio-serial version (penultimate episode on Monday) is now being successfully broadcast on the Light Programme, after a very good notice for Episode 1 from Paul Ferris in *The Observer*. I could guarantee delivery of the total MS within one month of signing the contract.

The only snag – should you wish to resume relations – is that I sold the paperback rights last summer to Four Square Books[1] (contract enclosed herewith).

I would be prepared, however, in return for an immediate advance on royalties, to assign to you the £75 payable on publication, plus £25 to be deducted from future royalties, making £100 in all; and agree to split 50/50 as with the other 2 novels.

I feel sure that you would be able to re-adjust the dates etc. with Frank Rudman[2] reference publication of the Four Square Edition.

I will telephone you tomorrow to find out your views[3] and, should your answer be 'No', will collect the Four Square Contract from your Reception Office. But it is my sincere wish that we will be able to continue as publisher & author.

Yours sincerely,

J. Maclaren-Ross

1 A paperback publishing firm, modelled on American paperback imprints such as Dell. The company was founded by Maclaren-Ross's friend Tony Van den Bergh. It was then taken over by Ace Books.

2 Rudman ran Ace Books, the company which had recently acquired Four Square Books.

3 On 10 November 1961, Machell wrote to Maclaren-Ross, returning the contract from Four Square Books and wishing him luck in finding a publisher to release a hardback edition of *The Girl in the Spotlight*.

to ROGER MACHELL

24 York Street[1] / London W1

10-12-61

Dear Mr Machell,

Should there be any news, proof-sheets of American *Doomsday Book* edition etc., my address until next Saturday is above.

After Dec. 16, I will be in Brighton,[2] but will let you know the address of my new flat there later.

Yours sincerely,

J. Maclaren-Ross

1 Maclaren-Ross and his family had taken up residence in one of numerous bedsits at this address.

2 On discovering that his mother-in-law was seriously ill, Maclaren-Ross made arrangements to move down to Brighton, so that Diane could be near the hospital to which she'd been taken. Along with Diane and their infant son, Maclaren-Ross moved into a flat at 24 Brunswick Terrace in Hove.

to ROGER MACHELL

24 Brunswick Terrace/Hove/Sussex

10-1-62

Dear Mr Machell,

Thank you for your letter of Feb. 9th explaining the mystery of the missing books: I'm glad that the explanation did not lie with me.

As for Obolensky, he is obviously extremely unbusinesslike and it's not to be hoped that the other half of the advance will very shortly materialise: the copyright affair will cost him something, which serves him right.

Likewise Rudman is unbusinesslike; last year he failed to turn up at an appointment which he himself had made, and sent me instead some boy who had not even read the contract concerning *The Girl in the Spotlight*.

I questioned this boy about publication of the paperback *Until the Day She Dies*, and could see that some delay was in the air; I telephoned your secretary warning her of this last September.

The re-organisation of Ace Books is entirely the concern of their firm, and it's to be hoped that Rudman can be made to pay up the rest of the advance now, as the delay in publication is of their own causing; I'm sure you will press for this.

I would be greatly obliged if you could have me sent 2 copies of *Until the Day She Dies* (2nd imp[ression]) to above address.

Yours sincerely,

J. Maclaren-Ross

to JOHN BROADBENT

24 Brunswick Terrace/Hove/Sussex

14-2-62

Dear Sir,

I should be grateful if you could forward to me at above address a form of application for the Royal Literary Fund.

Yours faithfully,

J. Maclaren-Ross

to MICHAEL BAKEWELL[1]

24 Brunswick Terrace / Hove / Sussex

23-2-62

Dear Bakewell,

Enclosed a new 40-minute radio play called *Farewell Mr Frankenstein*. If the length is any drawback (though there's a 40-minute play being done on the Home this Saturday) I can do a 20 min. play called *The Tip*,[2] which I have planned out and is quite funny, to go with it later and make a double-bill (like *Aurora's Room* and *They Put Me in Charge of A Squad*).

I'm hoping that you may be able to put this one through quickly and arrange a fee, as I've been finishing off a novel and have therefore not been able to do any other work at all. Therefore I have no money whatever and am facing eviction this week. After all I did help out about *The Girl in the Spotlight*[3] and now I need help myself very badly indeed.[4]

Coming along within a week or so will be the 60-minute play *The Painted Devil*, commissioned last year, which is not working out well; but if it doesn't work out in the end, I'll let you have a replacement for it in about 14 days, for the half-fee still due on *The Devil*.[5]

I will phone you up at 3.15 approx. on Monday afternoon to find out how the land lies re *Frankenstein*, so will you leave a message if you're out?[6]

Kindest regards,

Yours sincerely,

J. Maclaren-Ross

1 Michael Bakewell (1931–) had taken over from Barbara Bray as the BBC's Script Editor at Drama (Sound).
2 *The Tip* was never written.
3 He was probably alluding to the fact that, at the request of the BBC, he'd hurriedly expanded several episodes.
4 Even by their standards, Maclaren-Ross and his family were in a dire financial position.
5 Maclaren-Ross had delivered a completed script of *The Painted Devil*, commissioned on 13 October 1960, but the play was never produced.
6 Bakewell did not commission either of Maclaren-Ross's ideas.

to JOHN BROADBENT

24 Brunswick Terrace / Hove / Sussex
28-2-62

Dear Captain Broadbent,

Thank you for your letter of 23 February, I was delighted to hear from you.

As you will see from the enclosed form, I have got married since we last met and am now the father of a boy aged 3 ½. This naturally makes survival on the literary earnings more difficult, as I have explained in the enclosed letter to the Committee.

I also enclose copies of my two latest novels, and at the moment of writing I am awaiting letters from Sir John Waller, Bart.,[1] R.D. Smith, my BBC Producer, and – I hope – from Donald McWhinnie, now theatrical producer and formerly Assistant Director of BBC Sound Radio Drama, before I can post everything off.*

Quite frankly I can't afford even the fare to London at the moment; but soon I may get a trip up in someone else's car (I will telephone beforehand), though as yet the trip is uncertain.

With best wishes,

Yours sincerely,

J. Maclaren-Ross

* This letter not to hand: they may possibly be away, in that case I'll get someone else – meanwhile here is the rest to save time.

Enclosed:

1 copy *Until the Day She Dies*
1 copy (USA Edition) *The Doomsday Book*
1 completed form of application
1 separate letter outlining causes of distress
Authenticating letters from: Sir John Waller

To Whom It May Concern

While I have applied for, and received, the Royal Literary Fund in the past, I have not done so in the last ten years; although I married in the meantime and am now the father of a boy of three and a half years old (with wife also to support).

I managed, since his birth, to maintain financial equilibrium by writing plays and serials for Sound Radio, to the neglect of novels and books which I should have been writing; though novel versions of the two serials did in fact get written and copies of the respective books accompany this letter.

Since 1960, however, with the onset of Television, the face and sound of radio is gradually changing back to the old days of *Paul Temple*,[2] *P.C. 49*[3] etc., especially since Mrs Barbara Bray resigned from being head of the Script Department (she in fact commissioned the serial version of *Until the Day She Dies* from me purely on a conversational outline, and it proved a large success). Worse still, Donald McWhinnie, then Assistant Head of Drama and a man who understood completely the sort of work which I proposed to put before the public, also resigned to become a brilliant theatrical producer (Pinter's *The Caretaker* etc.) and at the same time a new Head of Programme Planning (I believe that was his title) was appointed: it has been tactfully hinted to me that henceforth fewer radio plays of my type would prove acceptable (even though many have been successfully repeated overseas and one serial was given World Transcription *before broadcast*, a distinction which I am told it shared with only the star-studded Production of *The Way of the World*.[4]

However, this means the virtual end of a profitable market, until I can get television drama people round to my way of thinking, which might take a year or even longer.

Last year was quite the worst financially for several past; and though my novel *The Doomsday Book* has, as you see, been published by Ivan Obolensky Inc. in the USA, they have still not paid the other half of the advance due on publication: it took 6 months before they paid the first half to Messrs Hamilton, although this had been promised on signature of contract.

I am also awaiting a decision on a possible Penguin edition of my autobiography *The Weeping and the Laughter*, but I have since been told that this may take another 4 weeks;[5] an advance of £50 payable on publication of a paperback edition of *Until the Day She Dies* (scheduled for March) has now been postponed until the Autumn due to re-organisation of the firm concerned; and the immediate financial situation has become in consequence extremely desperate, as I'm sure you will readily appreciate.

There is little to add, except that mine seems, to me at any rate, a case deserving of a Grant for Purposes of Alleviation: the novel on which I am now engaged, which I consider to be my best work, is extremely long and may take another six months to complete;[6] and the negotiations over the one which I have recently completed are held up over a dispute about paperback rights, sold by me in 1960 to a firm which has since been taken-over by an American combine, and disentanglement may again take too long, although I have offered every suggestion in my power to clear up the outstanding difficulties.

J. Maclaren-Ross.

1 Sir John Waller (1917–95), poet and friend of Maclaren-Ross.
2 BBC radio series, scripted by Francis Durbridge and broadcast between 1938 and 1968.
3 *P.C. 49: Incidents in the Career of Police Constable Archibald Berkeley-Willoughby* was a BBC radio series, broadcast between 1947 and 1953. Coincidentally, Eric Phillips (who played the character 'Sergeant Wright') was a fan of Maclaren-Ross's work. Phillips had interviewed him for the September 1961 issue of *The Writer*.
4 Comic play by William Congreve (1670–1729), first performed in 1700.
5 Penguin decided against bringing out a paperback edition of the book.
6 He was referring to *The Girl in the Spotlight*, which he had already finished. By lying about this, he must have hoped he'd increase his chances of securing a grant.

to JOHN BROADBENT

7-3-62

Dear Captain Broadbent,
Herewith the second authenticating letter, from Olivia Manning the novelist and R.D. Smith, her husband[1] and my BBC producer; Donald McWhinnie being away at the moment.
I'm afraid I still can't get up to London yet, as my mother-in-law is in a coma and in the hospital here and my wife needs me; but if I am able to I will let you know at once.
Yours sincerely,
J. Maclaren Ross.

1 'In order to keep his wife and child,' this jointly signed testimonial declared, 'he has had to lay aside his own creative writing to freelance, mainly in the field of sound radio. For some years he has managed successfully to keep going, but inevitably there are limits to the amount of work Sound Drama Service can absorb by any one person, and the rewards for such work are not so great that a writer can build up any reserve… for the last month or two he was able to withdraw to Hove and continue his long-delayed original novel, but now faces financial disaster. I am sure that you know his work, and know that he has a talent of a rare and original kind. Help now would certainly save, if not the total ruin, at least the delay of many years of a piece of work that really should be completed and published.'

to JOHN BROADBENT

24 Brunswick Terrace / Hove / Sussex
21-3-62

Dear Captain Broadbent,

Thank you for your letter of 13 March.

It was a great blow to me,[1] because as you realise things are quite desperate with me. At the moment we may not have anywhere to stay after next Monday. I am owed, as you know, £120 by my American publisher, but still this has not been sent although the novel was published in the USA in November and the second half of the advance due on publication.

My mother-in-law has partly recovered but she is still in a nursing-home and by no means well. I will try to let you know when I am able to come to London in advance, but the prospect seems remote at present.

I will let you know change of address if we have to vacate this flat, which of course, as the present situation is, will be disastrous.

With best wishes,

Yours sincerely,

J. Maclaren Ross

PS Re' medical reports,[2] none of us luckily *is* ill, except my mother-in-law and, even though she is Leonard's Woolf's sister, I fear that would not apply.

1 Broadbent had informed Maclaren-Ross that his application for another grant from the Royal Literary Fund had been rejected.
2 His application to the Royal Literary Fund would have been strengthened if he could demonstrate that his earnings had been reduced due to illness.

to ROGER MACHELL

Hotel Brunswick[1] / 69 Brunswick Place / Hove / Sussex
Early April 1962

Dear Mr Machell,

Should any news come through before Easter, my address until Good Friday is the above.

After Easter I will be able to give you a more permanent address.

Yours sincerely,

J. Maclaren-Ross

1   Owing the huge sum of £214 to Mrs Tanchan, their landlady at 24 Brunswick Terrace, Maclaren-Ross and his family had moved to the Hotel Brunswick, close to their previous address, on 8 April 1962.

to ROGER MACHELL

Easter Monday 1962

Dear Machell,

It was very kind of you to let me have that £10 for Easter. But if you could let me have another £25 – or even £15 – as an advance on the Obolensky money, I would (though I realise the drawbacks from your firm's point of view) be most grateful, as I am now in such a financial fix that I have not even anywhere to stay.

I will ring you up either on Tuesday or Wednesday at 4 o'clock for an answer.

(One of the reasons for this position is that I have as yet not found a publisher who will take *The Girl in the Spotlight*, now completed, when the paperback rights have been sold; but I have at last obtained a letter from Rudman agreeing to cancel their contract if the advance of £125 is repaid.)

Yours sincerely,

J. Maclaren-Ross

to JOHN BROADBENT

c/o Dr J. Schwartz[1] / 14 Chichester Terrace / Brighton / Sussex

8-4-62

Dear Captain Broadbent,

The above address will find me, as my friend Dr Schwartz, who collects my MSS, has kindly allowed me to have letters addressed to his house.

After Wednesday I have no idea where we will be staying; as we have to leave where we are at twelve noon and there is no money to deposit on another flat. The situation is simply desperate; and still the American publisher Obolensky has not paid the money he owes me. (Though my novel came out in USA in Nov.) I fear I won't be able to come to London before the meeting; but if I am able to come, I will contact you by phone.

With kindest regards,

Yours sincerely,

J. Maclaren-Ross

1   An American who lived in Brighton. He dealt in first editions and auto-graphs, not to mention literary manuscripts, which he sold to American universities. For several years Schwartz had been buying Maclaren-Ross's manuscripts, pro-viding Maclaren-Ross with invaluable extra cash.

to HAMISH HAMILTON

> c/o R.D. Smith/BBC Drama Dept/Broadcasting House[1]/
> Portland Place/London W1
> **26-4-62**

Dear Hamilton,

You signed the contract with Obolensky of New York for my novel *The Doomsday Book*, not I.

Nonetheless, it was *my* book which appeared under his imprint in the States 6 months ago, and the second half of the advance, due on publication, has still not been paid.

I know that you have done your best to obtain satisfaction, but the whole responsibility of the transaction with this obviously erratic firm rests with you.

Since my small request for £25 advance out of the sum of £119 was met with refusal, I must ask you to honour your responsibility by immediate payment of the total amount due to me.

I will telephone you tomorrow (Friday) morning at 12 a.m. to ask when it will be convenient to call for the cash. I think you will agree that I have been very patient up to now.[2]

Yours sincerely,

J. Maclaren-Ross

1   Back in London after the break-up of his second marriage, Maclaren-Ross was left homeless. Not for the first time, in defiance of a previous complaint he'd received from the BBC, he used Broadcasting House as his postal address.
2   On 17 May 1962, Machell wrote to Maclaren-Ross, announcing that Obolensky had at last sent the expected cheque. Maclaren-Ross's share of the money was £118 17s 11d. Realising how broke Maclaren-Ross was, Machell offered to give him the payment in cash, which could be collected from the offices of Hamish Hamilton the following afternoon.

to DOUGLAS CLEVERDON[1]

c/o The George[2]/Great Portland Street/London W1

13-5-62

Dear Cleverdon,

Appended herewith is a synopsis for the musical version of [*The Picture of*] *Dorian Gray* which we discussed the other day. The length would be about 75 minutes.

If I am commissioned for the work, I would then prepare a complete script ready for discussion (including proposed music-and-song cues etc.) with Humphrey Searle[3] and yourself when he returns from Germany in a fortnight's time.

For the lyrics I would suggest a collaboration between myself and Donald Cotton,[4] a great admirer of Wilde's and this novel in particular. (The lyrics would be done last of all.)

I give you above address since I am between flats at the moment and it is at any rate sure to find me.

Your sincerely,

J. Maclaren-Ross

1 Douglas Cleverdon (1903–87) was a producer in BBC Radio's Features Department.
2 This pub had become a favourite haunt of BBC staff as well as actors and writers seeking employment with the BBC. From around 1957, Maclaren-Ross was a regular customer there. Other regulars included Reggie Smith, Olivia Manning, the poet Louis MacNeice and the actor Patrick Magee.
3 The composer Humphrey Searle (1915–82) was a producer at the BBC.
4 Donald Cotton (?–2000), dramatist, novelist and journalist, whose credits include the script of 'The Gunfighters', a 1965 episode of BBC TV's *Doctor Who*.

to DIANE BROMLEY[1]

Draft, August 1962

Child,

Come and see me again – I can't bear it without you any longer. Next week, thank God, my novel goes through at last and about the middle I will draw an advance, but if you can afford it, send or bring me some money; things go from bad to worse, for Christ's sake. If you will ring me, I'll be in the George tomorrow lunchtime (LAN 1295)[2] seeing a man about a job. I don't properly understand what went wrong after last Monday night. Please let's stop being oblique and hurting each other to no purpose. I will never give you up, darling, so it's no use trying to get away from me.

I love you I love you I love you I love you

J.

1 Maclaren-Ross's wife, who was fourteen years his junior. Since the break-up of their relationship, she had reverted to her previous married name.
2 The telephone number of the George. The prefix indicated the local telephone exchange.

to CLAIRE[1]

16-9-62

Dear Claire,

Thank you for your two letters. Unfortunately, some 'nonsense' prevents me from coming to Dublin after all.

I did, however, meet your friends the Behans,[2] whilst they were over here.

So, as you yourself said in a poem: 'The dream, like a perfect crime, must remain in the head.'

Sincerely,

J.M.R.

1 Maclaren-Ross's latest girlfriend.
2 The Irish writers Brendan Behan (1923–64) and his brother Dominic (1928–89).

to ALAN ROSS[1]

Please reply to: Mrs E. Brill[2]/16 Chepstow Place/London W2

26-11-62

My dear Alan,

Enclosed herewith the essay on A.E.W. Mason which you commissioned from me, and which I hope you will find satisfactory.[3] It is 3,000 words in length.

Please send me the fee in cash, as I've no bank account and am damnably short of the ready.

Am now working on the long story of which I told you, and a portion of which I will soon have to show.

Any news about my novel from Collins yet?[4]

As ever,

Julian

1   Maclaren-Ross had been on friendly terms with the writer Alan Ross ever since the two of them had met in the Wheatsheaf during the latter stages of the Second World War. Since then, Ross had taken over from John Lehmann as editor of the *London Magazine*.

2   Maclaren-Ross had recently embarked on a romance with Eleanor Brill, a Northern Irish woman who worked for the Reuters news agency. She lived in a flat above Donald McWhinnie and his wife Pauline. Maclaren-Ross soon moved in with her. They remained together until his death in November 1964. Later she became the girlfriend of Maclaren-Ross's friend John Gawsworth.

3   Maclaren-Ross's essay 'The Black Romances of A.E.W. Mason' was published in the March 1963 issue of the *London Magazine*. He argued that 'Mason was prophetic in the light of present-day fictional trends, where the twisted and the damned are prone to rouse the reader's pity.'

4   Alan Ross had forwarded *The Girl in the Spotlight* to a contact at the publishing firm William Collins.

to CHARLES OSBORNE[1]

c/o Mrs E. Brill/16 Chepstow Place/London W2

3-1-63

Dear Osborne,

Thank you for sending me £10 and the documents referring to my novel from Walton Street.[2]

As Alan Ross presumably is still away, could you please send me the remainder of the fee, as I am engaged in writing a long story at the moment and find finance difficult to obtain.

With regard to the Mason article, there will be a short note to add in proof reference one of the novels which I was unable to get hold of at the time, but I don't think it will make for difficulty. If you send proofs to above address, I will attend to them without delay.

Best New Year wishes to you all and to the magazine (I enjoyed Brigid Brophy's pieces and the Graham Greene).[3]

Sincerely,

J. Maclaren-Ross

1   Charles Osborne (1927–) was the Australian-born assistant to Alan Ross at the *London Magazine*.

2   The *London Magazine* office was located there.

3   The November 1962 issue of the *London Magazine* had included 'May We Borrow Your Husband?', a lengthy Graham Greene short story. Brigid Brophy's essays on the novelist Ronald Firbank, Mozart's operas and the short-story writer Katherine Mansfield appeared in the October, November and December 1962 editions of the magazine.

to ALAN ROSS

c/o Mrs E. Brill/16 Chepstow Place/London W2

26-2-63

My dear Alan,

I expect you are now back from Australia.

If so, please drop me a card to above address when you are available for us to have a drink together; I've one or two things I'd like to talk to you about.

As I expect you know, Collins returned the MS of my novel to me. Hope all is going well.

As ever,

Julian

to ROGER MACHELL

c/o R.D. Smith/BBC Drama Dept/Broadcasting House/

Portland Place/London W1

27-2-63

Dear Mr Machell,

'Re Ace Books Edition of *Until the Day She Dies*.

You will recall that Ace proposed last year to postpone publication until this Spring.

The book is listed in the Spring *Bookseller* both under my name and under the title, as a Four Square Book (210), in the 'Index to Books Announced'; but no mention of it appears in the Four Square Spring Announcements (pp. 724–5).

Perhaps you could find out from the New English Library[1] when they plan to publish, and when I may expect to receive the other half of the advance, due on publication, as it is now nearly 3 years since the contract was signed?

Last month I asked for a copy of Barlow's *Hour of Maximum Danger*[2] to include mention of it in a middle article for the *TLS*; but I regret that the section devoted to it was cut by the Editors for reasons of space. (*TLS* Friday Feb. 8th.)

Yours sincerely,

J. Maclaren-Ross

1 Ace Books, which owned the Four Square Books imprint, had been taken over by New English Library, another paperback publisher.
2 James Barlow, *Hour of Maximum Danger* (1962).

to ROGER MACHELL

16 Chepstow Place/London W2

14-4-63

Dear Mr Machell,

Thank you for arranging the payment to me of £50 from Four Square Books.

I also note the news from Obolensky re *Doomsday Book*.

I see that *Until the Day She Dies* paperback is on sale in the bookshops. Could the Four Square people be asked to send me 6 complimentary copies to above address, please?

Yours sincerely,

J. Maclaren-Ross

to JACOB SCHWARTZ

16 Chepstow Place/London W2

25-4-63

My dear Jake,

Here is a corrected final proof of the middle on William Sansom for *Times Literary Supplement*, with MS additions which I had to make reference Elizabeth Bowen's Introduction.

Hope you received paperback edition of *Until the Day She Dies* sent to you last week. Please send something if you can, as I've just had to pay out large sum, leaving me broke.[1]

As ever,

Julian

1 On 27 April 1963, Schwartz responded to Maclaren-Ross's appeal with the following message: 'I enclose a pound note – not because the material you sent me is worth it but for friendship's sake.'

to ALAN ROSS

16 Chepstow Place/London W2

13-5-63

My dear Alan,

Enclosed, the article on Sexton Blake which you asked me to go ahead with in your postcard of 9th May.

It is 4,000 words (nearly twice the length I envisaged) and has necessitated a lot of reading and researching, so I hope it will amuse you.

Please send me the fee in cash to above address, as I need – as always – ready money.

Yours ever,

Julian

to ALAN ROSS

16 Chepstow Place/London W2

28-5-63

My dear Alan,

Hope you received the copies of Sexton Blake which I sent to you as requested.

More material (only a few points, but which must be mentioned) has turned up: so could I have the article again, to save correction on the proof, and I will return it within one day, necessary insertions made.

Two more things:

(1) Did anyone do *Raymond Chandler Speaking* (his letters) when it appeared early last year? If not, I suggest I do him, on the strength of the material contained therein plus my knowledge of his work, in your 'Reputations' series.

(2) Have you done an article on the outstanding American novel *The Recognitions* by William Gaddis (published USA 1955; here by Macgibbon and Kee last year)? If not, it certainly deserves one: except by Philip Toynbee, a monstrously neglected book.

As ever,

Julian

to ALAN ROSS

16 Chepstow Place/London W2

30-5-63

Dear Alan,

Enclosed the revised SB[1] article, with important additions (historical and otherwise).

Chandler follows shortly (perhaps over Whitsun).

There's also a book appeared today which (if possible) I'd like to review: *King of the Lags*, a biography of Charles Peace[2] (on whom I'd planned to write a musical) by David Ward (Elek 18s). This might be fun. I'm trying meantime to get more books by Robert Bloch.[3]

As ever,

Julian

PS When sending Blake proofs,[4] please remember to return MS.[5] Also you might, if you cared to, send me a fiver (cash) advance on Chandler, as some fees, expected before Whit, are now not coming in until after.

1 Sexton Blake.
2 Whilst wanted by the police on a murder charge, Charles Peace (1832–79) pursued a successful career as a burglar. After being arrested in London, he gave a false name and was sentenced to hard labour. When his secret was revealed, he had to face the original charge. He subsequently confessed to committing a second murder two years earlier. The victim had been a police officer. His trial culminated in him being sentenced to death, a sentence that he was unable to evade.
3 Alan Ross had commissioned Maclaren-Ross to write an article for the *London Magazine* on Robert Bloch (1917–94), the American science-fiction and thriller writer, best known for *Psycho*, the novel on which the Alfred Hitchcock film of that title was based. On 17 May 1963 Maclaren-Ross had written to Alan Ross, requesting help in obtaining review copies from Ace Books and Regency Books, Bloch's American publishers. Maclaren-Ross was keen to acquire the short-story collection *Yours Truly, Jack the Ripper* and five novels: *The Scarf, Spiderweb, The Kidnapper, Terror in the Night*, and *Kill for Kali*.
4 Maclaren-Ross's essay 'Seventy Years of Sexton Blake', appeared in the November 1963 issue of the *London Magazine*.
5 Maclaren-Ross probably hoped to sell the manuscript to Schwartz.

to ALAN ROSS

16 Chepstow Place / London W2

3-6-63

Dear Alan,

Here's the 'Reputations' article on Chandler, which has now become 'Chandler and Hammett' because it's almost impossible to write about one without the other if the job's to be done properly.

The essay is exactly 4,474 words in length.

Please send fee – cash or an *opened* cheque, to above address as soon as possible.

As ever,
Julian

to ALAN ROSS

16 Chepstow Place / London W2

20-7-63

My dear Alan,

Thank you for your news and the cheque for Robert Bloch[1] essay, received this morning. Please enclose MS when sending proofs of Chandler;[2] also drop me a line saying when you'd be free for a drink (I'd suggest the Bedford Head – is it? – in Pont Street), as I would very much like to have a chat with you sometime soon.

As ever,

Julian

1 Maclaren-Ross's essay 'The World of Robert Bloch', appeared in the July 1964 issue of the *London Magazine*.
2 Maclaren-Ross's essay 'Chandler and Hammett' was published in the March 1964 issue of the *London Magazine*. That issue also included a review by Maclaren-Ross of Raymond Chandler's *Killer in the Rain*.

to JAMES GRAHAM-MURRAY[1]

22-9-63

Poor Eleanor yesterday after leaving you either fell, or more probably was coshed, on the back of her head; also had her money stolen. She was stitched up at the hospital and seems all right now – or as well as can be expected; but you may get a visit from the police who are trying to find out about times, and I was unable to tell them when she left you, Eleanor herself being unable to remember. Sorry about that, but I had to give your name as having been with her (and us both). When I took a taxi to the West End, the time was 4.35, and I expect you left soon after.

Drop us a line if you find out anything from Gibbs' Girl?[2]

J.

1 The seedy Graham-Murray had been installed as Maclaren-Ross's new agent. Known as 'James the shit', Graham-Murray was, as the poet John Heath Stubbs recalled in conversation, 'no more of a shit than anyone else in that boozy circle'.
2 Probably a reference to one of the assistants to Anthony Gibbs, who ran Panther, the paperback publishing company. Gibbs had earlier worked with André Deutsch at Allan Wingate Ltd. Graham-Murray was trying to persuade Gibbs to buy the paperback rights to the novel of *The Girl in the Spotlight*.

to JAMES GRAHAM-MURRAY

16 Chepstow Place / London W2

1-10-63

Dear Graham-Murray,

You are hereby empowered to negotiate the film-rights of my novel *The Doomsday Book* (which are my sole property), provided that it is understood that I am not required in any way to work on a screen adaptation or on the script.

Yours very truly,

J. Maclaren-Ross

to JAMES GRAHAM-MURRAY

16 Chepstow Place / London W2

23-10-63

My dear James,

Thanks for letter-card received 2nd post today; don't put Roman numerals for W2: they read it as 'W11' which causes delay.

Okay, continue pressing, sounds hopeful, don't forget Van den Bergh's[1] plan re Four Square if you have to deal with Pacey. But the money situation here is dire; if I could only get a 'Yes' in writing and a definite payment-date, I might be able to raise a bit, however.

Also sounds good re paperback *Doomsday*, but may be a bit of a scuffle with prima-donna-behaving Roger Machell of Hamish Hamilton, who prevented me from selling pre-publication paperback rights to Van den Bergh, failed to sell them anywhere after, and thus was directly responsible for sale of *Girl in Spotlight* to Four Square: this deal replacing VDBs[2] offer to buy *DB*[3] and split 50-fifty with Hamilton. Machell by his stubbornness cost his firm £100 and also me £100. Treat him tough if you have to deal with him: by contract signed 1960 they are entitled to 50/50 share, but no doubt this could be got round as they haven't been able to sell 15 paperbacks since.

Now listen: ref. film rights of *Doomsday*.

The new Len Deighton, *Horse Under Water*, already sold to Salzman[4] and Broccoli,[5] has not only Neo-Nazis as villains, but the central theme (though book is set largely in Portugal) is exactly the same as *Doomsday Book*, depending on the recovery of a collaborators list such as Vogel's Book[6] was supposed to contain.[7]

'It contains the complete list of important persons, here in England, who would have collaborated if the Axis had won the war. Together with their dossiers and full documentary proofs.' (*Doomsday Book* p. 121.)

'It (the 'Weiss List') was about the size and shape of a paperback novel. It had thick grey card covers. Inside were the names of British Nationals and their addresses. They were in alphabetical order ... Each name was that of a person who would actively assist the Germans when they invaded Britain.' (*Horse Under Water*, pp. 198–99.)

The villain's motive (they are actual Neo-Nazis, which mine are *not*) is the same as Maxim's in my book:[8] blackmail of important persons named on the List (in Deighton's case, successfully practised on a Cabinet Minister etc.).

Broccoli and the *Dr No*[9] lot cannot bring out *Horse* until late next year at the earliest (they haven't even cast *The Ipcress*[10] yet); and if threatened with prior production of a film with the same basic plot (of which the source appeared 1961), I believe that they would put up rights of *Doomsday Book* rather than lose the money already paid to Deighton for *Horse*, by not making the latter.

A film company who owned *Doomsday* would therefore be in a position to sell out to Broccoli's mob (now among the richest producers in England) for any sum. I will sell for £3,000 or so and let them negotiate with the others: I'd be surprised if they didn't net £7,000 profit at least.

If you think you can swing this, go ahead – but it must be *quick* or the Broccoli gang will put *Horse* on the lot. If you don't think you can handle it, I will personally approach Vivian Cox[11] (D. Angel's[12] Associate Producer, who lives at Campden Towers, Notting Hill Broadway).

Let me know your opinion; I believe this is a 100% sure.

Love,

Julian

1 Tony Van den Bergh (1916–2000) was an actor with whom Maclaren-Ross had been friends since early 1947. During the 1950s, Van den Bergh had set up Four Square Books, a successful paperback publishing company based on the example of various American imprints, among them Avon and Dell. To promote its books, many of which were of high literary quality, Four Square sold them through tobacconists' shops, newsagents and other outlets previously overlooked by English publishers. What's more, the covers of the books featured garish paintings of the type seen on the jackets of American so-called 'pulp' novels. Coincidentally, Maclaren-Ross was an early collector and advocate of the virtues of American authors such as David Goodis and Robert Bloch, whose work first appeared in this format.

2 Tony Van den Bergh.

3 *The Doomsday Book*.

4 Harry Saltzman (1915–94), the Canadian film financier, had set up Woodfall Films with the director Tony Richardson and the playwright John Osborne. Their movies included *The Entertainer* (1960), *A Taste of Honey* (1960), and *Doctor No* (1962).

5 Albert R. 'Cubby' Broccoli (1909–96), the British-based American film producer whose credits include *Doctor No* (1962) and numerous other James Bond movies.

6 The plot of *The Doomsday Book* revolves around a writer's quest to locate a dossier kept by the mysterious Istvan Vogel.

7 Maclaren-Ross needn't have worried, because a film adaptation of Deighton's novel never went into production.

8 Known as 'the Man Who Cannot Die' and 'the King of the Night', 'Maxim' is a character in *The Doomsday Book*.

9 *Doctor No* (1962) was the first of the series of James Bond films, brought to the screen by Harry Saltzman and Albert Broccoli.

10 The film adaptation of Len Deighton's novel *The Ipcress File* was released in 1965. Produced by Harry Saltzman, it starred Michael Caine.

11 Vivian Cox (1915–?) was a British film producer whose credits include *The Clouded Yellow* (1951).

12 Daniel M. Angel (1911–99) ran Angel Productions, the firm responsible for films such as *Reach For The Sky* (1956).

to ALAN ROSS

16 Chepstow Place / London W2

29-10-63

Dear Alan,

Enclosed corrected proofs 'Chandler and Hammett' and 'Douglas Hayes'.[1] Thanks for sending MSS back.

How about the new collected Mikhail Zoshchenko[2] (great Soviet Russian humorist – remember his stories during war?) which Gollancz has just brought out? 1,500 words or so on this?[3]

Anyway, contact me soon for a drink: it's a long time I haven't seen you.

As ever,
Julian

1 Maclaren-Ross had written an essay on the comic novels of Douglas Hayes. The essay appeared in the December 1963 issue of the *London Magazine*.

2 Mikhail Zoshchenko (1895–1958).

3 Maclaren-Ross was commissioned to write about this once famous but now obscure Ukrainian writer. The consequent essay, entitled 'The Comic and Calico Masks of Zoshchenko', was published in the October 1964 issue of the *London Magazine*.

to JACOB SCHWARTZ

16 Chepstow Place / London W2

1-11-63

Dear Jake,

Thank you for letter and cash for Chandler and Hayes MSS enclosed.

Don't know Hayes personally, nor his private address; but write c/o his publishers, Messrs Abelard-Schuman, 8 King St, London WC3.

Sexton Blake article out in *London Mag*. Nov. issue, on sale Wed. next; just received complimentary copy, advertising 'Chandler & Hammett' for Dec. issue! Going to see Alan Ross this morning to get Chandler's last book of short stories for review.

Unlikely to come to Brighton until next summer to see my son, but do drop me a line when you're coming up before Xmas anyway.

Love to you both,

Julian

to JAMES GRAHAM-MURRAY

16 Chepstow Place / London W2

18-11-63

My dear James,

Thank you for your letter.

Not having heard from you, I phoned Gibbs' office last Friday to find out what was going on. I got the girl: Gibbs of course cowered in his office and pretended to be out, though I spoke very pleasantly. She promised to find out what had happened and to ring me back before 5 with the news. I sat and waited in the ML Club[1] for nearly 2 hours; no call came; and when I phoned the office again, they'd all buggered off. This is the kind of treatment I don't like, so I wrote a brief note to Gibbs, which he'll get this morning, calling the book in.

This may have the effect of getting some action or it may not: I've ceased to care. There was no suggestion in the girl's tone that anything had been, or was going to be, done at all. I took an excursion into various parts of the Lit. World last week, and there the impression was that I'd be a fool to appear under the Gibbs imprint anyway, and that even if I got any money from him at all, it would in any case do harm to the prospect of getting a properly established publisher for my next book, which I'm counting on for a firm future.

I also hear that *Until the Day She Dies* has gone into a 2nd edition with Four Square Books, which makes it very doubtful that they'll want to sell or surrender any rights to Panther.

Anyway, there it rests.

I too read *America*[2] and thought NFG.[3]

As ever,

Julian

1 Popular nickname for the Marie Lloyd Club, a basement drinking club frequented by many BBC staff from nearby Broadcasting House.
2 1927 novel by Franz Kafka.
3 'No fucking good'. A variant of the once-popular acronym 'NBG' ('no bloody good').

to JACOB SCHWARTZ

16 Chepstow Place / London W2

7-12-63

Dear Jake,

Thank you for yours and £3 enclosing glad to hear from you again. Thanks also for what you say about the criticism: my article on Hayes appears in the current *London Magazine*, and next day I received a card from Alan Ross, saying that he himself had read Douglas Hayes and that he was all I said he was – a real discovery. Next month, Mary McCarthy,[1] then 'Chandler and Hammett'; then Bloch and Sheridan Le Fanu.[2]

Now for some news – good for a change. I have at last sold my novel of which you have the rough of Parts II and III and which was serialised on radio as *The Girl in the Spotlight*, now re-titled *My Name Is Love*.

I'd difficulty about this because I sold the paperback rights before publication to Four Square Books; but now I have assigned these to a new firm which has started up from the Isle of Man and is beginning in a big new way next year: it is called The Times Press Ltd. I've only sold the rights of this one book, for an advance of £250: will soon have the cheque, so I can get ahead with my new long novel without so much worry. I will be getting back the MS of *My Name Is Love* in the New Year (they've already gone to press) and will then send it on to you.

Yes, by all means let's get together for a good old drink in the ML Club soon – before Xmas anyway.

Love to Anita[3] and yourself,

from

Julian

1 'Mary McCarthy and the Class of '33', Maclaren-Ross's essay on the author of *The Group* (1963), was published in the January 1964 issue of the *London Magazine*.
2 His essay, entitled 'The Dark Glass of Sheridan Le Fanu', featured in the February 1964 issue of the *London Magazine*.
3 Schwartz's wife, who was an actress, often in television drama.

to JAMES GRAHAM-MURRAY

16 Chepstow Place / London W2
11-12-63

Dear James,

Terribly sorry about the Uxbridge.[1] I had a nasty cut on my nose and felt rotten, but 1.30 on Thursday will be alright, I'm sure.

I'd a letter from Quayle[2] (written on Saturday) saying they would endeavour to follow my jacket-design;[3] nothing so far about the cheque, but I don't anticipate much trouble on getting it, because their accountants will see that we're in the right and we've Gibbs on our side.

Eleanor is okay now and I hope your cold's a thing of the past.

As ever,

Julian

1 The Uxbridge was a pub where Maclaren-Ross had arranged to meet Graham-Murray between 1.00 and 1.30 p.m. on 8 December 1964. Maclaren-Ross hadn't, however, turned up. This was the second time that he'd failed to show up for a drink with Graham-Murray. On the evening of 7 December 1964, they'd been due to meet, but Maclaren-Ross had had to stay at home because 'Eleanor definitely was not well... and the child was asleep' (letter from Maclaren-Ross to Graham-Murray, 8 December 1964). The child in question was Eleanor Brill's daughter Caroline.
2 Herbert Quayle was Maclaren-Ross's contact at the Times Press.
3 The front cover of the published book followed an idea sketched out by Maclaren-Ross.

to REGGIE SMITH

16 Chepstow Place / London W2
11-2-64

Re *The Midnight Men* (project for a TV Serial-version entitled *Midnight*)

My dear Reggie,

You may recall that in 1959 the BBC commissioned a radio serial of mine called *The Midnight Men*: first of all in 8 episodes, later lengthened to 12.

Of these episodes I wrote 10, which are still in MS form with the Script Dept. The project, according to Eric Ewens,[1] was finally – I think only temporarily – shelved; but about £400 was paid out over the period concerned, and I've now thought of a way by which this matter could be adjusted to the advantage of all.

Coming across some of the early episodes in rough form, it occurred to me that this story – a variant of the Tichborne Case[2] and a neo-Gothic mystery – would make an excellent TV serial. I started adapting it, and found it worked well, although I cannot write more than the first complete episode without reference to the others in existence.

I also thought that each episode should come within the 50–60-min. length, as I find when viewing that the 30-min. length does not give members of the audience enough idea of the plot and characters, especially in the case of a story as complicated as this.

I am willing to finish Episode 1 and submit it to the BBC TV Drama Dept. if the Sound Radio people, who at present own the copyright, will give me permission to do so. Also in order to adapt further episodes for TV I would have to have the scripts. But of course I would *make a contract arrangement by which the sums already paid can be deducted from payments made on signature of a BBC Television contract.*

Could you tell me what you think of this idea, and pass the proposal on to those executives concerned for a quick decision, as I either want to get on with the work involved or drop the project altogether as soon as possible?[3]

As ever,

Julian

1 Eric Ewens (1917–?) was an Assistant Script Editor in the BBC's Drama (Sound) Department. Even though he wasn't a heavy drinker, he had become a regular bar-room companion of Maclaren-Ross.
2 The so-called Tichborne case was a celebrated nineteenth-century legal case. It began when Arthur Orton (1834–98), a young butcher living in Australia, claimed to be Sir Roger Tichborne (1829–54), missing heir to the estates of the Doughty-Tichborne family.
3 The proposal was turned down.

to ROGER MACHELL[1]

16 Chepstow Place / London W2

20-2-64

Dear Mr Machell,

Thank you for sending me a copy of Ed McBain's *Like Love*, which I reviewed for the *London Magazine* together with Chandler's *Killer in the Rain* (this review should appear in the next issue, with my long article on Chandler and Hammett).

I should be glad to receive a copy of *Killer in the Rain*, also the new Dickson Carr[2] which I promised Alan Ross I would review as well, at above address.

Yours sincerely,

J. Maclaren-Ross

1 Many years after Maclaren-Ross's death, Machell was contacted by Peggy Rust, widow of the film producer Donald Taylor. Unaware that Maclaren-Ross had died, she requested his contact details. Machell, who was also unaware of Maclaren-Ross's death, responded with a letter that provided an amusing account of the writer's last dealings with the firm. See Appendix 3.

2 The crime writer John Dickson Carr, one of whose books Maclaren-Ross had earlier adapted into a BBC radio play.

to JACOB SCHWARTZ

16 Chepstow Place / London W2

24-2-64

My dear Jake,

The Times Press of the Isle of Man informs me that they have sent the MS of my novel which they are publishing, *My Name Is Love*, direct to you, as I asked them to do some time ago.

It seems to me that they will have sent it to Chichester Terrace[1] (the address I gave them in December), so if it hasn't been forwarded, can you get hold of it?

And please send me as much as you can for it, because the lease of this flat is up and I have to deposit £50 on a new one, otherwise I will have nowhere to stay and the need is desperate.

They've sent me a proof copy today, *with* the end of the book bound up in the middle, so it might be of some value as a curiosity and I will send it on to you directly when I get another copy for correction.

Best wishes to Anita and yourself,
from
Julian

I may have good news for Anita about a TV role.

1   Jacob Schwartz's old address.

to ALAN ROSS

16 Chepstow Place/London W2
5-3-64

Dear Alan,

I agree: most new publishers' lists consist of bloody old reprints or Henry James. A new novel of mine should come out from you first.

Let's meet and talk about this new book etc. as soon as possible, also future pieces for *LM*[1] (I hope you received the Dickson Carr review:[2] Machell sent me a copy of the book).

I'm going through the Spring *Bookseller* but haven't come across any subject for articles so far: have you any suggestions?

Anyway I'll ring you next Tuesday, or write to me better still before then and name a day for meeting.

I've received *My Name Is Love* in page proof (2 copies, one bound up so the end of the book came in the middle!); the dispute about the £50 they owe me continues, but I've already got myself out of the option clause (which in any case was for a future thriller only),[3] so we're in the clear.

As ever,
Julian

1   The *London Magazine*.
2   The review wasn't used.
3   The thriller was provisionally titled *My Father's Ghost*.

to JACOB SCHWARTZ

16 Chepstow Place / London W2

7-3-64

My dear Jake,

Thank you for letter and £1 for corrected proof of *My Name Is Love*. Glad you saw John Lehmann and that he's working hard; I hope to see him myself when taking him a printed copy of the novel.

I've had a letter from an editor called Gene Buro asking permission to reprint my *London Magazine* memoir of Frank Harris in an Avon Paperback Anthology of British Writing over last 30 years, for distribution in the states and elsewhere.

Have you seen 'Chandler and Hammett' in the current *London Mag.*, also review of Chandler's last stories with Professor Durham's introduction? I reviewed his book on Chandler in the *TLS* a few weeks ago.

Hope your cold is much better now.

With love to you both,

from

Julian

to ALAN ROSS

16 Chepstow Place / London W2

27-3-64

My dear Alan,

I'm frightfully sorry about the party on Wednesday; the time had apparently been put back from 6.30 to 5 p.m., so that when I arrived the whole thing was over and people were being turned away at the door by a practically non-English-speaking hotel porter.

The reason why I was not notified was that – according to boss-man at Times Press – the letter which I'd written to him accepting the invitation went astray and he did not believe that I intended to come. This letter also contained a list of critics etc. (including yourself) which I had asked him to invite, which explains why you received no invitation.

It all seems to me a typical Times Press balls-up: I have not even now received the usual 6 presentation copies of the book, and I am writing to them to send you one at once.

Please drop me a line after Easter and name a time and day when we can meet for drinks. I haven't, by the way, copies of Jean Rhys'

books now, so I'd have to have copies in order to do the introduction:[1]
I also want to talk to you about other things.

As ever,

Julian

1 Alan Ross appears to have been planning to republish one of the novels of
Jean Rhys (1890–1970). But no such reissue ever appeared under the Alan Ross Ltd
imprint.

to EDMUND HUGHES

16 Chepstow Place / London W2

20-4-64

My dear Edmund,

Thanks so much for fiver received this morning which will indeed
help me out.

I enjoyed our day together and hope you'll be able to come up
Saturday next about the same time, when things I trust will be better.
We could meet at the Alma:[1] I will wait for you there.

On Thursday I'm seeing Alan Ross. Will let you know what happens.

Eleanor joins me in thanks and love,

Also from the Small Saurus[?].

J. Maclaren-Ross

1 The Alma on Westbourne Grove had become Maclaren-Ross's favourite
pub. He was often to be found there with John Gawsworth and the publisher
Charles Wrey Gardiner. After Diane Maclaren-Ross had been widowed, she became
Gardiner's long-term girlfriend.

to JACOB SCHWARTZ

16 Chepstow Place / London W2

6-5-64

My dear Jake,

I'm enclosing a new article (rough copy) on M.P. Shiel[1] whose
centenary falls next February: it will be printed in the July *London
Magazine* (and Robert Bloch in June), and I will send you the fair copy
together with corrected proof when I receive them.

Alan Ross as you'll see from advertisement in current issue is starting
up early next year as a publisher, and he is going to publish a collection
of my critical pieces,[2] others of which will appear monthly in the *London*

Mag. (Wyndham Lewis next),[3] so that the MSS (including those of articles already published) will be in effect the MS of the book (they will be revised of course before publication). Ross is at the moment in London clinic having had minor operation, but Osborne says he's recovering well.

For the Shiel article, the King of Redonda[4] (John Gawsworth, who was speaking very kindly of you yesterday) has made me the *Grand Duke of Ragusa*,[5] the formal conferment of the title to be made in the Alma (a pub) in Westbourne Grove on my birthday, Tuesday July 7th, where I am having my 52nd celebration.

Why don't you come along? We could drink till 3, then travel down to Brighton together, as it is also my son's 6th birthday and I have promised Diane to come and see him in the afternoon.

Please thank Anita for her charming letter; I am writing to her very shortly, but will wait until next week when I hope to have definite news for her about one of the TV Plays on which I've been hard at work. I saw and enjoyed her performance in *The Old Lady Says No!*[6]

Love to you both,

from

Julian

1 The article, entitled 'The Strange Realm of M.P. Sheil', appeared in the December 1964 issue of the *London Magazine*. M.P. Shiel (1865–1947) was a science-fiction and fantasy writer who enjoyed great success in the early years of the twentieth century.

2 The book was never published.

3 Maclaren-Ross's essay on the novelist and painter Percy Wyndham-Lewis (1884–1957) never appeared in the *London Magazine*. The manuscript has been lost.

4 Santa Maria la Redonda is a tiny West Indian island with no permanent human inhabitants. M.P. Shiel claimed its non-existent throne. In the absence of an heir, he installed John Gawsworth as his successor. Gawsworth carried out the role with absurd zeal, issuing titles to people such as Diana Dors and Dirk Bogarde.

5 Alert to the comic potential of the titles he bestowed, previous ones including 'Duke of Guano', Gawsworth gave Maclaren-Ross a peerage that alluded to his taste for red wine from the region around the Sicilian town of Ragusa.

6 Written by Denis Johnson, *The Old Lady Says No!* (1929) is a romantic play set in the nineteenth century, its action punctuated by choral interludes.

to ALAN ROSS

16 Chepstow Place / London W2

1-6-64

Dear Alan,

Thank you for your card and the Zoshchenko cheque.

I'd like to do Hemingway for 'Reputations': indeed, I rang Cape's[1] and got a copy of the memoirs,[2] but said you or Osborne would be getting in touch re sending his other books to me (I'll need the novels and the one-volume collected short stories: the play *The Fifth Column*[3] is interesting as a piece of self-dramatisation, but I don't suppose they'll have a copy now and I'll try to get that out of the library).

Hope you are very much better now, and we must have a drink when you get back into circulation. Things are still tough with me, but I'm fighting back: just planning my book of *Memoirs of the Forties*.

As ever,

Julian

I've got *Alice B. Toklas*[4] to compare Miss Stein on Hem[ingway].

1 Jonathan Cape, the publishers.
2 *A Moveable Feast* (1964).
3 By a strange coincidence, the 1940 snapshot reproduced on the cover of this book shows Maclaren-Ross holding a copy of *The Fifth Column* (1939).
4 *The Autobiography of Alice B. Toklas* (1933), by Gertrude Stein (1874–1946), who had known Hemingway well.

to EDMUND HUGHES

16 Chepstow Place / London W2

5-6-64

My dear Edmund,

Unfortunately all the Hemingway books arrived this morning and I shall have to work on the article all weekend in order to get some money for next week, as we haven't any now.

But perhaps we could meet about midweek one evening if you let me know a date or time when you can come up, or else the *following* Saturday?

I enjoyed last time very much.

All the best,

from Julian

to ALAN ROSS

Flat 7/4 Dawson Place/London W2
13-6-64

Dear Alan,

Thank you for cheque for Graham Greene[1] and copy of the August magazine. Can you get Shiel[2] in Sept. issue as the King[3] is worrying me about it? Then the way's clear for Dylan.[4]

Let's meet one evening soon as I've some points to discuss before you go away. If you drop me a line here naming time and place I will come along. Just finishing first chapter (Jonathan Cape):[5] Greene comes after this.

As ever,
Julian

PS Please return Hemingway MS.[6]

1 A reference to 'Excursion in Greeneland', a memoir of an encounter with Graham Greene, commissioned for the *London Magazine*. The memoir, featured in the December 1964 issue, was destined to become the third chapter of Maclaren-Ross's posthumously published *Memoirs of the Forties* (1965).
2 Maclaren-Ross's essay about M.P Shiel's work.
3 Gawsworth, the King of Redonda.
4 Maclaren-Ross was planning to write about his time working as a screen-writer alongside Dylan Thomas.
5 'Meeting a Publisher', the opening chapter of *Memoirs of the Forties*, described Maclaren-Ross's pre-Second World War encounter with Jonathan Cape, founder of the eponymous publishing firm.
6 Maclaren-Ross's article on Hemingway, prompted by the publication of *A Moveable Feast*, appeared in the August 1964 issue of the *London Magazine*.

to EDMUND HUGHES

16 Chepstow Place/London W2
23-6-64

My dear Edmund,

Thank you for your letter and cheque received this morning: it will be a great help in providing Tom (actually it's 'Top') Cat[1] for Gogo[2] and strawberries for Little One.[3]

I had a good interview with Macgibbon of Gollancz Ltd about my *Memoirs*; asked for a part advance of £150 now, and will hear on Wednesday whether his colleagues agree. If so, he would like the book in MS by Nov. and will publish next March. So keep your fingers X'd;

and I will ring up and tell you the result and we can arrange to meet very soon, I hope.

Meanwhile I'm at work on the Dylan memoir for *Encounter*.[4]

Eleanor sends her love: as indeed I do.

J. Maclaren-Ross

1 A brand of cat food.
2 The cat owned by Maclaren-Ross and Eleanor Brill.
3 Maclaren-Ross's nickname for Eleanor Brill's daughter Caroline.
4 The piece was for the *London Magazine*, not *Encounter*.

to HAMISH HAMILTON

2-7-64

Dear Hamilton,

Enclosed herewith a plan of my proposed book of memoirs of Literary People met in the Forties, which I hope you might like to publish.

The Memoir of Dylan Thomas at Strand Films, where in 1943 we worked together as documentary scriptwriters, is already completed and in the hands of editors of literary reviews.[1]

Otherwise the book is not written, but could be completed and in your hands between September and October this year, subject to an *immediate* part-advance payment of £150: the sum of the total advance to be decided by yourself.

I hope that you will be able to let me have a decision letter by Saturday morning after perusing the enclosed plan.

The definitive title by the way is:

Everything They Said Has Been Taken in Evidence,[2] and the book would concentrate on memoirs of the persons concerned as *people* rather than in relation to their work.

Looking forward to hearing from you,

Yours sincerely,

J. Maclaren-Ross

Please enclose plan if proposition not acceptable.

1 The memoir, entitled 'The Polestar Neighbour', was published in the November 1964 issue of *London Magazine*. Later the piece was incorporated into Maclaren-Ross's *Memoirs of the Forties*.
2 The published book appeared under another title: *Memoirs of the Forties*.

to EDMUND HUGHES

16 Chepstow Place/London W2
8-8-64

My dear Edmund,

It may be too late to apologise for having turned you away the other week but I was working at tremendous pressure, and indeed still am, on a new novel.[1] However, here's a copy of the one that's just come out to make up for it.[2] Hope to see you soon; drop me a card and let me know when you'll next be about so we can have a drink or two together.

With love to Mary and yourself,

from Julian

1 The nature of the novel is unknown.
2 Maclaren-Ross sent him a copy of *My Name Is Love*, carrying the following inscription: 'For Edmund from Julian in memory of, and gratitude, for many good times. 4.8.64'.

* * *

This appears to be the last surviving letter penned by Maclaren-Ross. Just under three months later, during the early hours of 3 November 1964, he was at home with Eleanor Brill, drinking brandy to celebrate the arrival of an unexpected cheque. When he suffered chest pains, he tried to banish them by polishing off the bottle of brandy. But he continued to complain about these pains until daybreak. Worried by their persistence, Eleanor rushed him to the nearby St Charles Hospital. No sooner had she and Maclaren-Ross arrived there than he was struck by a fatal heart-attack. With remarkable insensitivity, one of the doctors informed Eleanor that Maclaren-Ross might have survived if he'd been brought in earlier. By then, the dying fifty-two-year-old writer had already blurted out his final words – 'Graham Greene' and, moments after that, 'I love you…'

RAF Stoke Holy Cross/Nr Norwich/Norfolk

11-5-43

Dear Captain Hart-Davis,

This is a rather sudden introduction I'm afraid, but I have had a letter today from Julian Maclaren-Ross asking me to write to you. He was sent back to his unit in Southend yesterday. I am Scylla Yates – he will have spoken of me to you I think.

About a fortnight ago, I went to Birmingham to see him and also had an interview with Major Ross, the psychiatrist. Apparently the Major wanted to see me and would in fact have sent for me, if I had not already been coming. I tell you this because Julian seems to think it important that you should know of this interview and what Major Ross had to say. I know that you also saw him, and the CO, and that you have been tremendously kind and energetic in your efforts to help Julian.

Major Ross seemed to take a very sympathetic view of the whole case. He told me that he thought a court martial was unavoidable as J. was quite responsible for his actions and that military law would take its course, etc. Also he might have to serve a sentence of detention, but at the end of this his case would come up before a reviewing board. He himself had recommended Julian's discharge from the army as he did not consider him to be temperamentally suited. The CO had made enquiries at the War Office about a job for him, but nothing appeared to be forthcoming. There remained only routine clerical work. He agreed with me when I said that J. would never settle down to that again in the army. In fact he seemed definitely of the opinion that J. needed a suitable job *out* of the army.

This all seemed very hopeful. When I said, 'Supposing the reviewing board doesn't act on your recommendations?' he smiled, and said that J. was bound to get discharged in time, as, if he was returned to the army, he would undoubtedly come up before a psychiatrist again. I said I was afraid of this happening as reviewing boards do not always seem to take the [long] view.

When I mentioned the fact that the CO of my unit had interrogated me about fascists, Major Ross got very interested. But when I asked him what it was all about, and got amused at the idea, particularly at J.'s alleged assertion that there were fascists in the War Office, he dismissed it and asked me no more about it.

He ended by assuring me he would do all he could.

Please excuse this long letter from a complete stranger but Julian wanted me to write you as soon as possible.

I must thank you so very much for all that you are doing, and have already done for him.

Yours sincerely,

Scylla Yates

APPENDIX 2

RAF Stoke Holy Cross/Nr Norwich/Norfolk
16-5-43

Dear Rupert Hart-Davis,

Thank you very much for your letter. You most probably heard from Julian before getting my telegram. I suppose he told me to let you know in case he could not. Unfortunately I was away from [camp], did not see his letter till last night and as it was late to phone you, to try and find out your number, and chance you being there, I sent the telegram.

J. asked me to contact Major Backus who, as you may know, took charge of his case after Major Ross left. I will do all I can though do not know what official action he is able to take now that J. has been RTU.

From what I have gathered, J. rather annoyed the MO (Southend) in his interview with him. But I don't understand what can have taken place to cause the MO to make such a recommendation where apparently there was no such suggestion in the psychiatrist's report. Also the MO had already told J. at the end of the interview that he would send him for a medical board.

Nothing that Major Ross said to me pointed to this idea of Mental Home treatment, in fact he said that J. would have to stand the CM as he could not declare him unfit to be tried. Curious if the MO has been inspired to take such action in order to spare J. a court martial! I believe it was Major Backus who wanted it all worked out without any more fuss and bother.

I hoped, with you, that the end of all this business was in sight. But this new development seems to have opened up more trouble. Let's hope it will clear up quickly.

Yours very sincerely,

Scylla Yates

APPENDIX 3

Hamish Hamilton Ltd/57–59 Long Acre/London WC2E 9JZ

4-2-81

Dear Mrs Rust,

I am sorry, but we cannot help you. We had incessant difficulties with Julian Maclaren-Ross and our rights to the two books of his which we published reverted to him many years ago. He used to give 'c/o the BBC' as his address but I think he exhausted their patience as well as ours; other addresses he gave us proved to be bombed out sites or non-existent. The last time he called on us he demanded his taxi-fare home before he would leave and when a guileless editor called a cab and gave him a few shillings to cover the fare, Ross threw the money in his face, ran off and never, I am glad to say, came to see us again.

A great pity as he wrote brilliantly and had the best handwriting I have ever seen. But I am sorry to have no practical advice for you.

Yours sincerely,

Roger Machell

APPENDIX 4

Threnody on a Gramophone

Anton Alexseyevitch

1.

When they slung us out of there we hadn't a sou left. They'd pinched the bloody lot. This was in Marseilles: a place down by the port and pretty tough.

'They are savages,' Laskov said to me, 'uncivilised savages'; his nose wouldn't stop bleeding where that big bastard hit him. He kept mopping it and saying they were savages, that he'd like to go back there and kill them all.

'Sure,' I said to him, 'same here.'

'No, but seriously,' Laskov said. 'I am quite serious. I should like to take a revolver and shoot them all dead.'

'Me too,' I told him.

We came back along the Cannebière where all the cafés were lit up, with people sitting at tables outside. It was high summer and hellish hot, but we hadn't even the price of a pernod.

'What'll we do without dough?' I asked Laskov. 'How about the hotel bill?'

'That's all right,' he said through the handkerchief he was holding over his nose; 'we can always pawn my gramophone. Besides, I get paid tomorrow.'

He'd got a pretty good job as a professional, dancing at the casino and doing well. That's because he was a prince, and all these old American dolls used to go mad about him. Me, Anton Chernikov, I haven't any kind of title, and let me tell you life in Europe for a Russian without a title is just plain hell, these days. Specially on the Côte, where I come from.

I went to Marseille with a Greek called Konstantin, who was in some racket or other, but he got slung downstairs by a sailor at a cinema he went to first night we got there, and had to go into hospital with a broken head; so I was left on my own till I ran into Laskov at the casino one evening, and I'd been living off him ever since.

2.

Back at the hotel, the patron looked up from his desk and beckoned us over.

'Listen,' he said. 'Your account. It's a month overdue. I can't let it run on much longer.'

'Don't worry,' Laskov told him. 'You shall have your money tomorrow morning. Without fail. There's no reason to worry yourself.'

'Tomorrow,' the patron said, 'Tomorrow. It's always some excuse. Promises and no payment.'

He turned away, muttering something that sounded like 'Lousy Russians', and we went on upstairs.

'I'd like to bust that bastard one,' I told Laskov, up in our room. 'One of these days I shall do it.'

'Don't for the love of God,' Laskov said. 'Do you want to get us thrown out?'

'Ah, shit,' I said. 'Give me a cigarette.'

'I've only got blues.'

'They'll do.'

I lay on the bed smoking, while Laskov bathed his nose at the basin. The bleeding had stopped but his nose had begun to swell up pretty bad. He looked at himself in the glass and swore.

'Those savages,' he said. 'Those swine.'

'Is there any cognac left?' I asked him.

He got the bottle out from under the bed and held it up to the light. 'Not a drop.'

'Damn.'

I drew a glass of tepid water from the tap and drank that. There wasn't any ice and I didn't like to ring for any, with us on credit and the patron turning snotty.

Laskov changed into his smoking jacket and said, 'You coming along?'

'Might as well.'

I put on a blazer and white flannels: it wasn't a gala night and you didn't have to dress; only Laskov did, being a dancer.

The band had began playing when we got there and Laskov went off at once. I sat down and told the garçon to bring a pernod and a packet of Chesterfields and charge them to Prince Laskov's account. I looked round and saw him doing a slow fox with some old jane who looked as though she'd had her face lifted. I didn't know any of the other janes dancing and began to feel I'd be better off back on the Côte where I did know people and had some kind of pull. I was sick of Marseille and that blasted hotel where the bugs bit you all night. I drank some pernod and started wishing I was back there at Henri's with Stepan and Boris and the rest of the bunch. After all, it was like home to me: I didn't remember Russia much, being only ten when the Revolution broke out and we had to scram.

Laskov was sitting down with this old tart, both of them drinking champagne, and it looked like he was fixed for the night. I finished my pernod and got out of there. A blonde over by the door grinned and gave me the eye as I went past, but what the hell, it isn't any good when you're broke. A girl's got to live, same as you and me.

3.

I got undressed and lay on the bed, but even with nothing on I was sweating like a bullock. I didn't turn out the light because the moment it was dark the bugs came out and started biting. They were scared of the light, it kept them away. I thought of playing the gramophone for a bit but most of Laskov's records were tangoes and I didn't care for tangoes. The other records he had were all last winter's tunes, and playing them would remind me of Sandra. I didn't want to be reminded of Sandra. That was the last thing I wanted.

So I lay there stark bollux on the bed and by and by I began to think of that blonde.

The blonde had a mouth like Sandra's. She smiled and said, 'Darling' and her voice was Sandra's voice. But Sandra was away in Paris so it couldn't be her. She put out her hand and touched my shoulder and then her face was Laskov's face and he was leaning over me with a bottle of cognac in his hand.

'Wake up, you old devil,' he said. 'I've been looking for you all evening. Listen we're in luck. I had a good client. Look!' And he pulled out a bundle of notes and shoved them across at me. 'We must celebrate,' he said, pouring out the cognac. 'We must absolutely celebrate.' He was a bit lit already.

'What's the time?' I said.

'It's nearly ten,' Laskov said. 'I've been out with the little Algerian. Listen, Anton, you must meet her. Absolutely. I will introduce you.' He poured me some more cognac. 'Only thirteen and yet a woman. You wouldn't believe it.'

'I don't. She must be more than thirteen.'

'Well, fourteen then. But certainly not more than that.'

'Listen,' I said to him, 'I've been thinking. I'm fed up with this place. I want to go back. Will you stake me for the train-fare home?'

'What?' he said. 'You're not leaving? You're not going to desert me?'

'I'd like to go back.'

'But look, I don't know another Russian in the whole damn town. If you go, I shan't have a soul to talk to. You can't do this!'

I didn't say anything. Laskov sat down on the bed beside me and put his hand on my shoulder.

'What is the matter, Anton? Why do you want to go?'

'I've told you. I'm sick of this town. And another thing: I've no money. It makes me feel low.'

'But I have plenty I can lend you. If it's a woman you want, I will arrange it. You can have the little Algerian. She's wonderful. Wait till you see her.'

'It's not altogether that.'

'Wait until the autumn, then. It's only three more months. When my contract's up, we can go back together.'

I thought three more months in Marseille would just about finish me, and said so.

Laskov sighed. 'Very well,' he said. 'I will let you have the money, if you really want to go.'

'That's damn good of you.'

'Not at all. I am sorry you are going, though.'

'So am I. But you understand how I feel.'

'Oh absolutely.'

He sat there with his nose all swollen, looking sad. I felt rotten about leaving him. He'd been a good friend to me, but what could I do, feeling the way I did?

'Have some more cognac,' I told him, 'and cheer up.' So we finished the bottle between us, but Laskov didn't cheer up. Drink always made him feel morbid, anyway.

Round about two we turned in. Neither of us could get to sleep, though. It was so hot, and the bugs started to bite. I rolled over, my body feeling on fire where they'd bitten me. I could hear Laskov threshing about in the other bed, scratching himself and cursing; and then he must have dozed off, because I could hear him snoring, with a sort of snuffling noise.

I lay awake, scratching myself and thinking about the Côte. It'd be good to get back. Now that Sandra had gone, there was no reason why I shouldn't get back.

Once Laskov shouted in his sleep, like he sometimes did. I reckon he was dreaming about Russia and the Revolution: being older than me, he could remember it better, and he'd told me he and his family had a tough time getting away.

4.

I caught the two o'clock train. Laskov saw me off at the station. His nose was still very swollen. It resembled rosbif.

'Give my compliments to Sandra when you get back. Don't forget.'

'Sandra's in Paris. I shan't be seeing her.'

'You might be seeing her.'

'I doubt it.'

'Well, if you do, say that I still remember her. She is always in my thoughts.'

'All right. I will.'

Laskov said: 'I am sorry you could not meet the little Algerian before you left. It is a great pity.'

'Are you seeing her tonight?'

'Naturally.'

Then the whistle went and I swung aboard. The train began to move and Laskov ran along the platform beside it, waving and shouting 'Goodbye, good luck.' Then as the train gathered speed he couldn't keep up with it, but as we went round the bend leaving the station out of sight I could still see him waving and maybe he was shouting too. I couldn't hear the words.

It was a five-hour journey, and in the train I must have gone to sleep, because when I woke up we were there, bumping over the iron bridge past the Russian church and the villa where we lived as kids, drawing slowly along the platform, under the glass roof, into the station.

I got down and it felt just like home, coming out into the sun with the smell of tar and the pavement sweating asphalt in wet black patches with the heat of the day. It was cooling a bit now, at seven o'clock, but still quite hot enough, the air moving slow and sticky and smelling of tar.

* * *

I swung onto the platform of a passing tram. It was the front platform, near the driver. The tram rattled and bounced over the Avenue de la Gare. The wind blew sparks from the cigarette I was smoking. It felt cool on my face, but the smell of tar was still blown along on it. The tram turned out into the Rue de Russia, with the café on the corner where we used to get credit before they clamped down on us. There was a new block of flats built on the corner and the café had a new awning up, but all the tables outside were empty. Rattling down the Rue de Russia past the public gardens and the Russian charcuterie where you could buy kvass, I didn't see anyone I knew. There weren't many people about. I wondered if there'd be any mail for me at the apartment. Sandra wouldn't write of course: she never wrote letters. But then I thought, suppose she *has* written. She might have written.

You bloody fool, I thought, you're not going to start that all over again. That's all over now. Finished and done with. But I couldn't stop it. I couldn't stop thinking, suppose she has written.

But Sandra never wrote. She couldn't write letters. She couldn't even spell. She spoke three languages, same's I did, but she couldn't spell. Not even in Russian.

The tram slowed down and I jumped off. The apartment was just over the way. I cut across the road, my valise banging against my legs.

The hall was cold and dark after the sun outside. There was sand strewn on the floor of it because they were tarring the road outside.

I couldn't get the letterbox open at first. I got the bloody key jammed in the lock. I pulled at it and the door came open and two letters fell out. One of them fell onto the floor. I groped for it in the sand and took them over to the door to read. It was too dark in the hall.

Both the letters were for her. I didn't know either of the hand-writings. One was postmarked two weeks before, from Cannes. It had been in the letterbox all this time. It looked like a man's handwriting. The other looked like a bill.

I could feel the sweat trickling down my face. It dried cold on me. So she hadn't written. Not even a line. I hadn't given her my address in Marseille but she could have written here. You bloody fool, I thought, you didn't want her to write, did you? Or did you?

I picked up my valise and went up the stairs to the second floor. The apartment was the same as I'd left it. There was a stale smell of Flit in the salon. I opened up the shutters and took the bottle of pernod out of the cupboard. My throat was dried up and I wanted a drink more than anything. There was no ice of course, so I drank it without. I had another drink and began to feel better. I thought I might have dinner downtown. There was nothing to eat in the apartment anyway.

The two letters were still on the table where I'd slung them. I looked at the one with the man's handwriting on it. I wondered who it was from. Not a Frenchman because 'rue' was spelt with a capital 'R'. A Frenchman would never write it that way. Most likely he was English. Or American. One of her bloody rich American boyfriends. She'd so many she couldn't count them.

Well, anyhow, she hadn't written. That let me out. I needn't think about her any more now. In Marseille I hadn't thought about her so much, but here in the apartment it wasn't so easy. After all, we'd lived here together three years. I began to think coming back hadn't been such a bright idea, after all. Still, I wasn't going to let her spoil it for me. There were other things to think about. Other women too. I'd find another girl to think about instead. There were plenty of them on the Côte. You'd only got to look. I thought, I'll start looking straightaway.

I poured out some more pernod, but drinking it made me feel hot again. I tried to put the electric fan on, but the blasted thing wouldn't work. I thought I'd have a bath. I turned on the taps and got into the tub. Splashing about in the tepid water, I began to sing 'Mama yo quiero un Novio'. It was Laskov's favourite tango. I wondered how he was getting on with his little Algerian. Good old Laskov. He'd lent me another five hundred on top of the train fare. That wouldn't last forever of course, but it'd see me through until I got some kind of job. In summer things were usually slack, but there was bound to be something the boys could put me on to.

Drying myself, I began to sing 'I Can't Give You Anything But Love, Baby'. I felt alright again now. The bath had washed it all away. Outside, the doorbell began to ring. I didn't bother about it. It couldn't be anyone for me because nobody knew I was back. I let them go on ringing. But then I thought, perhaps this is Love at the door. A beautiful maiden, preferably blonde. I might be missing my chance.

The ringing had stopped. I wrapped a towel round me and went to the door. Too late. They'd gone. Never mind. Love waiting at the door had been a beautiful thought. Pernod on an empty stomach was making me poetical. I felt I could write a poem. Or a song. A song would make more money.

I went into the bedroom and started to look for a clean shirt. Love, I sang, is at the door. And then I stopped singing. I felt as if everything had dropped out of me. Like when a lift starts falling, or on a switchback at the fair when it starts down the slope. Hot and cold with the feeling that seeing her suddenly always gave me. I'd forgotten the photograph which I'd put at the bottom of the drawer.

INDEX

Julian Maclaren-Ross
Collected Memoirs
with an introduction by
Paul Willetts
£8.95 paperback
ISBN 978-0-948238-30-7; 464pp

Julian Maclaren-Ross
Bitten by the Tarantula and other writing
with an introduction by
Paul Willetts
£9.95 paperback
ISBN 978-0-948238-32-1; 528pp

'Those who have yet to discover this wonderfully stylish and sardonic writer should start here'

PETER PARKER, *DAILY TELEGRAPH*

'Nothing has given me greater pleasure than the continuing revival of one of my favourite writers, Julian Maclaren-Ross, with his *Collected Memoirs*'

PHILIP FRENCH, BOOKS OF THE YEAR, *OBSERVER*

'a substantial account of his great talent'

INDEPENDENT ON SUNDAY

'excellent anthology'

MAIL ON SUNDAY

'Were he writing now…he would be a star'

IAIN FINLAYSON, *TIMES*

'accomplishment of a rare kind'

EVELYN WAUGH

'one of the most original and perceptive film critics this country has produced… His 1956 essay on Hitchcock, for instance, was a decade or more ahead of its time'

PHILIP FRENCH

'One of our very best writers'

JOHN BETJEMAN

'an author of outstanding gifts'

JOHN LEHMANN

'talent of a rare and original kind'

OLIVIA MANNING

---

www.blackspringpress.co.uk

the acclaimed biography

*Fear and Loathing
in Fitzrovia*
Paul Willetts
Dewi Lewis Publishing
£12.99 paperback
ISBN 978-1-904587-27-9; 352pp

'An inspiring read'
> JOHN KING, *NEW STATESMAN*
> BOOKS OF THE YEAR

'Diligent, painstaking and
bleakly hilarious'
> *GUARDIAN* BOOK OF THE WEEK

'Historical profiling of a high
order, richly and racily done'
> PHILIP OAKES, *LITERARY REVIEW*

'Very striking, very strange and
altogether fascinating'
> RICHARD HOLMES, AUTHOR OF
> *DR JOHNSON AND MR SAVAGE*

'Gloriously readable'
> *MAIL ON SUNDAY*

Julian Maclaren-Ross *Selected Stories*
Introduced by Paul Willetts
Dewi Lewis Publishing
£9.99 paperback
ISBN 978-1-904587-17-0; 256pp

The world of Maclaren-Ross's short fiction
tends to be the dingy, down-at-heel world
of smoke-veiled bars, rented lodgings,
blacked-out streets, and wartime army
garrisons, first-hand experience lending
his work a frisson of authenticity. Whether
they're narrated in the breathless, slangy
voice of an uneducated soldier, or the
clipped cadences of a colonial 'expat',
whether they're set on the French Riviera
or wartime England, they're imprinted
with Maclaren-Ross's unmistakable literary
logo. The prevailing tone is casual, matter-
of-fact and laconic, with his characteristically humorous asides failing to
conceal the melancholy that seeps through their hardboiled surfaces.

North Soho 999
A True Story of Gangs and
Gun-crime in 1940s London
Paul Willetts
Dewi Lewis Publishing
£9.99 paperback
ISBN 978-1-904587-45-3

'I urge you to read *North Soho 999* by Paul Willetts. It's the absolutely
gripping true story of an armed raid on a Fitzrovia jewellers/pawnbrokers
that escalated into a huge manhunt. The book drips with a fantastic
Austerity Britain atmosphere, a place of flick-knives and gangsters and a
capital awash with the plundered firearms of the recent war. It reads like a
novel and is amazingly relevant, showing how the same terrors and pre-
occupations about society spinning out of control have always been with us.'

MARK GATISS, INDEPENDENT ON SUNDAY

'...Paul Willetts's tour-de-force *North Soho 999*, a recreation of the
circumstances of a murder that took place on 29 April 1947...It is a
fascinating account of a vanished Britain.'

PHILIP FRENCH, TIMES LITERARY SUPPLEMENT

'A brilliant snapshot of '40s London, peopled by crooks, coppers and creeps.
Willetts slices through time with the skill of a razor-flashing wide boy.
Essential reading.'

JOHN KING

London Books

flying the flag for free-thinking literature

London Books is an independent publisher specialising in classic London
fiction, with a special interest in authors who operated beyond the
mainstream, maverick writers with something to say and an exciting way of
getting their ideas across.

Mixing substance and style, social concerns with a vibrant use of
language, the London Classics series kicks off with three titles. These consist
of James Curtis's cult 1930s crime novel *The Gilt Kid*; Gerald Kersh's *Night
and the City*, which anticipated the better-known novels of Patrick
Hamilton; and, striking a different yet equally resonant note, Alan Sillitoe's
A Start in Life, published with a new foreword by the author.

For further details and an overview of London literature, please visit
www.london-books.co.uk.